Advance Praise for
Contemporary American Poetry

"Representative and egalitarian in including what's really happening in poetry these days with regard to a balance between free and formal verse. It's a strong anthology at a good price. Better than any I've looked at in a while!"

Mark Todd
Western State College of Colorado

"This book seems best described as an attempt to survey the landscapes of contemporary poetry that doesn't take too many pictures from any one vantage. As such it has the real virtue of swiftness that is so often missing from oddly bloated anthologies."

John Emil Vincent
Wesleyan University

"The length of the book as a whole seems just right. I like the greater number of choices in this book."

Deborah G. Brown
University of New Hampshire at Manchester

"It's eminently usable. This text offers a reasonable sweep of contemporary poetry but is not so overbearingly expensive or backpack-filling as to make ordering other texts impossible."

Kathrine Varnes
University of Missouri

"This anthology looks like it might be very useful. It includes most of the poets I'd like my students to read, or to have a chance to read."

Herman Asarnow
University of Portland

"Many existing collections of contemporary poetry are 'balkanized' in terms of their coverage: they focus on a specific school or political issue. This book at least aims to achieve a broader coverage and open-mindedness about the dizzying array of poems produced by Americans today."

Jeff Westover
Howard University

R. S. Gwynn has edited several other books, including *Poetry: A Pocket Anthology; Fiction: A Pocket Anthology; Drama: A Pocket Anthology; The Longman Anthology of Short Fiction* (with Dana Gioia); and *Contemporary American Poetry: A Pocket Anthology* (with April Lindner). He has also authored five collections of poetry, including *No Word of Farewell: Selected Poems, 1970–2000*. In 2004 he was awarded the Michael Braude Award for verse from the American Academy of Arts and Letters. Gwynn is University Professor of English at Lamar University in Beaumont, Texas.

April Lindner's poetry collection, *Skin*, received the 2002 Walt McDonald First Book Prize from Texas Tech University Press. Her poems have appeared in numerous journals, including *The Paris Review, Prairie Schooner, Crazyhorse,* and *The Formalist*. She also has published two booklets—*Dana Gioia* and *New Formalists of the American West*—in Boise State University's Western Writers Series. She teaches at Saint Joseph's University in Philadelphia. Her photo was taken by Eli St. Amant.

For Our Students

Contemporary American Poetry

A Pocket Anthology

Edited by

R. S. Gwynn
Lamar University

April Lindner
Saint Joseph's University

PENGUIN ACADEMICS

PEARSON
Longman

New York • San Francisco • Boston
London • Toronto • Sydney • Tokyo • Singapore • Madrid
Mexico City • Munich • Paris • Cape Town • Hong Kong • Montreal

Vice President and Editor-in-Chief: Joseph P. Terry
Executive Marketing Manager: Ann Stypuloski
Production Manager: Eric Jorgensen
Project Coordination, Text Design, and Electronic Page Makeup:
  Pre-Press Co., Inc.
Senior Cover Design Manager/Designer: Nancy Danahy
Cover Image: © David Nicholls/Corbis-NY
Senior Manufacturing Buyer: Alfred C. Dorsey
Printer and Binder: RR Donnelley & Sons Company
Cover Printer: Phoenix Color Corp.

For permission to use copyrighted material, grateful acknowledgment is made
to the copyright holders on pp. 498–506, which are hereby made part of this
copyright page.

Library of Congress Cataloging-in-Publication Data

Contemporary American poetry : a pocket anthology / edited by R. S. Gwynn,
April Lindner.
     p. cm. — (Penguin academics)
  Includes indexes.
  ISBN 0-321-18282-0 (pbk.) — ISBN 0-321-27584-5 (exam copy)
     1. American poetry—21st century. 2. American poetry—20th century.
  I. Gwynn, R. S. II. Lindner, April. III. Series.

PS617.C65 2004
811'.608—dc22

                                                        2004050143

Visit us at http://www.ablongman.com

ISBN 0-321-18282-0

2345678910—DOH—07060504

Contents

Alphabetical List of Authors

Preface

The present collection builds on the proven success of *Poetry: A Pocket Anthology*, which has been used over the last decade by upwards of 25,000 students and is now in its fourth edition. Using many of the poems by recent American poets in that volume as the core, we have assembled a new anthology of contemporary American poetry that we hope will address many of the wishes and concerns of teachers of literature and creative writing and likewise will prove valuable to students and general readers.

Our primary concern was to compose an anthology that was truly contemporary, beginning with poets born in 1920 and concluding with poets born in the 1970s. (Dates for the first book publication and/or the composition dates of the selection are printed below each poem.) While we acknowledge that there are poets born before our time frame who continue to speak strongly to today's readers, we feel that the most important among them—Gwendolyn Brooks, Elizabeth Bishop, Robert Hayden, Weldon Kees, Robert Lowell, and May Swenson come first to mind—are now represented by complete editions of their works and might more profitably be studied in greater depth than the selections in a brief anthology can provide. At this writing, of the more than 150 poets who appear here, over 90 percent are still alive and productive, and all address the present situation of American life and letters.

Second, we have attempted to produce a collection that accurately reflects the diversity of contemporary American poetry. Reviewers of our table of contents have offered us many valuable suggestions about poets whom they would like to see included, and we have taken their recommendations—as far as the scope of our anthology allows—into account in making our final selections. To be sure, our primary focus has been to select representative poems that will provide a challenging and varied reading experience, but, in looking at the list of poets whom we have chosen, we are pleased to find that approximately one-third of them are women and that roughly one-quarter represent the ethnic and cultural complexities of American society—percentages, incidentally, that are substantially increased when one considers the poets born since 1940 who are now at the heights of their careers and who reflect the accelerated expansion of the poetic canon during the last three decades. We believe, however, that an accurate representation of poetic diversity should not be limited solely to matters of gender and ethnicity. Accordingly, we have tried to provide examples of poems from the many schools and styles that have appeared in American poetry in the last half-century, and we have done this in various ways. As an aid to readers, we have included an essay, written in the form of a "field guide" to contemporary American poetics, and following it a glossary detailing the many literary movements that seem to us most prominent in shaping the current scene. As a further assistance to users of the book, we have suggested, after entries in the glossary, lists of poets in the anthology on whom instructors might focus if they wish to examine the works of groups who share affinities of style and subject matter. Our selections, taken from the broadest base possible, range from avant-garde works to traditional styles, from prose poems to sonnets, from surrealism to neo-classicism, and from revolutionary political stances to conservative ones. We are especially happy to include examples of poetic genres often overlooked or under-represented in anthologies: mid-length and longer narrative poems, dramatic monologues, and a wide range of poems in both experimental and traditional forms. While geographical diversity, yet another of our concerns, may not play as large a role in American literature as it once did, we have nevertheless tried to reflect the regional qualities that have characterized American poetry since the nineteenth century and still lend it strength, including poets from virtually every state and major territory in the country. Additionally, we have included individual poems by a dozen poets born in the 1960s and 1970s, all of whom have already produced first and, in some cases, subsequent collections that indicate that these younger writers may well represent the best qualities to be found in the next generation of American poets.

Third, we aimed at compactness and affordability. Most of the competing anthologies run to twice the length and, in most cases, demand more than three times the price—while actually containing the works of fewer poets than included in *Contemporary American Poetry*. Our aim was to offer, with no sacrifices in format or overall production quality, an inexpensive anthology with a wide range of selections. In essence, we have provided a flexible core textbook which one group of instructors might find sufficient to their needs, or which another might wish to supplement with a second, more specialized anthology, or which another might combine with some sort of instructional or critical text, or which yet another might augment with individual collections of poets whom they wish to teach in depth—all with the aim of not saddling students with excessive demands on their budgets. Any anthology, we realize, reflects the many compromises that have shaped its final form, but we hope that *Contemporary American Poetry*'s "pocket" size, "pocketbook" net price, and the useful "pocketful"of extra material provided in the form of brief biographical introductions, explanatory essays, indexes, and appendices, will prove attractive to both instructors and students.

We wish to express our thanks to: Mary Gilman and Beverly Williams, whose hard work on this anthology was invaluable; The Saint Joseph's University English Department, with special thanks to Owen Gilman and Richard Fusco; Mary Martinson and Tamara Jackson of the Francis A. Drexel Library; and to the Research Council of Lamar University for a grant that aided in the completion of this project.

R. S. GWYNN
APRIL LINDNER

Introduction

No Arguing with the Future: Another Fifty Years of American Poetry

by
William Pritchard
Amherst College

In October 1962, as the Soviet fleet steamed toward Cuba and President Kennedy squared off with Premier Khrushchev, Washington's Library of Congress played host to a National Poetry Festival. Perhaps the major event of that festival was Randall Jarrell's talk, later published as "Fifty Years of American Poetry," in which, one after the other, he took the measure of twenty-four figures from roughly 1910 to the present: from Edwin Arlington Robinson, Robert Frost, and Ezra Pound, to Elizabeth Bishop, Richard Wilbur, and Robert Lowell. It was an astonishing performance, as Jarrell capsulized, in memorable paragraphs, the particular achievement of each writer, an achievement collectively that made American poetry, in his eyes, "the best and most influential in the English language." Forty-some years later, Jarrell's list of "American classics" as he called them still dazzles in its variety, even as the poets who make it up can be held together, if loosely, under the rubric of "modernism."

It will be agreed, I think, that no rubric can begin to hold together, even loosely, the 136 poets represented in this Pocket Anthology; nor is there likely to be agreement—as one pretty much agrees with Jarrell's list—about the top twenty or so poets born after 1919 who produced major work in the latter decades of the twentieth century. The editors of this anthology say of the poets represented that they all "address the present situation of American life and letters." And so they do, partly by being part of that situation. Has it ever been otherwise? In 1942, when Alfred Kazin published his groundbreaking survey of American prose writers from the early part of that century, he judged the greatest single fact about them to be "our writers' absorption in every last detail of their American world together with their deep and subtle alienation from it." Kazin's statement points to the necessary embrace of and detachment from "life" or "the present situation," that any imaginative writer, not just an American one, must practice. Frost put it another even more memorable way at the end of his preface to a posthumous volume of poetry by Robinson: "Give us immedicable woes—woes that nothing can be done for—woes flat and final. And then to play. The play's the thing. Play's the thing. All virtue in 'as if.'"

An anthology, this one certainly, attempts to be both discriminating and representative as it looks back over decades and selects, evenhandedly, interesting specimens of poetic play. How many of these poems, these poets, will be remembered fifty years from now? In this respect it may be instructive to compare an anthology from 1927, *The Oxford Book of American Verse*, edited by a now-forgotten poet, Bliss Carman, who included selections from one hundred poets born after 1841—so the span of years is roughly equivalent to that surveyed in *Contemporary American Poetry*. Only a very few of the poets Carman selected, such as Robinson, Frost, Amy Lowell, Ezra Pound, Edna St. Vincent Millay, would achieve classic status or even be familiar to a reader of today. The overwhelming majority have been honorably relegated to oblivion where rest such names as Richard Watson Gilder, Louise Imogen Guiney, Madison Cawein, Anna Hempstead Branch, Theodosia Garrison, and countless others. The moral seems clear and sobering.

Fifty years from now the majority of poets in this Pocket Anthology will be as forgotten as the ones Bliss Carman chose. This does not mean however that readers of the current anthology should treat the poems as historical phenomena to be "objectively" studied and classified. As the editors justly point out, their selections are, to say the least, wide-ranging—probably more so than would be an anthology made up from the poets Jarrell wrote about. Avant-garde and traditional, prose poems and sonnets, revolutionary and conservative politics—these and other names only gesture at the variety of affiliations in poems that share perhaps but a single quality: their words mean what they say and more often than not mean it intensely. It follows that, in dealing with this intensity in variety, readers should be encouraged to practice what Frost once called in a poem, "passionate preference such as love at sight." For it is only through such a committed exercise of taste that some of the names encountered here will still be alive a half century from now. Although Henry James in his great essay "The Art of Fiction" was directing his remarks at prose, they serve equally well to fit the world of verse: "Art lives upon discussion, upon experiment, upon curiosity, upon variety of attempt, upon the exchange of views and the comparison of standpoints." Such life can only be brought into activity by readers who make choices, have favorites, prefer this style to that, one way of looking at the world to another one. In fact, we choose among poems just as we choose among the people we meet in the course of our wordly adventure. In both cases, to reiterate Frost's words, the activity is passionate preference such as love at sight.

Howard Nemerov (1920–1991)

Howard Nemerov received both the National Book Award and the Pulitzer Prize for his Collected Poems *(1977). Nemerov was born in New York City. After graduating from Harvard in 1941, he served in World War II as a pilot in a unit of the Royal Canadian Air Force attached to the U.S. Army Air Forces. After the war he took a teaching job, and published his first volume of poems a year later. In 1969, he joined the English Department at Washington University in St. Louis, where he served as Distinguished Poet in Residence until his death. He also served as Poet Laureate of the United States from 1988 to 1990. Nemerov's body of work includes thirteen volumes of poetry, novels, stories, and criticism.*

History of a Literary Movement

After Margrave° died, nothing
Seemed worth while. I said as much
To Grumbach, who replied:
"The oscillations of fashion
Do not amuse me. There have been   5
Great men before, there will be
Other great men. Only man
Is important, man is ultimate."
I can still see him sitting there,
Sipping level by level his   10
Pousse-café.° He was a fat man.
Fat men are seldom the best
Creative writers.

       The rest of us
Slowly dispersed, hardly   15
Ever saw each other again,

---

1 **Margrave** fictitious writer, as are Grumbach and Impli   11 **Pousse-café** a layered drink featuring cream and liqueur

And did not correspond, for
There was little enough to say.
Only Impli and I
Hung on, feeling as we did   20
That the last word had not
Finally been said. Sometimes
I feel, I might say, cheated.
Life here at Bad Grandstein°
Is dull, is dull, what with   25
The eternal rocks and the river;
And Impli, though one of my
Dearest friends, can never,
I have decided, become great.

                                                  —1947

The Fourth of July

Because I am drunk, this Independence Night,
I watch the fireworks from far away,
From a high hill, across the moony green
Of lakes and other hills to the town harbor,
Where stately illuminations are flung aloft,   5
One light shattering in a hundred lights
Minute by minute. The reason I am crying,
Aside from only being country drunk,
That is, may be that I have just remembered
The sparklers, rockets, roman candles, and   10
So on, we used to be allowed to buy
When I was a boy, and set off by ourselves
At some peril to life and property.
Our freedom to abuse our freedom thus
Has since, I understand, been remedied   15
By legislation. Now the authorities
Arrange a perfectly safe public display
To be watched at a distance; and now also
The contribution of all the taxpayers

24 **Bad Grandstein** fictitious place

Together makes a more spectacular   20
Result than any could achieve alone
(A few pale pinwheels, or a firecracker
Fused at the dog's tail). It is, indeed, splendid:
Showers of roses in the sky, fountains
Of emeralds, and those profusely scattered zircons   25
Falling and falling, flowering as they fall
And followed distantly by a noise of thunder.
My eyes are half-afloat in happy tears.
God bless our Nation on a night like this,
And bless the careful and secure officials   30
Who celebrate our independence now.

—1958

A Primer of the Daily Round

A peels an apple, while B kneels to God,
C telephones to D, who has a hand
On E's knee, F coughs, G turns up the sod
For H's grave, I do not understand
But J is bringing one clay pigeon down   5
While K brings down a nightstick on L's head,
And M takes mustard, N drives into town,
O goes to bed with P, and Q drops dead,
R lies to S, but happens to be heard
By T, who tells U not to fire V   10
For having to give W the word
That X is now deceiving Y with Z,
    Who happens just now to remember A
    Peeling an apple somewhere far away.

—1958

The Human Condition

In this motel where I was told to wait,
The television screen is stood before
The picture window. Nothing could be more
Use to a man than knowing where he's at,
And I don't know, but pace the day in doubt   5
Between my looking in and looking out.

Through snow, along the snowy road, cars pass
Going both ways, and pass behind the screen
Where heads of heroes sometimes can be seen
And sometimes cars, that speed across the glass.   10
Once I saw world and thought exactly meet,
But only in a picture by Magritte.

A picture of a picture, by Magritte,°
Wherein a landscape on an easel stands
Before a window opening on a land-   15
scape, and the pair of them a perfect fit,
Silent and mad. You know right off, the room
Before that scene was always an empty room.

And that is now the room in which I stand
Waiting, or walk, and sometimes try to sleep.   20
The day falls into darkness while I keep
The TV going; headlights blaze behind
Its legendary traffic, love and hate,
In this motel where I was told to wait.

—1967

13 **Magritte** René Magritte (1898–1967) Belgian surrealist painter; his painting, *The Human Condition*, is described in the poem

Amy Clampitt (1920–1994)

Amy Clampitt set her lush yet exacting poems in a wide range of land-
scapes. Born and raised in New Providence, Iowa, she graduated from
Grinnell College and moved to New York City, where she spent most of
her life, earning her living as a secretary at the Oxford University Press, a
reference librarian at the Audubon Society, and a freelance editor.
Clampitt wrote poetry in high school, but abandoned poetry in favor of
fiction, and only resumed writing poetry in her forties. Her first poem was
published by the New Yorker *in 1978, and she published her first full-*
length collection, The Kingfisher *(1983), at the age of sixty-three. She*
*brought out four more collections—*What the Light Was Like *(1985),*
Archaic Figure *(1987),* Westward *(1990), and* A Silence Opens *(1994)—*
before her death.

The Kingfisher

In a year the nightingales were said to be so loud
they drowned out slumber, and peafowl strolled screaming
beside the ruined nunnery, through the long evening
of a dazzled pub crawl, the halcyon color, portholed
by those eye-spots' stunning tapestry, unsettled   5
the pastoral nightfall with amazements opening.

Months later, intermission in a pub on Fifty-fifth Street
found one of them still breathless, the other quizzical,
acting the philistine, puncturing Stravinsky°— "Tell
me, what *was* that racket in the orchestra about?"—   10
hauling down the Firebird,° harum-scarum, like a kite,
a burnished, breathing wreck that didn't hurt at all.

Among the Bronx Zoo's exiled jungle fowl, they heard
through headphones of a separating panic, the bellbird
reiterate its single *chong*, a scream nobody answered.   15
When he mourned, "The poetry is gone," she quailed,
seeing how his hands shook, sobered into feeling old.
By midnight, yet another fifth would have been killed.

---

9 Stravinsky Igor Stravinsky (1882–1971), Russian composer   **11 Firebird** *The Firebird*, a ballet
composed by Stravinsky for the Ballet Ruse

A Sunday morning, the November of their cataclysm
(Dylan Thomas° brought in *in extremis* to St. Vincent's,°   20
that same week, a symptomatic datum) found them
wandering a downtown churchyard. Among its headstones,
while from unruined choirs the noise of Christendom
poured over Wall Street, a benison in vestments,

a late thrush paused, in transit from some grizzled   25
spruce bog to the humid equatorial fireside: berry-
eyed, bark-brown above, with dark hints of trauma
in the stigmata of its underparts—or so, too bruised
just then to have invented anything so fancy,
later, re-embroidering a retrospect, she had supposed.   30

In gray England, years of muted recrimination (then
dead silence) later, she could not have said how many
spoiled takeoffs, how many entanglements gone sodden,
how many gaudy evenings made frantic by just one
insomniac nightingale, how many liaisons gone down   35
screaming in a stroll beside the ruined nunnery;

a kingfisher's burnished plunge, the color
of felicity afire, came glancing like an arrow
through landscapes of untended memory: ardor
illuminating with its terrifying currency   40
now no mere glimpse, no porthole vista
but, down on down, the uninhabitable sorrow.

—1983

What the Light Was Like

*For Louise Dickinson Rich and the family of
Ernest Woodward*

Every year in June—up here, that's the month for lilacs—
    almost his whole front yard,
with lobster traps stacked out in back, atop the rise
    that overlooks the inlet

20 Dylan Thomas Welsh poet (1914–1953) **20 St. Vincent's** hospital in New York where Thomas died

would be a Himalayan range of peaks of bloom,
     white or mauve-violet,

gusting a turbulence of perfume, and every year the same
     iridescent hummingbird,
or its descendant, would be at work among the mourning cloaks
     and swallowtails, its motor loud,   5
its burning gorget darkening at moments as though charred.
     He kept an eye out

for it, we learned one evening, as for everything that flapped
     or hopped or hovered
crepuscular under the firs: he'd heard the legendary
     trilling of the woodcock,
and watched the eiders, once rare along these coasts,
     making their comeback

so that now they're everywhere, in tribes, in families
     of aunts and cousins,   10
a knit-and-purl of irresistibly downy young behind them, riding
     every cove and inlet;
and yes, in answer to the question summer people always ask,
     he'd seen the puffins

that breed out on 'Tit Manan,° in summer improbably clown-faced
     behind the striped scarlet
of Commedia dell' Arte° masks we'll never see except in
     Roger Tory Peterson's°
field guide, or childish wishful thinking. There was much
     else I meant to ask about   15

another summer. But in June, when we came limping up here
     again, looking forward
to easing up from a mean, hard, unaccommodating winter,
     we heard how he'd gone out
at dawn, one morning in October, unmoored the dinghy
     and rowed to his boat

as usual, the harbor already chugging with half a dozen
     neighbors' revved-up craft,

13 'Tit Manan short for "Petit Manan," an island off of Maine   **14 Commedia dell' Arte** form of improvisational comedy that flourished during the sixteenth through eighteenth centuries
14 Roger Tory Peterson's Field Guide guide to bird species

wet decks stacked abaft with traps, the bait and kegs stowed
    forward, a lifting weft   20
of fog spooled off in pearl-pink fleeces overhead with the first
    daylight, and steered,

as usual, past first the inner and then the outer bar, where in
    whatever kind of weather,
the red reef-bell yells, in that interminable treble, *Trouble*,
    out past where the Groaner°
lolls, its tempo and forte changing with the chop, played on
    by every wind shift,

straight into the sunrise, a surge of burning turning the
    whole ocean iridescent   25
fool's-gold over molten emerald, into the core of that
    day-after-day amazement—
a clue, one must suppose, to why lobstermen are often
    naturally gracious:

maybe, out there beside the wheel, the Baptist spire
    shrunk to a compass-
point, the town an interrupted circlet, feeble as an apron-
    string, for all the labor
it took to put it there, it's finding, out in that ungirdled
    wallowing and glitter,   30

finally, that what you love most is the same as what you're
    most afraid of—God,
in a word; whereas it seems they think they've got it licked
    (or used to), back there
in the Restricted Area for instance, where that huge hush-
    hush thing they say is radar

sits sprawling on the heath like Stonehenge, belittling every
    other man-made thing
in view, even the gargantuan pods of the new boat hulls you
    now and then see lying,   35
stark naked, crimson on the inside as a just-skinned carcass,
    in Young's boatyard,

23 Groaner a whistling buoy

even the gray Grange Hall, wood-heated by a yardarm of stovepipe
    across the ceiling.
Out there, from that wallowing perspective, all comparisons
    amount to nothing,
though once you've hauled your last trap, things tend to wander
    into shorter focus

as, around noon, you head back in: first 'Tit Manan lighthouse,
    a ghostly gimlet   40
on its ledge by day, but on clear nights expanding to a
    shout, to starboard,
the sunstruck rock pile of Cranberry Point to port; then
    you see the hamlet

rainbowed, above the blurring of the spray shield, by the
    hurrying herring gulls'
insatiable fandango of excitement—the spire first, then
    the crimson boat hulls,
the struts of the ill-natured gadget on the heath behind them
    as the face of things expands,   45

the hide-and-seek behind the velvet-shouldered, sparse
    tree-spined profiles,
as first the outer, then the inner bar appears, then the scree-
    beach under Crowley Island's
crowding firs and spruces, and you detect among the chimneys
    and the TV aerials,

yours. But by midafternoon of that October day,
    when all his neighbors'
boats had chugged back through the inlet, his
    was still out; at evening,   50
with half the town out looking, and a hard frost
    settling in among the alders,

there'd been no sign of him. The next day, and the next,
    the search went on,
and widened, joined by planes and helicopters from as
    far away as Boston.
When, on the third day, his craft was sighted
    finally, it had drifted,

with its engine running, till the last gulp of fuel
    spluttered and ran out,   55
beyond the town's own speckled noose of buoys, past
    the furred crest of Schoodic,°
vivid in a skirt of aspens, the boglands cranberry-
    crimson at its foot,

past the bald brow the sunrise always strikes first, of
    the hulk of Cadillac,°
riding the current effortlessly as eiders tied to water
    by the summer molt,
for fifty miles southwestward to where, off Matinicus,°
    out past the rock   60

that, like 'Tit Manan, is a restricted area, off limits for
    all purposes but puffins',
they spotted him, slumped against the kegs. I find it
    tempting to imagine what,
when the blood roared, overflowing its cerebral sluiceway,
    and the iridescence

of his last perception, charring, gave way to unreversed,
    irrevocable dark,
the light out there was like, that's always shifting—from
    a nimbus gone berserk   65
to a single gorget, a cathedral train of blinking, or
    the fogbound shroud

that can turn anywhere into a nowhere. But it's useless.
    Among the mourning-cloak-
hovered-over lilac peaks, their whites and purples,
    when we pass his yard,
poignant to excess with fragrance, this year we haven't
    seen the hummingbird.

—1985

56 **Schoodic** a portion of Acadia National Park   58 **Cadillac** mountain in Acadia National Park
60 **Matinicus** island in Penobscot Bay

Nothing Stays Put

In memory of Father Flye, 1884–1985

The strange and wonderful are too much with us.
The protea of the antipodes—a great,
globed, blazing honeybee of a bloom—
for sale in the supermarket! We are in
our decadence, we are not entitled. 5
What have we done to deserve
all the produce of the tropics—
this fiery trove, the largesse of it
heaped up like cannonballs, these pineapples, bossed
and crested, standing like troops at attention, 10
these tiers, these balconies of green, festoons
grown sumptuous with stoop labor?

The exotic is everywhere, it comes to us
before there is a yen or a need for it. The green-
grocers, uptown and down, are from South Korea. 15
Orchids, opulence by the pailful, just slightly
fatigued by the plane trip from Hawaii, are
disposed on the sidewalks; alstroemerias, freesias
fattened a bit in translation from overseas; gladioli
likewise estranged from their piercing ancestral crimson; 20
as well as, less altered from the original blue cornflower
of the roadsides and railway embankments of Europe, these
bachelor's buttons. But it isn't the railway embankments
their featherweight wheels of cobalt remind me of, it's

a row of them among prim colonnades of cosmos, 25
snapdragon, nasturtium, bloodsilk red poppies,
in my grandmother's garden: a prairie childhood,
the grassland shorn, overlaid with a grid,
unsealed, furrowed, harrowed and sown with immigrant grasses,
their massive corduroy, their wavering feltings embroidered 30
here and there by the scarlet shoulder patch of cannas
on a courthouse lawn, by a love knot, a cross stitch
of living matter, sown and tended by women,
nurturers everywhere of the strange and wonderful,
beneath whose hands what had been alien begins, 35
as it alters, to grow as though it were indigenous.

But at this remove what I think of as
strange and wonderful, strolling the side streets of Manhattan
on an April afternoon, seeing hybrid pear trees in blossom,
a tossing, vertiginous colonnade of foam, up above—   40
is the white petalfall, the warm snowdrift
of the indigenous wild plum of my childhood.
Nothing stays put. The world is a wheel.
All that we know, that we're
made of, is motion.   45

—*1990*

Charles Bukowski (1920–1994)

Charles Bukowski was born in Andernach, Germany, and moved to the United States with his family at the age of three. Raised in Los Angeles, he spent much of his adult life as a drifter before eventually moving to San Pedro, California. Though never closely associated with Jack Kerouac and other Beat poets, Bukowski generally is considered an honorary "Beat writer" for his unconventional subject matter, blunt language, and iconoclastic approach to formal structure.

my father

was a truly amazing man
he pretended to be
rich
even though we lived on beans and mush and weenies
when we sat down to eat, he said,   5
"not everybody can eat like this."
and because he wanted to be rich or because he actually
thought he *was* rich
he always voted Republican
and he voted for Hoover against Roosevelt   10
and he lost
and then he voted for Alf Landon against Roosevelt
and he lost again
saying, "I don't know what this world is coming to,
now we've got that god damned Red in there again   15

and the Russians will be in our backyard next!"
I think it was my father who made me decide to
become a bum.
I decided that if a man like that wants to be rich
then I want to be poor.   20
and I became a bum.
I lived on nickles and dimes and in cheap rooms and
on park benches.
I thought maybe the bums knew something.
but I found out that most of the bums wanted to be   25
rich too.
they had just failed at that.
so caught between my father and the bums
I had no place to go
and I went there fast and slow.   30
never voted Republican
never voted.
buried him
like an oddity of the earth
like a hundred thousand oddities   35
like millions of other oddities,
wasted.

—1990

the great escape

listen, he said, you ever seen a bunch of crabs in a
bucket?
no, I told him.
well, what happens is that now and then one crab
will climb up on top of the others   5
and begin to climb toward the top of the bucket,
then, just as he's about to escape
another crab grabs him and pulls him back
down.
really? I asked.   10
really, he said, and this job is just like that, none

of the others want anybody to get out of
here. that's just the way it is
in the postal service!
I believe you, I said. 15

just then the supervisor walked up and said,
you fellows were talking.
there is no talking allowed on this
job.

I had been there for eleven and one-half 20
years.

I got up off my stool and climbed right up the
supervisor
and then I reached up and pulled myself right
out of there. 25

it was so easy it was unbelievable.
but none of the others followed me.

and after that, whenever I had crab legs
I thought about that place.
I must have thought about that place 30
maybe 5 or 6 times

before I switched to lobster.

—2002

Richard Wilbur (b. 1921)

*Richard Wilbur will be remembered by posterity as perhaps the most skill-
ful metricist and exponent of wit that American poetry has produced. His
highly polished poetry—against the grain of much contemporary writing—
is a monument to his craftsmanship and intelligence. Born in New York
City, Wilbur graduated from Amherst College and served in the army in
World War II. He has taught English at Harvard, Wellesley, Wesleyan, and
Smith. The recipient of two Pulitzer Prizes and a National Book Award,
Wilbur is perhaps the most honored of all living American poets. He
served as Poet Laureate of the United States in 1987, edited the poetry of
Shakespeare and Poe, and wrote song lyrics for* Candide, *a 1956 Broad-
way musical by Lillian Hellman and Leonard Bernstein. He also has writ-
ten literary criticism (collected in* Responses, *1976) and a children's story,*
Loudmouse *(1963). His translations of the verse dramas of Molière and
Racine are regularly performed throughout the world.*

The Pardon

My dog lay dead five days without a grave
In the thick of summer, hid in a clump of pine
And a jungle of grass and honeysuckle-vine.
I who had loved him while he kept alive

Went only close enough to where he was 5
To sniff the heavy honeysuckle-smell
Twined with another odor heavier still
And hear the flies' intolerable buzz.

Well, I was ten and very much afraid.
In my kind world the dead were out of range 10
And I could not forgive the sad or strange
In beast or man. My father took the spade

And buried him. Last night I saw the grass
Slowly divide (it was the same scene
But now it glowed a fierce and mortal green) 15
And saw the dog emerging. I confess

I felt afraid again, but still he came
In the carnal sun, clothed in a hymn of flies,

And death was breeding in his lively eyes.
I started in to cry and call his name,   20

Asking forgiveness of his tongueless head.
. . . I dreamt the past was never past redeeming:
But whether this was false or honest dreaming
I beg death's pardon now. And mourn the dead.

—1950

A Simile for Her Smile

Your smiling, or the hope, the thought of it,
Makes in my mind such pause and abrupt ease
As when the highway bridgegates fall,
Balking the hasty traffic, which must sit
On each side massed and staring, while   5
Deliberately the drawbridge starts to rise:

Then horns are hushed, the oilsmoke rarefies,
Above the idling motors one can tell
The packet's smooth approach, the slip,
Slip of the silken river past the sides,   10
The ringing of clear bells, the dip
And slow cascading of the paddle wheel.

—1950

Year's End

Now winter downs the dying of the year,
And night is all a settlement of snow;
From the soft street the rooms of houses show
A gathered light, a shapen atmosphere,
Like frozen-over lakes whose ice is thin   5
And still allows some stirring down within.

I've known the wind by water banks to shake
The late leaves down, which frozen where they fell
And held in ice as dancers in a spell

Fluttered all winter long into a lake;   10
Graved on the dark in gestures of descent,
They seemed their own most perfect monument.

There was perfection in the death of ferns
Which laid their fragile cheeks against the stone
A million years. Great mammoths overthrown   15
Composedly have made their long sojourns,
Like palaces of patience, in the gray
And changeless lands of ice. And at Pompeii°

The little dog lay curled and did not rise
But slept the deeper as the ashes rose   20
And found the people incomplete, and froze
The random hands, the loose unready eyes
Of men expecting yet another sun
To do the shapely thing they had not done.

These sudden ends of time must give us pause.   25
We fray into the future, rarely wrought
Save in the tapestries of afterthought.
More time, more time. Barrages of applause
Come muffled from a buried radio.
The New-year bells are wrangling with the snow.   30

—1950

Love Calls Us to the Things of This World

    The eyes open to a cry of pulleys,
And spirited from sleep, the astounded soul
Hangs for a moment bodiless and simple
As false dawn.
              Outside the open window
The morning air is all awash with angels.   5

    Some are in bed-sheets, some are in blouses,
Some are in smocks: but truly there they are.
Now they are rising together in calm swells

18 Pompeii Roman city destroyed by volcanic eruption in A.D. 79

Of halcyon feeling, filling whatever they wear
With the deep joy of their impersonal breathing;   10

   Now they are flying in place, conveying
The terrible speed of their omnipresence, moving
And staying like white water; and now of a sudden
They swoon down into so rapt a quiet
That nobody seems to be there.
                      The soul shrinks   15

   From all that it is about to remember,
From the punctual rape of every blessèd day,
And cries,
        "Oh, let there be nothing on earth but laundry,
Nothing but rosy hands in the rising steam
And clear dances done in the sight of heaven."   20

   Yet, as the sun acknowledges
With a warm look the world's hunks and colors,
The soul descends once more in bitter love
To accept the waking body, saying now
In a changed voice as the man yawns and rises,   25

   "Bring them down from their ruddy gallows;
Let there be clean linen for the backs of thieves;
Let lovers go fresh and sweet to be undone,
And the heaviest nuns walk in a pure floating
Of dark habits,
        keeping their difficult balance."   30

                    —*1956*

Mind

Mind in its purest play is like some bat
That beats about in caverns all alone,
Contriving by a kind of senseless wit
Not to conclude against a wall of stone.

It has no need to falter or explore;   5
Darkly it knows what obstacles are there,
And so may weave and flitter, dip and soar
In perfect courses through the blackest air.

And has this simile a like perfection?
The mind is like a bat. Precisely. Save   10
That in the very happiest intellection
A graceful error may correct the cave.

—*1956*

Advice to a Prophet

When you come, as you soon must, to the streets of our city,
Mad-eyed from stating the obvious,
Not proclaiming our fall but begging us
In God's name to have self-pity,

Spare us all word of the weapons, their force and range,   5
The long numbers that rocket the mind;
Our slow, unreckoning hearts will be left behind,
Unable to fear what is too strange.

Nor shall you scare us with talk of the death of the race.
How should we dream of this place without us?—   10
The sun mere fire, the leaves untroubled about us,
A stone look on the stone's face?

Speak of the world's own change. Though we cannot conceive
Of an undreamt thing, we know to our cost
How the dreamt cloud crumbles, the vines are blackened by frost, 15
How the view alters. We could believe,

If you told us so, that the white-tailed deer will slip
Into perfect shade, grown perfectly shy,
The lark avoid the reaches of our eye,
The jack-pine lose its knuckled grip   20

On the cold ledge, and every torrent burn
As Xanthus° once, its gliding trout
Stunned in a twinkling. What should we be without
The dolphin's arc, the dove's return,

These things in which we have seen ourselves and spoken?   25
Ask us, prophet, how we shall call
Our natures forth when that live tongue is all
Dispelled, that glass obscured or broken

22 Xanthus Hephaestus, invoked by Achilles, scalded the river Xanthus (Scamander) in *Iliad, xxi.*
[Wilbur's note]

In which we have said the rose of our love and the clean
Horse of our courage, in which beheld   30
The singing locust of the soul unshelled,
And all we mean or wish to mean.

Ask us, ask us whether with the worldless rose
Our hearts shall fail us; come demanding
Whether there shall be lofty or long standing   35
When the bronze annals of the oak-tree close.

—1961

The Writer

In her room at the prow of the house
Where light breaks, and the windows are tossed with linden,
My daughter is writing a story.

I pause in the stairwell, hearing
From her shut door a commotion of typewriter-keys   5
Like a chain hauled over a gunwale.

Young as she is, the stuff
Of her life is a great cargo, and some of it heavy:
I wish her a lucky passage.

But now it is she who pauses,   10
As if to reject my thought and its easy figure.
A stillness greatens, in which

The whole house seems to be thinking,
And then she is at it again with a bunched clamor
Of strokes, and again is silent.   15

I remember the dazed starling
Which was trapped in that very room, two years ago;
How we stole in, lifted a sash

And retreated, not to affright it;
And how for a helpless hour, through the crack of the door,   20
We watched the sleek, wild, dark

And iridescent creature
Batter against the brilliance, drop like a glove
To the hard floor, or the desk-top.

And wait then, humped and bloody, 25
For the wits to try it again; and how our spirits
Rose when, suddenly sure,

It lifted off from a chair-back,
Beating a smooth course for the right window
And clearing the sill of the world. 30

It is always a matter, my darling,
Of life or death, as I had forgotten. I wish
What I wished you before, but harder.

—1976

Hamlen Brook

At the alder-darkened brink
Where the stream slows to a lucid jet
I lean to the water, dinting its top with sweat,
And see, before I can drink,

A startled inchling trout 5
Of spotted near-transparency,
Trawling a shadow solider than he.
He swerves now, darting out

To where, in a flicked slew
Of sparks and glittering silt, he weaves 10
Through stream-bed rocks, disturbing foundered leaves,
And butts then out of view

Beneath a sliding glass
Crazed by the skimming of a brace
Of burnished dragon-flies across its face, 15
In which deep cloudlets pass

And a white precipice
Of mirrored birch-trees plunges down
Toward where the azures of the zenith drown.
How shall I drink all this? 20

Joy's trick is to supply
Dry lips with what can cool and slake,

Leaving them dumbstruck also with an ache
    Nothing can satisfy.

—*1988*

For C.

After the clash of elevator gates
And the long sinking, she emerges where,
A slight thing in the morning's crosstown glare,
She looks up toward the window where he waits,
Then in a fleeting taxi joins the rest   5
Of the huge traffic bound forever west.

On such grand scale do lovers say good-bye—
Even this other pair whose high romance
Had only the duration of a dance,
And who, now taking leave with stricken eye,   10
See each in each a whole new life forgone.
For them, above the darkling clubhouse lawn,

Bright Perseids flash and crumble; while for these
Who part now on the dock, weighed down by grief
And baggage, yet with something like relief,   15
It takes three thousand miles of knitting seas
To cancel out their crossing, and unmake
The amorous rough and tumble of their wake.

We are denied, my love, their fine tristesse
And bittersweet regrets, and cannot share   20
The frequent vistas of their large despair,
Where love and all are swept to nothingness;
Still, there's a certain scope in that long love
Which constant spirits are the keepers of,

And which, though taken to be tame and staid,   25
Is a wild sostenuto° of the heart,
A passion joined to courtesy and art
Which has the quality of something made,
Like a good fiddle, like the rose's scent,
Like a rose window or the firmament.   30

—*2000*

26 **sostenuto** musical direction: in a sustained or prolonged manner

Mona Van Duyn (b. 1921)

Mona Van Duyn is the author of nine books of poems including If It Be
Not I: Collected Poems 1959–1982 *(1993) and* Near Changes *(1990) for
which she received a Pulitzer Prize. Born in Waterloo, Iowa, Van Duyn
cofounded* Perspective: A Quarterly of Literature *in 1947, and coedited it,
with her husband, Jarvis Thurston, for over twenty years. She has served
as Poet Laureate of the United States, and lives in St Louis, Missouri.*

Letters from a Father

I

Ulcerated tooth keeps me awake, there is
such pain, would have to go to the hospital to have
it pulled or would bleed to death from the blood thinners,
but can't leave Mother, she falls and forgets her salve
and her tranquilizers, her ankles swell so and her bowels   5
are so bad, she almost had a stoppage and sometimes
what she passes is green as grass. There are big holes
in my thigh where my leg brace buckles the size of dimes.
My head pounds from the high pressure. It is awful
not to be able to get out, and I fell in the bathroom   10
and the girl could hardly get me up at all.
Sure thought my back was broken, it will be next time.
Prostate is bad and heart has given out,
feel bloated after supper. Have made my peace
because am just plain done for and have no doubt   15
that the Lord will come any day with my release.
You say you enjoy your feeder, I don't see why
you want to spend good money on grain for birds
and you say you have a hundred sparrows, I'd buy
poison and get rid of their diseases and turds.   20

II

We enjoyed your visit, it was nice of you to bring
the feeder but a terrible waste of your money
for that big bag of feed since we won't be living
more than a few weeks longer. We can see
them good from where we sit, big ones and little ones   25

but you know when I farmed I used to like to hunt
and we had many a good meal from pigeons
and quail and pheasant but these birds won't
be good for nothing and are dirty to have so near
the house. Mother likes the redbirds though.   30
My bad knee is so sore and I can't hardly hear
and Mother says she is hoarse from yelling but I know
it's too late for a hearing aid. I belch up all the time
and have a sour mouth and of course with my heart
it's no use to go to a doctor. Mother is the same.   35
Has a scab she thinks is going to turn to a wart.

III

The birds are eating and fighting, Ha! Ha! All shapes
and colors and sizes coming out of our woods
but we don't know what they are. Your Mother hopes
you can send us a kind of book that tells about birds.   40
There is one the folks called snowbirds, they eat on the ground,
we had the girl sprinkle extra there, but say,
they eat something awful. I sent the girl to town
to buy some more feed, she had to go anyway.

IV

Almost called you on the telephone   45
but it costs so much to call thought better write.
Say, the funniest thing is happening, one
day we had so many birds and they fight
and get excited at their feed you know
and it's really something to watch and two or three   50
flew right at us and crashed into our window
and bang, poor little things knocked themselves silly.
They come to after awhile on the ground and flew away.
And they been doing that. We felt awful
and didn't know what to do but the other day   55
a lady from our Church drove out to call
and a little bird knocked itself out while she sat
and she brought it in her hands right into the house,
it looked like dead. It had a kind of hat
of feathers sticking up on its head, kind of rose   60
or pinky color, don't know what it was,

and I petted it and it come to life right there
in her hands and she took it out and it flew. She says
they think the window is the sky on a fair
day, she feeds birds too but hasn't got   65
so many. She says to hang strips of aluminum foil
in the window so we'll do that. She raved about
our birds. P.S. The book just come in the mail.

     V

Say, that book is sure good, I study
in it every day and enjoy our birds.   70
Some of them I can't identify
for sure, I guess they're females, the Latin words
I just skip over. Bet you'd never guess
the sparrows I've got here, House Sparrows you wrote,
but I have Fox Sparrows, Song Sparrows, Vesper Sparrows,   75
Pine Woods and Tree and Chipping and White Throat
and White Crowned Sparrows. I have six Cardinals,
three pairs, they come at early morning and night,
the males at the feeder and on the ground the females.
Juncos, maybe 25, they fight   80
for the ground, that's what they used to call snowbirds. I miss
the Bluebirds since the weather warmed. Their breast
is the color of a good ripe muskmelon. Tufted Titmouse
is sort of blue with a little tiny crest.
And I have Flicker and Red-Bellied and Red-   85
Headed Woodpeckers, you would die laughing
to see Red-Bellied, he hangs on with his head
flat on the board, his tail braced up under,
wing out. And Dickcissel and Ruby Crowned Ringlet
and Nuthatch stands on his head and Veery on top   90
the color of a bird dog and Hermit Thrush with spot
on breast, Blue Jay so funny, he will hop
right on the backs of the other birds to get the grain.
We bought some sunflower seeds just for him.
And Purple Finch I bet you never seen,   95
color of a watermelon, sits on the rim
of the feeder with his streaky wife, and the squirrels,
you know, they are cute too, they sit tall
and eat with their little hands, they eat bucketfuls.
I pulled my own tooth, it didn't bleed at all.   100

VI

It's sure a surprise how well Mother is doing,
she forgets her laxative but bowels move fine.
Now that windows are open she says our birds sing
all day. The girl took a Book of Knowledge on loan
from the library and I am reading up   105
on the habits of birds, did you know some males have three
wives, some migrate some don't. I am going to keep
feeding all spring, maybe summer, you can see
they expect it. Will need thistle seed for Goldfinch and Pine
Siskin next winter. Some folks are going to come see us   110
from Church, some bird watchers, pretty soon.
They have birds in town but nothing to equal this.

So the world woos its children back for an evening kiss.

—1982

Hayden Carruth   (b. 1921)

Hayden Carruth received the National Book Critics' Circle Award for his Collected Shorter Poems, 1946–1991 *(1992) and the National Book Award for* Scrambled Eggs and Whiskey *(1996). Born in Waterbury, Connecticut, he studied at the University of North Carolina at Chapel Hill and the University of Chicago. Carruth lived for many years in northern Vermont, but now resides in upstate New York, where he taught until recently at Syracuse University. He has published many poetry collections, a novel, four books of criticism, and two anthologies. He also has served as editor of* Poetry, *poetry editor of* Harper's, *and advisory editor at* The Hudson Review. *Carruth's radical politics informs his poems, many of which depict life in impoverished rural communities.*

Woodsmoke at 70

How it is never the same
but always changing. How
sometimes nevertheless
you recognize it. How you
see it from your window   5
plunging down, flattening

across the frozen lawn,
then rising in a wild
swirl and it's gone . . .

—*1992*

Pittsburgh

And my beautiful daughter
had her liver cut open in Pittsburgh.
My god, my god! I rubbed
her back over the swollen and wounded
essentiality, I massaged   5
her legs, and we talked of death.
At the luckiest patients with liver cancer have
a 20% chance. We might have talked
of my death, not long to come. But no,
the falling into death of a beautiful   10
young woman is so much more important.
A wonderful hospital. If I must die
away from my cat Smudge and my Vermont Castings stove
let it be at Allegheny General.
I read to her, a novella by Allan Gurganus,°   15
a Russian serious flimsiness by Voinovich,°
and we talked. We laughed. We actually
laughed. I bought her a lipstick
which she wore though she disliked the color.
Helicopters took off and landed on the hospital pad,   20
bringing hearts and kidneys and maybe livers
from other places to be transplanted
into people in the shining household of technology
by shining technologists, wise and kindly.
The chances are so slight. Oh, my daughter,   25
my love for you has burgeoned—
an excess of singularity ever increasing—
you are my soul—for forty years. You
still beautiful and young. In my hotel
I could not sleep. In my woods, on my   30
little farm, in the blizzard on the mountain,

---

15 **Allan Gurganus** contemporary novelist   16 **Voinovich** Vladmir Voinovich, Soviet-era dissident
novelist

I could not sleep either, but scribbled
fast verses, very fast and
wet with my heartsblood and brainjuice
all my life, as now   35
in Pittsburgh. I don't know which of
us will live the longer, it's all a flick
of the wrist of the god mankind invented
and then had to deinvent, such a failure, like all
our failures, and the worst and best   40
is sentimentality after all. Let us go out together.
Here in brutal Pittsburgh. Let us
be together in the same room,
the old poet and the young painter,
holding hands, a calm touch, a whisper,   45
as the thumping helicopters go out and come in,
we in the crisis of forever inadequately medicated
pain, in the love of daughter and father.

—*1996*

Frederick Morgan (1922–2004)

Frederick Morgan made his poetic debut at age fifty, but had long been an important figure on the literary scene. A native New Yorker, Morgan grew up in Greenwich Village and graduated from Princeton University. During World War II, he served in the U.S. Army's Tank Destroyer Corps. He co-founded The Hudson Review *in 1947 and edited the journal for fifty years. Morgan published ten books of poems, as well as collections of prose fables and translations. His love poems to his wife, Paula Deitz, were collected in* Poems for Paula *(1995).*

The Step

From where you are at any moment you
may step off into death.
Is it not a clinching thought?
I do not mean a stoical bravado
of making the great decision blade in hand   5

but the awareness, all so simple, that
right in the middle of the day
you may be called to an adjoining room.

—1987

The Burial

How shall the difficult man
be buried? How indeed?
Who can track the difficult man
or know where he keeps himself hid?

You must catch him first if you can,   5
making certain he's safe in his box,
then put the whole works in that other—
the one with permanent locks.

Having settled him down once for all
in an absence that's yours to command   10
you may streamline his speech into scripture
and take all his meanings in hand—

you may smooth out the sense of his riddles
that taxed the dull wits of the tribe,
assign him a throne up in heaven   15
and yelp the good news far and wide—

but it's useless. Eluding your grasp,
he goes drifting away through the mist
as you stand there clutching the castoffs
from which he implausibly slipped—   20

and what have you gained for your trouble?
No enlightenment, no guarantee:
just this box which will rot in that other
while the difficult man roams free.

—2003

Anthony Hecht   (b. 1923)

Anthony Hecht is most often linked with Richard Wilbur as one of the American poets of the postwar era who have most effectively used traditional poetic forms. The brilliance of Hecht's technique, however, must be set beside the powerful moral intelligence that informs his poetry. Born in New York City, Hecht graduated from Bard College in 1944 and served in the army in both Europe and Japan. After World War II, he studied at Kenyon College and published his first book, A Summoning of Stones, *in 1954. Thirteen years later, Hecht brought out* The Hard Hours, *his second collection, which won the Pulitzer Prize in 1968. In addition to his poetry collections, Hecht has published critical essays, translations, and light verse. He currently lives in Washington, D.C.*

The Dover Bitch:
A Criticism of Life

for Andrews Wanning

So there stood Matthew Arnold° and this girl
With the cliffs of England crumbling away behind them,
And he said to her, "Try to be true to me,
And I'll do the same for you, for things are bad
All over, etc., etc."   5
Well now, I knew this girl. It's true she had read
Sophocles° in a fairly good translation
And caught that bitter allusion to the sea,
But all the time he was talking she had in mind
The notion of what his whiskers would feel like   10
On the back of her neck. She told me later on
That after a while she got to looking out
At the lights across the channel, and really felt sad,
Thinking of all the wine and enormous beds
And blandishments in French and the perfumes.   15
And then she got really angry. To have been brought

1 **Matthew Arnold** Victorian poet, author of "Dover Beach"   7 **Sophocles** Ancient Greek playwright

All the way down from London, and then be addressed
As a sort of mournful cosmic last resort
Is really tough on a girl, and she was pretty.
Anyway, she watched him pace the room   20
And finger his watch-chain and seem to sweat a bit,
And then she said one or two unprintable things.
But you mustn't judge her by that. What I mean to say is,
She's really all right. I still see her once in a while
And she always treats me right. We have a drink   25
And I give her a good time, and perhaps it's a year
Before I see her again, but there she is,
Running to fat, but dependable as they come.
And sometimes I bring her a bottle of *Nuit d'Amour.*

—*1967*

A Hill

In Italy, where this sort of thing can occur,
I had a vision once—though you understand
It was nothing at all like Dante's,° or the visions of saints.
And perhaps not a vision at all. I was with some friends.
Picking my way through a warm sunlit piazza   5
In the early morning. A clear fretwork of shadows
From huge umbrellas littered the pavement and made
A sort of lucent shallows in which was moored
A small navy of carts. Books, coins, old maps,
Cheap landscapes and ugly religious prints   10
Were all on sale. The colors and noise
Like the flying hands were gestures of exultation.
So that even the bargaining
Rose to the ear like a voluble godliness.
And then, when it happened, the noises suddenly stopped.   15
And it got darker; pushcarts and people dissolved
And even the great Farnese Palace° itself
Was gone, for all its marble; in its place
Was a hill, mole-colored and bare. It was very cold,
Close to freezing, with a promise of snow.   20

3 **Dante's** Dante Alighieri, author of *The Divine Comedy*   17 **Farnese Palace** Roman palace built in 1534

The trees were like old ironwork gathered for scrap
Outside a factory wall. There was no wind,
And the only sound for a while was the little click
Of ice as it broke in the mud under my feet.
I saw a piece of ribbon snagged on a hedge,   25
But no other sign of life. And then I heard
What seemed the crack of a rifle. A hunter, I guessed;
At least I was not alone. But just after that
Came the soft and papery crash
Of a great branch somewhere unseen falling to earth.   30

And that was all, except for the cold and silence
That promised to last forever, like the hill.

Then prices came through, and fingers, and I was restored
To the sunlight and my friends. But for more than a week
I was scared by the plain bitterness of what I had seen.   35
All this happened about ten years ago,
And it hasn't troubled me since, but at last, today,
I remembered that hill: it lies just to the left
Of the road north of Poughkeepsie; and as a boy
I stood before it for hours in wintertime.   40

—1967

"More Light! More Light!"°

For Heinrich Blücher and Hannah Arendt°

Composed in the Tower before his° execution
These moving verses, and being brought at that time
Painfully to the stake, submitted, declaring thus:
"I implore my God to witness that I have made no crime."

Nor was he forsaken of courage, but the death was horrible,   5
The sack of gunpowder failing to ignite.

"More Light! More Light!" reputed last words of Johann Wolfgang von Goethe (1749–1832), greatest German poet   **Heinrich Blücher and Hannah Arendt** husband and wife who escaped from Germany in 1941; Arendt wrote several books on the Holocaust   **1 his** a fictional English religious martyr (c. 1550), a composite of several actual cases

His legs were blistered sticks on which the black sap
Bubbled and burst as he howled for the Kindly Light.

And that was but one, and by no means one of the worst;
Permitted at least his pitiful dignity;   10
And such as were by made prayers in the name of Christ,
That shall judge all men, for his soul's tranquility.

We move now to outside a German wood.°
Three men are there commanded to dig a hole
In which the two Jews are ordered to lie down   15
And be buried alive by the third, who is a Pole.

Not light from the shrine at Weimar° beyond the hill
Nor light from heaven appeared. But he did refuse.
A Lüger° settled back deeply in its glove.
He was ordered to change places with the Jews.   20

Much casual death had drained away their souls.
The thick dirt mounted toward the quivering chin.
When only the head was exposed the order came
To dig him out again and to get back in.

No light, no light in the blue Polish eye.   25
When he finished a riding boot packed down the earth.
The Lüger hovered lightly in its glove.
He was shot in the belly and in three hours bled to death.

No prayers or incense rose up in those hours
Which grew to be years, and every day came mute   30
Ghosts from the ovens, sifting through crisp air,
And settled upon his eyes in a black soot.

—1967

Third Avenue in Sunlight

Third Avenue in sunlight. Nature's error.
Already the bars are filled and John is there.
Beneath a plentiful lady over the mirror
He tilts his glass in the mild mahogany air.

13 German wood Buchenwald ("beechen wood") was the site of a concentration camp   **17 shrine at Weimar** Goethe's home   **19 Lüger** German military pistol

I think of him when he first got out of college,   5
Serious, thin, unlikely to succeed;
For several months he hung around the Village,
Boldly T-shirted, unfettered but unfreed.

Now he confides to a stranger, "I was first scout,
And kept my glimmers peeled till after dark.   10
Our outfit had as its sign a bloody knout,
We met behind the museum in Central Park.

Of course, we were kids." But still those savages,
War-painted, a flap of leather at the loins,
File silently against him. Hostages   15
Are never taken. One summer, in Des Moines,

They entered his hotel room, tomahawks
Flashing like barracuda. He tried to pray.
Three years of treatment. Occasionally he talks
About how he almost didn't get away.   20

Daily the prowling sunlight whets its knife
Along the sidewalk. We almost never meet.
In the Rembrandt° dark he lifts his amber life.
My bar is somewhat further down the street.

—1967

The Book of Yolek

> Wir haben ein Gesetz,
> Und nach dem Gesetz soll er sterben.°

The dowsed coals fume and hiss after your meal
Of grilled brook trout, and you saunter off for a walk
Down the fern trail, it doesn't matter where to,
Just so you're weeks and worlds away from home,
And among midsummer hills have set up camp   5
In the deep bronze glories of declining day.

You remember, peacefully, an earlier day
In childhood, remember a quite specific meal:

23 Rembrandt Dutch Baroque-era painter and engraver (1606–1669)
Wir . . . er sterben "We have a law, and under that law he should die." John 19.7 (Martin Luther's German translation, c.1530)

A corn roast and bonfire in summer camp.
That summer you got lost on a Nature Walk;   10
More than you dared admit, you thought of home;
No one else knows where the mind wanders to.

The fifth of August, 1942.
It was morning and very hot. It was the day
They came at dawn with rifles to The Home   15
For Jewish Children, cutting short the meal
Of bread and soup, lining them up to walk
In close formation off to a special camp.

How often you have thought about that camp,
As though in some strange way you were driven to,   20
And about the children, and how they were made to walk,
Yolek who had bad lungs, who wasn't a day
Over five years old, commanded to leave his meal
And shamble between armed guards to his long home.

We're approaching August again. It will drive home   25
The regulation torments of that camp
Yolek was sent to, his small, unfinished meal,
The electric fences, the numeral tattoo,
The quite extraordinary heat of the day
They all were forced to take that terrible walk.   30

Whether on a silent, solitary walk
Or among crowds, far off or safe at home,
You will remember, helplessly, that day,
And the smell of smoke, and the loudspeakers of the camp.
Wherever you are, Yolek will be there, too.   35
His unuttered name will interrupt your meal.

Prepare to receive him in your home some day.
Though they killed him in the camp they sent him to,
He will walk in as you're sitting down to a meal.

—*1990*

James Dickey (1923–1997)

James Dickey wrote poems that daringly explore gray areas of morality, like "The Firebombing," narrated by a pilot who dropped incendiary devices on Japanese cities. He was born in a suburb of Atlanta, and played college football at the Clemson University, in South Carolina, until enlisting in the Army Air Corps. He served in the South Pacific as a radar observer and navigator during World War II, and as a flight-training instructor during the Korean conflict. After World War II, Dickey returned to school on the GI Bill and finished his education at Vanderbilt University. Dickey spent years in the advertising business, in his own words, "selling his soul to the devil in the daytime and buying it back at night." His first poetry collection, Into the Stone and Other Poems, *was published in 1960. He served for two years, 1966 and 1967, as consultant in poetry to the Library of Congress, and became a national celebrity with the success of his novel* Deliverance *(1970) and its celebrated film version. Dickey rarely strayed from the South for long, and he taught at the University of South Carolina for over two decades.*

The Heaven of Animals

Here they are. The soft eyes open
If they have lived in a wood
It is a wood.
If they have lived on plains
It is grass rolling   5
Under their feet forever.

Having no souls, they have come,
Anyway, beyond their knowing.
Their instincts wholly bloom
And they rise.   10
The soft eyes open.

To match them, the landscape flowers,
Outdoing, desperately
Outdoing what is required:
The richest wood,   15
The deepest field.

For some of these,
It could not be the place
It is, without blood.
These hunt, as they have done,   20
But with claws and teeth grown perfect,

More deadly than they can believe.
They stalk more silently,
And crouch on the limbs of trees,
And their descent   25
Upon the bright backs of their prey

May take years
In a sovereign floating of joy.
And those that are hunted
Know this as their life,   30
Their reward: to walk

Under such trees in full knowledge
Of what is in glory above them,
And to feel no fear,
But acceptance, compliance.   35
Fulfilling themselves without pain

At the cycle's center,
They tremble, they walk
Under the tree,
They fall, they are torn,   40
They rise, they walk again.

—*1962*

Adultery

We have all been in rooms
We cannot die in, and they are odd places, and sad.
Often Indians are standing eagle-armed on hills

In the sunrise   open wide to the Great Spirit
Or gliding in canoes   or cattle are browsing on the walls   5
Far away   gazing down with the eyes of our children

Not far away   or there are men driving
The last railspike, which has turned
Gold in their hands. Gigantic forepleasure lives

Among such scenes, and we are alone with it   10
At last. There is always some weeping
Between us   and someone is always checking

A wrist watch by the bed to see how much
Longer we have left. Nothing can come
Of this   nothing can come   15

Of us: of me with my grim techniques
Or you who have sealed your womb
With a ring of convulsive rubber:

Although we come together,
Nothing will come of us. But we would not give   20
It up, for death is beaten

By praying Indians   by distant cows   historical
Hammers   by hazardous meetings that bridge
A continent. One could never die here

Never die   never die   25
While crying. My lover, my dear one
I will see you next week

When I'm in town. I will call you
If I can. Please get hold of   please don't
Oh God, Please don't any more I can't bear . . . Listen: 30

We have done it again   we are
Still living. Sit up and smile,
God bless you. Guilt is magical.

—1968

The Sheep Child

Farm boys wild to couple
With anything   with soft-wooded trees
With mounds of earth   mounds
Of pinestraw   will keep themselves off

Animals by legends of their own: 5
In the hay-tunnel dark
And dung of barns, they will
Say   I have heard tell

That in a museum in Atlanta
Way back in a corner somewhere   10
There's this thing that's only half
Sheep   like a woolly baby
Pickled in alcohol   because
Those things can't live   his eyes
Are open   but you can't stand to look   15
I heard from somebody who . . .

But this is now almost all
Gone. The boys have taken
Their own true wives in the city,
The sheep are safe in the west hill   20
Pasture   but we who were born there
Still are not sure. Are we,
Because we remember, remembered
In the terrible dust of museums?

Merely with his eyes, the sheep-child may   25

Be saying   saying

> *I am here, in my father's house.*
> *I who am half of your world, came deeply*
> *To my mother in the long grass*
> *Of the west pasture, where she stood like moonlight*   30
> *Listening for foxes. It was something like love*
> *From another world that seized her*
> *From behind, and she gave, not lifting her head*
> *Out of dew, without ever looking, her best*
> *Self to that great need. Turned loose, she dipped her face*   35
> *Farther into the chill of the earth, and in a sound*
> *Of sobbing   of something stumbling*
> *Away, began, as she must do,*
> *To carry me. I woke, dying,*
>
> *In the summer sun of the hillside, with my eyes*   40
> *Far more than human. I saw for a blazing moment*
> *The great grassy world from both sides,*

Man and beast in the round of their need,
And the hill wind stirred in my wool,
My hoof and my hand clasped each other, 45
I ate my one meal
Of milk, and died
Staring. From dark grass I came straight

To my father's house, whose dust
Whirls up in the halls for no reason 50
When no one comes   piling deep in a hellish mild corner,
And, through my immortal waters,
I meet the sun's grains eye
To eye, and they fail at my closet of glass.
Dead, I am most surely living 55
In the minds of farm boys: I am he who drives
Them like wolves from the hound bitch and calf
And from the chaste ewe in the wind.
They go into woods   into bean fields   they go
Deep into their known right hands. Dreaming of me, 60
They groan   they wait   they suffer
Themselves, they marry, they raise their kind.

—1968

Alan Dugan (1923–2003)

*Alan Dugan was notable for his plainspoken poetic voice, often with sar-
donic overtones, and for the antiromantic stance of his most characteristic
poems. Born in Brooklyn, New York, he studied at Queens, Olivet, and
Mexico City Colleges. He served in the Army Air Corps during World War
II, and held jobs in advertising, publishing, and medical supply in New
York City. Dugan's first poetry collection,* Poems, *received the 1961 Yale
Younger Poets Award when he was nearly forty; it also won the National
Book Award and the Pulitzer Prize. Forty years later, Dugan won the National Book Award a second time, for his collection* Poems Seven: New
and Complete Poetry. *He lived in Paris, Rome, Mexico, and South America. Toward the end of his life, Dugan lived in Truro, Massachusetts, and
was associated with the Fine Arts Work Center in Provincetown.*

On a Seven-Day Diary

Oh I got up and went to work
and worked and came back home
and ate and talked and went to sleep.
Then I got up and went to work
and worked and came back home   5
from work and ate and slept.
Then I got up and went to work
and worked and came back home
and ate and watched a show and slept.
Then I got up and went to work   10
and worked and came back home
and ate steak and went to sleep.
Then I got up and went to work
and worked and came back home
and ate and fucked and went to sleep.   15
Then it was Saturday, Saturday, Saturday!
Love must be the reason for the week!
We went shopping! I saw clouds!
The children explained everything!
I could talk about the main thing!   20
What did I drink on Saturday night
that lost the first, best half of Sunday?
The last half wasn't worth this "word."
Then I got up and went to work

and worked and came back home   25
from work and ate and went to sleep,
refreshed but tired by the weekend.

—1963

Love Song: I and Thou

Nothing is plumb, level or square:
    the studs are bowed, the joists
are shaky by nature, no piece fits
    any other piece without a gap
or pinch, and bent nails
    dance all over the surfacing
like maggots. By Christ
    I am no carpenter. I built
the roof for myself, the walls
    for myself, the floors   5
for myself, and got
    hung up in it myself. I
danced with a purple thumb
    at this house-warming, drunk
with my prime whiskey: rage.
    Oh I spat rage's nails
into the frame-up of my work:
    it held. It settled plumb,
level, solid, square and true
    for that great moment. Then   10
it screamed and went on through,
    skewing as wrong the other way.
God damned it. This is hell,
    but I planned it, I sawed it,
I nailed it, and I
    will live in it until it kills me.
I can nail my left palm
    to the left-hand crosspiece but
I can't do everything myself.
    I need a hand to nail the right,   15
a help, a love, a you, a wife.

—1969

Tribute to Kafka° for Someone Taken

The party is going strong.
The doorbell rings. It's
for someone named me.
I'm coming. I take
a last drink, a last   5
puff on a cigarette,
a last kiss at a girl,
and step into the hall,
                              bang,
shutting out the laughter. "Is   10
your name you?" "Yes."
"Well come along then."
"See here. See here. See here."

—*1969*

Surviving the Hurricane

When the neighbor's outhouse went by
and landed upside down on my property,
unoccupied, I laughed and yelled, "It's mine,"
but what's so funny? the TV says
that many, many will get blown away   5
in the hurricane's uproarious humors,
and now the horizontal rain comes through
my wall, the wallpaper heaves and cries
and runs down to the floor as pulp
as the windows go out with the wind,   10
poof!, and the wind picks off the roof
two shingles at a time in love-me-nots,
and there is no difference inside or out:
Leaning against the wall or the wind
is the same. This wet is that wet.   15

Kafka Franz Kafka (1883–1924), Czech-born author known for depicting nightmarish alienation and dehumanization

There is no protection anywhere except
I go stand in the upside-down outhouse
with the crapper over my stinking head,
once it has dripped dry of its storm-borne shit,
and be the dry mummy of its sarcophagus   20
under the whole hurricane of the universe.
That's what's so funny: Egypt.

—*1989*

Louis Simpson (b. 1923)

Louis Simpson was born in Jamaica to a colonial lawyer father and an American mother, who was a Russian immigrant. He came to the United States in his teens and served in the U.S. Army in World War II in France, Belgium, Germany, and Holland. As a member of the 101st Airborne, he took part in D-Day. Two of his poems on the subject were set to music by the composer Aubert Lemeland and broadcast in France on the fiftieth anniversary of the battle. Simpson has written important critical studies of such major figures as Ezra Pound, T. S. Eliot, William Carlos Williams, and Allen Ginsberg, and has taught at Columbia, the University of California, Berkeley, and SUNY Stony Brook. He won the Pulitzer Prize in 1964 for At the End of the Open Road, *a volume that attempts to reexamine Walt Whitman's nineteenth-century definitions of the American experience. Subsequent collections have continued to demonstrate Simpson's unsentimental view of American suburban life.*

To the Western World

A siren sang, and Europe turned away
From the high castle and the shepherd's crook.
Three caravels went sailing to Cathay°
On the strange ocean, and the captains shook
Their banners out across the Mexique Bay.°   5

And in our early days we did the same.
Remembering our fathers in their wreck

3 **Cathay** China   5 **Mexique Bay** off the Oaxacan coast of Mexico

We crossed the sea from Palos° where they came
And saw, enormous to the little deck,
A shore in silence waiting for a name.   10

The treasures of Cathay were never found.
In this America, this wilderness
Where the axe echoes with a lonely sound,
The generations labor to possess
And grave by grave we civilize the ground.   15

—1959

American Poetry

Whatever it is, it must have
A stomach that can digest
Rubber, coal, uranium, moons, poems.

Like the shark, it contains a shoe.
It must swim for miles through the desert   5
Uttering cries that are almost human.

—1963

My Father in the Night Commanding No

My father in the night commanding No
Has work to do. Smoke issues from his lips;
    He reads in silence.
The frogs are croaking and the street lamps glow.

And then my mother winds the gramophone: 5
The Bride of Lammermoor° begins to shriek—

---

8 **Palos** in Greece   6 **Bride of Lammermoor** *Lucia di Lammermoor,* opera by Donizetti

Or reads a story
About a prince, a castle, and a dragon.

The moon is glittering above the hill.
I stand before the gateposts of the King—   10
So runs the story—
Of Thule,° at midnight when the mice are still.

And I have been in Thule! It has come true—
The journey and the danger of the world,
All that there is   15
To bear and to enjoy, endure and do.

Landscapes, seascapes . . . Where have I been led?
The names of cities—Paris, Venice, Rome—
Held out their arms.
A feathered god, seductive, went ahead.   20

Here is my house. Under a red rose tree
A child is swinging; another gravely plays.
They are not surprised
That I am here; they were expecting me.

And yet my father sits and reads in silence,   25
My mother sheds a tear, the moon is still,
And the dark wind
Is murmuring that nothing ever happens.

Beyond his jurisdiction as I move,
Do I not prove him wrong? And yet, it's true   30
They will not change
There, on the stage of terror and of love.

The actors in that playhouse always sit
In fixed positions—father, mother, child
With painted eyes.   35
How sad it is to be a little puppet!

Their heads are wooden. And you once pretended
To understand them! Shake them as you will,
They cannot speak.
Do what you will, the comedy is ended.   40

12 **Thule** a legendary realm in the far North

Father, why did you work? Why did you weep,
Mother? Was the story so important?
        "Listen!" the wind
Said to the children, and they fell asleep.

—1963

American Classic

It's a classic American scene—
a car stopped off the road
and a man trying to repair it.

The woman who stays in the car
in the classic American scene
stares back at the freeway traffic.

They look surprised, and ashamed
to be so helpless . . .
let down in the middle of the road!

To think that their car would do this!
They look like mountain people
whose son has gone against the law.

But every night they set out food
and the robber goes skulking back to the trees.
That's how it is with the car . . .

it's theirs, they're stuck with it.
Now they know what it's like to sit
and see the world go whizzing by.

In the fume of carbon monoxide and dust
they are not such good Americans
as they thought they were.

The feeling of being left out
through no fault of your own, is common.
That's why I say, an American classic.

—1980

Physical Universe

He woke at five and, unable
to go back to sleep,
went downstairs.

A book was lying on the table
where his son had done his homework.   5
He took it into the kitchen,
made coffee, poured himself a cup,
and settled down to read.

"There was a local eddy in the swirling gas
of the primordial galaxy,   10
and a cloud was formed, the protosun,
as wide as the present solar system.

"This contracted. Some of the gas
formed a diffuse, spherical nebula,
a thin disk, that cooled and flattened.   15
Pulled one way by its own gravity,
the other way by the sun,
it broke, forming smaller clouds,
the protoplanets. Earth
was 2,000 times as wide as it is now."   20

The earth was without form, and void,
and darkness was upon the face of the deep.

*

"Then the sun began to shine,
dispelling the gases and vapors,
shrinking the planets, melting earth,   25
separating iron and silicate
to form the core and mantle.
Continents appeared . . ."

history, civilization,
the discovery of America   30
and the settling of Green Harbor,
bringing us to Tuesday, the seventh of July.

Tuesday, the day they pick up the garbage!
He leapt into action,
took the garbage bag out of its container,   35
tied it with a twist of wire,
and carried it out to the toolshed,
taking care not to let the screen door slam,
and put it in the large garbage can
that was three-quarters full.   40
He kept it in the toolshed so the raccoons
couldn't get at it.

He carried the can out to the road,
then went back into the house
and walked around, picking up newspapers   45
and fliers for: "Thompson Seedless Grapes,
California's finest sweet eating";

"Scott Bathroom Tissue";

"Legislative report from Senator Ken LaValle."

He put all this paper in a box,   50
and emptied the waste baskets in the two
downstairs bathrooms,
and the basket in the study.

He carried the box out to the road,
taking care not to let the screen door slam,   55
and placed the box next to the garbage.

Now let the garbage men come!

                        *

He went back upstairs.
Mary said, "Did you put out the garbage?"
But her eyes were closed.   60
She was sleeping, yet could speak in her sleep,
ask a question, even answer one.

"Yes," he said, and climbed into bed.
She turned around to face him,
with her eyes still closed.   65
He thought, perhaps she's an oracle,

speaking from the Collective Unconscious.°
He said to her, "Do you agree with Darwin
that people and monkeys have a common ancestor?
Or should we stick to the Bible?"   70

She said, "Did you take out the garbage?"

"Yes," he said, for the second time.
Then thought about it. Her answer
had something in it of the sublime.
Like a *koan* . . . the kind of irrelevance   75
a Zen master says to the disciple
who is asking riddles of the universe.

He put his arm around her,
and she continued to breathe evenly
from the depths of sleep.   80

—1983

67 Collective Unconscious Swiss psychiatrist Carl Jung (1875–1961) postulated that certain pre-existing imaginary forms (or archetypes) are found in every culture, making up a collective psyche shared by all humans

Daniel Hoffman (b. 1923)

Daniel Hoffman has published ten books of poetry including Beyond Silence: Selected Shorter Poems 1948–2003 *(2003). He also has published a memoir, and seven volumes of criticism. W. H. Auden chose Hoffman's first poetry collection,* An Armada of Thirty Whales *(1954), for the Yale Series of Younger Poets. Hoffman served as Consultant in Poetry to the Library of Congress from 1973 to 1974, and as Poet in Residence of New York's Cathedral of St. John the Divine, overseeing the American Poet's Corner there from 1988 to 1999. He is the Felix E. Schelling Professor of English Emeritus at the University of Pennsylvania, and lives in Swarthmore, Pennsylvania, and Harborside, Maine.*

Rats

To rid your barn of rats
You need a watertight
Hogshead two-thirds full
You scatter your cornmeal
On the water   5
Scattered as though all
The barrel held was meal
And lean a plank against the rim
And then lay down—

This is *important!*   10

—A wooden chip the size
To keep one rat afloat.
He'll rid your barn of rats
He'll leap into your meal
He'll sink he'll swim then he'll   15
See the chip
He'll slither aboard and squeal
And another rat beneath your eaves
Will stop
            and listen,   20

And climb down to that barrel
And walk that plank and smell
The meal and see meal

And one rat
He'll hear that rat squeal
I'll get mine he'll think and he'll   25
Leap in and sink and swim
He'll scramble on that chip

—Now watch him!—

He'll shove the first rat down
In the water till he'll drown   30
He'll rid your barn of rats
He'll shiver and he'll squeal
And a rat up on your rafter
Will hear,
          and stop,
                    and start

Down the beam   35
Coming after
With one intent as in a dream—

He'll rid your barn of rats.

—1974

Bob

Hadn't been out of the house, except
once a week to the hospital, since
that day three months ago when they brought him
home from the mine, doubled over
in pain, no longer breathing acid fumes   5
or dust from the schists the copper ran in,
but sick, sick inside. So I didn't expect
while scraping and sanding my hourglass puller°
tipped keel-up above the tide-line
to see come, slowly down the hill   10
to the beach road, his big green pickup
with the front hitch for a snowplow and movable
spotlights on the cab, and him

8 hourglass puller a rowboat

driving. He stopped, rolled the window down,
looked out and said, Be sure you caulk 15
those seams around the keel. Beside him
Katherine gave a wan smile. Then, toward us
came that little red Toyota
of Hobie's, who'd had hard words from him
two winters past about cutting wrongside 20
of the line between their woodlots. Since then
they hadn't spoken, but Hobie stopped,
leaned from his window and called out, Hey there!
Good to see ya!! D'ya know the mackerel
are running? My boy hauled in a bucketful 25
at the town wharf last night. And next
Bing's empty dump truck roared and rattled
across the beach, then stopped, blocking
the road—Hiya (as though they'd spoken
only the day before)—We've finished 30
roofing that house on Varnumville
—talk whittled down to the dailiness
of living and the expectation of
tomorrow. I said, If you don't stop by,
Liz will be disappointed. So I got in 35
beside them. He winced, putting the truck
in gear. It rolled up to our drive.
At the table by the window we watched
the cove's arms embrace sun-deckled water
stirred by cat's-paw breezes as the gulls 40
swooped and terns dove. You can see
thirteen islands, he said, from here
(and, as his father had done for us
a quarter-century before, he called
their roll)—Pond Isle, and Beach, 45
Butter, Colt's Head, Horse's Head, North Haven,
Eagle Isle, Western, and Resolution . . . He said
the names as one who tolls his beads
before leaving on a long journey
so that never would he forget 50
this place, these islands,
wherever it is that he'll be gone.

—2002

Violence

After I'd read my poem about a brawl
between two sidewalk hustlers—one,
insulted, throws the other down and nearly
kills him—over coffee and cookies a grave

senior citizen reproved me: *How*   5
could you see such violence and you
didn't try to stop them?—Oh, I explained,
it wasn't like that, really—I saw

two guys in a shoving match and thought
I'd write about aggression, what   10
anger really feels like. . . . *Yes,*

and if the one got killed
it would be on your head.
You should've stopped them, he said.

—*2002*

Denise Levertov (1923–1999)

Denise Levertov was an outspoken opponent of U.S. involvement in the Vietnam War, an activity that has tended to overshadow her accomplishments as a lyric poet. Born of Jewish and Welsh parents in England, she emigrated to the United States during World War II. Educated at home, she published her first poem in Poetry Quarterly *at seventeen. During World War II, she served as a nurse in London during the bombings. Her first book,* The Double Image, *was published when she was twenty-three. In 1947, Levertov emigrated to the United States with her husband, the writer Mitchell Goodman. The couple moved to New York City and in 1956 Levertov became a naturalized U.S. citizen. While her early work was written in received poetic forms, Levertov eventually came to write experimental free verse and was associated with the American avant-garde, particularly with the Black Mountain movement, despite her claims not to belong to any particular school. Poetry editor of both* The Nation *and* Mother Jones *magazines, Levertov wrote more than twenty volumes of poetry and four books of prose, translated three volumes of poetry, and edited several anthologies. She taught at numerous universities, including Stanford University from 1982 to 1993.*

The Secret

Two girls discover
the secret of life
in a sudden line of
poetry.

I who don't know the   5
secret wrote
the line. They
told me

(through a third person)
they had found it   10
but not what it was
not even

what line it was. No doubt
by now, more than a week
later, they have forgotten   15
the secret,

the line, the name of
the poem. I love them
for finding what
I can't find,   20

and for loving me
for the line I wrote,
and for forgetting it
so that

a thousand times, till death   25
finds them, they may
discover it again, in other
lines

in other
happenings. And for   30
wanting to know it,
for

assuming there is
such a secret, yes,
for that   35
most of all.

—1964

What Were They Like?

1) Did the people of Viet Nam
    use lanterns of stone?
2) Did they hold ceremonies
    to reverence the opening of buds?
3) Were they inclined to quiet laughter?   5
4) Did they use bone and ivory,
    jade and silver, for ornament?
5) Had they an epic poem?
6) Did they distinguish between speech and singing?

1) Sir, their light hearts turned to stone.   10
    It is not remembered whether in gardens
    stone lanterns illumined pleasant ways.

2) Perhaps they gatherered once to delight in blossom,
    but after the children were killed
    there were no more buds.   15
3) Sir, laughter is bitter to the burned mouth.
4) A dream ago, perhaps. Ornament is for joy.
    All the bones were charred.
5) It is not remembered. Remember,
    most were peasants; their life   20
    was in rice and bamboo.
    When peaceful clouds were reflected in the paddies
    and the water buffalo stepped surely along terraces,
    maybe fathers told their sons old tales.
    When bombs smashed those mirrors   25
    there was time only to scream.
6) There is an echo yet
    of their speech which was like a song.
    It was reported their singing resembled
    the flight of moths in moonlight.   30
    Who can say? It is silent now.

—1967

Song for Ishtar°

The moon is a sow
and grunts in my throat
Her great shining shines through me
so the mud of my hollow gleams
and breaks in silver bubbles   5

She is a sow
and I a pig and a poet

When she opens her white
lips to devour me I bite back
and laughter rocks the moon   10

In the black of desire
we rock and grunt, grunt and
shine

—1972

Ishtar in ancient Babylonian mythology, the goddess of fertility

Richard Hugo (1923–1982)

Richard Hugo is best known for poems that depict the landscapes and people of his native Pacific Northwest. Born in a suburb of Seattle, Hugo was raised by his mother's parents after his father left the family; in 1942 he legally changed his name to Hugo, his stepfather's name. He volunteered for World War II, and served as a bombardier in the Mediterranean. Hugo studied creative writing at the University of Washington, and went on to work as a technical writer for Boeing. A Run of Jacks, his first poetry collection, was published in 1961. Hugo taught creative writing at the University of Montana in Missoula for nearly eighteen years. In 1977, he was named editor of the Yale Younger Poets Series.

Degrees of Gray in Philipsburg°

You might come here Sunday on a whim.
Say your life broke down. The last good kiss
you had was years ago. You walk these streets
laid out by the insane, past hotels
that didn't last, bars that did, the tortured try   5
of local drivers to accelerate their lives.
Only churches are kept up. The jail
turned 70 this year. The only prisoner
is always in, not knowing what he's done.

The principal supporting business now   10
is rage. Hatred of the various grays
the mountain sends, hatred of the mill,
The Silver Bill repeal, the best liked girls
who leave each year for Butte. One good
restaurant and bars can't wipe the boredom out.   15
The 1907 boom, eight going silver mines,
a dance floor built on springs—
all memory resolves itself in gaze,
in panoramic green you know the cattle eat
or two stacks high above the town,   20
two dead kilns, the huge mill in collapse
for fifty years that won't fall finally down.

Philipsburg in Montana

Isn't this your life? That ancient kiss
still burning out your eyes? Isn't this defeat
so accurate, the church bell simply seems   25
a pure announcement: ring and no one comes?
Don't empty houses ring? Are magnesium
and scorn sufficient to support a town,
not just Philipsburg, but towns
of towering blondes, good jazz and booze   30
the world will never let you have
until the town you came from dies inside?

Say no to yourself. The old man, twenty
when the jail was built, still laughs
although his lips collapse. Someday soon,   35
he says, I'll go to sleep and not wake up.
You tell him no. You're talking to yourself.
The car that brought you here still runs.
The money you buy lunch with,
no matter where it's mined, is silver   40
and the girl who serves you food
is slender and her red hair lights the wall.

                                                            —*1973*

My Buddy

This then buddy is the blue routine.
You chased a fox one noon.
She hid in a golden rain.
You ran through the gold until
a rainy chill.   5
If that's it buddy it's a bleak routine.
What happened to you there
may never happen again.

So say buddy it is a bleak routine.
The word caves in your skull.   10
All eyes give you chill.
The fox shows up on the moon
on the horizon, laughing you blind
painting the routine orange.
What happens to you now   15
happens again.

Say you deserve it. That's a good routine.
I'm nothing, see,
to the storming worms.
The fox died warm in ground.   20
Now she's gone tell what a bitch she was
loud in a red routine
and say it never happened to you.
Don't show no pain.

Sweet dear buddy it's a gray routine.   25
A girl rode in off the prairie
a very snuggly cuddly
had a neat twitch coming in
ran off with another man.
Sorry buddy for the brute routine.   30
For you it can never happen
over and over again.

One rain more and glory afternoon
complete with gin
and trees gone nuts in the gale   35
that's always whipping even in heat
when you sweat like the dog you are
when you sweat and swear at me buddy
in my underwear
hoping I have your hair.   40

Boogie boogie buddy. Scarey boo.
Here's a foxy ghost for you.
One with a heart big as a smirk
and a hot toe in your ear.
You're still my buddy   45
aren't you?
Sorry. A bizarre machine.
Stay away from my gears.

Hell old buddy back to the routine.
I mean routine routine.   50
The time clock tied to your dong.
The same bitch punching your card
that very snuggly cuddly
off with another man.
Someday buddy you'll say the wrong thing.   55
We'll never be friends again.

What to do blue buddy now you're gone?
Sing a song? Sing of a lost routine?
Buddy on skins and me in my cups
crying play it, play it again.   60
No sense losing a tear to the floor
with a mug of beer in your hand
and the blind proprietor yelling
go on, buddy, go on.

                                                        —1975

Bay of Recovery

This water started it all, this sullen arm
of gray wound loose about the islands
whipped in patches by the north wind white.
The girl on the cliff exposed her body
to wind and whispered "whip me whip me."   5
I was less than bird, awkward on my bad leg,
half drunk from last night, and maybe
you don't think I'm telling it all.
                         All right.
There was this sullen girl in tight pants   10
on the shore who whispered "love me"
at the stumps of broken pile.
                         All right.
There was this girl I could barely make out
alone in moonlight on a passing ship.   15
Sequins, I am sure. Even now I see the sparkle
of her skin.
              No. No. Let me try it again.
There was no girl and I was in good shape.
This water started it all, the dazzling arm   20
of blue blue promise and the dazzling gull.
Gull. Not girl. And it was less than dazzle,
it was more than being alone on the beach
young under the moon, started it all.

                                                        —1977

Edgar Bowers (1924–2000)

Edgar Bowers published sparingly, sometimes taking decades between books to perfect his carefully crafted poems. Born in Rome, Georgia, where his father ran a plant nursery, he left school during World War II to serve in the U.S. Army's Counter Intelligence Corps ending the war in Berchtesgaden, in the Bavarian Alps. After his discharge in 1946, he resumed his studies at the University of North Carolina and Stanford University. Bowers's first poetry collection, The Form of Loss, *appeared in 1956. His other books of poetry are* The Astronomers *(1965);* Living Together *(1973);* For Louis Pasteur *(1990), which won the Bollingen Prize for Poetry; and* Collected Poems *(1997). Bowers spent most of his career as a professor of English at the University of California, Santa Barbara.*

The Astronomers of Mont Blanc

Who are you there that, from your icy tower,
Explore the colder distances, the far
Escape of your whole universe to night;
That watch the moon's blue craters, shadowy crust,
And blunted mountains mildly drift and glare,   5
Ballooned in ghostly earnest on your sight;
Who are you, and what hope persuades your trust?

It is your hope that you will know the end
And compass of our ignorant restraint
There in lost time, where what was done is done   10
Forever as a havoc overhead.
Aging, you search to master in the faint
Persistent fortune which you gaze upon
The perfect order trusted to the dead.

—*1989*

Mary

The angel of self-discipline, her guardian
Since she first knew and had to go away
From home that spring to have her child with strangers,
Sustained her, till the vanished boy next door
And her ordeal seemed fiction, and the true   5
Her mother's firm insistence she was the mother
And the neighbors' acquiescence. So she taught school,
Walking a mile each way to ride the street car—
First books of the *Aeneid*° known by heart,
French, and the French Club Wednesday afternoon;   10
Then summer replacement typist in an office,
Her sister's family moving in with them,
Depression years and she the only earner.
Saturday, football game and opera broadcasts,
Sunday, staying at home to wash her hair,   15
The Business Women's Circle Monday night,
And, for a treat, birthdays and holidays,
Nelson Eddy and Jeanette McDonald.
The young blond sister long since gone to college,
Nephew and nieces gone, her mother dead,   20
Instead of Caesar, having to teach First Aid,
The students rowdy, she retired. The rent
For the empty rooms she gave to Thornwell Orphanage,
Unwed Mothers, Temperance, and Foster Parents
And never bought the car she meant to buy;   25
Too blind at last to do much more than sit
All day in the antique glider on the porch
Listening to cars pass up and down the street.
Each summer, on the grass behind the house—
Cape jasmine, with its scent of August nights   30
Humid and warm, the soft magnolia bloom
Marked lightly by a slow brown stain—she spread,
For airing, the same small intense collection,
Concert programs, worn trophies, years of yearbooks,
Letters from schoolgirl chums, bracelets of hair   35
And the same picture: black hair in a bun,

9 **Aeneid** Epic by the Roman poet Virgil (70–19 B.C.)

Puzzled eyes in an oval face as young
Or old as innocence, skirt to the ground,
And, seated on the high school steps, the class,
The ones to whom she would have said, "*Seigneur,*   40
Donnez-nous la force de supporter
La peine,"° as an example easy to remember,
Formal imperative, object first person plural.

—*1989*

A Fragment: the Cause

What I remember is the spell, a mask
Of numbness on the face and on the body
Attention to a silent foreign call,
Rapt murmuring on the lips the one reply;
Later, the fall, the cry profane and life-long,   5
Convulsion, and our helplessness—a pillow
Under the head, a blanket, and the waiting;
Medicinal hope's spent brevity, the spent
Bitterness of catastrophe's relief.
I could remember everything, if I would,   10
But do not wish to or to tell the story,
Though none will know it when I, too, am dead,
The last of those who shared and witnessed it.

—*1997*

40 **Seigneur, Donnez-nous** . . . God, give us the strength to bear trouble

Edward Field (b. 1924)

Edward Field was born in Brooklyn, New York, and grew up on Long Island. One of six children, he played cello in the Field Family Trio. A pilot in the European theater during World War II, Field later worked in a warehouse, in art production, as a machinist, and as a clerk-typist. In 1956, he began studying acting with Russian émigré Vera Soloviova of the Moscow Art Theatre. Field applied the method-acting technique to his poetry reading, and was able to support himself throughout the 1960s and '70s by giving public performances. Field, who currently resides in New York City, has taught poetry workshops, edited anthologies, translated Eskimo songs and stories, and written the narration for the Academy Award–winning short documentary To Be Alive! *Under the joint pseudonym Bruce Elliot, Field has cowritten three popular novels with his partner Neil Derrick.*

The Bride of Frankenstein

The Baron has decided to mate the monster,
to breed him perhaps,
in the interests of pure science, his only god.

So he goes up into his laboratory
which he has built in the tower of the castle   5
to be as near the interplanetary forces as possible,
and puts together the prettiest monster-woman you ever saw
with a body like a pin-up girl
and hardly any stitching at all
where he sewed on the head of a raped and murdered beauty
       queen.   10

He sets his liquids burping, and coils blinking and buzzing,
and waits for an electric storm to send through the equipment
the spark vital for life.
The storm breaks over the castle
and the equipment really goes crazy   15
like a kitchen full of modern appliances
as the lightning juice starts oozing right into that pretty corpse.

He goes to get the monster
so he will be right there when she opens her eyes,
for she might fall in love with the first thing she sees as ducklings
       do.   20

That monster is already straining at his chains and slurping,
ready to go right to it:
he has been well prepared for coupling
by his pinching leering keeper, who's been saying for weeks,
"Ya gonna get a little nookie, kid,"   25
or "How do you go for some poontang, baby?"
All the evil in him is focused on this one thing now
as he is led into her very presence.

She awakens slowly,
she bats her eyes,   30
she gets up out of the equipment,
and finally she stands in all her seamed glory,
a monster princess with a hairdo like a fright wig,
lightning flashing in the background
like a halo and a wedding veil,   35
like a photographer snapping pictures of great moments.

She stands and stares with her electric eyes,
beginning to understand that in this life too
she was just another body to be raped.
The monster is ready to go: 40
he roars with joy at the sight of her,
so they let him loose and he goes right for those knockers.
And she starts screaming to break your heart
and you realize that she was just born:
in spite of her big tits she was just a baby.   45

But her instincts are right—
rather death than that green slobber:
she jumps off the parapet.
And then the monster's sex drive goes wild.
Thwarted, it turns to violence, demonstrating sublimation crudely;   50
and he wrecks the lab, those burping acids and buzzing coils,
overturning the control panel so the equipment goes off like a
              bomb,
the stone castle crumbling and crashing in the storm,
destroying them all . . . perhaps.

Perhaps somehow the Baron got out of that wreckage of his
              dreams   55
with his evil intact, if not his good looks,
and more wicked than ever went on with his thrilling career.

And perhaps even the monster lived
to roam the earth, his desire still ungratified;
and lovers out walking in shadowy and deserted places   60
will see his shape loom up over them, their doom—
and children sleeping in their beds
will wake up in the dark night screaming
as his hideous body grabs them.

—1967

The Dog Sitters

for Stanley and Jane

Old friends, we tried so hard
to take care of your dogs.
We petted them, talked to them, even slept with them,
and followed all your instructions
about feeding and care—   5
but they were inconsolable.
The longer you were gone
the more they pined for you.
We were poor substitutes,
almost worse than nothing.   10

Until you returned, days of worry
as each fell ill with fever, diarrhoea and despair,
moving about all night restlessly on the bed we shared.
We wakened at dawn to walk them,
but there was a mess already on the rug.   15
We called the vet, coaxed them to eat,
tried to distract them
from the terrible sadness in their eyes
every time they lay down with their chins in their paws
in utter hopelessness, and the puppy   20
got manic, biting our hands.

Ten days in the house by the bay
trying to keep them alive, it was a nightmare,
for they were afraid to go anywhere with us, for fear
you would never come back,   25

that they must be there waiting when you did,
until you did . . . if you did. . . .

Then, the minute you got home
they turned away from us to you
and barely looked at us again, even when we left—   30
for you had filled the terrible empty
space that only you could fill,
and our desperate attempts
were dismissed without a thought.

We tried to tell each other it was a victory   35
keeping them alive, but the truth is
that when someone belongs so utterly to someone else,
stay out of it—that kind of love is a steamroller
and if you get in the way, even to help,
you can only get flattened.   40

—1992

John Haines   (b. 1924)

*John Haines spent twenty-five years homesteading in Alaska, an experi-
ence which provided much of the raw material for his ten-plus books of
poetry. The son of a naval officer, he spent his early life on a series of
naval bases. He served in the Navy and attended art school before building
a cabin in an isolated spot approximately seventy miles from Fairbanks.
There he survived by hunting and trapping, and used his solitude to write
poetry. At the age of forty-two, he published* Winter News *(1966), his first
book of poems. His first book of essays,* Living Off the Country, *appeared
in 1981. Haines currently lives in Helena, Montana.*

Life in an Ashtray

In our thin white paper skins
and freckled collars,
little brown shreds for bones,

we begin with our feet in ashes,
shaking our shoes   5
in a crazy, crippling dance;

then skate along the glassy
metal rim of our world,
to lean there, sour and reeking . . .

the only people born tall,   10
who shrink as they grow.

Prodded by hired matches,
we'd like to complain,

but all our efforts to speak
dissolve in smoke   15
and gales of coughing.

The yellow glare in our eyes
turning red as we age,
stomping our feet to put out the fire;

and always the old ones crumpling,   20
crushed from above
by enormous hands,

the young ones beginning to burn.

                                                                    —*1970*

Rain Country

> Earth. Nothing more.
> Earth. Nothing less.
> And let that be enough for you.
>
> —*Pedro Salinas*

I

The woods are sodden,
and the last leaves
tarnish and fall.

Thirty-one years ago
this rainy autumn   5
we walked home from the lake,

Campbell and Peg and I,
over the shrouded dome,
the Delta wind in our faces,
home through the drenched   10
and yellowing woodland.

Bone-chilled but with singing
hearts we struck our fire
from the stripped bark
and dry, shaved aspen;   15
and while the stove-iron
murmured and cracked
and our wet wool steamed,
we crossed again
the fire-kill of timber   20
in the saddle of Deadwood—

down the windfall slope,
by alder thicket, and now
by voice alone, to drink
from the lake at evening.   25

A mile and seven days
beyond the grayling pool
at Deep Creek, the promised
hunt told of a steepness
in the coming dusk.   30

        II

Light in the aspen wood
on Campbell's hill,
a fog trail clearing below,
as evenly the fall distance
stretched the summer sun.   35

Our faces strayed together
in the cold north window—
night, and the late cup
steaming before us . . .
Campbell, his passion   40

tamed by the tumbling years,
an old voice retelling.

As if a wind had stopped us
listening on the trail,
we turned to a sound   45
the earth made that morning—
a heavy rumble in the gray
hills toward Fairbanks;
our mountain shivered
underfoot, and all   50
the birds were still.

III

Shadows blur in the rain,
they are whispering straw
and talking leaves.

I see what does not exist,   55
hear voices that cannot speak
through the packed
earth that fills them.

Loma, in the third year
of the war, firing at night   60
from his pillow
for someone to waken.

Campbell, drawing a noose
in the dust at his feet:
"Creation was seven days,   65
no more, no less . . ."
Noah and the flooded earth
were clouded in his mind.

And Knute, who turned
from his radio one August   70
afternoon, impassioned
and astonished:
                    "Is that

the government? I ask you—
is *that* the government?"   75

Bitter Melvin, who nailed
his warning above the doorway:

Pleese dont shoot
the beevers
They are my friends.   80

IV

And all the stammering folly
aimed toward us
from the rigged pavilions—
malign dictations, insane
pride of the fox-eyed men   85
who align the earth
to a tax-bitten dream
of metal and smoke—

all drank of the silence
to which we turned: 90
one more yoke at the spring,
another birch rick balanced,
chilled odor and touch
of the killed meat quartered
and racked in the shade.   95

It was thirty-one years ago
this rainy autumn.

Of the fire we built to warm us,
and the singing heart
driven to darkness   100
on the time-bitten earth—

only a forest rumor
whispers through broken straw
and trodden leaves
how late in a far summer   105
three friends came home,

walking the soaked ground
of an ancient love.

V

Much rain has fallen. Fog
drifts in the spruce boughs,
heavy with alder smoke,
denser than I remember.

Campbell is gone, in old age
struck down one early winter;
and Peg in her slim youth
long since become a stranger.
The high, round hill of Buckeye
stands whitened and cold.

I am not old, not yet, though
like a wind-turned birch
spared by the axe,
I claim this clearing
in the one country I know.

Remembering, fitting names
to a rain-soaked map:
Gold Run, Minton, Tenderfoot,
McCoy. Here Melvin killed
his grizzly, there Wilkins
built his forge. All
that we knew, and everything
but for me forgotten.

VI

I write this down
in the brown ink of leaves,
of the changed pastoral
deepening to mist on my page.

I see in the shadow-pool
beneath my hand a mile

110

115

120

125

130

135

and thirty years beyond
this rain-driven autumn.

All that we loved: a fire   140
long dampened, the quenched
whispering down of faded
straw and yellowing leaves.

The names, and the voices
within them, speak now   145
for the slow rust of things
that are muttered in sleep.

There is ice on the water
I look through, the steep
rain turning to snow.   150

—*1978–1983*

Gerald Stern (b. 1925)

Gerald Stern writes poems informed by his working-class, Jewish-American background. Stern was born in Pittsburgh, Pennsylvania, in 1925. He published his first collection at the age of forty-six, and since has won many awards, including the National Book Award, and fellowships from The Academy of American Poets and the Guggenheim Foundation. Educated at the University of Pittsburgh and Columbia University, Stern taught for many years at the Iowa Writers' Workshop, before retiring to Lambertville, New Jersey, and being named the state's first poet laureate.

Behaving Like a Jew

When I got there the dead opossum looked like
an enormous baby sleeping on the road.
It took me only a few seconds—just
seeing him there—with the hole in his back
and the wind blowing through his hair   5
to get back again into my animal sorrow.

I am sick of the country, the bloodstained
bumpers, the stiff hairs sticking out of the grilles,
the slimy highways, the heavy birds
refusing to move;   10
I am sick of the spirit of Lindbergh° over everything,
that joy in death, that philosophical
understanding of carnage, that
concentration on the species.
—I am going to be unappeased at the opossum's death.   15
I am going to behave like a Jew
and touch his face, and stare into his eyes,
and pull him off the road.
I am not going to stand in a wet ditch
with the Toyotas and the Chevies passing over me   20
at sixty miles an hour
and praise the beauty and the balance
and lose myself in the immortal lifestream
when my hands are still a little shaky
from his stiffness and his bulk   25
and my eyes are still weak and misty
from his round belly and his curved fingers
and his black whiskers and his little dancing feet.

—1977

The Dancing

In all these rotten shops, in all this broken furniture
and wrinkled ties and baseball trophies and coffee pots
I have never seen a postwar Philco°
with the automatic eye
nor heard Ravel's° "Bolero" the way I did   5
in 1945 in that tiny living room
on Beechwood Boulevard, nor danced as I did
then, my knives all flashing, my hair all streaming,

---

11 Lindbergh (1902–1974) Charles A. Lindbergh in 1927 made the first solo nonstop transatlantic flight and became, late in life, a spokesperson for environmentalist causes
3 Philco brand of radio   **5 Ravel's** Maurice Ravel (1875–1937), French composer

my mother red with laughter, my father cupping
his left hand under his armpit, doing the dance   10
of old Ukraine, the sound of his skin half drum,
half fart, the world at last a meadow
the three of us whirling and singing, the three of us
screaming and falling, as if we were dying,
as if we could never stop—in 1945—   15
in Pittsburgh, beautiful filthy Pittsburgh, home
of the evil Mellons,° 5,000 miles away
from the other dancing—in Poland and Germany—
oh God of mercy, oh wild God.

—1984

The Sounds of Wagner°

You could call him a lachrymose animal
lying on his glasses at two in the morning
remembering the photograph of himself ice-skating
on his uncle's farm or eating hot sausages
and buttermilk or making a speech for Stevenson°   5
on Chestnut Street in Philadelphia or talking
to Auden° about Velveeta cheese or standing
for an hour in front of the Beacon Pharmacy
and pitching pennies or climbing all day long
above the Liberty Tunnel or swimming by himself   10
around the Steel Pier in his wool bathing suit.

He loved lavender more than anything else
and never forgot the sunsuit he wore, nor did he
ever forget looking into the tiny window
of a music listening room and seeing his darling   15
fucking someone else on the carpeted floor,

---

17 Mellons the Mellon family amassed one of the three biggest pre-World War I fortunes in the
United States
Richard Wagner (1813–1883), German composer of opera and other music, who considered himself
"the most German of men"   **5 Adlai Stevenson** (1900–1965), a two-time Democratic candidate for
president   **7 W. H. Auden** (1907–1973), British poet

her earphones still intact though his—her lover's—
an Air Corps Cadet—his hung askew and the sounds
of Wagner floated or scattered throughout the room,
and he could hear it, nor did he ever forget   20
his walk that day through the park and how ashamed
he felt, and bitter, and how he weathered it.

—1998

Maxine Kumin (b. 1925)

Maxine Kumin was born in Philadelphia and educated at Radcliffe. Kumin was an early literary ally and friend of Anne Sexton, with whom she coauthored several children's books. Kumin and Sexton met in 1957 in John Holmes's poetry class at the Boston Center for Adult Education, and their friendship continued until Sexton's suicide in 1974. Kumin, who makes frequent use of traditional poetic forms, has published more than eleven books of poetry, in addition to novels, essays, short stories, and children's novels. Winner of the 1973 Pulitzer Prize and a former Consultant in Poetry to the Library of Congress, Kumin has raised horses in rural New Hampshire for some years. Her increased interest in the natural world has paralleled the environmental awareness of many of her readers.

Morning Swim

Into my empty head there come
a cotton beach, a dock wherefrom

I set out, oily and nude
through mist, in chilly solitude.

There was no line, no roof or floor   5
to tell the water from the air.

Night fog thick as terry cloth
closed me in its fuzzy growth.

I hung my bathrobe on two pegs.
I took the lake between my legs.   10

Invaded and invader, I
went overhand on that flat sky.

Fish twitched beneath me, quick and tame.
In their green zone they sang my name

and in the rhythm of the swim   15
I hummed a two-four-time slow hymn.

I hummed *Abide with Me*. The beat
rose in the fine thrash of my feet,

rose in the bubbles I put out
slantwise, trailing through my mouth.   20

My bones drank water; water fell
through all my doors. I was the well

that fed the lake that met my sea
in which I sang *Abide with Me*.

—1982

Woodchucks

Gassing the woodchucks didn't turn out right.
The knockout bomb from the Feed and Grain Exchange
was featured as merciful, quick at the bone
and the case we had against them was airtight,
both exits shoehorned shut with puddingstone,   5
but they had a sub-sub-basement out of range.

Next morning they turned up again, no worse
for the cyanide than we for our cigarettes
and state-store Scotch, all of us up to scratch.
They brought down the marigolds as a matter of course   10
and then took over the vegetable patch
nipping the broccoli shoots, beheading the carrots.

The food from our mouths, I said, righteously thrilling
to the feel of the .22, the bullets' neat noses.
I, a lapsed pacifist fallen from grace   15

puffed with Darwinian pieties for killing,
now drew a bead on the littlest woodchuck's face.
He died down in the everbearing roses.

Ten minutes later I dropped the mother. She
flipflopped in the air and fell, her needle teeth   20
still hooked in a leaf of early Swiss chard.
Another baby next. O one-two-three
the murderer inside me rose up hard,
the hawkeye killer came on stage forthwith.

There's one chuck left. Old wily fellow, he keeps   25
me cocked and ready day after day after day.
All night I hunt his humped-up form. I dream
I sight along the barrel in my sleep.
If only they'd all consented to die unseen
gassed underground the quiet Nazi way.   30

—*1982*

Noted in the *New York Times*

Lake Buena Vista, Florida, June 16, 1987

Death claimed the last pure dusky seaside sparrow
today, whose coastal range was narrow,
as narrow as its two-part buzzy song.
From hummocks lost to Cape Canaveral°
this mouselike skulker in the matted grass,   5
a six-inch bird, plain brown, once thousands strong,
sang *toodle-raeee azhee,* ending on a trill
before the air gave way to rocket blasts.

It laid its dull white eggs (brown specked) in small
neat cups of grass on plots of pickleweed,   10
bulrushes, or salt hay. It dined
on caterpillars, beetles, ticks, the seeds

4 **Cape Canaveral** site of the John F. Kennedy Space Center

of sedges. Unremarkable
the life it led with others of its kind.

Tomorrow we can put it on a stamp,   15
a first-day cover with Key Largo rat,
Schaus swallowtail, Florida swamp
crocodile, and fading cotton mouse.
How simply symbols replace habitat!
The tower frames of Aerospace   20
quiver in the flush of another shot
where, once indigenous, the dusky sparrow
soared trilling twenty feet above its burrow.

—1989

Oblivion

The dozen ways they did it—
off a bridge, the back of a boat,
pills, head in the oven, or
wrapped in her mother's old mink coat
in the garage, a brick on the accelerator,   5
the Cougar's motor thrumming
while she crossed over,

What they left behind—
the outline of a stalled novel, diaries,
their best poems, the note that ends   10
now will you believe me,
offspring of various ages, spouses
who cared and weep and yet
admit relief now that it's over.

How they fester, the old details   15
held to the light like a stained-glass icon
—the shotgun in the mouth, the string
from toe to trigger; the tongue
a blue plum forced between his lips

when he hanged himself in her closet—   20
for us it is never over

who raced to the scene, cut the noose,
pulled the bathtub plug on pink water,
broke windows, turned off the gas,
rode in the ambulance, only minutes later   25
to take the body blow of bad news.
We are trapped in the plot, every one.
Left behind, there is no oblivion.

—*2002*

Donald Justice (1925–2004)

Donald Justice published more selectively than most of his contemporaries. His Pulitzer Prize–winning volume of selected poems displays considerable literary sophistication and reveals the poet's familiarity with the traditions of contemporary European and Latin American poetry. As an editor, he was responsible for rescuing the important work of Weldon Kees from obscurity. Born in Miami, Florida, Justice graduated from the University of Miami and obtained graduate degrees from the University of North Carolina and the University of Iowa. Before retiring in 1992, he taught at Syracuse University; the University of California, Irvine; Princeton University; the University of Virginia; the University of Iowa; and the University of Florida. His many honors included the Bollingen Prize in Poetry and the Lamont Prize.

Counting the Mad

This one was put in a jacket,
This one was sent home,
This one was given bread and meat
But would eat none,
And this one cried No No No No   5
All day long.

This one looked at the window
As though it were a wall,
This one saw things that were not there,

This one things that were,   10
And this one cried No No No No
All day long.

This one thought himself a bird,
This one a dog,
And this one thought himself a man,   15
An ordinary man,
And this one cried No No No No
All day long.

                                              —1960

But That Is Another Story

I do not think the ending can be right.
How can they marry and live happily
Forever, these who were so passionate
At chapter's end? Once they are settled in
The quiet country house, what will they do,   5
So many miles from anywhere?
Those blond ancestral ghosts crowding the stair,
Surely they disapprove? Ah me,
I fear love will catch cold and die
From pacing naked through those drafty halls   10
Night after night. Poor Frank! Poor Imogene!
Before them now their lives
Stretch empty as great Empire beds
After the lovers rise and the damp sheets
Are stripped by envious chambermaids.   15

And if the first night passes brightly enough,
What with the bonfires lit with old love letters,
That is no inexhaustible fuel, perhaps?
God knows how it must end, not I.
Will Frank walk out one day   20
Alone through the ruined orchard with his stick,
Strewing the path with lissome heads
Of buttercups? Will Imogene
Conceal in the crotches of old trees

Love notes for beardless gardeners and such? 25
Meanwhile they quarrel and make it up
Only to quarrel again. A sudden storm
Pulls the last fences down. Now moonstruck sheep
Stray through the garden all night peering in
At the exhausted lovers where they sleep. 30

—1967

Men at Forty

Men at forty
Learn to close softly
The doors to rooms they will not be
Coming back to.

At rest on a stair landing, 5
They feel it moving
Beneath them now like the deck of a ship,
Though the swell is gentle.

And deep in mirrors
They rediscover
The face of the boy as he practices tying 10
His father's tie there in secret,

And the face of that father,
Still warm with the mystery of lather.
They are more fathers than sons themselves now. 15
Something is filling them, something

That is like the twilight sound
Of the crickets, immense,
Filling the woods at the foot of the slope
Behind their mortgaged houses. 20

—1967

American Scenes (1904–1905)

I CAMBRIDGE IN WINTER

Immense pale houses! Sunshine just now and snow
Light up and pauperize the whole brave show—
Each fanlight, each veranda, each good address,
All a mere paint and pasteboard paltriness!

These winter sunsets are the one fine thing: 5
Blood on the snow, a last impassioned fling,
The wild frankness and sadness of surrender—
As if our cities ever could be tender!

2 RAILWAY JUNCTION SOUTH OF RICHMOND, PAST MIDNIGHT

Indistinguishable engines hooting, red
Fires flaring, vanishing; a formless shed   10
Just straggling lifeward before sinking back
Into Dantean° glooms beside the track,

All steam and smoke and earth—and even here,
Out of this little hell of spurts and hisses,
Come the first waftings of the Southern air,   15
Of open gates, of all but bland abysses.

3 ST. MICHAEL'S CEMETERY, CHARLESTON

One may depend on these old cemeteries
To say the one charmed thing there is to say—
So here the silvery seaward outlook carries
Hints of some other world beyond the bay,   20

The sun-warmed tombs, the flowers. Each faraway
Game-haunted inlet and reed-smothered isle
Speaks of lost Venices; and the South meanwhile
Has only to be tragic to beguile.

---

12 Dantean resembling Dante's vision of hell in his epic poem, *The Divine Comedy*

4 EPILOGUE: CORONADO BEACH, CALIFORNIA

In a hotel room by the sea, the Master   25
Sits brooding on the continent he has crossed.
Not that he foresees immediate disaster,
Only a sort of freshness being lost—
Or should he go on calling it Innocence?
The sad-faced monsters of the plains are gone;   30
Wall Street controls the wilderness. There's an immense
Novel in all this waiting to be done,
But not, not—sadly enough—by him. His talents,
Such as they may be, want an older theme,
One rather more civilized than this, on balance.   35
For him now always the consoling dream
Is just the mild dear light of Lamb House° falling
Beautifully down the pages of his calling.

AFTER HENRY JAMES

—1987

---

37 **Lamb House** East Sussex home of the American novelist Henry James (1843–1916), sometimes called "the Master"

Carolyn Kizer (b. 1925)

Carolyn Kizer has had a fascinating career that includes a year's study in Taiwan and another year in Pakistan, where she worked for the U.S. State Department. Her first collection, The Ungrateful Garden *(1961), demonstrates an equal facility with formal and free verse, but her subsequent books (including the Pulitzer Prize–winning* Yin *of 1984) have tended more toward the latter. A committed feminist, Kizer anticipated many of today's women's issues as early as the mid-1950s, just as the poem "The Ungrateful Garden" was published a decade before "ecology" became a household word. Born in Spokane, Washington, Kizer founded the literary magazine* Poetry Northwest *in 1959 and edited it until 1965. Kizer divides her time between Sonoma, California, and Paris.*

The Ungrateful Garden

Midas° watched the golden crust
That formed over his streaming sores,
Hugged his agues, loved his lust,
But damned to hell the out-of-doors

Where blazing motes of sun impaled   5
The serried° roses, metal-bright.
"Those famous flowers," Midas wailed,
"Have scorched my retina with light."

This gift, he'd thought, would gild his joys,
Silt up the waters of his grief;   10
His lawns a wilderness of noise,
The heavy clang of leaf on leaf.

Within, the golden cup is good
To heft, to sip the yellow mead.
Outside, in summer's rage, the rude   15
Gold thorn has made his fingers bleed.

"I strolled my halls in golden shift,
As ruddy as a lion's meat.

---

1 Midas legendary king whose touch turned everything to gold   **6 serried** crowded in rows

Then I rushed out to share my gift,
And golden stubble cut my feet."   20

Dazzled with wounds, he limped away
To climb into his golden bed.
Roses, roses can betray.
"Nature is evil," Midas said.

                                                        —*1961*

Bitch

Now, when he and I meet, after all these years,
I say to the bitch inside me, don't start growling.
He isn't a trespasser anymore,
Just an old acquaintance tipping his hat.
My voice says, "Nice to see you,"   5
As the bitch starts to bark hysterically.
He isn't an enemy now,
Where are your manners, I say, as I say,
"How are the children? They must be growing up."
At a kind word from him, a look like the old days,   10
The bitch changes her tone: she begins to whimper.
She wants to snuggle up to him, to cringe.
Down, girl! Keep your distance
Or I'll give you a taste of the choke-chain.
"Fine, I'm just fine," I tell him.   15
She slobbers and grovels.
After all, I am her mistress. She is basically loyal.
It's just that she remembers how she came running
Each evening, when she heard his step;
How she lay at his feet and looked up adoringly   20
Though he was absorbed in his paper;
Or, bored with her devotion, ordered her to the kitchen
Until he was ready to play.
But the small careless kindnesses
When he'd had a good day, or a couple of drinks,   25

Come back to her now, seem more important
Than the casual cruelties, the ultimate dismissal.
"It's nice to know you are doing so well," I say.
He couldn't have taken you with him;
You were too demonstrative, too clumsy,   30
Not like the well-groomed pets of his new friends.
"Give my regards to your wife," I say. You gag
As I drag you off by the scruff,
Saying, "Goodbye! Goodbye! Nice to have seen you again."

—1971

Pro Femina:° Part Three

I will speak about women of letters, for I'm in the racket.
Our biggest successes to date? Old maids to a woman.
And our saddest conspicuous failures? The married spinsters
On loan to the husbands they treated like surrogate fathers.
Think of that crew of self-pitiers, not-very-distant,   5
Who carried the torch for themselves and got first-degree burns.
Or the sad sonneteers, toast-and-teasdales° we loved at thirteen;
Middle-aged virgins seducing the puerile anthologists
Through lust-of-the-mind; barbiturate-drenched Camilles°
With continuous periods, murmuring softly on sofas   10
When poetry wasn't a craft but a sickly effluvium,
The air thick with incense, musk, and emotional blackmail.

I suppose they reacted from an earlier womanly modesty
When too many girls were scabs to their stricken sisterhood,
Impugning our sex to stay in good with the men,   15
Commencing their insecure bluster. How they must have swaggered
When women themselves endorsed their own inferiority!
Vestals, vassals and vessels, rolled into several,
They took notes in rolling syllabics, in careful journals,

Pro Femina (Latin) in favor of woman   7 teasdales poets like Sara Teasdale (1884–1933), a
sensitive, reclusive woman who ended her life by suicide   9 Camilles a reference to *Camille*, a
romantic tragedy by Alexandre Dumas *fils* (1824–95)

Aiming to please a posterity that despises them.   20
But we'll always have traitors who swear that a woman surrenders
Her Supreme Function, by equating Art with aggression
And failure with Femininity. Still it's just as unfair
To equate Art with Femininity, like a prettily-packaged commodity
When we are the custodians of the world's best-kept secret: 25
Merely the private lives of one-half of humanity.

But even with masculine dominance, we mares and mistresses
Produced some sleek saboteuses,° making their cracks
Which the porridge-brained males of the day were too thick to perceive,
Mistaking young hornets for perfectly harmless bumblebees.   30
Being thought innocuous rouses some women to frenzy;
They try to be ugly by aping the ways of the men
And succeed. Swearing, sucking cigars and scorching the bedspread,
Slopping straight shots, eyes blotted, vanity-blown
In the expectation of glory: *she writes like a man!*   35
This drives other women mad in a mist of chiffon
(one poetess draped her gauze over red flannels, a practical feminist).

But we're emerging from all that, more or less,
Except for some lady-like laggards and Quarterly priestesses
Who flog men for fun, and kick women to maim competition.   40
Now, if we struggle abnormally, we may almost seem normal;
If we submerge our self-pity in disciplined industry;
If we stand up and be hated, and swear not to sleep with editors;
If we regard ourselves formally, respecting our true limitations
Without making an unseemly show of trying to unfreeze our assets;   45
Keeping our heads and our pride while remaining unmarried;
And if wedded, kill guilt in its tracks when we stack up the dishes
And defect to the typewriter. And if mothers, believe in the luck of
     our children,
Whom we forbid to devour us, whom we shall not devour,
And the luck of our husbands and lovers, who keep free women.   50

—1984

28 **saboteuses** women who carry out acts of sabotage

W. D. Snodgrass (b. 1926)

W. D. Snodgrass won the Pulitzer Prize for his first collection, Heart's
Needle *(1959), and is generally considered one of the first important confessional poets. However, in his later career he has turned away from autobiographical subjects, writing, among other poems, a long sequence of
dramatic monologues spoken by leading Nazis during the final days of the
Hitler regime. Born into a Quaker family in Wilkinsburg, Pennsylvania,
Snodgrass studied at Geneva College and the University of Iowa. The author of more than twenty books of poetry and translations, he has served
as Distinguished Professor of Creative Writing at the University of
Delaware, and has taught at Cornell, Wayne State and Syracuse Universities, and at the University of Rochester. He lives in upstate New York.*

"After Experience Taught Me . . ."

After experience taught me that all the ordinary
Surroundings of social life are futile and vain;

> I'm going to show you something very
> Ugly: someday, it might save your life.

Seeing that none of the things I feared contain   5
In themselves anything either good or bad

> What if you get caught without a knife;
> Nothing—even a loop of piano wire;

Excepting only in the effect they had
Upon my mind, I resolved to inquire   10

> Take the first two fingers of this hand;
> Fork them out—kind of a "V for Victory"—

Whether there might be something whose discovery
Would grant me supreme, unending happiness.

> And jam them into the eyes of your enemy.   15
> You have to do this hard. Very hard. Then press

No virtue can be thought to have priority
Over this endeavor to preserve one's being.

Both fingers down around the cheekbone
And setting your foot high into the chest   20

No man can desire to act rightly, to be blessed,
To live rightly, without simultaneously

You must call up every strength you own
And you can rip off the whole facial mask.

Wishing to be, to act, to live. He must ask   25
First, in other words, to actually exist.

      And you, whiner, who wastes your time
         Dawdling over the remorseless earth,
      What evil, what unspeakable crime
         Have you made your life worth?   30

—1967

The Examination

Under the thick beams of that swirly smoking light,
    The black robes are clustering, huddled in together.
Hunching their shoulders, they spread short, broad sleeves like night-
    Black grackles' wings; then they reach bone-yellow leather-

y fingers, each to each. And are prepared. Each turns   5
    His single eye—or since one can't discern their eyes,
That reflective, single, moon-pale disc which burns
    Over each brow—to watch this uncouth shape that lies

Strapped to their table. One probes with his ragged nails
    The slate-sharp calf, explores the thigh and the lean thews   10
Of the groin. Others raise, red as piratic sails,
    His wing, stretching, trying the pectoral sinews.

One runs his finger down the whet of that cruel
    Golden beak, lifts back the horny lids from the eyes,
Peers down in one bright eye malign as a jewel,   15
    And steps back suddenly. "He is anaesthetized?"

"He is. He is. Yes. Yes." The tallest of them, bent
    Down by the head, rises: "This drug possesses powers
Sufficient to still all gods in this firmament.
    This is Garuda who was fierce. He's yours for hours.   20

"We shall continue, please." Now, once again, he bends
    To the skull, and its clamped tissues. Into the cran-
ial cavity, he plunges both of his hands
    Like obstetric forceps and lifts out the great brain,

Holds it aloft, then gives it to the next who stands   25
    Beside him. Each, in turn, accepts it, although loath,
Turns it this way, that way, feels it between his hands
    Like a wasp's nest or some sickening outsized growth.

They must decide what thoughts each part of it must think;
    They tap at, then listen beside, each suspect lobe;   30
Next, with a crow's quill dipped into India ink,
    Mark on its surface, as if on a map or globe,

Those dangerous areas which need to be excised.
    They rinse it, then apply antiseptics to it;
Now silver saws appear which, inch by inch, slice   35
    Through its ancient folds and ridges, like thick suet.

It's rinsed, dried, and daubed with thick salves. The smoky saws
    Are scrubbed, resterilized, and polished till they gleam.
The brain is repacked in its case. Pinched in their claws,
    Glimmering needles stitch it up, that leave no seam.   40

Meantime, one of them has set blinders to the eyes,
    Inserted light packing beneath each of the ears
And calked the nostrils in. One, with thin twine, ties
    The genitals off. With long wooden-handled shears,

Another chops pinions out of the scarlet wings.   45
    It's hoped that with disuse he will forget the sky
Or, at least, in time, learn, among other things,
    To fly no higher than his superiors fly.

Well; that's a beginning. The next time, they can split
    His tongue and teach him to talk correctly, can give   50
Him opinions on fine books and choose clothing fit
    For the integrated area where he'll live.

Their candidate may live to give them thanks one day.
    He will recover and may hope for such success
He might return to join their ranks. Bowing away,   55
    They nod, whispering, "One of ours; one of ours. Yes. Yes."

—1967

Mementos, I

Sorting out letters and piles of my old
 Canceled checks, old clippings, and yellow note cards
That meant something once, I happened to find
 Your picture. *That* picture. I stopped there cold,
Like a man raking piles of dead leaves in his yard   5
  Who has turned up a severed hand.

Still, that first second, I was glad: you stand
 Just as you stood—shy, delicate, slender,
In that long gown of green lace netting and daisies
 That you wore to our first dance. The sight of you stunned   10
Us all. Well, our needs were different, then,
  And our ideals came easy.

Then through the war and those two long years
 Overseas, the Japanese dead in their shacks
Among dishes, dolls, and lost shoes; I carried   15
 This glimpse of you, there, to choke down my fear,
Prove it had been, that it might come back.
  That was before we got married.

—Before we drained out one another's force
 With lies, self-denial, unspoken regret   20
And the sick eyes that blame; before the divorce
 And the treachery. Say it: before we met. Still,
I put back your picture. Someday, in due course,
  I will find that it's still there.

              —*1967*

A. R. Ammons (1926–2001)

A. R. Ammons wrote poetry for over fifty years, and published almost thirty books. Raised during the great depression on a subsistence farm in North Carolina, he began writing poetry while in the South Pacific aboard a U.S. Navy destroyer escort. Later, he studied science at Wake Forest College and worked as a real estate agent, an editor, an elementary school principal, and an executive in his father-in-law's glass company. A vanity press published his first book of poetry, which went largely unread. Ultimately, the reflective poetry of Archie Randolph Ammons earned him numerous honors, including two National Book Awards for Collected Poems 1951–1971 *(in 1973) and* Garbage *(in 1993), and the Bollingen Prize for* Sphere: The Form of a Motion *(in 1974). He lived in Ithaca, New York, where he was Goldwin Smith Professor of Poetry at Cornell University until his retirement in 1998. Ammons's poems range from the epigrammatic to the encyclopedic, and often have at their center an abiding fascination with nature.*

Corsons Inlet°

I went for a walk over the dunes again this morning
to the sea,
then turned right along
    the surf
              rounded a naked headland   5
              and returned

   along the inlet shore:

it was muggy sunny, the wind from the sea steady and high,
crisp in the running sand,
        some breakthroughs of sun   10
   but after a bit
continuous overcast:

the walk liberating, I was released from forms,
from the perpendiculars,
        straight lines, blocks, boxes, binds   15
of thought

Corsons Inlet on the New Jersey shore

into the hues, shadings, rises, flowing bends and blends
      of sight:

        I allow myself eddies of meaning:
yield to a direction of significance   20
running
like a stream through the geography of my work:
   you can find
in my sayings
       swerves of action   25
        like the inlet's cutting edge:
    there are dunes of motion,
organizations of grass, white sandy paths of remembrance
in the overall wandering of mirroring mind:

but Overall is beyond me: is the sum of these events   30
I cannot draw, the ledger I cannot keep, the accounting
beyond the account:

in nature there are few sharp lines: there are areas of
primrose
     more or less dispersed;   35
disorderly orders of bayberry; between the rows
of dunes,
irregular swamps of reeds,
though not reeds alone, but grass, bayberry, yarrow, all . . .
predominantly reeds: 40

I have reached no conclusions, have erected no boundaries,
shutting out and shutting in, separating inside
     from outside: I have
     drawn no lines:
     as   45

manifold events of sand
change the dune's shape that will not be the same shape
tomorrow.

so I am willing to go along, to accept
the becoming   50
thought, to stake off no beginnings or ends, establish
    no walls:

by transitions the land falls from grassy dunes to creek

to undercreek: but there are no lines, though
      change in that transition is clear   55
      as any sharpness: but "sharpness" spread out,
allowed to occur over a wider range
than mental lines can keep:

the moon was full last night: today, low tide was low:
black shoals of mussels exposed to the risk   60
of air
and, earlier, of sun,
waved in and out with the waterline, waterline inexact,
caught always in the event of change:
      a young mottled gull stood free on the shoals   65
      and ate
to vomiting: another gull, squawking possession, cracked a crab,
picked out the entrails, swallowed the soft-shelled legs, a ruddy
turnstone° running in to snatch leftover bits:

risk is full: every living thing in   70
siege: the demand is life, to keep life: the small
white blacklegged egret, how beautiful, quietly stalks and spears
      the shallows, darts to shore
          to stab—what? I couldn't
      see against the black mudflats—a frightened   75
      fiddler crab?

      the news to my left over the dunes and
reeds and bayberry clumps was
      fall: thousands of tree swallows
      gathering for flight: 80
      an order held
      in constant change: a congregation
rich with entropy: nevertheless, separable, noticeable
      as one event,
          not chaos: preparations for   85
flight from winter,
cheet, cheet, cheet, cheet, wings rifling the green clumps,
beaks

68–69 ruddy turnstone a type of wading bird

at the bayberries
     a perception full of wind, flight, curve,   90
     sound:
     the possibility of rule as the sum of rulelessness:
the "field" of action
with moving, incalculable center:

in the smaller view, order tight with shape: 95
blue tiny flowers on a leafless weed: carapace of crab:
snail shell:
          pulsations of order
          in the bellies of minnows: orders swallowed,
broken down, transferred through membranes   100
to strengthen larger orders: but in the large view, no
lines or changeless shapes: the working in and out, together
          and against, of millions of events: this,
                    so that I make
                    no form   105
                    formlessness:

orders as summaries, as outcomes of actions override
or in some way result, not predictably (seeing me gain
the top of a dune,
the swallows   110
could take flight—some other fields of bayberry
          could enter fall
          berryless) and there is serenity:

          no arranged terror: no forcing of image, plan,
or thought: 115
no propaganda, no humbling of reality to precept:

terror pervades but is not arranged, all possibilities
of escape open: no route shut, except in
     the sudden loss of all routes:

          I see narrow orders, limited tightness, but will   120
not run to that easy victory:
          still around the looser, wider forces work:
          I will try
     to fasten into order enlarging grasps of disorder, widening
scope, but enjoying the freedom that   125

Scope eludes my grasp, that there is no finality of vision,
that I have perceived nothing completely,
   that tomorrow a new walk is a new walk.

—*1965*

First Carolina Said-Song

as told me by an aunt

In them days
      they won't hardly no way to know if
            somebody way off
            died
                  till they'd be   5
                  dead and buried

            and Uncle Jim

hitched up a team of mules to the wagon
and he cracked the whip over them
            and run them their dead-level best   10
the whole thirty miles to your great grandma's funeral
                  down there in
                  Green Sea County

            and there come up this
awfulest rainstorm   15
            you ever saw in your whole life
            and your grandpa
            was setting
            in a goatskin-bottom chair

and them mules a-running   20
and him sloshing round in that chairful of water
                  till he got scalded
                  he said
                  and ev-
                  ery   25
anch of skin come off his behind:

we got there just in time to see her buried
      in an oak grove up

back of the field:
it's growed over with soapbushes and huckleberries now.   30

—*1966*

The Foot-Washing

Now you have come,
the roads
humbling your feet with dust:

I ask you to
sit by this   5
spring:

I will wash your feet
with springwater
and silver care:

I lift leaking handbowls   10
to your ankles:
O ablutions!

Who are you
sir
who are my brother?   15

I dry your feet
with sweetgum
and mint leaves:

the odor of your feet
is newly earthen,   20
honeysuckled:

bloodwork in blue
raisures over the white
skinny anklebone:

if I have wronged you   25
cleanse me with the falling
water of forgiveness.

And woman, your flat feet
yellow, gray with dust,

your orphaned udders flat,   30

lift your dress
up to your knees
and I will wash your feet:

feel the serenity
cool as cool springwater   35
and hard to find:

if I have failed to know
the grief in your gone time,
forgive me wakened now.

—*1966*

James Merrill (1926–1995)

James Merrill wrote The Changing Light at Sandover *(1982), a long poem that resulted from many years of sessions with a Ouija board. The book became his major work and, among many other things, a remarkable memoir of a long-term gay relationship. Merrill's shorter poems, collected in 2001, reveal meticulous craftsmanship and a play of wit unequaled among contemporary American poets. Merrill was born in New York City and grew up in Manhattan and Southhampton; he was the son of Charles Merrill, cofounder of the Merrill Lynch brokerage firm. Merrill studied at Amherst College, but took a leave of absence to serve in the Army during World War II.* First Poems *(1951), his first mature poetry collection, garnered mixed reviews, but his 1959 publication,* The Country of a Thousand Years of Peace, *brought him critical accolades. In 1956, Merrill founded the Ingram Merrill Foundation, which awards grants to artists and writers. Among his many honors are the Pulitzer Prize and two National Book Awards. His last book,* A Scattering of Salts *(1995), was published a few months after his death.*

Charles on Fire

Another evening we sprawled about discussing
Appearances. And it was the consensus
That while uncommon physical good looks
Continued to launch one, as before, in life

(Among its vaporous eddies and false calms),   5
Still, as one of us said into his beard,
"Without your intellectual and spiritual
Values, man, you are sunk." No one but squared
The shoulders of his own unloveliness.
Long-suffering Charles, having cooked and served the meal,   10
Now brought out little tumblers finely etched
He filled with amber liquor and then passed.
"Say," said the same young man, "in Paris, France,
They do it this way"—bounding to his feet
And touching a lit match to our host's full glass.   15
A blue flame, gentle, beautiful, came, went
Above the surface. In a hush that fell
We heard the vessel crack. The contents drained
As who should step down from a crystal coach.
Steward of spirits, Charles's glistening hand   20
All at once gloved itself in eeriness.
The moment passed. He made two quick sweeps and
Was flesh again. "It couldn't matter less,"
He said, but with a shocked, unconscious glance
Into the mirror. Finding nothing changed,   25
He filled a fresh glass and sank down among us.

                                                          —1966

The Broken Home

Crossing the street,
I saw the parents and the child
At their window, gleaming like fruit
With evening's mild gold leaf.

In a room on the floor below,   5
Sunless, cooler—a brimming
Saucer of wax, marbly and dim—
I have lit what's left of my life.

I have thrown out yesterday's milk
And opened a book of maxims.
The flame quickens. The word stirs.   10

Tell me, tongue of fire,

That you and I are as real
At least as the people upstairs.

My father, who had flown in World War I,   15
Might have continued to invest his life
In cloud banks well above Wall Street and wife.
But the race was run below, and the point was to win.

Too late now, I make out in his blue gaze
(Through the smoked glass of being thirty-six)   20
The soul eclipsed by twin black pupils, sex
And business: time was money in those days.

Each thirteenth year he married. When he died
There were already several chilled wives
In sable orbit—rings, cars, permanent waves.   25
We'd felt him warming up for a green bride.

He could afford it. He was "in his prime"
At three score ten. But money was not time.

When my parents were younger this was a popular act:
A veiled woman would leap from an electric, wine-dark car   30
To the steps of no matter what—the Senate or the Ritz Bar—
And bodily, at newsreel speed, attack

No matter whom—Al Smith° or José Maria Sert°
Or Clemenceau°—veins standing out on her throat
As she yelled *War mongerer! Pig! Give us the vote!*,   35
And would have to be hauled away in her hobble skirt.

What had the man done? Oh, made history.
Her business (he had implied) was giving birth,
Tending the house, mending the socks.

Always that same old story—   40
Father Time and Mother Earth,
A marriage on the rocks.

One afternoon, red, satyr-thighed
Michael, the Irish setter, head

33 Al Smith Democratic candidate for the presidency in 1928   **33 José Maria Sert** Spanish muralist
34 Clemenceau premier of France during World War I

Passionately lowered, led   45
The child I was to a shut door. Inside,

Blinds beat sun from the bed.
The green-gold room throbbed like a bruise.
Under a sheet, clad in taboos
Lay whom we sought, her hair undone, outspread,   50

And of a blackness found, if ever now, in old
Engravings where the acid bit.
I must have needed to touch it
Or the whiteness—was she dead?
Her eyes flew open, startled strange and cold.   55
The dog slumped to the floor. She reached for me. I fled.

Tonight they have stepped out onto the gravel.
The party is over. It's the fall
Of 1931. They love each other still.

She: Charlie, I can't stand the pace.   60
He: Come on, honey—why, you'll bury us all!

A lead soldier guards my windowsill:
Khaki rifle, uniform, and face.
Something in me grows heavy, silvery, pliable.

How intensely people used to feel!   65
Like metal poured at the close of a proletarian novel,
Refined and glowing from the crucible,
I see those two hearts, I'm afraid,
Still. Cool here in the graveyard of good and evil,
They are even so to be honored and obeyed.   70

. . . Obeyed, at least, inversely. Thus
I rarely buy a newspaper, or vote.
To do so, I have learned, is to invite
The tread of a stone guest° within my house.

Shooting this rusted bolt, though, against him,   75
I trust I am no less time's child than some
Who on the heath impersonate Poor Tom°

---

74 stone guest In Mozart's opera *Don Giovanni*, the legendary womanizer, is dragged to hell by the statue of a man he has murdered   **77 Poor Tom** In Shakespeare's *King Lear*, the name Edgar calls himself when he wanders the heath in disguise

Or on the barricades risk life and limb.

Nor do I try to keep a garden, only
An avocado in a glass of water—   80
Roots pallid, gemmed with air. And later,

When the small gilt leaves have grown
Fleshy and green, I let them die, yes, yes,
And start another. I am earth's no less.

A child, a red dog roam the corridors,   85
Still, of the broken home. No sound. The brilliant
Rag runners halt before wide-open doors.
My old room! Its wallpaper—cream, medallioned
With pink and brown—brings back the first nightmares,
Long summer colds, and Emma, sepia-faced,   90
Perspiring over broth carried upstairs
Aswim with golden fats I could not taste.

The real house became a boarding school.
Under the ballroom ceiling's allegory
Someone at last may actually be allowed   95
To learn something; or, from my window, cool
With the unstiflement of the entire story,
Watch a red setter stretch and sink in cloud.

—1969

Casual Wear

Your average tourist: Fifty. 2.3
Times married. Dressed, this year, in Ferdi Plinthbower°
Originals. Odds 1 to 9^{10}°
Against her strolling past the Embassy

Today at noon. Your average terrorist:
Twenty-five. Celibate. No use for trends,
At least in clothing. Mark, though, where it ends.
People have come forth made of colored mist

Unsmiling on one hundred million screens

2 **Ferdi Plinthbower** a fictional designer   3 **1 to 9^{10}** pronounced "one to nine to the tenth power"

To tell of his prompt phone call to the station,
"Claiming responsibility"—devastation
Signed with a flourish, like the dead wife's jeans.

—1984

Robert Creeley (b. 1926)

Robert Creeley is one of several important contemporary poets (Denise Levertov is another) associated with Black Mountain College, a small experimental school in North Carolina that attracted writers and artists during the 1950s. Born in Arlington, Massachusetts, Creeley was educated at Harvard University from 1943 to 1946, but took a year off from school to work for the American Field Service in Burma and India. In 1949, he started a correspondence with his poetic forbears William Carlos Williams and Ezra Pound; a year later he met the poet Charles Olson, the rector of Black Mountain College. Creeley joined the Black Mountain faculty and took up editorship of the Black Mountain Review, *thereby helping to shape an emerging literary counter-tradition. The author of more than sixty books of poetry, he has been affiliated with the State University of New York–Buffalo since 1989.*

Naughty Boy

When he brings home a whale
she laughs and says, that's not for real.

And if he won the Irish sweepstakes,
she would say, where were you last night?

Where are you now, for that matter? Am   5
I always (she says) to be looking

at you? She says,
if I thought it would get any better I

would shoot you, you
nut, you. Then pats her hair   10

into place, and waits
for Uncle Jim's deep-fired, all-fat, real gone

whale steaks.

—1959

I Know a Man

As I sd to my
friend, because I am
always talking,— John, I

sd, which was not his
name, the darkness sur-   5
rounds us, what

can we do against
it, or else, shall we &
why not, buy a goddamn big car,

drive, he sd, for   10
christ's sake, look
out where yr going.

—1962

Oh No

If you wander far enough
you will come to it
and when you get there
they will give you a place to sit

for yourself only, in a nice chair,   5
and all your friends will be there
with smiles on their faces
and they will likewise all have places.

—1962

The Language

Locate *I*
love you some-
where in

teeth and
eyes, bite
it but   5

take care not
to hurt, you
want so

much so   10
little. Words
say everything.

I
love you
again,   15

then what
is emptiness
for. To

fill, fill.
I heard words   20
and words full
of holes
aching. Speech
is a mouth.

—1967

Allen Ginsberg (1926–1997)

Allen Ginsberg became the chief poetic spokesman of the Beat Generation. He was a force—as poet and celebrity—who continued to outrage and delight four decades after the 1956 appearance of Howl, *the monumental poem describing how Ginsberg saw "the best minds of my generation destroyed by madness." Born in Newark, New Jersey, Ginsberg attended Columbia University, where he became friends with Jack Kerouac, William S. Burroughs, and Neal Cassady, key figures in the Beat movement. Ginsberg moved to San Francisco in 1954 and studied with Zen masters and gurus in the 1960s and '70s. He founded and directed the Jack Kerouac School of Disembodied Poetics at Colorado's Naropa Institute, and served as Distinguished Professor at Brooklyn College. He died in 1997 in New York City. Ginsberg's poems are cultural documents that provide a key to understanding the radical changes in American life, particularly among youth, that began in the mid-1950s.*

America

America I've given you all and now I'm nothing.
American two dollars and twentyseven cents January 17, 1956.
I can't stand my own mind.
America when will we end the human war?
Go fuck yourself with your atom bomb.   5
I don't feel good don't bother me.
I won't write my poem till I'm in my right mind.
America when will you be angelic?
When will you take off your clothes?
When will you look at yourself through the grave?   10
When will you be worthy of your million Trotskyites?°
America why are your libraries full of tears?
America when will you send your eggs to India?
I'm sick of your insane demands.
When can I go into the supermarket and buy what I need with my
    good looks?   15
America after all it is you and I who are perfect not the next world.
Your machinery is too much for me.

---

11 Trotskyites American communists. Leon Trotsky advocated a world revolution by the working class

You made me want to be a saint.
There must be some other way to settle this argument.
Burroughs° is in Tangiers I don't think he'll come back it's sinister.   20
Are you being sinister or is this some form of practical joke?
I'm trying to come to the point.
I refuse to give up my obsession.
America stop pushing I know what I'm doing.
America the plum blossoms are falling.   25
I haven't read the newspapers for months, everyday somebody goes
    on trial for murder.
America I feel sentimental about the Wobblies°.
America I used to be a communist when I was a kid I'm not sorry.
I smoke marijuana every chance I get.
I sit in my house for days on end and stare at the roses in the closet. 30
When I go to Chinatown I get drunk and never get laid.
My mind is made up there's going to be trouble.
You should have seen me reading Marx.
My psychoanalyst thinks I'm perfectly right.
I won't say the Lord's Prayer.
I have mystical visions and cosmic vibrations.   35

America I still haven't told you what you did to Uncle Max after he
    came over from Russia.
I'm addressing you.
Are you going to let your emotional life be run by Time Magazine?
I'm obsessed by Time Magazine.   40
I read it every week.
Its cover stares at me every time I slink past the corner candystore.
I read it in the basement of the Berkeley Public Library.
It's always telling me about responsibility. Businessmen are serious.
    Movie producers are serious. Everybody's serious but me.
It occurs to me that I am America.   45
I am talking to myself again.

Asia is rising against me.
I haven't got a chinaman's chance.

---

20 Burroughs William S. Burroughs, author of *Naked Lunch* (1959)   **27 Wobblies** members of the
Industrial Workers of the World, a radical labor organization

I'd better consider my national resources.
My national resources consist of two joints of marijuana millions of
    genitals an unpublishable private literature that jetplanes 1400
    miles an hour and twentyfive-thousand mental institutions.   50
I say nothing about my prisons nor the millions of underprivileged
    who live in my flowerpots under the light of five hundred suns.
I have abolished the whorehouses of France, Tangiers is the next
    to go.
My ambition is to be President despite the fact that I'm a Catholic.

America how can I write a holy litany in your silly mood?
I will continue like Henry Ford my strophes° are as individual as his
    automobiles more so they're all different sexes.   55
America I will sell you strophes $2500 apiece $500 down on
    your old strophe
America free Tom Mooney°
America save the Spanish Loyalists°
America Sacco & Vanzetti must not die°
America I am the Scottsboro boys.°   60
America when I was seven momma took me to Communist Cell
    meetings they sold us garbanzos a handful per ticket a ticket
    costs a nickel and the speeches were free everybody was angelic
    and sentimental about the workers it was all so sincere you
    have no idea what a good thing the party was in 1935 Scott
    Nearing° was a grand old man a real mensch Mother Bloor°
    the Silk-strikers' Ewig-Weibliche° made me cry I once saw the
    Yiddish orator Israel Amter° plain. Everybody must have been
    a spy.
America you don't really want to go to war.
America it's them bad Russians.
Them Russians them Russians and them Chinamen. And them
    Russians.

---

55 strophes stanzas in a ode   57 **Tom Mooney** a labor organizer jailed for allegedly exploding a bomb; condemned to death, he was freed after 23 years in prison   58 **Spanish Loyalists** in the Spanish Civil War, supporters of the Socialist government of Republican Spain who fought against fascist revolutionaries   59 **Sacco & Vanzetti** anarchists executed in 1927   60 **Scottsboro boys** nine African-American men tried for allegedly gang raping two white women. After an unfair trial in Scottsboro, Alabama, eight of the accused men were condemned to death   61 **Scott Nearing** radical economist and socialist   61 **Mother Bloor** Ella Reeve Bloor, a Communist party leader   61 **Ewig-Weibliche** in German, the eternal feminine   61 **Israel Amter** a Communist party leader

The Russia wants to eat us alive. The Russia's power mad. She wants
   to take our cars from out our garages.   65
Her wants to grab Chicago. Her needs a Red *Readers' Digest.* Her
   wants our auto plants in Siberia. Him big bureaucracy running
   our filling-stations.
That no good. Ugh. Him make Indians learn read. Him need big
   black niggers. Hah. Her make us all work sixteen hours a day.
   Help.
America this is quite serious.
America this is the impression I get from looking in the television set.
America is this correct?   70
I'd better get right down to the job.
It's true I don't want to join the Army or turn lathes in precision parts
   factories, I'm nearsighted and psychopathic anyway.
America I'm putting my queer shoulder to the wheel.

—1956

Howl

For Carl Solomon°

I

I saw the best minds of my generation destroyed by madness,
   starving hysterical naked,
dragging themselves through the negro streets at dawn looking for
   an angry fix,
angelheaded hipsters burning for the ancient heavenly connection
   to the starry dynamo in the machinery of night,
who poverty and tatters and hollow-eyed and high sat up smoking
   in the supernatural darkness of cold-water flats floating across
   the tops of cities contemplating jazz,
who bared their brains to Heaven under the El° and saw Moham-   5
   medan angels staggering on tenement roofs illuminated,

Carl Solomon Ginsberg and Solomon met in 1949 when both men were patients at the Columbia
Presbyterian Psychiatric Institute   **5 El** New York's elevated railway

who passed through universities with radiant cool eyes hallucinating
Arkansas and Blake-light° tragedy among the scholars of war,

who were expelled from the academies for crazy & publishing
obscene odes on the windows of the skull,

who cowered in unshaven rooms in underwear, burning their money
in wastebaskets and listening to the Terror through the wall,

who got busted in their pubic beards returning through Laredo with
a belt of marijuana for New York,

who ate fire in paint hotels or drank turpentine in Paradise Alley,°   10
death, or purgatoried their torsos night after night

with dreams, with drugs, with waking nightmares, alcohol and cock
and endless balls,

incomparable blind streets of shuddering cloud and lightning in the
mind leaping toward poles of Canada & Paterson,° illuminating
all the motionless world of Time between,

Peyote solidities of halls, backyard green tree cemetery dawns, wine
drunkenness over the rooftops, storefront boroughs of teahead
joyride neon blinking traffic light, sun and moon and tree
vibrations in the roaring winter dusks of Brooklyn, ashcan
rantings and kind king light of mind.

who chained themselves to subways for the endless ride from Battery
to holy Bronx on benzedrine until the noise of wheels and
children brought them down shuddering mouth-wracked and
battered bleak of brain all drained of brilliance in the drear light
of Zoo,°

who sank all night in submarine light of Bickford's° floated out and   15
sat through the stale beer afternoon in desolate Fugazzi's,°
listening to the crack of doom on the hydrogen jukebox,

who talked continuously seventy hours from park to pad to bar to
Bellevue° to museum to the Brooklyn Bridge,

a lost battalion of platonic conversationalists jumping down the
stoops off fire escapes off windowsills off Empire State out of the
moon,

yacketayakking screaming vomiting whispering facts and memories
and anecdotes and eyeball kicks and shocks of hospitals and jails
and wars,

---

6 **Blake-light** William Blake, English Romantic poet   10 **Paradise Alley** an alleyway running
between tenement buildings in New York's Lower East Side   12 **Paterson** in New Jersey; the town
in which Ginsberg was raised   14 **Zoo** the Bronx Zoo   15 **Bickford's** a chain of cafeterias
15 **Fugazzi's** a bar near Greenwich Village in New York City   16 **Bellevue** a New York City
hospital known for its psychiatric ward

whole intellects disgorged in total recall for seven days and nights
with brilliant eyes, meat for the Synagogue cast on the pavement,
who vanished into nowhere Zen New Jersey leaving a trail of   20
ambiguous picture postcards of Atlantic City Hall,
suffering Eastern sweats and Tangerian bone-grindings and migraines
of China under junk-withdrawal in Newark's bleak furnished
room,
who wandered around and around at midnight in the railroad yard
wondering where to go, and went, leaving no broken hearts,
who lit cigarettes in boxcars boxcars boxcars racketing through
snow toward lonesome farms in grandfather night,
who studied Plotinus Poe St. John of the Cross° telepathy and bop°
kabbalah° because the cosmos instinctively vibrated at their feet
in Kansas,
who loned it through the streets of Idaho seeking visionary indian   25
angels who were visionary indian angels,
who thought they were only mad when Baltimore gleamed in
supernatural ecstasy,
who jumped in limousines with the Chinaman of Oklahoma on the
impulse of winter midnight streetlight smalltown rain,
who lounged hungry and lonesome through Houston seeking jazz or
sex or soup, and followed the brilliant Spaniard to converse about
America and Eternity, a hopeless task, and so took ship to Africa,
who disappeared into the volcanoes of Mexico leaving behind
nothing but the shadow of dungarees and the lava and ash of
poetry scattered in fireplace Chicago,
who reappeared on the West Coast investigating the FBI in beards   30
and shorts with big pacifist eyes sexy in their dark skin passing
out incomprehensible leaflets,
who burned cigarette holes in their arms protesting the narcotic
tobacco haze of Capitalism,
who distributed Supercommunist pamphlets in Union Square°
weeping and undressing while the sirens of Los Alamos° wailed
them down, and wailed down Wall,° and the Staten Island ferry
also wailed,

---

24 **Plotinus Poe St. John of the Cross** visionary writers   24 **bop** a jazz style   24 **Kaballah** a body of mystical Jewish teachings, also spelled Cabbala   32 **Union Square** in New York City, the site of radical political demonstrations in the 1930s   32 **Los Alamos** in New Mexico, where the atomic bomb was developed   32 **Wall Street** in New York, home to the New York Stock Exchange

who broke down crying in white gymnasiums naked and trembling
before the machinery of other skeletons,

who bit detectives in the neck and shrieked with delight in policecars
for committing no crime but their own wild cooking pederasty
and intoxication,

who howled on their knees in the subway and were dragged off the 35
roof waving genitals and manuscripts,

who let themselves be fucked in the ass by saintly motorcyclists,
and screamed with joy,

who blew and were blown by those human seraphim, the sailors,
caresses of Atlantic and Caribbean love,

who balled in the morning in the evenings in rosegardens and the
grass of public parks and cemeteries scattering their semen freely
to whomever come who may,

who hiccupped endlessly trying to giggle but wound up with a sob
behind a partition in a Turkish Bath when the blond & naked
angel came to pierce them with a sword,

who lost their loveboys to the three old shrews of fate the one eyed 40
shrew of the heterosexual dollar the one eyed shrew that winks
out of the womb and the one eyed shrew that does nothing but
sit on her ass and snip the intellectual golden threads of the
craftsman's loom,

who copulated ecstatic and insatiate with a bottle of beer a
sweetheart a package of cigarettes a candle and fell off the bed,
and continued along the floor and down the hall and ended
fainting on the wall with a vision of ultimate cunt and come
eluding the last gyzym of consciousness,

who sweetened the snatches of a million girls trembling in the sunset,
and were red eyed in the morning but prepared to sweeten the
snatch of the sunrise, flashing buttocks under barns and naked in
the lake,

who went out whoring through Colorado in myriad stolen night-
cars, N.C.,° secret hero of these poems, cocksman and Adonis
of Denver—joy to the memory of his innumerable lays of girls
in empty lots & diner backyards, moviehouses' rickety rows, on
mountaintops in caves or with gaunt waitresses in familiar
roadside lonely petticoat upliftings & especially secret gas-station
solipsisms of johns, & hometown alleys too,

---

43 N. C. Neal Cassady, whose travels with novelist Jack Kerouac are the basis for the novel *On the Road* (1957)

who faded out in vast sordid movies, were shifted in dreams, woke
on a sudden Manhattan, and picked themselves up out of
basements hungover with heartless Tokay° and horrors of Third
Avenue iron dreams & stumbled to unemployment offices,
who walked all night with their shoes full of blood on the snowbank 45
docks waiting for a door in the East River to open to a room
full of steamheat and opium,
who created great suicidal dramas on the apartment cliff-banks of
the Hudson under the wartime blue floodlight of the moon &
their heads shall be crowned with laurel in oblivion,
who ate the lamb stew of the imagination or digested the crab at
the muddy bottom of the rivers of Bowery,°
who wept at the romance of the streets with their pushcarts full of
onions and bad music,
who sat in boxes breathing in the darkness under the bridge, and rose
up to build harpsichords in their lofts,
who coughed on the sixth floor of Harlem crowned with flame under 50
the tubercular sky surrounded by orange crates of theology,
who scribbled all night rocking and rolling over lofty incantations
which in the yellow morning were stanzas of gibberish,
who cooked rotten animals lung heart feet tail borsht & tortillas
dreaming of the pure vegetable kingdom,
who plunged themselves under meat trucks looking for an egg,
who threw their watches off the roof to cast their ballot for Eternity
outside of Time, & alarm clocks fell on their heads every day
for the next decade,
who cut their wrists three times successively unsuccessfully, gave up 55
and were forced to open antique stores where they thought they
were growing old and cried,
who were burned alive in their innocent flannel suits on Madison
Avenue° amid blasts of leaden verse & the tanked-up clatter of
the iron regiments of fashion & the nitroglycerine shrieks of the
fairies of advertising & the mustard gas of sinister intelligent
editors, or were run down by the drunken taxicabs of Absolute
Reality,
who jumped off the Brooklyn Bridge this actually happened and
walked away unknown and forgotten into the ghostly daze of
Chinatown soup alleyways & firetrucks, not even one free beer,

---

43 **Tokay** a cheap wine   47 **Bowery** a section of lower Manhattan, associated with vagrants and
alcoholics   56 **Madison Avenue** in New York, the hub of America's advertising industry

who sang out of their windows in despair, fell out of the subway window, jumped in the filthy Passaic,° leaped on negroes, cried all over the street, danced on broken wineglasses barefoot smashed phonograph records of nostalgic European 1930s German jazz finished the whiskey and threw up groaning into the bloody toilet, moans in their ears and the blast of colossal steam-whistles,

who barreled down the highways of the past journeying to each other's hotrod-Golgotha° jail-solitude watch or Birmingham jazz incarnation,

who drove crosscountry seventytwo hours to find out if I had a vision 60 or you had a vision or he had a vision to find out Eternity,

who journeyed to Denver, who died in Denver, who came back to Denver & waited in vain, who watched over Denver & brooded & loned in Denver and finally went away to find out the Time, & now Denver is lonesome for her heroes,

who fell on their knees in hopeless cathedrals praying for each other's salvation and light and breasts, until the soul illuminated its hair for a second,

who crashed through their minds in jail waiting for impossible criminals with golden heads and the charm of reality in their hearts who sang sweet blues to Alcatraz,°

who retired to Mexico to cultivate a habit, or Rocky Mount to tender Buddha or Tangiers to boys or Southern Pacific to the black locomotive or Harvard to Narcissus to Woodlawn° to the daisychain or grave,

who demanded sanity trials accusing the radio of hypnotism & were 65 left with their insanity & their hands & a hung jury,

who threw potato salad at CCNY° lecturers on Dadaism° and subsequently presented themselves on the granite steps of the madhouse with shaven heads and harlequin speech of suicide, demanding instantaneous lobotomy,

and who were given instead the concrete void of insulin Metrazol electricity hydrotherapy psychotherapy occupational therapy pingpong & amnesia,

who in humorless protest overturned only one symbolic pingpong table, resting briefly in catatonia,

58 Passaic river in New Jersey   **59 Golgotha** site of Jesus Christ's crucifixion   **63 Alcatraz** federal prison in San Francisco Bay   **64 Woodlawn** cemetery in the Bronx   **66 CCNY** City College of New York   **66 Dadaism** iconoclastic literary and artistic movement that embraced the bizarre and accidental

returning years later truly bald except for a wig of blood, and tears and fingers, to the visible madman doom of the wards of the madtowns of the East,

Pilgrim State's Rockland's and Greystone's° foetid halls, bickering 70 with the echoes of the soul, rocking and rolling in the midnight solitude-bench dolmen-realms of love, dream of life a nightmare, bodies turned to stone as heavy as the moon,

with mother finally ******,° and the last fantastic book flung out of the tenement window, and the last door closed at 4 A.M. and the last telephone slammed at the wall in reply and the last furnished room emptied down to the last piece of mental furniture, a yellow paper rose twisted on a wire hanger in the closet, and even that imaginary, nothing but a hopeful little bit of hallucination—

ah, Carl, while you are not safe I am not safe, and now you're really in the total animal soup of time—

and who therefore ran through the icy streets obsessed with a sudden flash of the alchemy of the use of the ellipse the catalog the meter & the vibrating plane,

who dreamt and made incarnate gaps in Time & Space through images juxtaposed, and trapped the archangel of the soul between 2 visual images and joined the elemental verbs and set the noun and dash of consciousness together jumping with sensation of Pater Omnipotens Aeterna Deus°

to recreate the syntax and measure of poor human prose and stand 75 before you speechless and intelligent and shaking with shame, rejected yet confessing out the soul to conform to the rhythm of thought in his naked and endless head,

the madman bum and angel beat in Time, unknown, yet putting down here what might be left to say in time come after death,

and rose reincarnate in the ghostly clothes of jazz in the goldhorn shadow of the band and blew the suffering of America's naked mind for love into an eli eli lamma lamma sabacthani° saxophone cry that shivered the cities down to the last radio

with the absolute heart of the poem of life butchered out of their own bodies good to eat a thousand years.

—1956

70 **Pilgrim State's Rockland's and Greystone's** mental hospitals   71 ****** originally "fucked"; Ginsberg eventually replaced the obscenity with asterisks   74 **Pater Omnipotens Aeterna Deus** eternal god omnipotent father   77 **eli eli lamma lamma sabacthani** My god, my god, why has thou forsaken me?

A Supermarket in California

What thoughts I have of you tonight, Walt Whitman, for I walked down the sidestreets under the trees with a headache self-conscious looking at the full moon.

In my hungry fatigue, and shopping for images, I went into the neon fruit supermarket, dreaming of your enumerations!

What peaches and what penumbras?° Whole families shopping at night! Aisles full of husbands! Wives in the avocados, babies in the tomatoes!—and you, García Lorca,° what were you doing down by the watermelons?

I saw you, Walt Whitman, childless, lonely old grubber, poking among the meats in the refrigerator and eyeing the grocery boys.

I heard you asking questions of each: Who killed the pork chops? What price bananas? Are you my Angel?   5

I wandered in and out of the brilliant stacks of cans following you, and followed in my imagination by the store detective.

We strode down the open corridors together in our solitary fancy tasting artichokes, possessing every frozen delicacy, and never passing the cashier.

Where are we going, Walt Whitman? The doors close in an hour. Which way does your beard point tonight?

(I touch your book and dream of our odyssey in the supermarket and feel absurd.)

Will we walk all night through solitary streets? The trees add shade to shade, lights out in the houses, we'll both be lonely.   10

Will we stroll dreaming of the lost America of love past blue automobiles in driveways, home to our silent cottage?

Ah, dear father, graybeard, lonely old courage-teacher, what America did you have when Charon° quit poling his ferry and you got out on a smoking bank and stood watching the boat disappear on the black waters of Lethe?°

—1956

---

3 **penumbras** shadows   3 **García Lorca** Federico García Lorca, Spanish poet (1898–1936)
12 **Charon** ferryman of Hades   12 **Lethe** river in Hades, means forgetfulness

Frank O'Hara (1926–1966)

Frank O'Hara's untimely death in a dune buggy accident on Fire Island robbed American poetry of one of its most refreshing talents. An authority on modern art, O'Hara incorporated many of the spontaneous techniques of abstract expressionist painting in his own poetry, which often was written as an immediate reaction to the events of his daily life. Born in Baltimore and raised in Massachusetts, O'Hara studied piano at Boston's New England Conservatory and served in the South Pacific and Japan as a sonarman on the destroyer USS Nicholas. After the war, O'Hara majored in music at Harvard, where he met the poet John Ashbery and soon began writing poems and publishing them in the Harvard Advocate. O'Hara changed his major to English, and went on to earn an M.A. from the University of Michigan. He then moved to New York City where he began to write both poetry and essays on contemporary art for the publication ArtNews. Firmly associated with the New York School of Poets (a group which includes Ashbery, James Schuyler, and Kenneth Koch), O'Hara associated with the artists Larry Rivers, Jackson Pollock, and Jasper Johns, and on occasion collaborated on "poem-paintings," which incorporated written text into paintings.

Why I Am Not a Painter

I am not a painter, I am a poet.
Why? I think I would rather be
a painter, but I am not. Well,

for instance, Mike Goldberg°
is starting a painting. I drop in.   5
"Sit down and have a drink" he
says. I drink; we drink. I look
up. "You have SARDINES in it."
"Yes, it needed something there."
"Oh." I go and the days go by   10
and I drop in again. The painting
is going on, and I go, and the days
go by. I drop in. The painting is
finished. "Where's SARDINES?"

---

4 **Mike Goldberg** New York painter

All that's left is just   15
letters, "It was too much," Mike says.

But me? One day I am thinking of
a color: orange. I write a line
about orange. Pretty soon it is a
whole page of words, not lines.   20
Then another page. There should be
so much more, not of orange, of
words, of how terrible orange is
and life. Days go by. It is even in
prose, I am a real poet. My poem   25
is finished and I haven't mentioned
orange yet. It's twelve poems, I call
it ORANGES. And one day in a gallery
I see Mike's painting, called SARDINES.

—1958

The Day Lady° Died

It is 12:20 in New York a Friday
three days after Bastille day,° yes
it is 1959 and I go get a shoeshine
because I will get off the 4:19 in Easthampton
at 7:15 and then go straight to dinner   5
and I don't know the people who will feed me

I walk up the muggy street beginning to sun
and have a hamburger and a malted and buy
an ugly NEW WORLD WRITING to see what the poets
in Ghana are doing these days   10
                              I go on to the bank
and Miss Stillwagon (first name Linda I once heard)
doesn't even look up my balance for once in her life
and in the GOLDEN GRIFFIN I get a little Verlaine°
for Patsy with drawings by Bonnard° although I do   15
think of Hesiod,° trans. Richard Lattimore or

Lady Billie Holiday (1915–1959), blues singer   **2 Bastille day** July 14   **14 Verlaine** Paul Verlaine
(1844–1896), French Poet   **15 Bonnard** Pierre Bonnard (1867–1947), French painter   **16 Hesiod**
Greek poet, thought to have lived around 700 BC

Brendan Behan's° new play or *Le Balcon* or *Les Nègres*
of Genet,° but I don't, I stick with Verlaine°
after practically going to sleep with quandariness

and for Mike I just stroll into the PARK LANE   20
Liquor Store and ask for a bottle of Strega° and
then I go back where I came from to 6th Avenue
and the tobacconist in the Ziegfeld Theatre and
casually ask for a carton of Gauloises° and a carton
of Picayunes, and a NEW YORK POST with her face on it   25

and I am sweating a lot by now and thinking of
leaning on the john door in the 5 SPOT
while she whispered a song along the keyboard
to Mal Waldron° and everyone and I stopped breathing.

—*1964*

Poem

The eager note on my door said "Call me,
call when you get in!" so I quickly threw
a few tangerines into my overnight bag,
straightened my eyelids and shoulders, and

headed straight for the door. It was autumn   5
by the time I got around the corner, oh all
unwilling to be either pertinent or bemused, but
the leaves were brighter than grass on the sidewalk!

Funny, I thought, that the lights are on this late
and the hall door open; still up at this hour, a   10
champion jai-alai player like himself? Oh fie!
for shame! What a host, so zealous! And he was

there in the hall, flat on a sheet of blood that
ran down the stairs. I did appreciate it. There are few
hosts who so thoroughly prepare to greet a guest   15
only casually invited, and that several months ago.

—*1964*

17 **Behan** Brendan Behan (1923–1964), Irish writer   18 **Genet** Jean Genet (1910–1986), French
playwright   18 **Verlaine** Paul Verlaine (1844–1896), French poet   21 **Strega** Italian liqueur
24 **Gauloises** like Picayunes, a brand of cigarettes   29 **Mal Waldron** Holiday's accompanist

Robert Bly (b. 1926)

Robert Bly is best known as the author of the nonfiction best-seller Iron John: A Book About Men *(1990), a cornerstone of the mythopoetic men's movement that argues for a new ideal of masculinity. Also a poet, editor, and translator, Bly was born in western Minnesota to parents of Norwegian heritage. He served two years in the Navy, and studied at St. Olaf College, Harvard, and the Iowa Writers' Workshop. In 1956, a Fulbright grant brought him to Norway, where he discovered the work of Latin American and European poets like Pablo Neruda, Cesar Vallejo, and Georg Trakl, and resolved to win for them an American audience. Back in Minnesota, he started the literary magazine titled, successively,* The Fifties, The Sixties, *and* The Seventies, *which included many translations. In 1966, he cofounded American Writers Against the Vietnam War and was a vocal antiwar activist. More recently, Bly has conducted self-help workshops for men and women and seminars on European fairy tales.*

After Drinking All Night with a Friend, We Go Out in a Boat at Dawn to See Who Can Write the Best Poem

These pines, these fall oaks, these rocks,
This water dark and touched by wind—
I am like you, you dark boat,
Drifting over water fed by cool springs.

Beneath the waters, since I was a boy,   5
I have dreamt of strange and dark treasures,
Not of gold, or strange stones, but the true
Gift, beneath the pale lakes of Minnesota.

This morning also, drifting in the dawn wind,
I sense my hands, and my shoes, and this ink—   10

Drifting, as all of this body drifts,
Above the clouds of the flesh and the stone.

A few friendships, a few dawns, a few glimpses of grass,
A few oars weathered by the snow and the heat,
So we drift toward shore, over cold waters,   15
No longer caring if we drift or go straight.

—1953

For My Son, Noah, Ten Years Old

Night and day arrive, and day after day goes by,
and what is old remains old, and what is young remains
    young, and grows old,
and the lumber pile does not grow younger, nor the
    weathered two by fours lose their darkness,
but the old tree goes on, the barn stands without help so
    many years,
the advocate of darkness and night is not lost.   5

The horse swings around on one leg, steps, and turns,
the chicken flapping claws onto the roost, its wings whelping
    and whalloping,
but what is primitive is not to be shot out into the night and
    the dark.
And slowly the kind man comes closer, loses his rage, sits
    down at table.

So I am proud only of those days that we pass in undivided
    tenderness,   10
when you sit drawing, or making books, stapled, with
    messages to the world . . .
or coloring a man with fire coming out of his hair.
Or we sit at a table, with small tea carefully poured;
so we pass our time together, calm and delighted.

—1981

The Scandal

The day the minister ran off with the choir director
The bindlestiffs° felt some gaiety in their arms.
Spike-pitchers° threw their bundles higher on the load
And the County Assessor drove with a tiny smile.

Actually the minister's wife felt relieved that
    morning,   5
Though afraid too. She walked out by the slough,
And admired the beaver's house, partly above
Water, partly beneath. That seemed right.

The minister felt dizzy as the two of them drove
For hours: country music and the loose ribbon   10
Mingled in his mind with the *Song of Songs*.
They stopped at a small motel near Bismarck.

For the threshers, the stubble was still dry,
The oat dust itchy, the big belt needed grease,
The loads pulled up to the machine. This story
    happens   15
Over and over, and it's a good story.

—*1997*

---

2 bindlestiffs hoboes   **3 Spike-pitchers** grain harvesters

Galway Kinnell (b. 1927)

*Galway Kinnell was born in Providence, Rhode Island. He studied at
Princeton University—where he roomed with the poet W. S. Merwin—and
at the University of Rochester. A two-time Fulbright scholar, Kinnell has
been employed in Chicago as a director of adult education and in Iran as a
journalist. In the 1960s he worked with the Congress of Racial Equality,
helping to register Southern black voters; during the Vietnam era, he was
active in the antiwar movement. His* Selected Poems *(1982), received both
the Pulitzer Prize and the National Book Award. Erich Maria Remarque
Professor of Creative Writing at New York University, Kinnell divides his
time between Vermont and New York City. His poems display a keen interest in the natural world, and a pervasive sense of the fragility of life.*

After Making Love
We Hear Footsteps

For I can snore like a bullhorn
or play loud music
or sit up talking with any reasonably sober Irishman
and Fergus will only sink deeper
into his dreamless sleep, which goes by all in one flash,   5
but let there be that heavy breathing
or a stifled come-cry anywhere in the house
and he will wrench himself awake
and make for it on the run—as now, we lie together,
after making love, quiet, touching along the length of our bodies,   10
familiar touch of the long-married,
and he appears—in his baseball pajamas, it happens,
the neck opening so small
he has to screw them on, which one day may make him wonder
about the mental capacity of baseball players—   15
and flops down between us and hugs us and snuggles himself to sleep,
his face gleaming with satisfaction at being this very child.

In the half darkness we look at each other
and smile
and touch arms across his little, startlingly muscled body—   20
this one whom habit of memory propels to the ground of his making,

sleeper only the mortal sounds can sing awake,
this blessing love gives again into our arms.

—1964

Goodbye

1

My mother, poor woman, lies tonight
in her last bed. It's snowing, for her, in her darkness.
I swallow down the goodbyes I won't get to use,
tasteless, with wretched mouth-water;
whatever we are, she and I, we're nearly cured.   5

The night years ago when I walked away
from that final class of junior high school students
in Pittsburgh, the youngest of them ran
after me down the dark street. "Goodbye!" she called,
snow swirling across her face, tears falling.   10

2

Tears have kept on falling. History
has taught them its slanted understanding
of the human face. At each last embrace
the snow brings down its disintegrating curtain.
The mind shreds the present, once the past is over.   15

In the Derry graveyard where only her longings sleep
and armfuls of flowers go out in the drizzle
the bodies not yet risen must lie nearly forever . . .
"Sprouting good Irish grass," the graveskeeper blarneys,
he can't help it, "A sprig of shamrock, if they were young."   20

3

In Pittsburgh tonight, those who were young
will be less young, those who were old, more old, or more likely
no more; and the street where Syllest,
fleetest of my darlings, caught up with me
and hugged me and said goodbye, will be empty. Well,   25

one day the streets all over the world will be empty—
already in heaven, listen, the golden cobblestones have fallen still—
everyone's arms will be empty, everyone's mouth, the Derry earth.
It is written in our hearts, the emptiness is all.
That is how we have learned, the embrace is all.   30

—1980

Saint Francis and the Sow

The bud
stands for all things,
even for those things that don't flower,
for everything flowers, from within, of self-blessing;
though sometimes it is necessary   5
to reteach a thing its loveliness,
to put a hand on its brow
of the flower
and retell it in words and in touch
it is lovely   10
until it flowers again from within, of self-blessing;
as Saint Francis
put his hand on the creased forehead
of the sow, and told her in words and in touch
blessings of earth on the sow, and the sow   15
began remembering all down her thick length,
from the earthen snout all the way
through the fodder and slops to the spiritual curl of the tail,
from the hard spininess spiked out from the spine
down through the great broken heart   20
to the sheer blue milken dreaminess spurting and shuddering
from the fourteen teats into the fourteen mouths sucking and
    blowing beneath them:
the long, perfect loveliness of sow.

—1980

John Ashbery (b. 1927)

John Ashbery has said of his own poetry, "I'm trying to accurately portray states of mind, ones of my own that I think might have a general application, and the movement of the mind and the way we think and forget and discover and forget some more." His enigmatic poems have intrigued readers for so long that much contemporary literary theory seems to have been created expressly for explicating them. Ashbery was born in upstate New York and educated at Harvard University. His first full-length book, Some Trees, *was chosen by W. H. Auden for the Yale Younger Poets Award in 1956. In addition to his significant body of poetry, Ashbery has published art criticism and a novel,* A Nest of Ninnies *(1969), coauthored with poet James Schuyler. His collection* Self-Portrait in a Convex Mirror *(1975) received the Pulitzer Prize for poetry, the National Book Critics Circle Award, and the National Book Award. Impossible to dismiss, he is now seen as the chief inheritor of the symbolist tradition brought to American locales by Wallace Stevens.*

Farm Implements and Rutabagas in a Landscape

The first of the undecoded messages read: "Popeye sits in thunder,
Unthought of. From that shoebox of an apartment,
From livid curtain's hue, a tangram° emerges: a country."
Meanwhile the Sea Hag was relaxing on a green couch: "How
    pleasant
To spend one's vacation *en la casa de Popeye,*"° she scratched   5
Her cleft chin's solitary hair. She remembered spinach

And was going to ask Wimpy if he had bought any spinach.
"M'love," he intercepted, "the plains are decked out in thunder
Today, and it shall be as you wish." He scratched
The part of his head under his hat. The apartment   10
Seemed to grow smaller. "But what if no pleasant
Inspiration plunge us now to the stars? *For this is my country.*"

---

3 tangram a Chinese puzzle consisting of a square cut into smaller shapes, to be reassembled into different figures   **5 . . . casa de Popeye** (Spanish), in Popeye's house

Suddenly they remembered how it was cheaper in the country.
Wimpy was thoughtfully cutting open a number 2 can of
   spinach
When the door opened and Swee'pea crept in. "How
   pleasant!"   15
But Swee'pea looked morose. A note was pinned to his bib.
   "Thunder
And tears are unavailing," it read. "Henceforth shall Popeye's
   apartment
Be but remembered space, toxic or salubrious, whole or scratched."

Olive came hurtling through the window; its geraniums scratched
Her long thigh. "I have news!" she gasped. "Popeye, forced as you
   know to flee the country   20
One musty gusty evening, by the schemes of his wizened, duplicate
   father, jealous of the apartment
And all that it contains, myself and spinach
In particular, heaves bolts of loving thunder
At his own astonished becoming, rupturing the pleasant

Arpeggio of our years. No more shall pleasant   25
Rays of the sun refresh your sense of growing old, nor the scratched
Tree-trunks and mossy foliage, only immaculate darkness and
   thunder."
She grabbed Swee'pea. "I'm taking the brat to the country."
"But you can't do that—he hasn't even finished his spinach,"
Urged the Sea Hag, looking fearfully around at the apartment.   30

But Olive was already out of earshot. Now the apartment
Succumbed to a strange new hush. "Actually it's quite pleasant
Here," thought the Sea Hag. "If this is all we need fear from spinach
Then I don't mind so much. Perhaps we could invite Alice the Goon
   over"—she scratched
One dug pensively—"but Wimpy is such a country   35
Bumpkin, always burping like that." Minute at first, the thunder

Soon filled the apartment. It was domestic thunder,
The color of spinach. Popeye chuckled and scratched
His balls: it sure was pleasant to spend a day in the country.

                                                                —1966

The Other Tradition

They all came, some wore sentiments
Emblazoned on T-shirts, proclaiming the lateness
Of the hour, and indeed the sun slanted its rays
Through branches of Norfolk Island pine as though
Politely clearing its throat, and all ideas settled   5
In a fuzz of dust under trees when it's drizzling:
The endless games of Scrabble, the boosters,
The celebrated omelette au Cantal,° and through it
The roar of time plunging unchecked through the sluices
Of the days, dragging every sexual moment of it   10
Past the lenses: the end of something.
Only then did you glance up from your book,
Unable to comprehend what had been taking place, or
Say what you had been reading. More chairs
Were brought, and lamps were lit, but it tells   15
Nothing of how all this proceeded to materialize
Before you and the people waiting outside and in the next
Street, repeating its name over and over, until silence
Moved halfway up the darkened trunks.
And the meeting was called to order.   20
                                        I still remember
How they found you, after a dream, in your thimble hat,
Studious as a butterfly in a parking lot.
The road home was nicer then. Dispersing, each of the
Troubadours had something to say about how charity   25
Had run its race and won, leaving you the ex-president
Of the event, and how, though many of those present
Had wished something to come of it, if only a distant
Wisp of smoke, yet none was so deceived as to hanker
After that cool non-being of just a few minutes before,   30
Now that the idea of a forest had clamped itself
Over the minutiae of the scene. You found this
Charming, but turned your face fully toward night,
Speaking into it like a megaphone, not hearing

8 **omelette au Cantal** cheese omelet

Or caring, although these still live and are generous   35
And all ways contained, allowed to come and go
Indefinitely in and out of the stockade
They have so much trouble remembering, when your
    forgetting
Rescues them at last, as a star absorbs the night.

—1977

Paradoxes and Oxymorons

The poem is concerned with language on a very plain level.
Look at it talking to you. You look out a window
Or pretend to fidget. You have it but you don't have it.
You miss it, it misses you. You miss each other.

The poem is sad because it wants to be yours, and cannot.   5
What's a plain level? It is that and other things,
Bringing a system of them into play. Play?
Well, actually, yes, but I consider play to be

A deeper outside thing, a dreamed role-pattern,
As in the division of grace these long August days   10
Without proof. Open-ended. And before you know
It gets lost in the steam and chatter of typewriters.

It has been played once more. I think you exist only
To tease me into doing it, on your level, and then you aren't there
Or have adopted a different attitude. And the poem   15
Has set me softly down beside you. The poem is you.

—1981

The Gods of Fairness

The failure to see God is not a problem
God has a problem with. Sure, he could see us
if he had a hankering to do so, but that's
not the point. The point is his concern
for us and for biscuits. For the loaf   5
of bread that turns in the night sky over Stockholm.

Not there, over *there*. And I yelled them
what I had told them before. The affair is no one's business.
The peeing man seemed not to notice either.
We came up the strand with carbuncles   10
and chessmen fetched from the wreck. Finally the surplus buzz
did notice, and it was fatal to our project.
We just gave up then and there, some of us dying, others walking
wearily but contentedly away. God had had his little joke,
but who was to say it wasn't ours? Nobody, apparently,   15
which could be why the subject was never raised
in discussion groups in old houses along the harbor,
some of them practically falling into it.
Yet still they chatter a little ruefully: "I know
your grace's preference." There are times   20
when I even think I can read his mind,
coated with seed-pearls and diamonds.
There they are, for the taking. Take them away.
Deposit them in whatever suburban bank you choose.
Hurry, before he changes his mind—again.   25

But all they did was lean on their shovels, dreaming
of spring planting, and the marvelous harvests to come.

—*2000*

This Room

The room I entered was a dream of this room.
Surely all those feet on the sofa were mine.
The oval portrait

of a dog was me at an early age.
Something shimmers, something is hushed up.   5

We had macaroni for lunch every day
except Sunday, when a small quail was induced
to be served to us. Why do I tell you these things?
You are not even here.

—2000

Toy Symphony

> Palms and fiery plants populate the glorious lev-
> els of the unrecognizable mountains.
> —*Valéry*, Alphabet

Out on the terrace the projector had begun
making a shuttling sound like that of land crabs.
On Thursdays, Miss Marple° burped, picking up her knitting
again, it's always Boston Blackie or the Saint—
the one who was a detective   5
who came from far across the sea
to rescue the likes of you and me
from a horde of ill-favored seducers.

Well, let's get on with it
since we must. Work, it's true   10
suctions off the joy. Autumn's density moves down
though no one in his right mind would wish for spring—
winter's match is enough. The widening spaces
between the days.

I sip the sap of fools.   15
Another time I found some pretty rags
in the downtown district. They'd make nice slipcovers,
my wife thought, if they could be cleaned up.
I don't hold with that.
Why not leave everything exposed, out in the cold   20
till the next great drought of this century?
I say it mills me down,

---

3 **Miss Marple** fictional detective, as are Boston Blackie and the Saint

and everything is hand selected here: the cheeses,
oranges wrapped in pale blue tissue paper
with the oak-leaf pattern, letting their tint through   25
as it was meant to be, not according to the calculations
of some wounded genius, before he limped off
to the woods.

The stair of autumn is to climb
backward perhaps, into a cab.   30

—*2000*

W. S. Merwin (b. 1927)

*W. S. Merwin often displays the environmental concerns that have moti-
vated much poetry in recent years. Even in earlier work, his fears of the re-
sults of uncontrolled destruction of the natural world are presented alle-
gorically. Born in New York City, and the son of a Presbyterian minister,
he grew up in Union City, New Jersey, and Scranton, Pennsylvania. He
studied at Princeton University and traveled in France, Spain, and England, eventually settling in Majorca as a tutor to the son of poet Robert
Graves, whose neoclassical influence is evident in Merwin's early poems.
In 1951, Merwin moved to London, where he worked as a translator for
several years. During this time, his first poetry book,* A Mask for Janus
*(1952), was selected by W. H. Auden for the Yale Series of Younger Poets.
In addition to poetry, Merwin has published translations and prose, including a memoir of his life in the south of France. His 1970 collection,*
The Carrier of Ladders, *received the Pulitzer Prize. Merwin currently resides in Hawaii.*

The Drunk in the Furnace

      For a good decade
The furnace stood in the naked gully, fireless
And vacant as any hat. Then when it was
No more to them than a hulking black fossil
To erode unnoticed with the rest of the junk-hill   5
By the poisonous creek, and rapidly to be added
      To their ignorance,

They were afterwards astonished
To confirm, one morning, a twist of smoke like a pale
Resurrection, staggering out of its chewed hole, 10
And to remark then other tokens that someone,
Cosily bolted behind the eye-holed iron
Door of the drafty burner, had there established
His bad castle.

Where he gets his spirits 15
It's a mystery. But the stuff keeps him musical:
Hammer-and-anvilling with poker and bottle
To his jugged bellowings, till the last groaning clang
As he collapses onto the rioting
Springs of a litter of car-seats ranged on the grates, 20
To sleep like an iron pig.

In their tar-paper church
On a text about stoke-holes that are sated never
Their Reverend lingers. They nod and hate trespassers.
When the furnace wakes, though, all afternoon 25
Their witless offspring flock like piped rats to its siren
Crescendo, and agape on the crumbling ridge
Stand in a row and learn.

—*1960*

For the Anniversary of My Death

Every year without knowing it I have passed the day
When the last fires will wave to me
And the silence will set out
Tireless traveller
Like the beam of a lightless star 5

Then I will no longer
Find myself in life as in a strange garment
Surprised at the earth
And the love of one woman
And the shamelessness of men 10

As today writing after three days of rain
Hearing the wren sing and the falling cease
And bowing not knowing to what

—1969

The Last One

Well they'd make up their minds to be everywhere because why not.
Everywhere was theirs because they thought so.
They with two leaves they whom the birds despise.
In the middle of stones they made up their minds.
They started to cut.   5

Well they cut everything because why not.
Everything was theirs because they thought so.
It fell into its shadows and they took both away.
Some to have some for burning.

Well cutting everything they came to the water.   10
They came to the end of the day there was one left standing.
They would cut it tomorrow they went away.
The night gathered in the last branches.
The shadow of the night gathered in the shadow on the water.
The night and the shadow put on the same head.   15
And it said Now.

Well in the morning they cut the last one.
Like the others the last one fell into its shadow.
It fell into its shadow on the water.
They took it away its shadow stayed on the water.   20

Well they shrugged they started trying to get the shadow away.
They cut right to the ground the shadow stayed whole.
They laid boards on it the shadow came out on top.
They shone lights on it the shadow got blacker and clearer.
They exploded the water the shadow rocked.   25
They built a huge fire on the roots.
They sent up black smoke between the shadow and the sun.
The new shadow flowed without changing the old one.
They shrugged they went away to get stones.

They came back the shadow was growing. 30
They started setting up stones it was growing.
They looked the other way it went on growing.
They decided they would make a stone out of it.
They took stones to the water they poured them into the shadow.
They poured them in they poured them in the stones vanished. 35
The shadow was not filled it went on growing.
That was one day.

The next day was just the same it went on growing.
They did all the same things it was just the same.
They decided to take its water from under it. 40
They took away water they took it away the water went down.
The shadow stayed where it was before.
It went on growing it grew onto the land.
They started to scrape the shadow with machines.
When it touched the machines it stayed on them. 45
They started to beat the shadow with sticks.
Where it touched the sticks it stayed on them.
They started to beat the shadow with hands.
Where it touched the hands it stayed on them.
That was another day. 50

Well the next day started about the same it went on growing.
They pushed lights into the shadow.
Where the shadow got onto them they went out.
They began to stomp on the edge it got their feet.
And when it got their feet they fell down. 55
It got into eyes the eyes went blind.
The ones that fell down it grew over and they vanished.
The ones that went blind and walked into it vanished.
The ones that could see and stood still
It swallowed their shadows. 60
Then it swallowed them too and they vanished.
Well the others ran.

The ones that were left went away to live if it would let them.
They went as far as they could.
The lucky ones with their shadows. 65

—1969

The Judgment of Paris°

Long afterwards
the intelligent could deduce what had been offered
and not recognized
and they suggest that bitterness should be confined
to the fact that the gods chose for their arbiter   5
a mind and character so ordinary
albeit a prince

and brought up as a shepherd
a calling he must have liked
for he had returned to it   10

when they stood before him
the three
naked feminine deathless
and he realized that he was clothed
in nothing but mortality   15
the strap of his quiver of arrows crossing
between his nipples
making it seem stranger

and he knew he must choose
and on that day   20

the one with the gray eyes spoke first
and whatever she said he kept
thinking he remembered
but remembered it woven with confusion and fear
the two faces that he called father   25
the first sight of the palace
where the brothers were strangers
and the dogs watched him and refused to know him
she made everything clear she was dazzling she
offered it to him   30
to have for his own but what he saw
was the scorn above her eyes

Paris From Greek mythology. Summoned to choose the most beautiful of three goddesses, the young Trojan prince Paris chose Aphrodite, who promised him the most beautiful woman in the world, Helen, daughter of Tyndareaus (or, in some myths, of Zeus and the nymph Leda), as his reward. Paris seduced and married Helen and brought her to Troy, thus setting the Trojan war in motion

and her words of which he understood few
all said to him *Take wisdom*
take power   35
you will forget anyway

the one with the dark eyes spoke
and everything she said
he imagined he had once wished for
but in confusion and cowardice   40
the crown
of his father the crowns the crowns bowing to him
his name everywhere like grass
only he and the sea
triumphant   45
she made everything sound possible she was
dazzling she offered it to him
to hold high but what he saw
was the cruelty around her mouth
and her words of which he understood more   50
all said to him *Take pride*
take glory
you will suffer anyway

the third one the color of whose eyes
later he could not remember   55
spoke last and slowly and
of desire and it was his
though up until then he had been
happy with his river nymph°
here was his mind   60
filled utterly with one girl gathering
yellow flowers
and no one like her
the words
made everything seem present   65
almost present
present
they said to him *Take*

---

59 **his river nymph** Oenone, Paris's lover before Helen

her
you will lose her anyway 70

it was only when he reached out to the voice
as though he could take the speaker
herself
that his hand filled with
something to give 75
but to give to only one of the three
an apple as it is told
discord itself in a single fruit its skin
already carved
To the fairest 80

then a mason working above the gates of Troy
in the sunlight thought he felt the stone
shiver

in the quiver on Paris's back the head
of the arrow for Achilles' heel 85
smiled in its sleep

and Helen stepped from the palace to gather
as she would do every day in that season
from the grove the yellow ray flowers tall
as herself 90

whose roots are said to dispel pain

—1970

James Wright (1927–1980)

James Wright showed compassion for losers and underdogs of all types, an attitude evident everywhere in his poetry. A native of the steel-producing town of Martins Ferry, Ohio, he often described lives of quiet desperation in the blue-collar towns of his youth. Wright studied at Kenyon College and the University of Washington, and spent a year in Vienna on a Fulbright fellowship. While Wright was still a graduate student, W. H. Auden selected his first manuscript, The Green Wall *(1957), for the Yale Younger Poets series. Like many poets of his generation, Wright wrote formal verse in his early career and shifted to open forms during the 1960s. His 1963 volume,* The Branch Will Not Break, *proved influential to a new generation of poets, signaling the movement of American poetry away from neoclassicism and traditional forms.*

Saint Judas

When I went out to kill myself, I caught
A pack of hoodlums beating up a man.
Running to spare his suffering, I forgot
My name, my number, how my day began,
How soldiers milled around the garden stone   5
And sang amusing songs; how all that day
Their javelins measured crowds; how I alone
Bargained the proper coins, and slipped away.

Banished from heaven, I found this victim beaten,
Stripped, kneed, and left to cry. Dropping my rope   10
Aside, I ran, ignored the uniforms:
Then I remembered bread my flesh had eaten,
The kiss that ate my flesh. Flayed without hope,
I held the man for nothing in my arms.

—1959

Autumn Begins in Martins Ferry, Ohio

In the Shreve High football stadium,
I think of Polacks nursing long beers in Tiltonsville,
And gray faces of Negroes in the blast furnace at Benwood,
And the ruptured night watchman of Wheeling Steel,
Dreaming of heroes.   5

All the proud fathers are ashamed to go home.
Their women cluck like starved pullets,
Dying for love.

Therefore,
Their sons grow suicidally beautiful   10
At the beginning of October,
And gallop terribly against each other's bodies.

—1963

A Blessing

Just off the highway to Rochester, Minnesota,
Twilight bounds softly forth on the grass.
And the eyes of those two Indian ponies
Darken with kindness.
They have come gladly out of the willows   5
To welcome my friend and me.
We step over the barbed wire into the pasture
Where they have been grazing all day, alone.
They ripple tensely, they can hardly contain their happiness
That we have come.   10
They bow shyly as wet swans. They love each other.
There is no loneliness like theirs.
At home once more,
They begin munching the young tufts of spring in the darkness.
I would like to hold the slenderer one in my arms,   15
For she has walked over to me

And nuzzled my left hand.
She is black and white,
Her mane falls wild on her forehead,
And the light breeze moves me to caress her long ear   20
That is delicate as the skin over a girl's wrist.
Suddenly I realize
That if I stepped out of my body I would break
Into blossom.

—*1963*

Lying in a Hammock at William Duffy's Farm in Pine Island, Minnesota

Over my head, I see the bronze butterfly,
Asleep on the black trunk,
Blowing like a leaf in green shadow.
Down the ravine behind the empty house,
The cowbells follow one another   5
Into the distances of the afternoon.
To my right,
In a field of sunlight between two pines,
The droppings of last year's horses
Blaze up into golden stones.   10
I lean back, as the evening darkens and comes on.
A chicken hawk floats over, looking for home.
I have wasted my life.

—*1963*

Two Poems About President Harding°

ONE: *HIS DEATH*

In Marion,° the honey locust trees are falling.
Everybody in town remembers the white hair,
The campaign of a lost summer, the front porch
Open to the public, and the vaguely stunned smile   5
Of a lucky man.

"Neighbor, I want to be helpful," he said once.
Later, "You think I'm honest, don't you?"
Weeping drunk.

I am drunk this evening in 1961,   10
In a jag for my countryman,
Who died of crab meat on the way back from Alaska.
Everyone knows that joke.

How many honey locusts have fallen,
Pitched rootlong into the open graves of strip mines,   15
Since the First World War ended
And Wilson° the gaunt deacon jogged sullenly
Into silence?
Tonight,
The cancerous ghosts of old con men   20
Shed their leaves.
For a proud man,
Lost between the turnpike near Cleveland
And the chiropractors' signs looming among dead mul-
       berry trees,
There is no place left to go   25
But home.

"Warren lacks mentality," one of his friends said.

Harding Warren G. Harding (1865–1923), the twenty-ninth president of the United States. His
administration was wracked by scandal, and he died before completing his term **2 Marion** in Ohio,
Harding's childhood home **17 Wilson** Woodrow Wilson (1856–1924), the twenty-eighth president

Yet he was beautiful, he was the snowfall
Turned to white stallions standing still
Under dark elm trees.   30

He died in public. He claimed the secret right
To be ashamed.

TWO: *HIS TOMB IN OHIO*

> "... he died of a busted gut."
> —MENCKEN,° on BRYAN.°

A hundred slag piles north of us,
At the mercy of the moon and rain,
He lies in his ridiculous
Tomb, our fellow citizen.
No, I have never seen that place,   40
Where many shadows of faceless thieves
Chuckle and stumble and embrace
On beer cans, stogie butts, and graves.

One holiday, one rainy week
After the country fell apart,   45
Hoover° and Coolidge° came to speak
And snivel about his broken heart.
His grave, a huge absurdity,
Embarrassed cops and visitors.
Hoover and Coolidge crept away   50
By night, and women closed their doors.

Now junkmen call their children in
Before they catch their death of cold;
Young lovers let the moon begin
Its quick spring; and the day grows old;   55
The mean one-legger who rakes up leaves
Has chased the loafers out of the park;
Minnegan Leonard° half-believes
In God, and the poolroom goes dark;

60

America goes on, goes on
Laughing, and Harding was a fool.
Even his big pretentious stone
Lays him bare to ridicule.
I know it. But don't look at me.
By God, I didn't start this mess.   65
Whatever moon and rain may be,
The hearts of men are merciless.

—1963

Philip Levine (b. 1928)

Philip Levine was born in Detroit, Michigan, and educated at Wayne State University. He is one of the many contemporary poets to hold a degree from the Iowa Writers' Workshop. Levine has lived on and off in Spain, and his poems reflect a strong, left-leaning populism informed by his sympathy for the antifascists in the Spanish Civil War. The gritty urban landscapes and characters trapped in dead-end industrial jobs that provide Levine with subjects for many of his poems match exactly his unadorned, informal idiom. Like the deceptively simple William Carlos Williams, Levine has influenced many younger poets.

Animals Are Passing from Our Lives

It's wonderful how I jog
on four honed-down ivory toes
my massive buttocks slipping
like oiled parts with each light step.

I'm to market. I can smell   5
the sour, grooved block, I can smell
the blade that opens the hole
and the pudgy white fingers

that shake out the intestines
like a hankie. In my dreams   10

the snouts drool on the marble,
suffering children, suffering flies,

suffering the consumers
who won't meet their steady eyes
for fear they could see. The boy   15
who drives me along believes

that any moment I'll fall
on my side and drum my toes
like a typewriter or squeal
and shit like a new housewife   20

discovering television,
or that I'll turn like a beast
cleverly to hook his teeth
with my teeth. No. Not this pig.

—1968

They Feed They Lion

Out of burlap sacks, out of bearing butter,
Out of black bean and wet slate bread,
Out of the acids of rage, the candor of tar,
Out of creosote, gasoline, drive shafts, wooden dollies,
They Lion grow.   5
   Out of the gray hills
Of industrial barns, out of rain, out of bus ride,
West Virginia to Kiss My Ass, out of buried aunties,
Mothers hardening like pounded stumps, out of stumps,
Out of the bones' need to sharpen and the muscles' to stretch,   10
They Lion grow.
   Earth is eating trees, fence posts,
Gutted cars, earth is calling in her little ones,
"Come home, Come home!" From pig balls,
From the ferocity of pig driven to holiness,   15
From the furred ear and the full jowl come
The repose of the hung belly, from the purpose
They Lion grow.
   From the sweet glues of the trotters

Come the sweet kinks of the fist, from the full flower   20
Of the hams the thorax of caves,
From "Bow Down" come "Rise Up,"
Come they Lion from the reeds of shovels,
The grained arm that pulls the hands,
They Lion grow.   25
        From my five arms and all my hands,
From all my white sins forgiven, they feed,
From my car passing under the stars,
They Lion, from my children inherit,
From the oak turned to a wall, they Lion,   30
From they sack and they belly opened
And all that was hidden burning on the oil-stained earth
They feed they Lion and he comes.

—*1972*

You Can Have It

My brother comes home from work
and climbs the stairs to our room.
I can hear the bed groan and his shoes drop
one by one. You can have it, he says.

The moonlight streams in the window   5
and his unshaven face is whitened
like the face of the moon. He will sleep
long after noon and waken to find me gone.

Thirty years will pass before I remember
that moment when suddenly I knew each man   10
has one brother who dies when he sleeps
and sleeps when he rises to face this life,

and that together they are only one man
sharing a heart that always labors, hands
yellowed and cracked, a mouth that gasps   15
for breath and asks, Am I gonna make it?

All night at the ice plant he had fed
the chute its silvery blocks, and then I

stacked cases of orange soda for the children
of Kentucky, one gray box-car at a time   20

with always two more waiting. We were twenty
for such a short time and always in
the wrong clothes, crusted with dirt
and sweat. I think now we were never twenty.

In 1948 the city of Detroit, founded   25
by de la Mothe Cadillac° for the distant purposes
of Henry Ford, no one wakened or died,
no one walked the streets or stoked a furnace,

for there was no such year, and now
that year has fallen off all the old newspapers,   30
calendars, doctors' appointments, bonds,
wedding certificates, drivers licenses.

The city slept. The snow turned to ice.
The ice to standing pools or rivers
racing in the gutters. Then the bright grass rose   35
between the thousands of cracked squares,

and that grass died. I give you back 1948.
I give you all the years from then
to the coming one. Give me back the moon
with its frail light falling across a face.   40

Give me back my young brother, hard
and furious, with wide shoulders and a curse
for God and burning eyes that look upon
all creation and say, You can have it.

—*1979*

What Work Is

We stand in the rain in a long line
waiting at Ford Highland Park. For work.
You know what work is—if you're
old enough to read this you know what

---

26 Cadillac Antoine de la Mothe Cadillac (1658–1730)

work is, although you may not do it.   5
Forget you. This is about waiting,
shifting from one foot to another.
Feeling the light rain falling like mist
into your hair, blurring your vision
until you think you see your own brother   10
ahead of you, maybe ten places.
You rub your glasses with your fingers,
and of course it's someone else's brother,
narrower across the shoulders than
yours but with the same sad slouch, the grin   15
that does not hide the stubbornness,
the sad refusal to give in to
rain, to the hours wasted waiting,
to the knowledge that somewhere ahead
a man is waiting who will say, "No,   20
we're not hiring today," for any
reason he wants. You love your brother,
now suddenly you can hardly stand
the love flooding you for your brother,
who's not beside you or behind or   25
ahead because he's home trying to
sleep off a miserable night shift
at Cadillac so he can get up
before noon to study his German.
Works eight hours a night so he can sing   30
Wagner, the opera you hate most,
the worst music ever invented.
How long has it been since you told him
you loved him, held his wide shoulders,
opened your eyes wide and said those words,   35
and maybe kissed his cheek? You've never
done something so simple, so obvious,
not because you're too young or too dumb,
not because you're jealous or even mean
or incapable of crying in   40
the presence of another man, no,
just because you don't know what work is.

—1991

Anne Sexton (1928–1974)

Anne Sexton lived a tortured life of mental illness and family troubles, becoming the model of the confessional poet. Born in Newton, Massachusetts, into a comfortably middle-class family, she married at age nineteen, suffered from severe postpartum depression and nervous breakdowns after the births of her two daughters, and was repeatedly admitted to Westwood Lodge, a neuropsychiatric hospital. She began writing poetry as the result of a program on public television, later taking a workshop from Robert Lowell in which Sylvia Plath was a fellow student. Her first book, To Bedlam and Part Way Back *(1960), received positive reviews, and her subsequent books won her a large audience and numerous honors. She taught at Colgate and Boston University, and wrote a play,* Mercy Street, *that was produced off-Broadway. For fifteen years, until her suicide, she was a vibrant, exciting presence in American poetry.*

Unknown Girl in the Maternity Ward

Child, the current of your breath is six days long.
You lie, a small knuckle on my white bed;
lie, fisted like a snail, so small and strong
at my breast. Your lips are animals; you are fed
with love. At first hunger is not wrong.   5
The nurses nod their caps; you are shepherded
down starch halls with the other unnested throng
in wheeling baskets. You tip like a cup; your head
moving to my touch. You sense the way we belong.
But this is an institution bed.   10
You will not know me very long.

The doctors are enamel. They want to know
the facts. They guess about the man who left me,
some pendulum soul, going the way men go
and leave you full of child. But our case history   15
stays blank. All I did was let you grow.
Now we are here for all the ward to see.
They thought I was strange, although

I never spoke a word. I burst empty
of you, letting you learn how the air is so.   20
The doctors chart the riddle they ask of me
and I turn my head away. I do not know.

Yours is the only face I recognize.
Bone at my bone, you drink my answers in.
Six times a day I prize   25
your need, the animals of your lips, your skin
growing warm and plump. I see your eyes
lifting their tents. They are blue stones, they begin
to outgrow their moss. You blink in surprise
and I wonder what you can see, my funny kin,   30
as you trouble my silence. I am a shelter of lies.
Should I learn to speak again, or hopeless in
such sanity will I touch some face I recognize?

Down the hall the baskets start back. My arms
fit you like a sleeve, they hold   35
catkins of your willows, the wild bee farms
of your nerves, each muscle and fold
of your first days. Your old man's face disarms
the nurses. But the doctors return to scold
me. I speak. It is you my silence harms.   40
I should have known; I should have told
them something to write down. My voice alarms
my throat. "Name of father—none." I hold
you and name you bastard in my arms.

And now that's that. There is nothing more   45
that I can say or lose.
Others have traded life before
and could not speak. I tighten to refuse
your owling eyes, my fragile visitor.
I touch your cheeks, like flowers. You bruise   50
against me. We unlearn. I am a shore
rocking you off. You break from me. I choose
your only way, my small inheritor
and hand you off, trembling the selves we lose.
Go child, who is my sin and nothing more.   55

—*1960*

All My Pretty Ones

> All my pretty ones?
> Did you say all? O hell-kite! All?
> What! all my pretty chickens and their dam
> At one fell swoop? . . .
> I cannot but remember such things were,
> That were most precious to me.
>
> —*Macbeth*

Father, this year's jinx rides us apart
where you followed our mother to her cold slumber;
a second shock boiling its stone to your heart,
leaving me here to shuffle and disencumber
you from the residence you could not afford: 5
a gold key, your half of a woolen mill,
twenty suits from Dunne's, an English Ford,
the love and legal verbiage of another will,
boxes of pictures of people I do not know.
I touch their cardboard faces. They must go.   10

But the eyes, as thick as wood in this album,
hold me. I stop here, where a small boy
waits in a ruffled dress for someone to come . . .
for this soldier who holds his bugle like a toy
or for this velvet lady who cannot smile.   15
Is this your father's father, this commodore
in a mailman suit? My father, time meanwhile
has made it unimportant who you are looking for.
I'll never know what these faces are all about.
I lock them into their book and throw them out.   20

This is the yellow scrapbook that you began
the year I was born; as crackling now and wrinkly
as tobacco leaves: clippings where Hoover° outran
the Democrats, wiggling his dry finger at me
and Prohibition; news where the *Hindenburg*° went   25
down and recent years where you went flush
on war. This year, solvent but sick, you meant

---

23 **Hoover** Herbert Hoover (1874–1964), thirty-first president. Sexton refers to the 1928
presidential election   25 **Hindenburg** German dirigible destroyed by fire

to marry that pretty widow in a one-month rush.
But before you had that second chance, I cried
on your fat shoulder. Three days later you died.   30

These are the snapshots of marriage, stopped in places.
Side by side at the rail toward Nassau° now;
here, with the winner's cup at the speedboat races,
here, in tails at the Cotillion, you take a bow,
here, by our kennel of dogs with their pink eyes,   35
running like show-bred pigs in their chain-link pen;
here, at the horseshow where my sister wins a prize;
and here, standing like a duke among groups of men.
Now I fold you down, my drunkard, my navigator,
my first lost keeper, to love or look at later.   40

I hold a five-year diary that my mother kept
for three years, telling all she does not say
of your alcoholic tendency. You overslept,
she writes. My God, father, each Christmas Day
with your blood, will I drink down your glass   45
of wine? The diary of your hurly-burly years
goes to my shelf to wait for my age to pass.
Only in this hoarded span will love persevere.
Whether you are pretty or not, I outlive you,
bend down my strange face to yours and forgive you.   50

—*1962*

In Celebration
of My Uterus

Everyone in me is a bird.
I am beating all my wings.
They wanted to cut you out
but they will not.
They said you were immeasurably empty   5
but you are not.
They said you were sick unto dying

32 Nassau in the Bahamas

but they were wrong.
You are singing like a school girl.
You are not torn.   10

Sweet weight,
in celebration of the woman I am
and of the soul of the woman I am
and of the central creature and its delight
I sing for you. I dare to live.   15

Hello, spirit. Hello, cup.
Fasten, cover. Cover that does contain.
Hello to the soil of the fields.
Welcome, roots.

Each cell has a life.   20
There is enough here to please a nation.
It is enough that the populace own these goods.

Any person, any commonwealth would say of it,
"It is good this year that we may plant again
and think forward to a harvest.   25
A blight had been forecast and has been cast out."
Many women are singing together of this:
one is in a shoe factory cursing the machine,
one is at the aquarium tending a seal,
one is dull at the wheel of her Ford,   30
one is at the toll gate collecting,
one is tying the cord of a calf in Arizona,
one is straddling a cello in Russia,
one is shifting pots on the stove in Egypt,
one is painting her bedroom walls moon color,   35
one is dying but remembering a breakfast,
one is stretching on her mat in Thailand,
one is wiping the ass of her child,
one is staring out the window of a train
in the middle of Wyoming and one is   40
anywhere and some are everywhere and all
seem to be singing, although some can not
sing a note.

Sweet weight,
in celebration of the woman I am   45

let me carry a ten-foot scarf,
let me drum for the nineteen-year-olds,
let me carry bowls for the offering
(if that is my part).

Let me study the cardiovascular tissue,   50
let me examine the angular distance of meteors,
let me suck on the stems of flowers
(if that is my part).
Let me make certain tribal figures
(if that is my part).   55
For this thing the body needs
let me sing
for the supper,
for the kissing,
for the correct   60
yes.

—*1969*

Cinderella

You always read about it:
the plumber with twelve children
who wins the Irish Sweepstakes.
From toilets to riches.
That story.   5

Or the nursemaid,
some luscious sweet from Denmark
who captures the oldest son's heart.
From diapers to Dior.°
That story.   10

Or a milkman who serves the wealthy,
eggs, cream, butter, yogurt, milk,
the white truck like an ambulance
who goes into real estate
and makes a pile.   15
From homogenized to martinis at lunch.

9 Dior French clothing designer

Or the charwoman
who is on the bus when it cracks up
and collects enough from the insurance.
From mops to Bonwit Teller.°   20
That story.

Once
the wife of a rich man was on her deathbed
and she said to her daughter Cinderella:
Be devout. Be good. Then I will smile   25
down from heaven in the seam of a cloud.
The man took another wife who had
two daughters, pretty enough
but with hearts like blackjacks.
Cinderella was their maid.   30
She slept on the sooty hearth each night
and walked around looking like Al Jolson.°
Her father brought presents home from town,
jewels and gowns for the other women
but the twig of a tree for Cinderella.   35
She planted that twig on her mother's grave
and it grew to a tree where a white dove sat.
Whenever she wished for anything the dove
would drop it like an egg upon the ground.
The bird is important, my dears, so heed him.   40

Next came the ball, as you all know.
It was a marriage market.
The prince was looking for a wife.
All but Cinderella were preparing
and gussying up for the big event.   45
Cinderella begged to go too.
Her stepmother threw a dish of lentils
into the cinders and said: Pick them
up in an hour and you shall go.
The white dove brought all his friends;   50
all the warm wings of the fatherland came,
and picked up the lentils in a jiffy.
No, Cinderella, said the stepmother,

---

20 Bonwit Teller upscale department store   **32 Al Jolson** a white vaudevillian known for
performing in "blackface," makeup designed to make him appear black

you have no clothes and cannot dance.
That's the way with stepmothers.   55

Cinderella went to the tree at the grave
and cried forth like a gospel singer:
Mama! Mama! My turtledove,
send me to the prince's ball!
The bird dropped down a golden dress   60
and delicate little gold slippers.
Rather a large package for a simple bird.
So she went. Which is no surprise.
Her stepmother and sisters didn't
recognize her without her cinder face   65
and the prince took her hand on the spot
and danced with no other the whole day.

As nightfall came she thought she'd
better get home. The prince walked her home
and she disappeared into the pigeon house   70
and although the prince took an axe and broke
it open she was gone. Back to her cinders.
These events repeated themselves for three days.
However on the third day the prince
covered the palace steps with cobbler's wax   75
And Cinderella's gold shoe stuck upon it.
Now he would find whom the shoe fit
and find his strange dancing girl for keeps.
He went to their house and the two sisters
were delighted because they had lovely feet.   80
The eldest went into a room to try the slipper on
but her big toe got in the way so she simply
sliced it off and put on the slipper.
The prince rode away with her until the white dove
told him to look at the blood pouring forth.   85
That is the way with amputations.
They don't just heal up like a wish.
The other sister cut off her heel
but the blood told as blood will.
The prince was getting tired.   90
He began to feel like a shoe salesman.
But he gave it one last try.

This time Cinderella fit into the shoe
like a love letter into its envelope.

At the wedding ceremony   95
the two sisters came to curry favor
and the white dove pecked their eyes out.
Two hollow spots were left
like soup spoons.

Cinderella and the prince   100
lived, they say, happily ever after,
like two dolls in a museum case
never bothered by diapers or dust,
never arguing over the timing of an egg,
never telling the same story twice,   105
never getting a middle-aged spread,
their darling smiles pasted on for eternity
Regular Bobbsey Twins.°
That story.

—*1971*

---

108 **Bobbsey Twins** a series of relentlessly cheerful children's books featuring the adventures of two sets of twins

Adrienne Rich (b. 1929)

*Born in Baltimore, Maryland, Rich began writing poetry under the tute-
lage of her father, a doctor and pathology professor. She received the Yale
Younger Poet's Award at age twenty-one for work that was formally regular, restrained, and elegant. By her third book,* Snapshots of a Daughter-in-
Law *(1963), Rich had moved toward free verse and had begun addressing
more intimate subject matter. Ever since, her poetry and her essays have
sought to reconcile the personal and lyric with the political and social
realms. Rich's many awards include The Lannan Foundation's Lifetime
Achievement Award, the National Book Award, a MacArthur fellowship,
and in 2003, the Bollingen Prize. She lives in Northern California.*

Aunt Jennifer's Tigers

Aunt Jennifer's tigers prance across a screen,
Bright topaz denizens of a world of green.
They do not fear the men beneath the tree;
They pace in sleek chivalric certainty.

Aunt Jennifer's fingers fluttering through her wool   5
Find even the ivory needle hard to pull.
The massive weight of Uncle's wedding band
Sits heavily upon Aunt Jennifer's hand.

When Aunt is dead, her terrified hands will lie
Still ringed with ordeals she was mastered by.   10
The tigers in the panel that she made
Will go on prancing, proud and unafraid.

—*1951*

Living in Sin

She had thought the studio would keep itself;
no dust upon the furniture of love.
Half heresy, to wish the taps less vocal,
the panes relieved of grime. A plate of pears,

a piano with a Persian shawl, a cat 5
stalking the picturesque amusing mouse
had risen at his urging.
Not that at five each separate stair would writhe
under the milkman's tramp; that morning light
so coldly would delineate the scraps 10
of last night's cheese and three sepulchral bottles;
that on the kitchen shelf among the saucers
a pair of beetle-eyes would fix her own—
envoy from some village in the moldings . . .
Meanwhile, he, with a yawn, 15
sounded a dozen notes upon the keyboard,
declared it out of tune, shrugged at the mirror,
rubbed at his beard, went out for cigarettes;
while she, jeered by the minor demons,
pulled back the sheets and made the bed and found 20
a towel to dust the table-top,
and let the coffee-pot boil over on the stove.
By evening she was back in love again,
though not so wholly but throughout the night
she woke sometimes to feel the daylight coming 25
like a relentless milkman up the stairs.

—*1955*

Diving into the Wreck

First having read the book of myths,
and loaded the camera,
and checked the edge of the knife-blade,
I put on
the body-armor of black rubber 5
the absurd flippers
the grave and awkward mask.
I am having to do this
not like Cousteau° with his
assiduous team 10

9 **Cousteau** Jacques-Yves Cousteau (1910–1997), underwater explorer

aboard the sun-flooded schooner
but here alone.

There is a ladder.
The ladder is always there
hanging innocently   15
close to the side of the schooner.
We know what it is for,
we who have used it.
Otherwise
it is a piece of maritime floss   20
some sundry equipment.

I go down.
Rung after rung and still
the oxygen immerses me
the blue light   25
the clear atoms
of our human air.
I go down.
My flippers cripple me,
I crawl like an insect down the ladder   30
and there is no one
to tell me when the ocean
will begin.

First the air is blue and then
it is bluer and then green and then   35
black I am blacking out and yet
my mask is powerful
it pumps my blood with power
the sea is another story
the sea is not a question of power   40
I have to learn alone
to turn my body without force
in the deep element.

And now: it is easy to forget
what I came for   45
among so many who have always
lived here
swaying their crenellated fans
between the reefs

and besides   50
you breathe differently down here.

I came to explore the wreck.
The words are purposes.
The words are maps.
I came to see the damage that was done   55
and the treasures that prevail.
I stroke the beam of my lamp
slowly along the flank
of something more permanent
than fish or weed   60

the thing I came for:
the wreck and not the story of the wreck
the thing itself and not the myth
the drowned face always staring
toward the sun   65
the evidence of damage
worn by salt and sway into this threadbare beauty
the ribs of the disaster
curving their assertion
among the tentative haunters.   70

This is the place.
And I am here, the mermaid whose dark hair
streams black, the merman in his armored body.
We circle silently
about the wreck   75
we dive into the hold.
I am she: I am he

whose drowned face sleeps with open eyes
whose breasts still bear the stress
whose silver, copper, vermeil cargo lies   80
obscurely inside barrels
half-wedged and left to rot
we are the half-destroyed instruments
that once held to a course
the water-eaten log   85
the fouled compass

We are, I am, you are
by cowardice or courage

the one who find our way
back to this scene   90
carrying a knife, a camera
a book of myths
in which
our names do not appear.

—1973

Rape

There is a cop who is both prowler and father:
he comes from your block, grew up with your brothers,
had certain ideals.
You hardly know him in his boots and silver badge,
on horseback, one hand touching his gun.   5

You hardly know him but you have to get to know him:
he has access to machinery that could kill you.
He and his stallion clop like warlords among the trash,
his ideals stand in the air, a frozen cloud
from between his unsmiling lips.   10

And so, when the time comes, you have to turn to him,
the maniac's sperm still greasing your thighs,
your mind whirling like crazy. You have to confess
to him, you are guilty of the crime
of having been forced.   15

And you see his blue eyes, the blue eyes of all the family
whom you used to know, grow narrow and glisten,
his hand types out the details
and he wants them all
but the hysteria in your voice pleases him best.   20

You hardly know him but now he thinks he knows you:
he has taken down your worst moment
on a machine and filed it in a file.
He knows, or thinks he knows, how much you imagined;
he knows, or thinks he knows, what you secretly wanted.   25

He has access to machinery that could get you put away;
and if, in the sickening light of the precinct,

and if, in the sickening light of the precinct,
your details sound like a portrait of your confessor,
will you swallow, will you deny them, will you lie your way home? 30

—1973

from An Atlas of the Difficult World

XIII (Dedications)

I know you are reading this poem
late, before leaving your office
of the one intense yellow lamp-spot and the darkening window
in the lassitude of a building faded to quiet
long after rush-hour. I know you are reading this poem   5
standing up in a bookstore far from the ocean
on a grey day of early spring, faint flakes driven
across the plains' enormous spaces around you.
I know you are reading this poem
in a room where too much has happened to you to bear   10
where the bedclothes lie in stagnant coils on the bed
and the open valise speaks of flight
but you cannot leave yet. I know you are reading this poem
as the underground train loses momentum and before running up
      the stairs
toward a new kind of love   15
your life has never allowed.
I know you are reading this poem by the light
of the television screen where soundless images jerk and slide
while you wait for the newscast from the intifada.°
I know you are reading this poem in a waiting-room   20
of eyes met and unmeeting, of identity with strangers.
I know you are reading this poem by fluorescent light
in the boredom and fatigue of the young who are counted out,

19 intifada uprising, specifically the Palestinian protest against the Israeli occupation of the West Bank and Gaza strip

count themselves out, at too early an age. I know   25
you are reading this poem through your failing sight, the thick
lens enlarging these letters beyond all meaning yet you read on
because even the alphabet is precious.
I know you are reading this poem as you pace beside the stove
warming milk, a crying child on your shoulder, a book in your hand
because life is short and you too are thirsty.   30
I know you are reading this poem which is not in your language
guessing at some words while others keep you reading
and I want to know which words they are.
I know you are reading this poem listening for something, torn
    between bitterness and hope
turning back once again to the task you cannot refuse.   35
I know you are reading this poem because there is nothing else left to
    read
there where you have landed, stripped as you are.

—1991

Final Notations

it will not be simple, it will not be long
it will take little time, it will take all your thought
it will take all your heart, it will take all your breath
it will be short, it will not be simple

it will touch through your ribs, it will take all your heart   5
it will not be long, it will occupy your thought
as a city is occupied, as a bed is occupied
it will take all your flesh, it will not be simple

You are coming into us who cannot withstand you
you are coming into us who never wanted to withstand you   10
you are taking parts of us into places never planned
you are going far away with pieces of our lives

it will be short, it will take all your breath
it will not be simple, it will become your will

—1991

X. J. Kennedy (b. 1929)

X. J. Kennedy is one of the few contemporary America poets who have not been attracted by free verse, preferring to remain what he calls a "dinosaur," one of those poets who continue to write in meter. He also is rare among his contemporaries in his commitment to writing poems with strong ties to song. Kennedy is the editor of Literature: An Introduction to Fiction, Poetry, and Drama, *perhaps the most widely used college literature text ever written. Born Joseph Kennedy in Dover, New Jersey, he added the initial "X" to his name to differentiate himself from the patriarch of the political Kennedys. His career has included teaching stints at numerous universities, but he has been a freelance writer and editor since 1978. He lives in Lexington, Massachusetts.*

First Confession

Blood thudded in my ears. I scuffed,
    Steps stubborn, to the telltale booth
Beyond whose curtained portal coughed
    The robed repositor of truth.

The slat shot back. The universe 5
    Bowed down his cratered dome to hear
Enumerated my each curse,
    The sip snitched from my old man's beer,

My sloth pride envy lechery,
    The dime held back from Peter's Pence° 10
With which I'd bribed my girl to pee
    That I might spy her instruments.

Hovering scale-pans when I'd done
    Settled their balance slow as silt
While in the restless dark I burned 15
    Bright as a brimstone in my guilt

Until as one feeds birds he doled
    Seven Our Fathers and a Hail

10 **Peter's Pence** in the Roman Catholic Church, a yearly voluntary contribution to the pope

Which I to double-scrub my soul
    Intoned twice at the altar rail   20

Where Sunday in seraphic light
    I knelt, as full of grace as most,
And stuck my tongue out at the priest:
    A fresh roost for the Holy Ghost.

—1961

In a Prominent Bar in Secaucus One Day

To the tune of "The Old Orange Flute" or the
tune of "Sweet Betsy from Pike"

In a prominent bar in Secaucus one day
Rose a lady in skunk with a topheavy sway,
Raised a knobby red finger—all turned from their beer—
While with eyes bright as snowcrust she sang high and clear:

"Now who of you'd think from an eyeload of me   5
That I once was a lady as proud as could be?
Oh I'd never sit down by a tumbledown drunk
If it wasn't, my dears, for the high cost of junk.

"All the gents used to swear that the white of my calf
Beat the down of the swan by a length and a half.   10
In the kerchief of linen I caught to my nose
Ah, there never fell snot, but a little gold rose.

"I had seven gold teeth and a toothpick of gold,
My Virginia cheroot° was a leaf of it rolled
And I'd light it each time with a thousand in cash—   15
Why the bums used to fight if I flicked them an ash.

"Once the toast of the Biltmore, the belle of the Taft,
I would drink bottle beer at the Drake, never draft,

---

14 cheroot a thin cigar

And dine at the Astor on Salisbury steak
With a clean tablecloth for each bite I did take.   20

"In a car like the Roxy I'd roll to the track,
A steel-guitar trio, a bar in the back,
And the wheels made no noise, they turned over so fast,
Still it took you ten minutes to see me go past.

"When the horses bowed down to me that I might choose,   25
I bet on them all, for I hated to lose.
Now I'm saddled each night for my butter and eggs
And the broken threads race down the backs of my legs.

"Let you hold in mind, girls, that your beauty must pass
Like a lovely white clover that rusts with its grass.   30
Keep your bottoms off barstools and marry you young
Or be left—an old barrel with many a bung.

"For when time takes you out for a spin in his car
You'll be hard-pressed to stop him from going too far
And be left by the roadside, for all your good deeds,   35
Two toadstools for tits and a face full of weeds."

All the house raised a cheer, but the man at the bar
Made a phonecall and up pulled a red patrol car
And she blew us a kiss as they copped her away
From that prominent bar in Secaucus, N.J.   40

—1961

Little Elegy

for a child who skipped rope

Here lies resting, out of breath,
Out of turns, Elizabeth
Whose quicksilver toes not quite
Cleared the whirring edge of night.

Earth whose circles round us skim   5
Till they catch the lightest limb,

Shelter now Elizabeth
And for her sake trip up Death.

—1961

Cross Ties

Out walking ties left over from a track
Where nothing travels now but rust and grass,
I could take stock in something that would pass
Bearing down Hell-bent from behind my back:
A thing to sidestep or go down before,   5
Far-off, indifferent as that curfew's wail
The evening wind flings like a sack of mail
Or close up as the moon whose headbeam stirs
A flock of cloud to make tracks. Down to strafe
Bristle-backed grass a hawk falls—there's a screech   10
Like steel wrenched taut till severed. Out of reach
Or else beneath desiring, I go safe,
Walk on, tensed for a leap, unreconciled
To a dark void all kindness.
      When I spill   15
The salt I throw the Devil some and, still,
I let them sprinkle water on my child.

—1985

September Twelfth, 2001

Two caught on film who hurtle
From the eighty-second floor,
Choosing between a fireball
And to jump holding hands,

Aren't us. I wake beside you,   5
Stretch, scratch, taste the air,
The incredible joy of coffee
And the morning light.

Alive, we open eyelids
On our pitiful share of time,   10
We bubbles rising and bursting
In a boiling pot.

—2002

Thom Gunn (1929–2004)

Thom Gunn published more than thirty books in the United States and Britain. Born in Gravesend, Kent, he moved to London when he was eight. After leaving school, he spent two years in the National Service before studying at Cambridge University. His first collection, Fighting Terms, *received much acclaim when it appeared in 1954. Soon after graduating, Gunn moved to the United States and studied with Yvor Winters at Stanford. In 1992, he published* The Man with Night Sweats, *a collection of poems memorializing friends and acquaintances who had succumbed to* AIDS.

In the Tank

A man sat in the felon's tank, alone,
Fearful, ungrateful, in a cell for two.
And from his metal bunk, the lower one,
He studied where he was, as felons do.

The cell was clean and cornered, and contained   5
A bowl, grey gritty soap, and paper towels,
A mattress lumpy and not over-stained,
Also a toilet, for the felon's bowels.

He could see clearly all there was to see,
And later when the lights flicked off at nine   10
He saw as clearly all there was to see:
An order without colour, bulk, or line.

And then he knew exactly where he sat.
For though the total riches could not fail
—Red weathered brick, fountains, wisteria—yet   15
Still they contained the silence of a jail,

The jail contained a tank, the tank contained
A box, a mere suspension, at the centre,
Where there was nothing left to understand,
And where he must re-enter and re-enter.   20

—1967

From the Wave

It mounts at sea, a concave wall
    Down-ribbed with shine,
And pushes forward, building tall
    Its steep incline.

Then from their hiding rise to sight   5
    Black shapes on boards
Bearing before the fringe of white
    It mottles towards.

Their pale feet curl, they poise their weight
    With a learn'd skill.   10
It is the wave they imitate
    Keeps them so still.

The marbling bodies have become
    Half wave, half men,
Grafted it seems by feet of foam   15
    Some seconds, then,

Late as they can, they slice the face
    In timed procession:
Balance is triumph in this place,
    Triumph possession.   20

The mindless heave of which they rode
    A fluid shelf
Breaks as they leave it, falls and, slowed,
    Loses itself.

Clear, the sheathed bodies slick as seals   25
    Loosen and tingle;
And by the board the bare foot feels
    The suck of shingle.

They paddle in the shallows still;
    Two splash each other;   30
Then all swim out to wait until
    The right waves gather.

—1971

Terminal

The eight years difference in age seems now
Disparity so wide between the two
That when I see the man who armoured stood
Resistant to all help however good
Now helped through day itself, eased into chairs,   5
Or else led step by step down the long stairs
With firm and gentle guidance by his friend,
Who loves him, through each effort to descend,
Each wavering, each attempt made to complete
An arc of movement and bring down the feet   10
As if with that spare strength he used to enjoy,
I think of Oedipus, old, led by a boy.

—1992

Gregory Corso (1930–2001)

Gregory Corso was born in New York City to a sixteen-year-old mother, and spent much of his childhood in orphanages and foster homes. He grew into a troubled adolescent, spending several months in the Tombs, the New York City jail, and under observation at Bellevue Hospital. At seventeen, he was convicted of theft and sentenced to three years in Clinton State Prison, where he began writing poetry. Once released, he met Allen Ginsberg, William Burroughs, and Jack Kerouac, and moved to San Francisco, where Lawrence Ferlinghetti published Gasoline *(1958), Corso's first poetry collection. Corso traveled in Mexico and Eastern Europe, and taught at the State University of New York at Buffalo and the Naropa University in Boulder, Colorado. The idiosyncratic "Marriage" is his best-known poem.*

Marriage

Should I get married? Should I be good?
Astound the girl next door with my velvet suit and faustus° hood?
Don't take her to movies but to cemeteries
tell all about werewolf bathtubs and forked clarinets
then desire her and kiss her and all the preliminaries   5
and she going just so far and I understanding why
not getting angry saying You must feel! It's beautiful to feel!
Instead take her in my arms lean against an old crooked tombstone
and woo her the entire night the constellations in the sky—

When she introduces me to her parents   10
back straightened, hair finally combed, strangled by a tie,
should I sit knees together on their 3rd degree sofa
and not ask Where's the bathroom?
How else to feel other than I am,
often thinking Flash Gordon° soap—   15
O how terrible it must be for a young man
seated before a family and the family thinking
We never saw him before! He wants our Mary Lou!
After tea and homemade cookies they ask What do you do for a living?

---

2 faustus In German legend, Faust, a medieval necromancer and astrologer, sells his soul to the devil in exchange for knowledge and power   **15 Flash Gordon** popular science fiction comic, radio, and movie serials in the 1930s

Should I tell them? Would they like me then?   20
Say All right get married, we're losing a daughter
but we're gaining a son—
And should I then ask Where's the bathroom?

O God, and the wedding! All her family and her friends
and only a handful of mine all scroungy and bearded   25
just wait to get at the drinks and food—
And the priest! he looking at me as if I masturbated
asking me Do you take this woman for your lawful wedded wife?
And I trembling what to say say Pie Glue!
I kiss the bride all those corny men slapping me on the back   30
She's all yours, boy! Ha-ha-ha!
And in their eyes you could see some obscene honeymoon going on—
Then all that absurd rice and clanky cans and shoes
Niagara Falls! Hordes of us! Husbands! Wives! Flowers! Chocolates!
All streaming into cozy hotels   35
All going to do the same thing tonight
The indifferent clerk he knowing what was going to happen
The lobby zombies they knowing what
The whistling elevator man he knowing
The winking bellboy knowing   40
Everybody knowing! I'd be almost inclined not to do anything!
Stay up all night! Stare that hotel clerk in the eye!
Screaming: I deny honeymoon! I deny honeymoon!
running rampant into those almost climactic suites
yelling Radio belly! Cat shovel!   45
O I'd live in Niagara forever! in a dark cave beneath the Falls
I'd sit there the Mad Honeymooner
devising ways to break marriages, a scourge of bigamy
a saint of divorce—

But I should get married I should be good   50
How nice it'd be to come home to her
and sit by the fireplace and she in the kitchen
aproned young and lovely wanting my baby
and so happy about me she burns the roast beef
and comes crying to me and I get up from my big papa chair   55
saying Christmas teeth! Radiant brains! Apple deaf!
God what a husband I'd make! Yes, I should get married!
So much to do! like sneaking into Mr Jones' house late at night

and cover his golf clubs with 1920 Norwegian books
Like hanging a picture of Rimbaud° on the lawnmower   60
like pasting Tannu Tuva° postage stamps all over the picket fence
like when Mrs Kindhead comes to collect for the Community Chest
grab her and tell her There are unfavorable omens in the sky!
And when the mayor comes to get my vote tell him
When are you going to stop people killing whales!   65
And when the milkman comes leave him a note in the bottle
Penguin dust, bring me penguin dust, I want penguin dust—

Yet if I should get married and it's Connecticut and snow
and she gives birth to a child and I am sleepless, worn,
up for nights, head bowed against a quiet window, the past behind me, 70
finding myself in the most common of situations a trembling man
knowledged with responsibility not twig-smear nor Roman coin soup—
O what would that be like!
Surely I'd give it for a nipple a rubber Tacitus°
For a rattle a bag of broken Bach° records   75
Tack Della Francesca° all over its crib
Sew the Greek alphabet on its bib
And build for its playpen a roofless Parthenon

No, I doubt I'd be that kind of father
Not rural not snow no quiet window   80
but hot smelly tight New York City
seven flights up, roaches and rats in the walls
a fat Reichian° wife screeching over potatoes Get a job!
And five nose running brats in love with Batman
And the neighbors all toothless and dry haired   85
like those hag masses of the 18th century
all wanting to come in and watch TV
The landlord wants his rent
Grocery store Blue Cross Gas & Electric Knights of Columbus
Impossible to lie back and dream Telephone snow, ghost parking— 90
No! I should not get married I should never get married!

---

60 **Rimbaud** Arthur Rimbaud (1854–1891), French symbolist poet   61 **Tannu Tuva** a country in southern Siberia absorbed by the former USSR in 1944, Tuva is known for its attractive postal stamps   74 **Tacitus** (55?–117?), Roman historian   75 **Bach** Johann Sebastian Bach (1665–1750), German composer   76 **Della Francesca** Piero della Francesca (1420?–1492), painter of the Italian Renaissance   83 **Reichian** Willhelm Reich (1897–1957), Austrian psychiatrist whose theories linked sexual pleasure to mental health; or, perhaps, German

But—imagine If I were married to a beautiful sophisticated woman
tall and pale wearing an elegant black dress and long black gloves
holding a cigarette holder in one hand and a highball in the other
and we lived high up in a penthouse with a huge window   95
from which we could see all of New York and ever farther on clearer days
No, can't imagine myself married to that pleasant prison dream—

O but what about love? I forget love
not that I am incapable of love
it's just that I see love as odd as wearing shoes—   100
I never wanted to marry a girl who was like my mother
And Ingrid Bergman° was always impossible
And there's maybe a girl now but she's already married
And I don't like men and—
but there's got to be somebody!   105
Because what if I'm 60 years old and not married,
all alone in a furnished room with pee stains on my underwear
and everybody else is married! All the universe married but me!

Ah, yet well I know that were a woman possible as I am possible
then marriage would be possible—   110
Like SHE° in her lonely alien gaud waiting her Egyptian lover
so I wait—bereft of 2,000 years and the bath of life.

—*1960*

---

102 **Ingrid Bergman** (1915–1982) American movie star, born in Sweden   111 **SHE** Ayesha, a
sorceress in H. Rider Haggard's novel *She*

Miller Williams (b. 1930)

Miller Williams won the Poets' Prize in 1990 for Living on the Surface, *a volume of selected poems. The author of poems, stories, and critical essays, Williams served as a faculty member at the Bread Loaf Writers' Conference for seven years, and has taught at the University of Chile, the National University of Mexico, and, for many years, at the University of Arkansas. A skillful translator of both Giuseppe Belli, a Roman poet of the early nineteenth century, and of Nicanor Parra, a contemporary Chilean, Williams has written many poems about his travels throughout the world, yet has retained the relaxed idiom of his native Arkansas. Father of acclaimed singer-songwriter Lucinda Williams, he is himself no stranger to the national spotlight, having read his poem "Of History and Hope" at Bill Clinton's 1997 presidential inauguration.*

Let Me Tell You

how to do it from the beginning.
First notice everything:
The stain on the wallpaper
of the vacant house,
the mothball smell   5
of a Greyhound toilet.
Miss nothing. Memorize it.
You cannot twist the fact you do not know.

Remember
the blonde girl you saw in the bar.   10
Put a scar on her breast.
Say she left home to get away from her father.
Invent whatever will support your line.
Leave out the rest.

Use metaphors: The mayor is a pig   15
is a metaphor
which is not to suggest
it is not a fact.
Which is irrelevant.
Nothing is less important   20
than a fact.

Be suspicious of any word you learned
and were proud of learning.

It will go bad.
It will fall off the page.   25

When your father lies
in the last light
and your mother cries for him,
listen to the sound of her crying.
When your father dies   30
take notes
somewhere inside.

If there is a heaven
he will forgive you
if the line you found was a good line.   35

It does not have to be worth the dying.

—1971

The Book

I held it in my hands while he told the story.

He had found it in a fallen bunker,
a book for notes with all the pages blank.
He took it to keep for a sketchbook and diary.

He learned years later, when he showed the book   5
to an old bookbinder, who paled, and stepped back
a long step and told him what he held,
what he had laid the days of his life in.
It's bound, the binder said, in human skin.

I stood turning it over in my hands,   10
turning it in my head. Human skin.

What child did this skin fit? What man, what woman?
Dragged still full of its flesh from what dream?

Who took it off the meat? Some other one
who stayed alive by knowing how to do this?   15

I stared at the changing book and a horror grew,
I stared and a horror grew, which was, which is,
how beautiful it was until I knew.

—1989

The Curator

We thought it would come, we thought the Germans would come,
were almost certain they would. I was thirty-two,
the youngest assistant curator in the country.
I had some good ideas in those days.

Well, what we did was this. We had boxes   5
precisely built to every size of canvas.
We put the boxes in the basement and waited.

When word came that the Germans were coming in,
we got each painting put in the proper box
and out of Leningrad in less than a week.   10
They were stored somewhere in southern Russia.

But what we did, you see, besides the boxes
waiting in the basement, which was fine,
a grand idea, you'll agree, and it saved the art—
but what we did was leave the frames hanging,   15
so after the war it would be a simple thing
to put the paintings back where they belonged.

Nothing will seem surprised or sad again
compared to those imperious, vacant frames.

Well, the staff stayed on to clean the rubble   20
after the daily bombardments. We didn't dream—
You know it lasted nine hundred days.
Much of the roof was lost and snow would lie
sometimes a foot deep on this very floor,
but the walls stood firm and hardly a frame fell.   25

Here is the story, now, that I want to tell you.
Early one day, a dark December morning,
we came on three young soldiers waiting outside,
pacing and swinging their arms against the cold.
They told us this: in three homes far from here   30
all dreamed of one day coming to Leningrad
to see the Hermitage,° as they supposed
every Soviet citizen dreamed of doing.

---

32 Hermitage the State Hermitage art museum in St. Petersburg, formerly Leningrad

Now they had been sent to defend the city,
a turn of fortune the three could hardly believe.   35

I had to tell them there was nothing to see
but hundreds and hundreds of frames where the paintings had hung.

"Please, sir," one of them said, "let us see them."

And so we did. It didn't seem any stranger
than all of us being here in the first place,   40
inside such a building, strolling in snow.

We led them around most of the major rooms,
what they could take the time for, wall by wall.
Now and then we stopped and tried to tell them
part of what they would see if they saw the paintings.   45
I told them how those colors would come together,
described a brushstroke here, a dollop there,
mentioned a model and why she seemed to pout
and why this painter got the roses wrong.

The next day a dozen waited for us,   50
then thirty or more, gathered in twos and threes.
Each of us took a group in a different direction:
Castagno, Caravaggio, Brueghel, Cézanne, Matisse,
Orozco, Manet, da Vinci, Goya, Vermeer,
Picasso, Uccello, your Whistler, Wood, and Gropper.°   55
We pointed to more details about the paintings,
I venture to say, than if we had had them there,
some unexpected use of line or light,
balance or movement, facing the cluster of faces
the same way we'd done it every morning   60
before the war, but then we didn't pay
so much attention to what we talked about.
People could see for themselves. As a matter of fact
we'd sometimes said our lines as if they were learned
out of a book, with hardly a look at the paintings.   65

But now the guide and the listeners paid attention
to everything—the simple differences
between the first and post-impressionists,
romantic and heroic, shade and shadow.

53-55 **Castagno . . . and Gropper** painters

Maybe this was a way to forget the war   70
a little while. Maybe more than that.
Whatever it was, the people continued to come.
It came to be called The Unseen Collection.

Here. Here is the story I want to tell you.

Slowly, blind people began to come.   75
A few at first then more of them every morning,
some led and some alone, some swaying a little.
They leaned and listened hard, they screwed their faces,
they seemed to shift their eyes, those that had them,
to see better what was being said.   80
And a cock of the head. My God, they paid attention.

After the siege was lifted and the Germans left
and the roof was fixed and the paintings were in their places,
the blind never came again. Not like before.
This seems strange, but what I think it was,   85
they couldn't see the paintings anymore.
They could still have listened, but the lectures became
a little matter-of-fact. What can I say?
Confluences come when they will and they go away.

                                                    —*1992*

Folding His *USA Today* He Makes His Point in the Blue Star Café

There's this bird I saw in the paper, they said
was a long time on that endangered list
but isn't now because they're all dead.
It didn't have a place to put its nest.
So what we're out is, we're out a bird.   5
It never weighed an ounce, and what I read,
the thing was hardly seen or even heard
by much of anyone. So now it's spread
across a half a page. Do-gooders, they'll
undo us yet. If it was, say, a deer,   10

that did some good. Or bass. OK. Or quail.
We are talking about a sparrow here.
Maybe there's something I don't understand.
Anyone's cooked a sparrow, raise your hand.

—1992

Gary Snyder (b. 1930)

Gary Snyder was deeply involved in poetic activity in his hometown, San Francisco, when that city became the locus of the Beat Generation in the mid-1950s. Yet Snyder, whose studies in Zen Buddhism and Oriental cultures preceded his acquaintance with Allen Ginsberg and Jack Kerouac, has always exhibited a seriousness of purpose that sets him apart from his peers. His long familiarity with the mountains of the Pacific Northwest dates from his jobs with logging crews during his days at Reed College. Snyder took part in a number of left-wing activities during the Sixties, including the original San Francisco Be-In in 1967. His book Turtle Island *won the 1974 Pulitzer Prize;* Axe Handles *(1983) garnered an American Book Award. Snyder teaches at the University of California at Davis.*

Hay for the Horses

He had driven half the night
From far down San Joaquin
Through Mariposa, up the
Dangerous mountain roads,
And pulled in at eight a.m.   5
With his big truckload of hay
      behind the barn.
With winch and ropes and hooks
We stacked the bales up clean
To splintery redwood rafters   10
High in the dark, flecks of alfalfa
Whirling through shingle-cracks of light,
Itch of haydust in the
      sweaty shirt and shoes.

At lunchtime under Black oak   15
Out in the hot corral,
—The old mare nosing lunchpails,
Grasshoppers crackling in the weeds—
"I'm sixty-eight" he said,
"I first bucked hay when I was seventeen.   20
I thought, that day I started,
I sure would hate to do this all my life.
And dammit, that's just what
I've gone and done."

—*1959*

Riprap

Lay down these words
Before your mind like rocks.
                placed solid, by hands
In choice of place, set
Before the body of the mind   5
                in space and time:
Solidity of bark, leaf, or wall
                riprap of things:
Cobble of milky way,
                straying planets,   10
These poems, people,
                lost ponies with
Dragging saddles—
                and rocky sure-foot trails.
The worlds like an endless   15
                four-dimensional
Game of *Go*.°
                ants and pebbles
In the thin loam, each rock a word
                a creek-washed stone   20
Granite: ingrained
                with torment of fire and weight
Crystal and sediment linked hot

17 *Go* Japanese board game

all change, in thoughts,
As well as things.   25

—*1959*

A Walk

Sunday the only day we don't work:
Mules farting around the meadow,
         Murphy fishing,
The tent flaps in the warm
Early sun: I've eaten breakfast and I'll   5
         take a walk
To Benson Lake. Packed a lunch,
Goodbye. Hopping on creekbed boulders
Up the rock throat three miles
         Piute Creek—   10
In steep gorge glacier-slick rattlesnake country
Jump, land by a pool, trout skitter,
The clear sky. Deer tracks.
Bad place by a falls, boulders big as houses,
Lunch tied to belt,   15
I stemmed up a crack and almost fell
But rolled out safe on a ledge
         and ambled on.
Quail chicks freeze underfoot, color of stone
Then run cheep! away, hen quail fussing.   20
Craggy west end of Benson Lake—after edging
Past dark creek pools on a long white slope—
Lookt down in the ice-black lake
         lined with cliff
From far above: deep shimmering trout.   25
A lone duck in a gunsightpass
         steep side hill
Through slide-aspen and talus, to the east end
Down to grass, wading a wide smooth stream
Into camp. At last.   30
      By the rusty three-year-
Ago left-behind cookstove

Of the old trail crew,
Stoppt and swam and ate my lunch.

—1967

The Bath

Washing Kai in the sauna,
The kerosene lantern set on a box
    outside the ground-level window,
Lights up the edge of the iron stove and the
    washtub down on the slab   5
Steaming air and crackle of waterdrops
    brushed by on the pile of rocks on top
He stands in warm water
Soap all over the smooth of his thigh and stomach
    "Gary don't soap my hair!"   10
    —his eye-sting fear—
    the soapy hand feeling
    through and around the globes and curves of his body
    up in the crotch,
And washing-tickling out the scrotum, little anus,   15
    his penis curving up and getting hard
    as I pull back skin and try to wash it
Laughing and jumping, flinging arms around,
    I squat all naked too,
                is this our body?   20

Sweating and panting in the stove-steam hot-stone
    cedar-planking wooden bucket water-splashing
    kerosene lantern-flicker wind-in-the-pines-out
    sierra forest ridges night—
Masa comes in, letting fresh cool air   25
    sweep down from the door
    a deep sweet breath
And she tips him over gripping neatly, one knee down
    her hair falling hiding one whole side of
    shoulder, breast, and belly,   30
Washes deftly Kai's head-hair
    as he gets mad and yells—

The body of my lady, the winding valley spine,
    the space between the thighs I reach through,
    cup her curving vulva arch and hold it from behind,   35
    a soapy tickle   a hand of grail
The gates of Awe
That open back a turning double-mirror world of
    wombs in wombs, in rings,
    that start in music,   40
                is this our body?

The hidden place of seed
The veins net flow across the ribs, that gathers
    milk and peaks up in a nipple—fits
    our mouth—   45
The sucking milk from this our body sends through
    jolts of light; the son, the father,
    sharing mother's joy
That brings a softness to the flower of the awesome
    open curling lotus gate I cup and kiss   50
As Kai laughs at his mother's breast he now is weaned
    from, we
    wash each other,
                this our body

Kai's little scrotum up close to his groin,   55
    the seed still tucked away, that moved from us to him
In flows that lifted with the same joys forces
    as his nursing Masa later,
    playing with her breast,
Or me within her,   60
Or him emerging,
                this is our body:

Clean, and rinsed, and sweating more, we stretch
    out on the redwood benches hearts all beating
Quiet to the simmer of the stove,   65
    the scent of cedar
And then turn over,
    murmuring gossip of the grasses,
    talking firewood,
Wondering how Gen's napping, how to bring him in   70

soon wash him too—
These boys who love their mother
 who loves men, who passes on
 her sons to other women;

The cloud across the sky. The windy pines,   75
 the trickle gurgle in the swampy meadow

 this is our body.

Fire inside and boiling water on the stove
We sigh and slide ourselves down from the benches
 wrap the babies, step outside,   80

black night & all the stars.

Pour cold water on the back and thighs
Go in the house—stand steaming by the center fire
Kai scampers on the sheepskin
Gen standing hanging on and shouting,   85

"Bao! bao! bao! bao! bao!"

This is our body. Drawn up crosslegged by the flames
 drinking icy water
 hugging babies, kissing bellies,

Laughing on the Great Earth   90

Come out from the bath.

       —1974

Rhina P. Espaillat (b. 1932)

Rhina P. Espaillat published her first poetry collection at age sixty. Born in the Dominican Republic, she has lived in the United States since 1939, and writes in both English and Spanish. Her first publication, Lapsing to Grace, *was published by Bennett & Kitchel in 1992, and her second,* Where Horizons Go, *received the 1998 T. S. Eliot Prize and was published by New Odyssey Press. Espaillat runs The Powow River Poets, a monthly workshop, and conducts a reading series and poetry contest sponsored by the Newburyport Art Association, in Massachusetts. A past winner of the Howard Nemerov Award and the* Sparrow Sonnet Award, *she writes intimate, carefully crafted poems in traditional poetic forms.*

Visiting Day

She still remembers me, she strokes my face.
She made me in her body's deepest place

and fed me from herself. I was her moon.
I comb her hair and feed her with a spoon

and dress her in clean clothes. She understands;   5
she pats her empty purse with eager hands

and walks about the grounds with me. She knows
but cannot always say this is a rose.

The words she taught me are the shapes I see:
because she spoke the sun, it came to be;   10

she called me out of nothing, and I came.
Will I still be when she forgets my name?

—1992

Bra

What a good fit! But the label says Honduras:
Alas, I am Union forever, yes, both breasts
and the heart between them committed to U.S. labor.

But such a splendid fit! And the label tells me
the woman who made it, bronze as the breasts now in it,   5
speaks the language I dream in; I count in Spanish

the pesos she made stitching this breast-divider:
will they go for her son's tuition, her daughter's wedding?
The thought is a lovely fit, but oh, the label!

And oh, those pesos that may be pennies, and hard-earned.   10
Was it son or daughter who made this, unschooled, unwedded?
How old? Fourteen? Ten? That fear is a tight fit.

If only the heart could be worn like the breast, divided,
nosing in two directions for news of the wide world,
sniffing here and there for justice, for mercy.   15

How burdened every choice is with politics, guilt,
expensive with duty, heavy as breasts in need of
this perfect fit whose label says Honduras.

—1998

Reservation

As if he has decided on a nap
but feels too pressed for time to find his bed
or even shift the napkin from his lap,
the man across the table drops his head
mid-anecdote, just managing to clear   5
a basket of warm rolls and butter stacked
like little golden dice beside his ear.
The lady seems embarrassed to attract
such swift attention from the formal stranger
who leaves his dinner, bends as if to wake   10
the sleeper, seeks a pulse. Others arrange her
coat about her, gather round to take
the plates, the quiet form, her name, her hand.
Now slowly she begins to understand.

—1998

Linda Pastan (b. 1932)

Linda Pastan served as poet laureate of Maryland, where she has lived and taught for many years. Born in New York City, she studied at Radcliffe College and Brandeis University. Her first book, A Perfect Circle of Sun, appeared in 1971, and she has since won many honors, including the Pushcart Prize, a Dylan Thomas Award, the Di Castagnola Award, and the Charity Randall Citation. On the Bread Loaf Writers' Conference poetry faculty for twenty years, Pastan also has taught at American University. Her voice stands out among contemporary poets for its straightforward, conversational diction.

Ethics

In ethics class so many years ago
our teacher asked this question every fall:
if there were a fire in a museum
which would you save, a Rembrandt° painting
or an old woman who hadn't many   5
years left anyhow? Restless on hard chairs
caring little for pictures or old age
we'd opt one year for life, the next for art
and always half-heartedly. Sometimes
the woman borrowed my grandmother's face   10
leaving her usual kitchen to wander
some drafty, half-imagined museum.
One year, feeling clever, I replied
why not let the woman decide herself?
Linda, the teacher would report, eschews   15
the burdens of responsibility.
This fall in a real museum I stand
before a real Rembrandt, old woman,
or nearly so, myself. The colors
within this frame are darker than autumn,   20
darker even than winter—the browns of earth,
though earth's most radiant elements burn
through the canvas. I know now that woman

---

4 Rembrandt Rembrandt van Rijn (1606–1669), Dutch painter

and painting and season are almost one
and all beyond saving by children.   25

—1981

Crocuses

They come
by stealth, spreading
the rumor of spring—
near the hedge . . .
by the gate . . .   5
at our chilly feet . . .
mothers of saffron, fathers
of insurrection, purple
and yellow scouts
of an army still massing   10
just to the south.

—1991

1932–

I saw my name in print the other day
with 1932 and then a blank
and knew that even now some grassy bank
just waited for my grave. And somewhere a grey

slab of marble existed already   5
on which the final number would be carved—
as if the stone itself were somehow starved
for definition. When I went steady

in high school years ago, my boyfriend's name
was what I tried out, hearing how it fit   10
with mine; then names of film stars in some hit.
My husband was anonymous as rain.

There is a number out there, odd or even
that will become familiar to my sons

and daughter. (They are the living ones   15
I think of now: Peter, Rachel, Stephen.)

I picture it, four integers in a row
5 or 7, 6 or 2 or 9:
a period; silence; an end-stopped line;
a hammer poised . . . delivering its blow.   20

—1991

Sylvia Plath (1932–1963)

Sylvia Plath, whose troubled personal life is often difficult to separate from her poetry, is almost always read as an autobiographical and confessional poet. Born in Jamaica Plain, Massachusetts, she was eight years old when her father, a biology professor specializing in bees, died from complications from undiagnosed diabetes, an event that left her with permanent emotional scars. Plath attended Smith College on a scholarship, and in her junior year was awarded a guest editorship at Mademoiselle *magazine. Brilliant and precocious, she served a long apprenticeship to the tradition of modern poetry before attaining her mature style in the final two years of her life. Only one collection,* The Colossus *(1960), appeared in her lifetime, and her fame mainly rests on her posthumous books of poetry and the success of her lone novel,* The Bell Jar *(1963). She committed suicide in 1963. Plath has been the subject of many biographical studies, reflecting the intense interest that readers have in her life and work.*

The Colossus

I shall never get you put together entirely,
Pieced, glued, and properly jointed.
Mule-bray, pig-grunt and bawdy cackles
Proceed from your great lips.
It's worse than a barnyard.   5

Perhaps you consider yourself an oracle,
Mouthpiece of the dead, or of some god or other.
Thirty years now I have labored
To dredge the silt from your throat.
I am none the wiser.   10

Scaling little ladders with gluepots and pails of lysol
I crawl like an ant in mourning
Over the weedy acres of your brow
To mend the immense skull plates and clear
The bald, white tumuli° of your eyes.   15

A blue sky out of the Oresteia°
Arches above us. O father, all by yourself
You are pithy and historical as the Roman Forum.
I open my lunch on a hill of black cypress.
Your fluted bones and acanthine° hair are littered   20

In their old anarchy to the horizon-line.
It would take more than a lightning-stroke
To create such a ruin.
Nights, I squat in the cornucopia
Of your left ear, out of the wind,   25

Counting the red stars and those of plum-color.
The sun rises under the pillar of your tongue.
My hours are married to shadow.
No longer do I listen for the scrape of a keel
On the blank stones of the landing.   30

—1960

Daddy

You do not do, you do not do
Any more, black shoe
In which I have lived like a foot
For thirty years, poor and white,
Barely daring to breathe or Achoo.   5

Daddy, I have had to kill you.
You died before I had time—
Marble-heavy, a bag full of God,
Ghastly statue with one gray toe
Big as a Frisco seal   10

---

15 tumuli mounds of earth above prehistoric tombs   **16 Oresteia** trilogy by Greek playwright
Aeschylus (526–456 B.C.)   **20 acanthine** like an acanthus, a Mediterranean shrub with spiny leaves

And a head in the freakish Atlantic
Where it pours bean green over blue
In the waters off beautiful Nauset.
I used to pray to recover you.
Ach, du.°   15

In the German tongue, in the Polish town
Scraped flat by the roller
Of wars, wars, wars.
But the name of the town is common.
My Polack friend   20

Says there are a dozen or two.
So I never could tell where you
Put your foot, your root,
I never could talk to you.
The tongue stuck in my jaw.   25

It stuck in a barb wire snare.
Ich, ich, ich, ich,°
I could hardly speak.
I thought every German was you.
And the language obscene   30

An engine, an engine
Chuffing me off like a Jew.
A Jew to Dachau, Auschwitz, Belsen.°
I began to talk like a Jew.
I think I may well be a Jew.   35

The snows of the Tyrol, the clear beer of Vienna
Are not very pure or true.
With my gypsy ancestress and my weird luck
And my Taroc pack and my Taroc pack
I may be a bit of a Jew.   40

I have always been scared of *you*,
With your Luftwaffe,° your gobbledygoo.
And your neat mustache

---

15 **Ach, du** "Oh, you"   27 **Ich, ich, ich, ich** "I, I, I, I"   33 **Dachau, Auschwitz, Belsen** German concentration camps   42 **Luftwaffe** German Air Force

And your Aryan eye, bright blue.
Panzer-man, panzer-man, O You—   45

Not God but a swastika
So black no sky could squeak through.
Every woman adores a Fascist,
The boot in the face, the brute
Brute heart of a brute like you.   50

You stand at the blackboard, daddy,
In the picture I have of you,
A cleft in your chin instead of your foot
But no less a devil for that, no not
Any less the black man who   55

Bit my pretty red heart in two.
I was ten when they buried you.
At twenty I tried to die
And get back, back, back to you.
I thought even the bones would do.   60

But they pulled me out of the sack,
And they stuck me together with glue.
And then I knew what to do.
I made a model of you,
A man in black with a Meinkampf° look   65

And a love of the rack and the screw.
And I said I do, I do.
So daddy, I'm finally through.
The black telephone's off at the root,
The voices just can't worm through.   70

If I've killed one man, I've killed two—
The vampire who said he was you
And drank my blood for a year,
Seven years, if you want to know.
Daddy, you can lie back now.   75

65 Meinkampf title of Hitler's autobiography ("My Struggle")

There's a stake in your fat black heart
And the villagers never liked you.
They are dancing and stamping on you.
They always *knew* it was you.
Daddy, daddy, you bastard, I'm through.   80

—1965

Edge

The woman is perfected.
Her dead

Body wears the smile of accomplishment,
The illusion of a Greek necessity

Flows in the scrolls of her toga,   5
Her bare

Feet seem to be saying:
We have come so far, it is over.

Each dead child coiled, a white serpent,
One at each little   10

Pitcher of milk, now empty.
She has folded

Them back into her body as petals
Of a rose close when the garden

Stiffens and odors bleed   15
From the sweet, deep throats of the night flower.

The moon has nothing to be sad about,
Staring from her hood of bone.

She is used to this sort of thing.
Her blacks crackle and drag.   20

—1965

Lady Lazarus°

I have done it again.
One year in every ten
I manage it—

A sort of walking miracle, my skin
Bright as a Nazi lampshade,   5
My right foot

A paperweight,
My face a featureless, fine
Jew linen.

Peel off the napkin   10
O my enemy.
Do I terrify?—

The nose, the eye pits, the full set of teeth?
The sour breath
Will vanish in a day.   15

Soon, soon the flesh
The grave cave ate will be
At home on me

And I a smiling woman.
I am only thirty.   20
And like the cat I have nine times to die.

This is Number Three.
What a trash
To annihilate each decade.

What a million filaments.   25
The peanut-crunching crowd
Shoves in to see

Them unwrap me hand and foot—
The big strip tease.
Gentleman, ladies,   30

Lazarus in the New Testament, man raised from the dead by Jesus

These are my hands,
My knees.
I may be skin and bone,

Nevertheless, I am the same, identical woman.
The first time it happened I was ten.   35
It was an accident.

The second time I meant
To last it out and not come back at all.
I rocked shut

As a seashell.   40
They had to call and call
And pick the worms off me like sticky pearls.

Dying
Is an art, like everything else.
I do it exceptionally well.   45

I do it so it feels like hell.
I do it so it feels real.
I guess you could say I've a call.

It's easy enough to do it in a cell.
It's easy enough to do it and stay put.   50
It's the theatrical

Comeback in broad day
To the same place, the same face, the same brute
Amused shout:

"A miracle!"   55
That knocks me out.
There is a charge

For the eyeing of my scars, there is a charge
For the hearing of my heart—
It really goes.   60

And there is a charge, a very large charge,
For a word or a touch
Or a bit of blood

Or a piece of my hair or my clothes.
So, so, Herr° Doktor.   65
So, Herr Enemy.

I am your opus,
I am your valuable,
The pure gold baby

That melts to a shriek.   70
I turn and burn.
Do not think I underestimate your great concern.

Ash, ash—
You poke and stir.
Flesh, bone, there is nothing there—   75

A cake of soap,
A wedding ring,
A gold filling.

Herr God, Herr Lucifer,
Beware   80
Beware.

Out of the ash
I rise with my red hair
And I eat men like air.

—*1965*

The Moon and the Yew Tree

This is the light of the mind, cold and planetary.
The trees of the mind are black. The light is blue.
The grasses unload their griefs on my feet as if I were God,
Prickling my ankles and murmuring of their humility.
Fumy, spiritous mists inhabit this place   5

---

65 Herr (German), Mister

Separated from my house by a row of headstones.
I simply cannot see where there is to get to.

The moon is no door. It is a face in its own right,
White as a knuckle and terribly upset.
It drags the sea after it like a dark crime; it is quiet   10
With the O-gape of complete despair. I live here.
Twice on Sunday, the bells startle the sky—
Eight great tongues affirming the Resurrection.
At the end, they soberly bong out their names.

The yew tree points up. It has a Gothic shape.   15
The eyes lift after it and find the moon.
The moon is my mother. She is not sweet like Mary.
Her blue garments unloose small bats and owls.
How I would like to believe in tenderness—
The face of the effigy, gentled by candles,   20
Bending, on me in particular, its mild eyes.

I have fallen a long way. Clouds are flowering
Blue and mystical over the face of the stars.
Inside the church, the saints will be all blue,
Floating on their delicate feet over the cold pews,   25
Their hands and faces stiff with holiness.
The moon sees nothing of this. She is bald and wild.
And the message of the yew tree is blackness—blackness and silence.

—1965

Morning Song

Love set you going like a fat gold watch.
The midwife slapped your footsoles, and your bald cry
Took its place among the elements.

Our voices echo, magnifying your arrival. New statue.
In a drafty museum, your nakedness   5
Shadows our safety. We stand round blankly as walls.

I'm no more your mother
Than the cloud that distills a mirror to reflect its own slow
Effacement at the wind's hand.

All night your moth-breath 10
Flickers among the flat pink roses. I wake to listen:
A far sea moves in my ear.

One cry, and I stumble from bed, cow-heavy and floral
In my Victorian nightgown.
Your mouth opens clean as a cat's. The window square 15

Whitens and swallows its dull stars. And now you try
Your handful of notes;
The clear vowels rise like balloons.

—1965

Gerald Barrax (b. 1933)

Gerald Barrax has been poetry editor for the journals Obsidian *and* Callaloo. *Influenced early in his career by the political poetry of the Black Arts Movement, Barrax's later poems explore issues of family and community. Born in Attalla, Alabama, Barrax was raised in Alabama and Pittsburgh, Pennsylvania. He studied at Duquesne University and the University of Pittsburgh. From a Person Sitting in Darkness: New and Selected Poems was published in 1998. Barrax taught at North Carolina State University and lives in Raleigh, North Carolina.*

Strangers Like Us: Pittsburgh, Raleigh, 1945–1985

The sounds our parents heard echoing over
housetops while listening to evening radios
were the uninterrupted cries running and cycling
we sent through the streets and yards, where spring summer
fall we were entrusted to the night, boys 5
and girls together, to send us home for bath
and bed after the dark had drifted down and eased
contests between pitcher and batter, hider and seeker.

Our own children live imprisoned in light.
They are cycloned into our yards and hearts,   10
whose gates flutter shut on unfamiliar smiles.
At the rumor of a moon, we call them in
before the monsters who hunt, who hurt, who haunt
us, rise up from our own dim streets.

—*1992*

Pittsburgh, 1948: The Music Teacher

I don't know where my mother got him—
whose caricature he was—or how
he found me, to travel by streetcars
on Saturday mornings to the Negro
home, our two rooms and bath on the Hornsby's   5
second floor. His name was Professor
Something-or-Other Slavic, portly,
florid man, bald pate surrounded
by stringy gray hair. Everything
about him was threadbare: wing collar,   10
string tie, French cuffs, cut-away coat.
His sausage fingers were grimy, his nails
dirty. I think, now, he was one of the War's
Displaced Persons, who accepted with grace
coming to give violin lessons   15
to a 15-year-old alien boy
(displaced here myself from a continent,
from a country I couldn't name,
and a defector from Alabama).
I was the debt he had to pay   20
on the short end of a Refugee's desperate
wager, or prayer, to redeem the body
before the soul. I don't know why
my mother didn't give him
his paltry three dollars. I had to do it.   25

One morning he stood
at my side waving his bow
in time to my playing, swayed
once and crumpled to the kitchen
floor that she had made   30
spotless for him, taking
the music stand down.
I stood terrified until she
ran in and we helped him to his feet.

He finished my lesson in dignified shame,   35
and I knew, from pure intuition,
he had not eluded the hounds of hunger.

Outside of death camps I'd seen liberated
in newsreels and *Life*, it was the first time, I think,
I'd felt sorry for anyone white.   40

—1998

Mark Stran∂ (b. 1934)

Mark Strand displays a simplicity in his best poems that reveals the influence of Spanish-language poets like Nicanor Parra, the father of "antipoetry," and Rafael Alberti, whom Strand has translated. Born on Canada's Prince Edward Island, he was raised in the United States and South America. He did his undergraduate work at Antioch College and earned an M.A. from the University of Iowa. Fulbright scholarships and lectureships took him to Italy and Brazil. Strand has taught at many American universities, among them Columbia, Princeton, Harvard, and the University of Utah. His ninth collection, Blizzard of One *(1998), received the Pulitzer Prize, and he was named U.S. Poet Laureate in 1990.*

Eating Poetry

Ink runs from the corners of my mouth.
There is no happiness like mine.
I have been eating poetry.

The librarian does not believe what she sees.
Her eyes are sad   5
and she walks with her hands in her dress.

The poems are gone.
The light is dim.
The dogs are on the basement stairs and coming up.

Their eyeballs roll,   10
their blond legs burn like brush.
The poor librarian begins to stamp her feet and weep.

She does not understand.
When I get on my knees and lick her hand,
she screams.   15

I am a new man.
I snarl at her and bark.
I romp with joy in the bookish dark.

—1968

Keeping Things Whole

In a field
I am the absence
of field.

This is
always the case.   5
Wherever I am
I am what is missing.

When I walk
I part the air
and always   10
the air moves in
to fill the spaces
where my body's been.

We all have reasons
for moving.   15
I move
to keep things whole.

—*1968*

The Tunnel

A man has been standing
in front of my house
for days. I peek at him
from the living room
window and at night,   5
unable to sleep,
I shine my flashlight
down on the lawn.
He is always there.

After a while   10
I open the front door
just a crack and order
him out of my yard.
He narrows his eyes
and moans. I slam   15
the door and dash back
to the kitchen, then up
to the bedroom, then down.

I weep like a schoolgirl
and make obscene gestures   20
through the window. I
write large suicide notes
and place them so he
can read them easily.
I destroy the living   25
room furniture to prove
I own nothing of value.

When he seems unmoved
I decide to dig a tunnel

to a neighboring yard. 30
I seal the basement off
from the upstairs with
a brick wall. I dig hard
and in no time the tunnel
is done. Leaving my pick 35
and shovel below,

I come out in front of a house
and stand there too tired to
move or even speak, hoping
someone will help me. 40
I feel I'm being watched
and sometimes I hear
a man's voice,
but nothing is done
and I have been waiting for days. 45

—1968

The Great Poet Returns

When the light poured down through a hole in the clouds,
We knew the great poet was going to show. And he did.
A limousine with all white tires and stained-glass windows
Dropped him off. And then, with a clear and soundless fluency,
He strode into the hall. There was a hush. His wings were big. 5
The cut of his suit, the width of his tie, were out of date.
When he spoke, the air seemed whitened by imagined cries.
The worm of desire bore into the heart of everyone there.
There were tears in their eyes. The great one was better than ever.
"No need to rush," he said at the close of the reading, "the end 10
Of the world is only the end of the world as you know it."
How like him, everyone thought. Then he was gone,
And the world was a blank. It was cold and the air was still.
Tell me, you people out there, what is poetry anyway?
Can anyone die without even a little? 15

—1998

Robert Mezey (b. 1935)

Robert Mezey received the Poets' Prize for his Collected Poems 1952–1999 *(2000) and the Lamont Prize for* The Lovemaker *(1961). Born in Philadelphia, he was educated at the University of Iowa, Kenyon College, and Stanford University. He has edited and coedited a number of anthologies, including* Naked Poetry *(1969);* Poems from the Hebrew *(1973); and* Poems of the American West *(2002). Mezey lives in Claremont, California, and is professor emeritus at Pomona College.*

Hardy°

Thrown away at birth, he was recovered,
Plucked from the swaddling-shroud, and chafed and slapped,
The crone implacable. At last he shivered,
Drew the first breath, and howled, and lay there, trapped
In a world from which there is but one escape   5
And that forestalled now almost ninety years.
In such a scene as he himself might shape,
The maker of a thousand songs appears.

From this it follows, all the ironies
Life plays on one whose fate it is to follow   10
The way of things, the suffering one sees,
The many cups of bitterness he must swallow
Before he is permitted to be gone
Where he was headed in that early dawn.

—*1965*

My Mother

My mother writes from Trenton,
a comedian to the bone
but underneath serious
and all heart. "Honey," she says,

Hardy Thomas Hardy (1840–1928), British novelist and poet

"be a mensch and Mary too,   5
its no good, to worry, you
are doing the best you can
your Dad, and everyone
thinks you turned out very well
as long as you pay your bills   10
nobody can say a word
you can tell them, to drop dead
so save a dollar it cant
hurt—remember Frank you went
to high school with? he still lives   15
with his wife's mother, his wife
works, while he writes his books and
did he ever sell a one,
four kids run around, naked
36 and he's never had,   20
you'll forgive my expression
even a pot to piss in
or a window to throw it,
such a smart boy he couldnt
read the footprints on the wall   25
honey you think you know all
the answers you don't, please, try,
to put some money away
believe me it wouldn't hurt,
artist, shmartist life's too short,   30
for that kind of, forgive me
horseshit, I know what you want,
better than you, all that counts
is to make a good living
and the best of everything   35
as Sholem Aleichem° said,
he was a great writer did
you ever read his books dear,
you should make what he makes a year,
anyhow he says, some place   40
Poverty is no disgrace
but, it's no honor either

---

36 **Sholem Aleichem** (1859–1916), Russian author who wrote popular books in Yiddish

that's what I say,
     love,
          Mother"   45

—*1987*

Russell Edson (b. 1935)

Russell Edson has been writing wildly surrealistic prose poems since before the form came into fashion. The son of cartoonist Gus Edson, he attended the Art Students League, the New School for Social Research, Columbia University, and Black Mountain College. He has published eleven books of prose poems and one novel, The Song of Percival Peacock *(1992). Known for being reclusive, Edson lives in Connecticut, where he was born.*

An Old Man in Love

An old man decided to fall in love with himself. He gave himself a flower.

No no, I do not want to marry you, he said, you're old enough to be my father.

—*1964*

When the Ceiling Cries

A mother tosses her infant so that it hits the ceiling.

Father says, why are you doing that to the ceiling?

Do you want my baby to fly away to heaven? the ceiling is there so that the baby will come back to me, says mother.

Father says, you are hurting the ceiling, can't you hear it crying?

So mother and father climb a ladder and kiss the ceiling.   5

—*1964*

Ape

You haven't finished your ape, said mother to father, who had monkey hair and blood on his whiskers.

I've had enough monkey, cried father.

You didn't eat the hands, and I went to all the trouble to make onion rings for its fingers, said mother.

I'll just nibble on its forehead, and then I've had enough, said father.   5

I stuffed its nose with garlic, just like you like it, said mother.

Why don't you have the butcher cut these apes up? You lay the whole thing on the table every night; the same fractured skull, the same singed fur; like someone who died horribly. These aren't dinners, these are postmortem dissections.   10

Try a piece of its gum, I've stuffed its mouth with bread, said mother.

Ugh, it looks like a mouth full of vomit. How can I bite into its cheek with bread spilling out of its mouth? cried father.

Break one of the ears off, they're so crispy, said mother.

I wish to hell you'd put underpants on these apes; even a jockstrap,   15
screamed father.

Father, how dare you insinuate that I see the ape as anything more than simple meat, screamed mother.

Well, what's with this ribbon tied in a bow on its privates? screamed father.   20

Are you saying that I am in love with this vicious creature? That I would submit my female opening to this brute? That after we had love on the kitchen floor I would put him in the oven, after breaking his head with a frying pan; and then serve him to my husband, that my husband might eat the evidence of my infidelity . . . ?   25

I'm just saying that I'm damn sick of ape every night, cried father.

—1973

Mary Oliver (b. 1935)

Mary Oliver is widely respected for the clarity and precision of her poetry, which often explores the relationship between human beings and the natural world. She was born in Cleveland, Ohio, and educated at Ohio State University and Vassar College, and has served as a visiting professor at a number of universities and at the Fine Arts Work Center in Provincetown, Massachusetts. She has won both the Pulitzer Prize for American Primitive *(1983) and the National Book Award for her work, which first appeared in* No Voyage and Other Poems *in 1963.*

The Black Snake

When the black snake
flashed onto the morning road,
and the truck could not swerve—
death, that is how it happens.

Now he lies looped and useless   5
as an old bicycle tire.
I stop the car
and carry him into the bushes.

He is as cool and gleaming
as a braided whip, he is as beautiful and quiet   10
as a dead brother.
I leave him under the leaves

and drive on, thinking
about *death:* its suddenness,
its terrible weight,   15
its certain coming. Yet under

reason burns a brighter fire, which the bones
have always preferred.
It is the story of endless good fortune.
It says to oblivion: not me!   20

It is the light at the center of every cell.
It is what sent the snake coiling and flowing forward

happily all spring through the green leaves before
he came to the road.

—1979

University Hospital, Boston

The trees on the hospital lawn
are lush and thriving. They too
are getting the best of care,
like you, and the anonymous many,
in the clean rooms high above this city,   5
where day and night the doctors keep
arriving, where intricate machines
chart with cool devotion
the murmur of the blood,
the slow patching-up of bone,   10
the despair of the mind.

When I come to visit and we walk out
into the light of a summer day,
we sit under the trees—
buckeyes, a sycamore and one   15
black walnut brooding
high over a hedge of lilacs
as old as the red-brick building
behind them, the original
hospital built before the Civil War.   20
We sit on the lawn together, holding hands
while you tell me: you are better.

How many young men, I wonder,
came here, wheeled on cots off the slow trains
from the red and hideous battlefields   25
to lie all summer in the small and stuffy chambers
while doctors did what they could, longing
for tools still unimagined, medicines still unfound,
wisdoms still unguessed at, and how many died

staring at the leaves of the trees, blind   30
to the terrible effort around them to keep them alive?
I look into your eyes

which are sometimes green and sometimes gray,
and sometimes full of humor, but often not,
and tell myself, you are better,   35
because my life without you would be
a place of parched and broken trees.
Later, walking the corridors down to the street,
I turn and step inside an empty room.
Yesterday someone was here with a gasping face.   40
Now the bed is made all new,
the machines have been rolled away. The silence
continues, deep and neutral,
as I stand there, loving you.

—1983

The Buddha's Last Instruction

"Make of yourself a light,"
said the Buddha,
before he died.
I think of this every morning
as the east begins   5
to tear off its many clouds
of darkness, to send up the first
signal—a white fan
streaked with pink and violet,
even green.   10
An old man, he lay down
between two sala trees,
and he might have said anything,
knowing it was his final hour.
The light burns upward,   15
it thickens and settles over the fields.
Around him, the villagers gathered

and stretched forward to listen.
Even before the sun itself
hangs, disattached, in the blue air,   20
I am touched everywhere
by its ocean of yellow waves.
No doubt he thought of everything
that had happened in his difficult life.
And then I feel the sun itself   25
as it blazes over the hills,
like a million flowers on fire—
clearly I'm not needed,
yet I feel myself turning
into something of inexplicable value.   30
Slowly, beneath the branches,
he raised his head.
He looked into the faces of that frightened crowd.

—1990

Fred Chappell (b. 1936)

Fred Chappell wrote the epic-length poem Midquest *(1981), and his achievement was recognized when he was awarded the Bollingen Prize in 1985. A four-part poem written over a decade,* Midquest *uses the occasion of the poet's thirty-fifth birthday as a departure for a complex sequence of autobiographical poems that are heavily indebted to Dante for their formal structure. A versatile writer of poetry and prose, Chappell displays his classical learning brilliantly and in unusual contexts. Born in Canton, North Carolina, and educated at Duke University, he was appointed North Carolina's poet laureate in 1997.*

My Grandmother Washes Her Feet

I see her still, unsteadily riding the edge
Of the clawfoot tub, mumbling to her feet,
Musing bloodrust water about her ankles.

Cotton skirt pulled up, displaying bony
Bruised patchy calves that would make you weep.   5

Rinds of her soles had darkened, crust-colored—
Not yellow now—like the tough outer belly
Of an adder. In fourteen hours the most refreshment
She'd given herself was dabbling her feet in the water.

"You mightn't've liked John-Giles. Everybody knew   10
He was a mean one, galloping whiskey and bad women
All night. Tried to testify dead drunk
In church one time. That was a ruckus. Later
Came back a War Hero, and all the young men
Took to doing the things he did. And failed.   15
Finally one of his women's men shot him."

"What for?"

            "Stealing milk through fences. . . . That part
Of Family nobody wants to speak of.
They'd rather talk about fine men, brick houses,   20
Money. Maybe you ought to know, teach you
Something."

            "What do they talk about?"

                        "Generals,
And the damn Civil War, and marriages.   25
Things you brag about in the front of Bibles.
You'd think there was arms and legs of Family
On every battlefield from Chickamauga
To Atlanta."

            "That's not the way it is?"   30

"Don't matter how it is. No proper way
To talk, is all. It was nothing they ever did.
And plenty they won't talk about . . . John-Giles!"

Her cracked toes thumped the tub wall, spreading
Shocklets. Amber toenails curled like shavings.   35
She twisted the worn knob to pour in coolness
I felt suffuse her body like a whiskey.

"Bubba Martin, he was another, and no
Kind of man. Jackleg preacher with the brains

Of a toad. Read the Bible upsidedown and crazy   40
Till it drove him crazy, making crazy marks
On doorsills, windows, sides of Luther's barn.
He killed hisself at last with a shotgun.
No gratitude for Luther putting him up
All those years. Shot so he'd fall down the well."   45

"I never heard."

        "They never mention him.
Nor Aunt Annie, that everybody called
Paregoric Annie, that roamed the highways
Thumbing cars and begging change to keep   50
Even with her craving. She claimed she was saving up
To buy a glass eye. It finally shamed them
Enough, they went together and got her one.
That didn't stop her. She lugged it around
In a velvet-lined case, asking strangers   55
Please to drop it in the socket for her.
They had her put away. And that was that.
There's places Family ties just won't stretch to."

Born then in my mind a race of beings
Unknown and monstrous. I named them Shadow-Cousins,   60
A linked long dark line of them,
Peering from mirrors and gleaming in closets, agog
To manifest themselves inside myself.
Like discovering a father's cancer.
I wanted to search my body for telltale streaks.   65

"Sounds like a bunch of cow thieves."

        "Those too, I reckon,
But they're forgotten or covered over so well
Not even I can make them out. Gets foggy
When folks decide they're coming on respectable.   70
First thing you know, you'll have a Family Tree."

(I imagined a wind-stunted horse-apple.)

She raised her face. The moons of the naked bulb
Flared in her spectacles, painting out her eyes.
In dirty water light bobbed like round soap.   75
A countenance matter-of-fact, age-engraved,
Mulling in peaceful wonder petty annals

Of embarrassment. Gray but edged with brown
Like an old photograph, her hair shone yellow.
A tiredness mantled her fine energy.   80
She shifted, sluicing water under instep.

"O what's the use," she said. "Water seeks
Its level. If your daddy thinks that teaching school
In a white shirt makes him a likelier man,
What's to blame? Leastways, he won't smother   85
Of mule-farts or have to starve for a pinch of rainfall.
Nothing new gets started without the old's
Plowed under, or halfway under. We sprouted from dirt,
Though, and it's with you, and dirt you'll never forget."

"No Mam."   90

              "Don't you say me No Mam yet.
Wait till you get your chance to deny it."

Once she giggled, a sound like stroking muslin.

"You're bookish. I can see you easy a lawyer
Or a county clerk in a big white suit and tie,   95
Feeding the preacher and bribing the sheriff and the judge.
Second-generation-respectable
Don't come to any better destiny.
But it's dirt you rose from, dirt you'll bury in.
Just about the time you'll think your blood   100
Is clean, here will come dirt in a natural shape
You never dreamed. It'll rise up saying, Fred,
Where's that mule you're supposed to march behind?
Where's your overalls and roll-your-owns?
Where's your Blue Tick hounds and Domineckers?°   105
Not all the money in this world can wash true-poor
True rich. Fatback just won't change to artichokes."

"What's artichokes?"

              "Pray Jesus you'll never know.
For if you do it'll be a sign you've grown   110
Away from what you are, can fly to flinders
Like a touch-me-not° . . . I may have errored
When I said *true-poor*. It ain't the same

105 Domineckers breed of chicken   **112 touch-me-not** a plant whose ripened seed pod bursts when
touched

As dirt-poor. When you got true dirt you got
Everything you need . . . And don't you say me   115
Yes Mam again. You just wait."

                              She leaned
And pulled the plug. The water circled gagging
To a bloody eye and poured in the hole like a rat.
I thought maybe their spirits had gathered there,   120
All my Shadow-Cousins clouding the water,
And now they ran to earth and would cloud the earth.
Effigies of soil, I could seek them out
By clasping soil, forcing warm rude fingers
Into ancestral jelly my father wouldn't plow.   125
I strained to follow them, and never did.
I never had the grit to stir those guts.
I never had the guts to stir that earth.

                                        —*1981*

Narcissus and Echo°

Shall the water not remember   *Ember*
my hand's slow gesture, tracing above   *of*
its mirror my half-imaginary   *airy*
portrait? My only belonging   *longing*
is my beauty, which I take   *ache*   5
away and then return as love   *of*
teasing playfully the one being   *unbeing*.

whose gratitude I treasure   *Is your*
moves me. I live apart   *heart*
from myself, yet cannot   *not*   10
live apart. In the water's tone,   *stone?*
that brilliant silence, a flower   *Hour,*
whispers my name with such slight   *light,*
moment, it seems filament of air,   *fare*
the world become cloudswell.   *well.*   15

                                        —*1985*

Narcissus and Echo in the myth, the vain Narcissus drowned attempting to embrace his own reflection in the water. Echo, a nymph who loved him, pined away until only her voice remained

Ave Atque Vale°

Weeping, I mended the broken wing
Of Love and calmed his shuddering
And bound his wounded hand and then
I watched him fly away again.

—1993

Lucille Clifton (b. 1936)

*Lucille Clifton has commented succinctly about her own work, "I am a
Black woman poet, and I sound like one." A native of Depew, New York,
she began college at age sixteen, as a drama major at Howard University.
After transferring to SUNY–Fredonia, she began to find her poetic voice.
Entered into competition by the poet Robert Hayden, her first poetry
manuscript won the 1969 YW-YMHA Poetry Center Discovery Award,
and the resulting book,* Good Times, *was cited by the* New York Times *as
one of the year's best books. Clifton has written many children's books,
aimed specifically at an African-American audience. A former poet laureate of Maryland, she has taught at several colleges, including St. Mary's
College of Maryland. Clifton won a National Book Award in 2000.*

homage to my hips

these hips are big hips
they need space to
move around in.
they don't fit into little
petty places. these hips   5
are free hips.
they don't like to be held back.
these hips have never been enslaved,
they go where they want to go
they do what they want to do.   10
these hips are mighty hips.
these hips are magic hips.

Ave Atque Vale hail and farewell (Latin)

i have known them
to put a spell on a man and
spin him like a top!   15

—*1980*

wishes for sons

i wish them cramps.
i wish them a strange town
and the last tampon.
i wish them no 7-11.

i wish them one week early   5
and wearing a white skirt.
i wish them one week late.

later i wish them hot flashes
and clots like you
wouldn't believe. let the   10
flashes come when they
meet someone special.
let the clots come
when they want to.

let them think they have accepted   15
arrogance in the universe,
then bring them to gynecologists
not unlike themselves.

—*1991*

lee°

my mother's people
belonged to the lees
my father would say
then spout a litany

lee Robert E. Lee (1807–1870), Confederate general in American Civil War

of names   old lighthorse harry 5
old robert e

my father
who lied on his deathbed
who knew the truth
but didn't always choose it 10
who saw himself an honorable man

was proud of lee
that man of honor
praised by grant and lincoln
worshipped by his men 15
revered by the state of virginia
which he loved almost as much
as my father did

it may have been a lie
it may have been 20
one of my father's tales
if so there was an honor in it
if he was indeed to be
the child of slaves
he would decide himself 25
that proud old man

i can see him now
chaining his mother to lee

—1996

C. K. Williams (b. 1936)

C. K. Williams received the 2000 Pulitzer Prize for Repair (1999). *Born in Newark, New Jersey, Charles Kenneth Williams studied at the University of Pennsylvania. His first book,* Lies, *appeared in 1969. Williams teaches creative writing at Princeton University and divides his time between New Jersey and Paris. Williams has published translations of Francis Ponge, Issa, and Sophocles. His own recent poems use long, discursive lines to explore the moral complexities of daily life.*

Hood

Remember me? I was the one
in high school you were always afraid of.
I kept cigarettes in my sleeve, wore
engineer's boots, long hair, my collar
up in back and there were always   5
girls with me in the hallways.

You were nothing. I had it in for you—
when I peeled rubber at the lights
you cringed like a teacher.
And when I crashed and broke both lungs   10
on the wheel, you were so relieved
that you stroked the hard Ford paint
like a breast and your hands shook.

—1969

Hooks

Possibly because she's already so striking—tall, well dressed, very
        clear, pure skin—
when the girl gets on the subway at Lafayette Street everyone notices
        her artificial hand
but we also manage, as we almost always do, not to be noticed
        noticing, except one sleeping woman,

who hasn't budged since Brooklyn but who lifts her head now, opens
     up, forgets herself,
and frankly stares at those intimidating twists of steel, the homely   5
     leather sock and laces,
so that the girl, as she comes through the door, has to do in turn now
     what is to be done,
which is to look down at it, too, a bit askance, with an air of tolerant,
     bemused annoyance,
the way someone would glance at their unruly, apparently ferocious
     but really quite friendly dog.

—1987

Harm

With his shopping cart, his bags of booty and his wine, I'd always
     found him inoffensive.
Every neighborhood has one or two these days; ours never rants at
     you at least or begs.

He just forages the trash all day, drinks and sings and shadowboxes,
     then at nightfall
finds a doorway to make camp, set out his battered little radio and
     slab of rotting foam.

The other day, though, as I was going by, he stepped abruptly out
     between parked cars,   5
undid his pants, and, not even bothering to squat, sputtered out a
     noxious, almost liquid stream.

There was that, and that his bony shanks and buttocks were already
     stained beyond redemption,
that his scarlet testicles were blown up bigger than a bull's with some
     sorrowful disease,

and that a slender adolescent girl from down the block happened by
     right then, and looked,
and looked away, and looked at me, and looked away again, and
     made me want to say to her,   10

because I imagined what she must have felt, It's not like this, really, it's
    not this,
but she was gone, so I could think, But isn't it like this, isn't this just
    what it is?

—1992

Susan Howe (b. 1937)

*Susan Howe has said of her work, "My poems always seem to be con-
cerned with history. No matter what I thought my original intentions were
that's where they go. The past is present when I write." Born in Boston,
she has published several collections of experimental poetry. Her books of
criticism include* My Emily Dickinson *(1985). Howe lives in Guilford,
Connecticut, and has taught at SUNY–Buffalo since 1989.*

Closed Fist Withholding an Open Palm

The great fleet of Unready
floats on the waves

concealed and exposed

all argonauts

soever sweeping   5

existing dwarf wall once a garden

belligerent

the redcoats land.

Immigrant ship
the hour is late   10

up from my cabin
my sea-gown scarfed around me in the dark

belly that will bear a child forward into battle

the hieratic night is violent and visible.

Who will bring some pardon?   15
pushed to the side of the crowd.

Trembling fathers futile in the emptiness of matter
howl "wilderness"

at the waste
a preliminary geste   20

leap for some spot where a foot may jump

and cease from falling.

Nothing else exists or nothing exists
coming to be

passing away   25

we go to sea
we build houses

sleep our last sleep in a land of strangers

troops of marble messengers move before our eyes

predecessors   30

at the vague dawn
where fusion was born

no time, no space, no motion

arrow itself an illusion

fuel to keep from freezing   35

a sunbeam touches
the austere hymn

of jeopardy

blown through gaps in our community
our lives were wind   40

the rigor of it
fleece of the lamb of God

torn off

Numerous singularities

slight stutter   45
a short letter

embrace at departure

body backward
in a tremendous forward direction

house and host   50

vanished.

—1996

Robert Phillips   (b. 1938)

Robert Phillips labored for over thirty years as a New York advertising executive, a remarkable fact when one considers his many books of poetry, fiction, and criticism, and the numerous books he has edited. Phillips obtained his undergraduate and graduate degrees in English and American literature from Syracuse University. He currently lives in Houston, teaches in the creative writing program at the University of Houston, and serves as poetry editor of the Texas Review *and as a councilor of the Texas Institute of Letters.*

Running on Empty

As a teenager I would drive Father's
Chevrolet cross-county, given me

reluctantly: "Always keep the tank
half full, boy, half full, ya hear?"

The fuel gauge dipping, dipping   5
toward Empty, hitting Empty, then

—thrilling!—'way below Empty,
myself driving cross-county

mile after mile, faster and faster,
all night long, this crazy kid driving   10

the earth's rolling surface,
against all laws, defying chemistry,

rules, and time, riding on nothing
but fumes, pushing luck harder

than anyone pushed before, the wind   15
screaming past like the Furies° . . .

I stranded myself only once, a white
night with no gas station open, ninety miles

from nowhere. Panicked for a while,
at standstill, myself stalled.   20

At dawn the car and I both refilled. But,
Father, I am running on empty still.

—*1981*

The Stone Crab: A Love Poem

> Joe's serves approximately 1,000 pounds of crab
> claws each day.
> —*Florida Gold Coast Leisure Guide*

Delicacy of warm Florida waters,
his body is undesirable. One giant claw
is his claim to fame, and we claim it,

more than once. Meat sweeter than lobster,
less dear than his life, when grown that claw   5
is lifted, broken off at the joint.

Mutilated, the crustacean is thrown back
into the water, back upon his own resources.
One of nature's rarities, he replaces

an entire appendage as you or I   10
grow a nail. (No one asks how he survives
that crabby sea with just one claw;

two-fisted menaces real as nightmares, ten-tentacled nights cold
as fright.) In time he grows another,   15

large, meaty, magnificent as the first.
And one astonished day, *snap!* it too
is twigged off, the cripple dropped

16 Furies in Greek mythology, deities who pursue and torment evildoers

back into treachery. Unlike a twig,
it sprouts again. How many losses   20
can he endure? Well,

his shell is hard, the sea is wide.
Something vital broken off, he doesn't
nurse the wound; develops something new.

—1994

Compartments

Which shall be final?
      Pine box in a concrete vault,
urn on a mantel?

Last breath a rattle,
      stuffed in a black body bag,   5
he's zipped head to toe.

At the nursing home,
      side drawn to prevent a fall—
in a crib again.

His dead wife's false teeth   10
      underfoot in their bedroom.
Feel the piercing chill.

Pink flamingo lawn,
      a Florida trailer park:
one space he'll avoid.   15

The box they gave him
      on retirement held a watch
that measures decades.

The new bifocals
      rest in their satin-lined case,   20
his body coffined.

Move to the suburbs.
      Crowded train at seven-oh-two,
empty head at night.

New playpen, new crib,
  can't compete with the newness
of the newborn child.   25

Oak four-poster bed
  inherited from family—
Jack Frost defrosted.   30

Once he was pink-slipped.
  Dad helped out: "A son's a son,
Son, from womb to tomb."

Fourteen-foot ceilings,
  parquet floors, marble fireplace, 35
proud first apartment.

The Jack Frost Motel,
  its very name a portent
for their honeymoon.

Backseat of a car,   40
  cursing the inventor of
nylon pantyhose.

First-job cubicle.
  Just how many years before
a window office?   45

College quad at noon,
  chapel bells, frat men, coeds,
no pocket money.

his grandfather's barn.
  After it burned to the ground, 50
the moon filled its space.

His favorite tree—
  the leaves return to branches?
No, butterflies light.

Closet where he hid   55
  to play with himself. None knew?
Mothball orgasms.

Chimney that he scaled
  naked to sweep for his Dad:
Blake's soot-black urchin.   60

The town's swimming pool
      instructor, throwing him in
again and again . . .

Kindergarten play
      ground: swings, slides, rings, jungle gym.   65
Scraped knees, molester.

Red, blue and green birds
      mobilize over his crib,
its sides a tall fence.

Two months premature,   70
      he incubates by light bulbs,
like a baby chick.

He is impatient,
      curled in foetal position,
floating in darkness.   75

—2000

Michael S. Harper (b. 1938)

Michael S. Harper listened as a child to his parents' off-limits record collection, and his poems often incorporate jazz rhythms. Born in Brooklyn, New York, to a postal worker father and a medical stenographer mother, Harper moved to Los Angeles in 1951. He studied at the City College of Los Angeles, California State University at Los Angeles, and the Iowa Writers' Workshop, where he lived in segregated housing and was the only black student in both his poetry and fiction classes. The author of many books of poetry and the editor of several anthologies of African-American poetry, Harper has taught at Brown University since 1970, and lives in Barrington, Rhode Island.

Black Study

No one's been told
that black men
went first to the moon
the dark side

for dark brothers 5
without space ship
gravity complex
in our computer centers
government campuses
instant play and replay 10
white mice and pig-guineas
in concentric digital rows.

Someone has been
pulling brother's curls
into fancy barbed wire, 15
measuring his forelegs,
caressing his dense innards
into formaldehyde
pruning the jellied marrow:
a certain formula is appearing: 20
someone has been studying you.

—*1970*

Dear John, Dear Coltrane°

a love supreme, a love supreme°
a love supreme, a love supreme

Sex fingers toes
in the marketplace
near your father's church
in Hamlet, North Carolina—
witness to this love 5
in this calm fallow
of these minds,
there is no substitute for pain:
genitals gone or going,
seed burned out, 10
you tuck the roots in the earth,
turn back, and move

Coltrane John Coltrane (1926–1967), jazz saxophone player   **a love supreme** title of Coltrane album

by river through the swamps,
singing: *a love supreme, a love supreme*;
what does it all mean?   15
Loss, so great each black
woman expects your failure
in mute change, the seed gone.
You plod up into the electric city—
your song now crystal and   20
the blues. You pick up the horn
with some will and blow
into the freezing night:
a love supreme, a love supreme—

Dawn comes and you cook   25
up the thick sin 'tween
impotence and death, fuel
the tenor sax cannibal
heart, genitals, and sweat
that makes you clean—   30
a love supreme, a love supreme—

Why you so black?
cause I am
why you so funky?
cause I am   35
why you so black?
cause I am
why you so sweet?
cause I am
why you so black?   40
cause I am
a love supreme, a love supreme:

So sick
you couldn't play *Naima*,°
so flat we ached   45
for song you'd concealed
with your own blood,
your diseased liver gave
out its purity,

45 **Naima** a Coltrane composition

the inflated heart   50
pumps out, the tenor kiss,
tenor love:
a love supreme, a love supreme—
a love supreme, a love supreme—

—*1970*

We Assume: On the Death of Our Son, Reuben Masai Harper

We assume
that in twenty-eight hours,
lived in a collapsible isolette,°
you learned to accept pure oxygen
as the natural sky;   5
the scant shallow breaths
that filled those hours
cannot, did not make you fly—
but dreams were there
like crooked palmprints on   10
the twin-thick windows of the nursery—
in the glands of your mother.

We assume
the sterile hands
drank chemicals in and out   15
from lungs opaque with mucus,
pumped your stomach,
eeked the bicarbonate in
crooked, green-winged veins,
out in a plastic mask;   20

A woman who'd lost her first son
consoled us with an angel gone ahead
to pray for our family—
gone into that sky

3 **isolette** incubator

seeking oxygen,   25
gone into autopsy,
a fine brown powdered sugar,
a disposable cremation:

We assume
you did not know we loved you.   30

—2000

Charles Simic (b. 1938)

Charles Simic was born in Belgrade, Yugoslavia, and came with his parents to Chicago in 1949. Educated at New York University, he began publishing poetry at the age of twenty-one. Simic was drafted into the U.S. Army in 1961. Since the publication of his first full-length collection of poems, What the Grass Says *(1967), Simic has written over sixty books.* The World Doesn't End, *a collection of prose poems, won the Pulitzer Prize in 1990. He also has received fellowships from the Guggenheim and MacArthur foundations. Claiming influences as diverse as Emily Dickinson, the Surrealists, Pablo Neruda, and Fats Waller, Simic has taught English at the University of New Hampshire since 1973.*

Fork

This strange thing must have crept
Right out of hell.
It resembles a bird's foot
Worn around the cannibal's neck.

As you hold it in your hand,   5
As you stab with it into a piece of meat,
It is possible to imagine the rest of the bird:
Its head which like your fist
Is large, bald, beakless, and blind.

—1971

Stone

Go inside a stone
That would be my way.
Let somebody else become a dove
Or gnash with a tiger's tooth.
I am happy to be a stone.   5

From the outside the stone is a riddle:
No one knows how to answer it.
Yet within, it must be cool and quiet
Even though a cow steps on it full weight,
Even though a child throws it in a river;   10
The stone sinks, slow, unperturbed
To the river bottom
Where the fishes come to knock on it
And listen.

I have seen sparks fly out   15
When two stones are rubbed,
So perhaps it is not dark inside after all;
Perhaps there is a moon shining
From somewhere, as though behind a hill—
Just enough light to make out   20
The strange writings, the star charts
On the inner walls.

—1971

I was stolen . . .

I was stolen by the gypsies. My parents stole
me right back. Then the gypsies stole me again.
This went on for some time. One minute I was
in the caravan suckling the dark teat of my new
mother, the next I sat at the long dining room table   5
eating my breakfast with a silver spoon.

It was the first day of spring. One of my

fathers was singing in the bathtub; the other one
was painting a live sparrow the colors of a tropical
bird.   10

—*1989*

Betty Adcock (b. 1938)

*Betty Adcock was born in San Augustine, Texas. She has lived for many
years in Raleigh, North Carolina, where she is poet-in-residence at Meredith College. The author of five books of poetry, she received both the
Texas Institute of Letters Prize for Poetry and the North Carolina Award
for Literature in 1996. Her volume of selected poems,* Intervale, *appeared
in 2001 and won the Poets' Prize.*

Digression on the Nuclear Age

In some difficult part of Africa, a termite tribe
builds elaborate tenements that might be called
cathedrals, were they for anything so terminal
as Milton's° God. Who was it said
the perfect arch will always separate   5
the civilized from the not? Never mind.
These creatures are quite blind and soft
and hard at labor chemically induced.
Beginning with a dish-like hollow, groups
of workers pile up earthen pellets.   10
A few such piles will reach a certain height;
fewer still, a just proximity.
That's when direction changes, or a change
directs: the correct two bands of laborers
will make their towers bow toward each other.   15
Like saved and savior, they will meet in air.

---

4 Milton's John Milton (1608–1674), author of *Paradise Lost*, an epic poem retelling the biblical
story of Adam and Eve

It is unambiguously an arch and it will serve,
among the others rising and the waste,
an arch's purposes. Experts are sure
a specific moment comes when the very structure   20
triggers the response that will perfect it.

I've got this far and don't know what
termites can be made to mean. Or this poem:
a joke, a play on arrogance, nothing
but language? Untranslated, the world gets on   25
with dark, flawless constructions rising,
rising even where we think we are. And think
how we must hope convergences will fail this time,
that whatever it is we're working on won't work.

                                          —1988

To a Young Feminist Who Wants to Be Free

You describe your grandmothers walking straight
off the boats from Finland, Latvia
too late, early in this century, to bear blame
for sins we're bound to expiate:
in their funny hats, a potato in each pocket,   5
what possible American shame
could they hand down to me? You have your own
angers, you say. So much for the nineteenth
century's slavery, lynchings, native massacre, and the teeth
of cities still gnawing off the feet of survivors,   10
those gigantic traps still set.
You blame the men and free yourself of time
and fathers, displaced from more
than countries lost. Or never claimed.

I can't help thinking of the miserably hot summer   15
I taught in Michigan, where a July Fourth

was the whole *treasury of virtue*° hammered home
in speeches praising Michigan and the lever of the war
that undid slavery and joined the union back.
Yet that whole campus was the record of a severing: 20
not one face in any class was black.
And only a few miles distant, our Detroit
was roiling and afire.
The students laughed at my slow southern accent,
joked that I'd brought the unaccustomed heat.   25

Perhaps I know too much, living as I must
with the lives (in letters) of great- and twice-great-
grandmothers,
southern women talking about their slaves
as if it were ordinary. It was. Sometimes the wills are there: 30
whole black families listed with the mules. It's terrible enough
to die about, and people did: the saviors and the guilty
and the simple poor. Never believe it's gone.
The stain is mine and I can't pass it anywhere but on,
and to my own. I live with what the past will not stop   35
proffering. I think it makes me wiser than you are,
who measure by the careful inch your accident
of time here and your innocence.
It lets you be only the victim,
lets you find the gold-   40
eyed goat still waiting in the bushes
to be bled.

Anyone who came here anytime
came here to take this country's gifts.
Not even you may refuse this one: 45
what's built on darkness rests on it.
And there is wisdom yet, though hard to see
in this peculiar light. It is the only light
we've got. And when was it *not* the case
(except in hell) that land and history   50
wear another's face?
Here is the necessary, fearsome, precious,
backward whole embrace.

—1995

17 *treasury of virtue* since the Civil War, the north's sense of itself as morally superior to the south

Voyages

We were five girls prowling alleyways behind the houses,
having skipped math class for any and no reason.
Equipped with too many camelhair coats, too many cashmeres,
we were privileged and sure and dumb, isolated
without knowing it, smug in our small crime, playing   5
hooky from Miss Hockaday's Boarding School for young ladies.
Looking for anything that wouldn't be boring
as we defined that, we'd gone off exploring the going-downhill
neighborhoods around our tight Victorian schoolgrounds.
The houses were fronted with concrete porches,   10
venetian blinds drawn tight against the sun.

Somebody had told us an eccentric lived where one
back fence got strangely high and something stuck over
the top. We didn't care what it was, but we went anyway,
giggling with hope for the freakish: bodies stashed and decaying,   15
a madwoman pulling her hair, maybe a maniac in a cage.
Anything sufficiently awful would have done.

But when we came close enough to look through
the inch of space between two badly placed fenceboards,
we saw only the ordinary, grown grotesque and huge: 20
somebody was building a sailboat bigger than most city backyards,
bigger almost than the house it belonged to,
mast towering high in a brass-and-blue afternoon.
This was in the middle of Dallas, Texas—
the middle of the 1950s, which had us   25
(though we didn't yet know this) by the throat.
Here was a backyard entirely full of boat,
out of scale, out of the Bible, maybe out of a movie,
all rescue and ornament. It looked to be something between
a galleon and a Viking ship, larger than we could imagine   30
in such a space, with sails and riggings and a face on the prow
(about which we made much but which neither smiled nor frowned).
Gasping, overplaying the scene, we guessed at the kind
of old fool who would give a lifetime to building this thing.
Then one of us asked for a light for a cigarette   35
and we all knew how easy it would be to swipe

a newspaper, light it, and toss it onto the deck
of that great wooden landlocked ark, watch it go up.

But of course we didn't do it and nobody of course came out
of that house and we of course went back   40
in time for English and to sneak out of P.E. later
for hamburgers at Mitch's, where the blue-collar boys
leaned in their ducktails against the bar.

But before we did that, we stood for a while clumped
and smoking, pushed into silence by palpable obsession   45
where it sat as if it belonged on parched Dallas grass,
a stunned, unfinished restlessness.

And didn't the ground just then, under our penny-
loafers, give the tiniest heave? Didn't we feel how thin
the grass was, like a coat of light paint, like green ice   50
over something unmanageable? How thin the sun
became for a minute, the rest of our future dimming
and wavy and vast, even tomorrow's pop quiz and softball practice—

as if all around us were depths we really could drown in.

—1995

Jared Carter (b. 1939)

Jared Carter received the 1980 Walt Whitman Award for his first collection, Work, for the Night is Coming, *published when its author was forty-two. Chosen by Galway Kinnell, the volume collects poems set in fictional Mississinewa County, in rural Indiana, and is noteworthy for its focus and maturity. Carter's second book,* After the Rain, *was awarded the Poets' Prize for 1995.* Les Barricades Mysterieuses *(1999), Carter's third volume, is composed of thirty-two villanelles. Carter has received grants from the National Endowment for the Arts and the John Simon Guggenheim Memorial Foundation. Originally from Elwood, Indiana, Carter studied at Goddard College and Yale University. He lives in Indianapolis.*

Drawing the Antique

> The Victoria and Albert° . . . still displays its great
> collection of casts. American art museums destroyed
> theirs—the Chicago Art Institute did so, I believe, in
> the 1950s—or, as in the case of the Metropolitan
> Museum of Art, has them in storage in a highway
> viaduct. . . .
>
> > Henry Hope Reed, *letter to the* New York
> > Review of Books, *17 August 1989.*

On the third floor of the old high school—
up a stairway fenced off in the late sixties
due to rising costs and squabbles over turf—
through an iron gate, with the principal's key,
down a barrel-vaulted hallway, along doors   5
nailed shut now, past rows of display cases
displaying nothing—
                    after turning a corner
in our explorations, we come face to face
with three life-sized plaster casts acquired   10
when the local art league put them up for grabs
back during the fifties.

The Victoria and Albert museum in London

          Copies of copies,
on pedestals, their dim, dust-mantled features
glossy in places, luminous in the bleak light: 15
a Venus of some forgotten school, nipples
rubbed smooth, pudenda hammered and dented;
a wounded gladiator, fallen, overwhelmed
by marking-pencil swastikas; a statesman,
uplifted hand corroded, structural wires   20
bleeding through.
                    They wait here, faces battered,
noses chipped away, lips stained yellow where
countless cigarette butts, moistened with spit,
were carefully stuck.   25
                    Left in this dark place,
they become more like their lost originals,
true to some idea we can barely imagine now.
Yet we are shocked, we know them instantly—
recognizable as victims everywhere, shapes   30
destroyed and timeless,
                    still able to instruct.

                                                        —1993

Interview

Now this here rag is the one they used to call
the lost rag.

Sort of thing everybody knew and nobody ever bothered
to write down.

It was just a few licks, something you'd sit and play
by yourself,   5

when there was nobody else around. Maybe it was
some old man

showed you how to play it, a long time ago. You turn off
that machine,   10

I'm going to play it for you now. I said
turn it off.

—1993

The Purpose of Poetry

This old man grazed thirty head of cattle
in a valley just north of the covered bridge
on the Mississinewa,° where the reservoir
stands today. Had a black border collie
and a half-breed sheep dog with one eye.   5
The dogs took the cows to pasture each morning
and brought them home again at night
and herded them into the barn. The old man
would slip a wooden bar across both doors.
One dog slept on the front porch, one on the back.   10

He was waiting there one evening
listening to the animals coming home
when a man from the courthouse stopped
to tell him how the new reservoir
was going to flood all his property.   15
They both knew he was too far up in years
to farm anywhere else. He had a daughter
who lived in Florida, in a trailer park.
He should sell now and go stay with her.
The man helped bar the doors before he left.   20

He had only known dirt under his fingernails
and trips to town on Saturday mornings
since he was a boy. Always he had been around
cattle, and trees, and land near the river.
Evenings by the barn he could hear the dogs   25
talking to each other as they brought in
the herd; and the cows answering them.
It was the clearest thing he knew. That night

---

3 **Mississinewa** river that runs from Ohio to the Wabash river in Indiana

he shot both dogs and then himself.
The purpose of poetry is to tell us about life.   30

—*1993*

Ted Kooser (b. 1939)

Ted Kooser, who lives in Nebraska, writes plainspoken poems about life in America's heartland. Born in Iowa, Kooser studied at Iowa State University and the University of Nebraska. His poetry collections include Winter Morning Walks: One Hundred Postcards to Jim Harrison, *which was written during Kooser's recovery from cancer surgery and radiation treatment. It received the 2001 Nebraska Book Award for poetry. Kooser is editor and publisher of Windflower Press, a small press specializing in contemporary poetry. A retired vice president of Lincoln Benefit Life, an insurance company, Kooser teaches at the University of Nebraska, Lincoln. In 2004, Kooser was appointed U.S. Poet Laureate.*

Abandoned Farmhouse

He was a big man, says the size of his shoes
on a pile of broken dishes by the house;
a tall man too, says the length of the bed
in an upstairs room; and a good, God-fearing man,
says the Bible with a broken back   5
on the floor below the window, dusty with sun;
but not a man for farming, say the fields
cluttered with boulders and the leaky barn.

A woman lived with him, says the bedroom wall
papered with lilacs and the kitchen shelves   10
covered with oilcloth, and they had a child,
says the sandbox made from a tractor tire.
Money was scarce, say the jars of plum preserves
and canned tomatoes sealed in the cellar hole.
And the winters cold, say the rags in the window frames.   15
It was lonely here, says the narrow country road.

Something went wrong, says the empty house
in the weed-choked yard. Stones in the fields

say he was not a farmer; the still-sealed jars
in the cellar say she left in a nervous haste.   20
And the child? Its toys are strewn in the yard
like branches after a storm—a rubber cow,
a rusty tractor with a broken plow,
a doll in overalls. Something went wrong, they say.

—1980

The Salesman

Today he's wearing his vinyl shoes,
shiny and white as little Karmann Ghias°
fresh from the body shop, and as he moves
in his door-to-door glide, these shoes fly round
each other, honking the horns of their soles.   5
His hose are black and ribbed and tight, as thin
as an old umbrella or the wing of a bat.
(They leave a pucker when he pulls them off.)
He's got on his double-knit leisure suit
in a pond-scum green, with a tight white belt   10
that matches his shoes but suffers with cracks
at the golden buckle. His shirt is brown
and green, like a pile of leaves, and it opens
onto the neck at a Brillo pad
of graying hair which tosses a cross and chain   15
as he walks. The collar is splayed out over
the jacket's lapels yet leaves a lodge pin
taking the sun like a silver spike.
He's swinging a briefcase full of the things
of this world, a leather cornucopia   20
heavy with promise. Through those dark lenses,
each of the doors along your sunny street
looks slightly ajar, and in your quiet house
the dog of your willpower cowers and growls,
then crawls in under the basement steps,   25
making the jingle of coin with its tags.

—1980

2 **Karmann Ghias** a sporty Volkswagen model popular in the 1960s and 70s

Selecting a Reader

First, I would have her be beautiful,
and walking carefully up on my poetry
at the loneliest moment of an afternoon,
her hair still damp at the neck
from washing it. She should be wearing   5
a raincoat, an old one, dirty
from not having money enough for the cleaners.
She will take out her glasses, and there
in the bookstore, she will thumb
over my poems, then put the book back   10
up on its shelf. She will say to herself,
"For that kind of money, I can get
my raincoat cleaned." And she will.

—*1980*

Stephen Dunn (b. 1939)

*Stephen Dunn writes poems that blend ordinary experience with larger
significance, as illustrated in the duality of his book titles like* Full of Lust
and Good Usage *(1976),* Work and Love *(1981), and* Between Angels
*(1989). Born in New York City, Dunn is a graduate of the creative writing
program at Syracuse University. He has played professional basketball and
has been an advertising copywriter and an editor, as well as a professor of
creative writing, most recently at The Richard Stockton College of New
Jersey in Pomona, New Jersey. His book* Different Hours *(2000) won the
2001 Pulitzer Prize.*

The Sacred

After the teacher asked if anyone had
          a sacred place
and the students fidgeted and shrank

in their chairs, the most serious of them all
          said it was his car,   5
being in it alone, his tape deck playing

things he'd chosen, and others knew the truth
      had been spoken
and began speaking about their rooms,

their hiding places, but the car kept coming up,   10
      the car in motion,
music filling it, and sometimes one other person

who understood the bright altar of the dashboard
      and how far away
a car could take him from the need   15

to speak, or to answer, the key
      in having a key
and putting it in, and going.

—1989

A Secret Life

Why you need to have one
is not much more mysterious than
why you don't say what you think
at the birth of an ugly baby.
Or, you've just made love   5
and feel you'd rather have been
in a dark booth where your partner
was nodding, whispering yes, yes,
you're brilliant. The secret life
begins early, is kept alive   10
by all that's unpopular
in you, all that you know
a Baptist, say, or some other
accountant would object to.
It becomes what you'd most protect   15
if the government said you can protect
one thing, all else is ours.
When you write late at night
it's like a small fire
in a clearing, it's what   20
radiates and what can hurt
if you get too close to it.

It's why your silence is a kind of truth.
Even when you speak to your best friend,
the one who'll never betray you,   25
you always leave out one thing;
a secret life is that important.

—1991

The Sexual Revolution

In that time of great freedom to touch
        and get in touch,
we lived on the prairie amid polite

moral certainty. The sensate world seemed
        elsewhere, and was.   5
On our color television the president's body

admitted he was lying. There was marching
        in the suddenly charged streets,
and what a girl in a headband and miniskirt

called *communication*. A faraway friend wrote   10
        to say the erotic life
was the only life. Get with it, he said.

But many must have been slow-witted
        during The Age of Enlightenment,
led artless lives during The Golden Age.   15

We watched the revolution on the evening news.
        It was 1972
when the sixties reached all the way

to where we were. The air became alive
        with incense and license.   20
The stores sold permission and I bought

and my wife bought until we were left
        with almost nothing.
Even the prairie itself changed;

people began to call it the Land, and once again   25
   it was impossibly green
and stretched endlessly ahead of us.

—*2000*

Tom Disch (b. 1940)

Tom Disch is a science fiction writer, author of interactive computer fiction, resident critic for magazines as diverse as Playboy *and* The Nation, *and possibly the most brilliant satirist in contemporary American poetry.* Yes, Let's, *a collection of his selected poems, appeared in 1989. Born in Des Moines, Iowa, Disch moved to New York City after high school and held a wide variety of jobs including extra at the Metropolitan Opera, bookstore clerk, journalist, insurance claims adjuster, bank teller, and mortuary attendant. His children's book,* The Brave Little Toaster *(1986), was made into a feature-length cartoon by Disney.*

The Rapist's Villanelle

She spent her money with such perfect style
The clerks would gasp at each new thing she'd choose.
I couldn't help myself: I had to smile

Or burst. Her slender purse was crocodile,
Her blouse was from Bendel's,° as were her shoes.   5
She spent her money with such perfect style!

I loved her so! She shopped—and all the while
My soul that bustling image would perfuse.
I couldn't help myself: I had to smile

At her hand-knitted sweater from the Isle   10
Of Skye, at après-skis° of bold chartreuse.
She spent her money with such perfect style.

Enchanted by her, mile on weary mile
I tracked my darling down the avenues.
I couldn't help myself. I had to smile   15

5 **Bendel's** upscale department store   11 **après-ski** outfits to be worn after skiing

At how she never once surmised my guile.
My heart was hers—I'd nothing else to lose.
She spent her money with such perfect style
I couldn't help myself. I had to smile.

—1981

Zewhyexary

Z is the Zenith from which we decline,
While Y is your Yelp as you're twisting your spine.
X is for Xmas; the alternative
Is an X-ray that gives you just one year to live.
So three cheers for Santa, and onward to W.   5
W's Worry, but don't let it trouble you:
W easily might have been Worse.
V, unavoidably, has to be Verse.
U is Uncertainty. T is a Trial
At which every objection is met with denial.   10
S is a Sentence of "Guilty as Charged."
R is a Russian whose nose is enlarged
By inveterate drinking, while Q is the Quiet
That falls on a neighborhood after a riot.
P is a Pauper with nary a hope   15
Of lining his pockets or learning to cope.
O is an Organ transplanted in vain,
While N is the Number of "Enemies Slain":
Three thousand three hundred and seventy-three.
If no one else wants it, could M be for Me?   20
No, M is reserved for a mad Millionaire,
And L is his Likewise, and goes to his heir.
K is a Kick in the seat of your pants,
And J is the Jury whose gross ignorance
Guaranteed the debacle referred to above.   25
I's the Inevitability of
Continued inflation and runaway crime,
So draw out your savings and have a good time.
H is your Heart at the moment it breaks,
And G is the Guile it initially takes   30

To pretend to believe that it someday will heal.
F is the strange Fascination we feel
For whatever's Evil—Yes, Evil is E—
And D is our Dread at the sight of a C,
Which is Corpse, as you've surely foreseen. B is Bone.   35
A could be anything. A is unknown.

—1981

Ballade of the New God

I have decided I'm divine.
Caligula and Nero° knew
A godliness akin to mine,
But they are strictly hitherto.
They're dead, and what can dead gods do?   5
I'm here and now. I'm dynamite.
I'd worship me if I were you.
A new religion starts tonight!

No booze, no pot, no sex, no swine:
I have decreed them all taboo.   10
My words will be your only wine,
The thought of me your honeydew.
All other thoughts you will eschew
And call yourself a Thomasite
And hymn my praise with loud yahoo.   15
A new religion starts tonight.

But (you might think) that's asinine!
I'm just as much a god as you.
You may have built yourself a shrine
But I won't bend my knee. Who   20
Asked you to be my god? I do,
Who am, as god, divinely right.
Now you must join my retinue:
A new religion starts tonight.

2 **Caligula and Nero** Roman emperors

All that I have said is true.   25
I'm god and you're my acolyte.
Surrender's bliss: I envy you
A new religion starts tonight.

—*1995*

Pattiann Rogers (b. 1940)

*Pattiann Rogers is the foremost naturalist among contemporary American
poets. Her poems resound with the rich names of unfamiliar species of
plants and animals, most of which she seems to know on intimate terms.
Rogers has published eleven books, including* Song of the World Becoming: New and Collected Poems, 1981–2001. *Born in Joplin, Missouri, she
studied at the University of Missouri and the University of Houston, and
has taught at a number of schools, including Washington University of
St. Louis and the University of Montana. Her many awards include a
Guggenheim fellowship and a poetry fellowship from the Lannan Foundation. The mother of two sons, Rogers lives in Colorado with her husband,
a retired geophysicist.*

Discovering Your Subject

Painting a picture of the same shrimp boat
Every day of your life might not be so boring.
For a while you could paint only in the mornings,
Each one different, the boat gold in the new sun
On your left, or the boat in predawn fog condensing   5
Mist. You might have to wait years, rising early
Over and over, to catch that one winter morning when frost
Becomes a boat. You could attempt to capture
The fragile potential inherent in that event.

You might want to depict the easy half-circle   10
Movements of the boat's shadows crossing over themselves
Through the day. You could examine every line
At every moment—the tangle of nets caught
In the orange turning of evening, the drape of the ropes
Over the rising moon.   15

You could spend considerable time just concentrating
On boat and birds—Boat with Birds Perched on Bow,

Boat with Birds Overhead, Shadows of Birds Covering
Hull and Deck, or Boat the Size of a Bird,
Bird in the Heart of the Boat, Boat with Wings,   20
Boat in Flight. Any endeavor pursued long enough
Assumes a momentum and direction all its own.

Or you might decide to lie down one day behind a clump
Of marsh rosemary on the beach, to see the boat embedded
In the blades of the saltwort or show how strangely   25
The stalk of the clotbur can rise higher than the mast.
Boat Caught like a Flower in the Crotch of the Sand Verbena.

After picturing the boat among stars, after discovering
The boat as revealed by rain, you might try painting
The boat in the eye of the gull or the boat in the eye   30
Of the sun or the boat in the eye of a storm
Or the eye trapped in the window of the boat.
You could begin a series of self-portraits—The Boat
In the Eye of the Remorseful Painter, The Boat in the Eye
Of the Blissful Painter, The Boat in the Eye of the Blind Painter,   35
The Boat in the Lazy Painter Forgetting His Eye.

Finally one day when the boat's lines are drawn in completely,
It will begin to move away, gradually changing its size,
Enlarging the ocean, requiring less sky, and suddenly it might
       seem
That you are the one moving. You are the one altering space,   40
Gliding easily over rough surfaces toward the mark
Between the ocean and the sky. You might see clearly,
For the first time, the boat inside the painter inside the boat
Inside the eye watching the painter moving beyond himself.
You must remember for us the exact color and design of that.   45

—1986

Foreplay

When it first begins, as you might expect,
the lips and thin folds are closed, the pouting
layers pressed, lapped lightly,
almost languidly, against one another
in a sealed bud.   5

However, with certain prolonged
and random strokings of care
along each binding line, with soft
intrusions traced beneath each pursed
gathering and edge, with inquiring   10
intensities of gesture—as the sun
swinging slowly from winter back
to spring, touches briefly,
between moments of moon and masking
clouds, certain stunning points   15
and inner nubs of earth—so
with such ministrations, a slight
swelling, a quiver of reaching,
a tendency toward space,
might be noticed to commence.   20

Then with dampness from the dark,
with moisture from the falling
night of morning, from hidden places
within the hills, each seal begins
to loosen, each recalcitrant clasp   25
sinks away into itself, and every tucked
grasp, every silk tack willingly relents,
releases, gives way, proclaims a turning,
declares a revolution, assumes,
in plain sight, a surging position   30
that offers, an audacious offering
that beseeches, every petal parted wide.

Remember the spiraling, blue
valerian, remember the violet, sucking
larkspur, the laurel and rosebay   35
and pea cockle flung backwards, remember
the fragrant, funnelling lily, the lifted
honeysuckle, the sweet, open pucker
of the ground ivy blossom?

Now even the darkest crease possessed,   40
the most guarded, pulsing, least drop
of pearl bead, moon grain trembling
deep within is fully revealed, fully exposed
to any penetrating wind or shaking fur

or mad hunger or searing, plunging surprise   45
the wild descending sky in delirium
has to offer.

—*1994*

Robert Pinsky (b. 1940)

*Robert Pinsky was named United States Poet Laureate in 1997, and
served an unprecedented three terms in that position. To underscore his
belief that poetry is an auditory, even bodily art, Pinsky created the Favorite Poem Project. His original plan was to make audio recordings of
Americans reading their favorite poems, but the call for submissions garnered 18,000 responses, and the project grew to include live readings
across the United States and a series of short audio and video recordings.
Born in Long Branch, New Jersey, Pinsky has received the Lenore Marshall Prize and the William Carlos Williams Prize for his own poetry. A
professor of creative writing and English at Boston University, he lives in
Newton Corner, Massachusetts.*

Shirt

The back, the yoke, the yardage. Lapped seams,
The nearly invisible stitches along the collar
Turned in a sweatshop by Koreans or Malaysians

Gossiping over tea and noodles on their break
Or talking money or politics while one fitted   5
This armpiece with its overseam to the band

Of cuff I button at my wrist. The presser, the cutter,
The wringer, the mangle. The needle, the union,
The treadle, the bobbin. The code. The infamous blaze

At the Triangle Factory in nineteen-eleven.   10
One hundred and forty-six died in the flames
On the ninth floor, no hydrants, no fire escapes—

The witness in a building across the street
Who watched how a young man helped a girl to step
Up to the windowsill, then held her out   15

Away from the masonry wall and let her drop.
And then another. As if he were helping them up
To enter a streetcar, and not eternity.

A third before he dropped her put her arms
Around his neck and kissed him. Then he held   20
Her into space, and dropped her. Almost at once

He stepped to the sill himself, his jacket flared
And fluttered up from his shirt as he came down,
Air filling up the legs of his gray trousers—

Like Hart Crane's Bedlamite,° "shrill shirt ballooning."   25
Wonderful how the pattern matches perfectly
Across the placket and over the twin bar-tacked

Corners of both pockets, like a strict rhyme
Or a major chord. Prints, plaids, checks,
Houndstooth, Tattersall, Madras. The clan tartans   30

Invented by mill-owners inspired by the hoax of Ossian,°
To control their savage Scottish workers, tamed
By a fabricated heraldry: MacGregor,

Bailey, MacMartin.° The kilt, devised for workers
To wear among the dusty clattering looms.   35
Weavers, carders, spinners. The loader,

The docker, the navvy. The planter, the picker, the sorter
Sweating at her machine in a litter of cotton
As slaves in calico headrags sweated in fields:

George Herbert,° your descendant is a Black   40
Lady in South Carolina, her name is Irma
And she inspected my shirt. Its color and fit

And feel and its clean smell have satisfied
Both her and me. We have culled its cost and quality
Down to the buttons of simulated bone,   45

---

25 Hart Crane's Bedlamite In "To Brooklyn Bridge" by Hart Crane (1899–1932), an American poet. A bedlamite is a lunatic; the next phrase is a quote from the poem   **31 Ossian** in the 1760s, the Scottish poet James Macpherson falsely claimed to have translated fragments of an ancient epic written by "Ossian, the Son of Fingal"   **33 MacGregor, Bailey, MacMartin** Scottish clans
40 George Herbert British poet (1593–1633)

The buttonholes, the sizing, the facing, the characters
Printed in black on neckband and tail. The shape,
The label, the labor, the color, the shade. The shirt.

—1990

The Want Bone

The tongue of the waves tolled in the earth's bell.
Blue rippled and soaked in the fire of blue.
The dried mouthbones of a shark in the hot swale
Gaped on nothing but sand on either side.

The bone tasted of nothing and smelled of nothing,   5
A scalded toothless harp, uncrushed, unstrung.
The joined arcs made the shape of birth and craving
And the welded-open shape kept mouthing O.

Ossified cords held the corners together
In groined spirals pleated like a summer dress.   10
But where was the limber grin, the gash of pleasure?
Infinitesimal mouths bore it away.

The beach scrubbed and etched and pickled it clean.
But O I love you it sings, my little my country
My food my parent my child I want you my own   15
My flower my fin my life my lightness my O.

—1990

ABC

Any body can die, evidently. Few
Go happily, irradiating joy,

Knowledge, love. Most
Need oblivion, painkillers,
Quickest respite.   5

Sweet time unafflicted,
Various world:

X = your zenith.

—2000

Peter Makuck (b. 1940)

Peter Makuck has published five poetry collections: Where We Live
(1982), Pilgrims *(1987),* The Sunken Lightship *(1990),* Shorelines *(1995),*
and Against Distance *(1997), and two story collections,* Breaking and Entering *(1981) and* Costly Habits *(2000). He has also coedited a book of essays on the Welsh poet Leslie Norris. Makuck has edited the journal* Tar
River Poetry *since 1976, and teaches at East Carolina University. He lives
in Pine Knoll Shores, North Carolina.*

Catsail°

Out on the edge
between ocean and a sky
that swallows light
    red, yellow, and green,
bright as a foreign flag,   5
it catches the wind
and something inside
about color,
the secret of difference,
how it changes   10
what we are,
makes us feel
we could walk out
on that watery sunpath
into another country   15
where, like children,
we would do little but
play with the quiet
and learn our colors again.

—1997

Catsail a small sailing catamaran

Leaning Against the Bar at Wrong-way Corrigan's in Greenville, North Carolina

after James Wright

Over my head, I see the green toucan,
taunted into squawking, "Go for it!"
by a red-faced juicer with jesus hair and a pool cue.
Down two smoky stairs by the jukebox
pool balls follow one another   5
from the table's green field into long dark tunnels.
To my right,
on her bare shoulder, behind a scrim
of long bleached hair, a tattooed butterfly,
the color of crankcase oil, sleeps on and on.   10
I lean back, as the late news comes on overhead.
A drunk staggers out the door, blind for home.
I have wasted my cash.

—1997

Robert Hass (b. 1941)

Robert Hass is known for subtle meditative lyrics that often reveal Asian influences. Born in San Francisco and raised in San Rafael, California, he teaches at the University of California at Berkeley. His first book, Field Guide, *was chosen by Stanley Kunitz for the Yale Series of Younger Poets in 1973. Hass, who studied at St. Mary's College in Moraga, California, and at Stanford University, has received a MacArthur fellowship and two National Book Critics Circle Awards. Recently, he has collaborated with Nobel Prize winner Czeslaw Milosz on English translations of the latter's poetry. He served as U.S. Poet Laureate from 1995 to 1997 and used the position to fight illiteracy and promote ecological awareness.*

Meditation at Lagunitas°

All the new thinking is about loss.
In this it resembles all the old thinking.
The idea, for example, that each particular erases
the luminous clarity of a general idea. That the clown-
faced woodpecker probing the dead sculpted trunk   5
of that black birch is, by his presence,
some tragic falling off from a first world
of undivided light. Or the other notion that,
because there is in this world no one thing
to which the bramble of *blackberry* corresponds,   10
a word is elegy to what it signifies.
We talked about it late last night and in the voice
of my friend, there was a thin wire of grief, a tone
almost querulous. After a while I understood that,
talking this way, everything dissolves: *justice,*   15
pine, hair, woman, you and *I.* There was a woman
I made love to and I remembered how, holding
her small shoulders in my hands sometimes,
I felt a violent wonder at her presence
like a thirst for salt, for my childhood river   20
with its island willows, silly music from the pleasure boat,
muddy places where we caught the little orange-silver fish
called *pumpkinseed.* It hardly had to do with her.

Lagunitas in California

Longing, we say, because desire is full
of endless distances. I must have been the same to her.   25
But I remember so much, the way her hands dismantled bread,
the thing her father said that hurt her, what
she dreamed. There are moments when the body is as numinous
as words, days that are the good flesh continuing.
Such tenderness, those afternoons and evenings,   30
saying *blackberry, blackberry, blackberry.*

—*1979*

A Story About the Body

The young composer, working that summer at an artist's colony,
had watched her for a week. She was Japanese, a painter, almost
sixty, and he thought he was in love with her. He loved her work,
and her work was like the way she moved her body, used her hands,
looked at him directly when she made amused and considered an-   5
swers to his questions. One night, walking back from a concert,
they came to her door and she turned to him and said, "I think you
would like to have me. I would like that too, but I must tell you that
I have had a double mastectomy," and when he didn't understand,
"I've lost both my breasts." The radiance that he had carried   10
around in his belly and chest cavity—like music—withered very
quickly, and he made himself look at her when he said, "I'm sorry. I
don't think I could." He walked back to his own cabin through the
pines, and in the morning he found a small blue bowl on the porch
outside his door. It looked to be full of rose petals, but he found   15
when he picked it up that the rose petals were on top; the rest of the
bowl—she must have swept them from the corners of her studio—
was full of dead bees.

—*1989*

Forty Something

She says to him, musing, "If you ever leave me,
and marry a younger woman and have another baby,
I'll put a knife in your heart." They are in bed,
so she climbs onto his chest, and looks directly
down into his eyes. "You understand? Your heart."   5

—1996

Billy Collins (b. 1941)

*Billy Collins is widely read for his work's immediacy and wit, and has
been pronounced "the most popular poet in America" in a* New York
Times *profile. His six books of poetry include a collection of new and se-
lected poems,* Sailing Alone Around the Room *(2001), and* Questions
About Angels *(1991), selected for the National Poetry Series. Named
United States Poet Laureate in 2001, Collins has recorded a spoken-word
CD,* The Best Cigarette *(1997), and has received much attention in the
mainstream media. He has conducted summer poetry workshops at Na-
tional University of Ireland, Galway, and has taught for many years at
Lehman College, City University of New York.*

Schoolsville

Glancing over my shoulder at the past
I realize the number of students I have taught
is enough to populate a small town.

I can see it nestled in a paper landscape,
chalk dust flurrying down in winter,   5
nights dark as a blackboard.

The population ages but never graduates.
On hot afternoons they sweat the final in the park
and when it's cold they shiver around stoves
reading disorganized essays out loud.   10
A bell rings on the hour and everybody zigzags
into the streets with their books.

I forgot all their last names first and their
first names last in alphabetical order.
But the boy who always had his hand up   15
is an alderman and owns the haberdashery.
The girl who signed her papers in lipstick
leans against the drugstore, smoking,
brushing her hair like a machine.

Their grades are sewn into their clothes   20
like references to Hawthorne.
The A's stroll along with other A's.
The D's honk whenever they pass another D.

All the creative writing students recline
on the courthouse lawn and play the lute.   25
Wherever they go, they form a big circle.

Needless to say, I am the mayor.
I live in the white colonial at Maple and Main.
I rarely leave the house. The car deflates
in the driveway. Vines twirl around the porch swing.   30

Once in a while a student knocks on the door
with a term paper fifteen years late
or a question about Yeats or double-spacing.
And sometimes one will appear in a windowpane
to watch me lecturing the wallpaper,   35
quizzing the chandelier, reprimanding the air.

—1988

Nostalgia

Remember the 1340s? We were doing a dance called the
    Catapult.
You always wore brown, the color craze of the decade,
and I was draped in one of those capes that were popular,
the ones with unicorns and pomegranates in needlework.
Everyone would pause for beer and onions in the afternoon,   5
and at night we would play a game called "Find the Cow."
Everything was hand-lettered then, not like today.

Where has the summer of 1572 gone? Brocade and sonnet
marathons were the rage. We used to dress up in the flags
of rival baronies and conquer one another in cold rooms of
    stone.   10
Out on the dance floor we were all doing the Struggle
while your sister practiced the Daphne all alone in her
    room.
We borrowed the jargon of farriers for our slang.
These days language seems transparent, a badly broken
    code.

The 1790s will never come again. Childhood was big.   15
People would take walks to the very tops of hills
and write down what they saw in their journals without
    speaking.
Our collars were high and our hats were extremely soft.
We would surprise each other with alphabets made of
    twigs.
It was a wonderful time to be alive, or even dead.   20

I am very fond of the period between 1815 and 1821.
Europe trembled while we sat still for our portraits.
And I would love to return to 1901 if only for a moment,
time enough to wind up a music box and do a few dance
    steps,
or shoot me back to 1922 or 1941, or at least let me   25
recapture the serenity of last month when we picked
berries and glided through afternoons in a canoe.

Even this morning would be an improvement over the
    present.
I was in the garden then, surrounded by the hum of bees
and the Latin names of flowers, watching the early light   30
flash off the slanted windows of the greenhouse
and silver the limbs on the rows of dark hemlocks.

As usual, I was thinking about the moments of the past,
letting my memory rush over them like water
rushing over the stones on the bottom of a stream.   35
I was even thinking a little about the future, that place
where people are doing a dance we cannot imagine,
a dance whose name we can only guess.

                                                —1991

Litany

> You are the bread and the knife,
> The crystal goblet and the wine.
> —*Jacques Crickillon*

You are the bread and the knife,
the crystal goblet and the wine.
You are the dew on the morning grass,
and the burning wheel of the sun.
You are the white apron of the baker   5
and the marsh birds suddenly in flight.

However, you are not the wind in the orchard,
the plums on the counter,
or the house of cards.
And you are certainly not the pine-scented air.   10
There is no way you are the pine-scented air.

It is possible that you are the fish under the bridge,
maybe even the pigeon on the general's head,
but you are not even close
to being the field of cornflowers at dusk.   15

And a quick look in the mirror will show
that you are neither the boots in the corner
nor the boat asleep in its boathouse.

It might interest you to know,
speaking of the plentiful imagery of the world,   20
that I am the sound of rain on the roof.

I also happen to be the shooting star,
the evening paper blowing down an alley,
and the basket of chestnuts on the kitchen table.

I am also the moon in the trees   25
and the blind woman's teacup.
But don't worry, I am not the bread and the knife.
You are still the bread and the knife.
You will always be the bread and the knife,
not to mention the crystal goblet and—somehow—
   the wine.   30

—*2002*

Toi Derricotte (b. 1941)

*Toi Derricotte has written, "My skin causes certain problems continu-
ously, problems that open the issue of racism over and over like a wound."
Born in Hamtramck, Michigan, she studied at Wayne State University and
New York University. She teaches at the University of Pittsburgh. With the
poet Cornelius Eady, Derricotte cofounded Cave Canem, a workshop and
retreat that supports the work of new voices in African-American poetry.*

The Feeding

My grandmother
haunted the halls
above Webster's Funeral
Home like a red-
gowned ghost. Till dawn   5
I'd see her spectral
form—henna-hair
blown back,
green eyes:
tameless.   10

She was proud.
Like God,
I swore I'd love her.
At night we whispered
how we hated mother   15
and wished that I could
live with *her*.

In the morning while she slept,
I'd pluck
costume diamonds   20
from a heart-shaped chest,
try her tortoise combs
and hairpins in my hair.
She'd wake
and take me to her bed.   25

Maroon-quilted, eider-downed,
I drowned.

Rocking on her wasted breast.
I'd hear her tell me
how she nursed my father   30
till he was old enough to ask.

Then, she'd draw me
to her—ask me
if she still had milk.
Yes. I said, yes.   35
Feeding on the sapless
lie,
even now
the taste of emptiness
weights my mouth.   40

                                                    —1978

On the Turning Up
of Unidentified Black
Female Corpses

Mowing his three acres with a tractor,
a man notices something ahead—a mannequin—
he thinks someone threw it from a car. Closer
he sees it is the body of a black woman.

The medics come and turn her with pitchforks.   5
Her gaze shoots past him to nothing. Nothing
is explained. How many black women
have been turned up to stare at us blankly,
in weedy fields, off highways,
pushed out in plastic bags,   10
shot, knifed, unclothed partially, raped,
their wounds sealed with a powdery crust.

Last week on TV, a gruesome face, eyes bloated shut.
No one will say, "She looks like she's sleeping," ropes
of blue-black slashes at the mouth. Does anybody   15
know this woman? Will anyone come forth? Silence

like a backwave rushes into that field
where, just the week before, four other black girls
had been found. The gritty image hangs in the air
just a few seconds, but it strikes me,   20

a black woman, there is a question being asked
about my life. How can I
protect myself? Even if I lock my doors,
walk only in the light, someone wants me dead.

Am I wrong to think   25
if five white women had been stripped,
broken, the sirens would wail until
someone was named?

Is it any wonder I walk over these bodies
pretending they are not mine, that I do not know   30
the killer, that I am just like any woman—
if not wanted, at least tolerated.

Part of me wants to disappear, to pull
the earth on top of me. Then there is this part
that digs me up with this pen   35
and turns my sad black face to the light.

—1989

Black Boys Play the Classics

The most popular "act" in
Penn Station°
is the three black kids in ratty
sneakers & T-shirts playing
two violins and a cello —Brahms.°   5
White men in business suits
have already dug into their pockets
as they pass and they toss in

---

2 Penn Station bus station in New York City   **5 Brahms** Johannes Brahms (1833–1897), classical German composer

a dollar or two without stopping.
Brown men in work-soiled khakis   10
stand with their mouths open,
arms crossed on their bellies
as if they themselves have always
wanted to attempt those bars.
One white boy, three, sits   15
cross-legged in front of his
idols —in ecstasy—
their slick, dark faces,
their thin, wiry arms,
who must begin to look   20
like angels!
Why does this trembling
pull us?
A: Beneath the surface we are one.
B: Amazing! I did not think that they could speak this tongue.   25

—*1996*

Gibbons Ruark (b. 1941)

Gibbons Ruark recently published Passing Through Customs: New and
Selected Poems *(1999), which collects thirty years' worth of his work. His
poems, which often deal with daily life, are remarkable for their music and
precision. Ruark has taught English at the University of Delaware since
1968, and lives in Landenberg, Pennsylvania.*

Polio

The snore of midsummer flies at the screen,
Afternoon's tepid fog crawling my sleep.
In my unrelenting dream the fire truck
Peals round the corner, and when I wake
The sirens still confound me. From the wobbly   5
Room I stumble to my mother's door,
A shifting blur in the wall before me.
Her limbs are weak and rumpled on the sheet.
The empty braces glint. Their brightness hurts.

Pale pillow, damp hair, my father's shadow   10
Straining over her, sweat at his armpits,
Straightening, bending, straightening her leg.
Like knives her shrill cries peel the heavy air,
But he keeps at it, forcing tears back till
His eyes ache. The veins map out his anguish.   15
His false teeth tighten on that work of love.

—1971

The Visitor

Holding the arm of his helper, the blind
Piano tuner comes to our piano.
He hesitates at first, but once he finds
The keyboard, his hands glide over the slow
Keys, ringing changes finer than the eye   5
Can see. The dusty wires he touches, row
On row, quiver like bowstrings as he
Twists them one notch tighter. He runs his
Finger along a wire, touches the dry
Rust to his tongue, breaks into a pure bliss   10
And tells us, "One year more of damp weather
Would have done you in, but I've saved it this
Time. Would one of you play now, please? I hear
It better at a distance." My wife plays
Stardust.° The blind man stands and smiles in her   15
Direction, then disappears into the blaze
Of new October. Now the afternoon,
The long afternoon that blurs in a haze
Of music . . . Chopin° nocturnes, Clair de Lune,°
All the old familiar, unfamiliar   20
Music-lesson pieces, Papa's Haydn's°
Dead and gone, gently down the stream . . . Hours later,
After the latest car has doused its beams,
Has cooled down and stopped its ticking, I hear

15 *Stardust* popular song by Hoagy Carmichael (1899–1981), American composer and bandleader
19 **Chopin** Frederic Chopin (1810-1849), Polish composer   19 *Clair de Lune* song by Claude
Debussy (1862–1918), French composer   21 **Haydn** Joseph Haydn (1732–1809), Austrian
composer

Our cat, with the grace of animals free   25
To move in darkness, strike one key only,
And a single lucid drop of water stars my dream.

—*1971*

Lecturing My Daughters

Listen a little. When my lone father
Called me down in love or hardly in anger,
I felt my own eyes shamefully flaring
      Under his mildness.

Sometimes he sang, and when he said scarcely   5
Anything but what he wanted me to hear,
I heard the sound of his own palm falling
      Asleep on my shoulder.

He took me walking in early morning,
In early evening, pausing in the lamplight.   10
Climbing a ladder, he let a swing down
      From a tree we lived by.

Last time but one I traveled home to him,
He took me walking just to show me where
A great tree hung its branches half a block   15
      No higher than a man.

Though there's not one tree where we are living
Strong or straight enough to hang a swing from,
With a little luck we will still do something
      Harmless together.   20

Little ones, I have raised the one father's voice
You know in anger. I will be quieter.
We will all walk quietly out together
      Under the lamplight,

And I will lower my own unsteady voice,   25
Hardly as musical as the one father's voice
I know, one rung at a time down the scarcely
      Audible ladder.

Maybe I am calling you home in time.
Given a little chance I had a father,   30
You are my children, walking in lamplight,
        This is your childhood.

                                             —*1978*

Henry Taylor   (b. 1942)

Henry Taylor received the 1986 Pulitzer Prize for The Flying Change, *his third poetry collection. He was born in Loudoun County, Virginia, and studied at the University of Virginia and Hollins College. He has published translations from the Bulgarian, French, Hebrew, Italian, and Russian, as well as from Greek and Roman classical drama. Codirector of the M.F.A. program in creative writing at American University in Washington, D.C., he was inducted into the Fellowship of Southern Writers in 2001.*

Artichoke

> If poetry did not exist, would you
> have had the wit to invent it?
> —*Howard Nemerov*

He had studied in private years ago
the way to eat these things, and was prepared
when she set the clipped green globe before him.
He only wondered (as he always did
when he plucked from the base the first thick leaf,   5
dipped it into the sauce and caught her eye
as he deftly set the velvet curve against
the inside edges of his lower teeth
and drew the tender pulp toward his tongue
while she made some predictable remark   10
about the sensuality of this act
then sheared away the spines and ate the heart)
what mind, what hunger, first saw this as food.

                                             —*1986*

Understanding Fiction

What brings it to mind this time? The decal
from East Stroudsburg State in the window
ahead of me as traffic winds to the airport?

Maybe we pass the Stroudwater Landing apartments.
Whatever it is, you who are with me get to hear it   5
all over again: how once, just out of college

or maybe a year or two later, into the first
teaching job, some circumstance found me
in the home of an old friend, one of the mentors

to whom I owe what I am, on one of those days   10
when the airwaves are filled with football.
We remember it now as four games, and swear

to one another, and to others, that this
is what happened. In the second game,
as men unpiled from a crowded scramble,   15

a calm voice remarked that Mike Stroud
had been in on the tackle, and we told
ourselves that we had heard the same thing

in the first game. Odd. So we listened,
or claimed to be listening, and drank,   20
and took what we were pleased to call notice.

Never an isolating or identifying shot,
just these brief observations of crowds:
Mike Stroud was in all four games.

An astonishing trick, a terrific story—   25
some plot of the color commentators,
a tribute to a friend with a birthday,

or maybe just a joke on the world.
I tell it at least four times a year,
and each time it is longer ago.   30

Mike Stroud, if he ever played football,
does not do so now, but he might
even have played only one game

that late fall day in—oh, 1967, let's say.
We were drinking. God knows what we heard.   35
But I tell it again, and see how

to help you believe it, so I make
some adjustment of voice or detail,
and the story strides into the future.

—*1996*

Charles Martin (b. 1942)

*Charles Martin has trained his cool, neoclassical eye on such postmodern
subjects as the Victoria's Secret catalog, the ESL classroom, and the game
show* Jeopardy! *A lifelong resident of New York City, Martin has taught
English as a second language for many years at Queensborough College,
and also has taught in the Writing Seminars at Johns Hopkins University.
Martin writes criticism and does translations, including a widely praised
volume of Catullus. His original collections,* Steal the Bacon *(1987) and*
What the Darkness Proposes *(1996), have been finalists for the Pulitzer
Prize.*

E.S.L.°

My frowning students carve
Me monsters out of prose:
This one—a gargoyle—thumbs its contemptuous nose
At how, in English, subject must agree
With verb—for any such agreement shows   5
    Too great a willingness to serve,
        A docility

    Which wiry Miss Choi
    Finds un-American.
She steals a hard look at me. I wink. Her grin   10
Is my reward. *In his will, our peace, our Pass:*
Gargoyle erased, subject and verb now in
    Agreement, reach object, enjoy
        Temporary truce.

E.S.L. English as a Second Language

Tonight my students must   15
   Agree or disagree:
America is still a land of opportunity.
The answer is always, uniformly, *Yes*—even though
"It has no doubt that here were to much free,"
   As Miss Torrico will insist.   20
      She and I both know

   That Language binds us fast,
    And those of us without
Are bound and gagged by those within. Each fledgling
Polyglot must shake old habits: tapping her sneakered feet,   25
Miss Choi exorcises incensed ancestors, flout-
   ing the ghosts of her Chinese past.
      Writhing in the seat

   Next to Miss Choi, Mister
    Fedakis, in anguish   30
Labors to express himself in a tongue which
Proves *Linear B* to me, when I attempt to read it
Later. They're here for English as a Second Language,
   Which I'm teaching this semester.
      God knows they need it,   35

   And so, thank God, do they.
    The night's made easier
By our agreement: I am here to help deliver
Them into the good life they write me papers about.
English is pre-requisite for that endeavor,   40
   Explored in their nightly essays
      Boldly setting out

   To reconnoiter the fair
    New World they would enter:
Suburban Paradise, the endless shopping center   45
Where one may browse for hours before one chooses
Some new necessity—gold-flecked magenta
   Wallpaper to re-do the spare
      Bath no one uses,

   Or a machine which can,   50
    In seven seconds, crush

A newborn calf into such seamless mush
As a *mousse* might be made of—or our true sublime:
The gleaming counters where frosted cosmeticians brush
    Decades from the allotted span,   55
        Abrogating Time

    As the spring tide brushes
    A single sinister
Footprint from the otherwise unwrinkled shore
Of America the Blank. In absolute confusion   60
Poor Mister Fedakis rumbles with despair
    And puts the finishing smutches
        To his conclusion

    While Miss Choi erases:
    One more gargoyle routed.   65
Their pure, erroneous lines yield an illuminated
Map of the new found land. We will never arrive there,
Since it exists only in what we say about it,
    As all the rest of my class is
        Bound to discover.   70

                             —*1983*

How My Queer Uncle Came to Die at Last

(i.m. Frederick Martin 1908–1957)

    I

Dear, debonair, intemperate,
Exotic, open, ordinary,
Precariously overweight,
Self-educated *bon vivant*,
Soft, sybaritic emissary   5
Of Dionysus to the Bronx,
And slyly uninhibited
Life of the party, Uncle Fred—

Dropped by a massive heart attack
Quite plausibly, the truth to tell,   10

One afternoon on his way back
From a late lunch at Child's or Schrafft's:°
As he lay dying where he fell,
His large ironic spirit passed
Through gawkers gathered at curbside   15
And hailed a cab for his last ride . . .

I'd seen your death certificate,
Signed by the famous coroner:
Who would have ever questioned it?
—Surely not anyone aware   20
Of your strong predilection for
The good life, served up bloody rare
Along with bottomless cocktails
And your unfiltered "coffin nails."

It was the good life did you in,   25
As I assumed—the appetite
Whose cheerful servant you had been
Until the good life cut yours short
One winter afternoon. That night
I listened to the wind's report   30
And hid myself away and cried.
I learned of dying when you died.

Other lessons were more subtle,
Were even open to debate;
This one alone brooked no rebuttal,   35
As though some mindless hand erased
The chalked-on figures from a slate,
And all the lines a lifetime traced
Were altogether swept away
Late on one lightless winter day . . .   40

II

My legacy from Uncle Fred?
The bookish boy whose vision you
Sought to correct inherited
Some books of yours (which some years later
Helped to explain a thing or two)   45

12 **Child's, Schrafft's** restaurants in New York City

By Oscar Wilde° and Walter Pater,°
And two bronze candlesticks with *putti°*—
A pair, in truth, of no great beauty,

But emblematic, I still knew,
Of what were called "the finer things—"   50
Though what *these* were, I had no clue.
Your angels now present themselves
In memory to try their wings,
Fly to forgotten kitchen shelves
And point out what I'd long misplaced,   55
The hidden origins of taste

In every bottle, tin, or jar:
Wild berries crushed to silken jam,
The bright black beads of caviar,
Rock lobster tails, imported beer,   60
Asparagus and Smithfield ham,°
So unfamiliar and so dear!
Even a can—can it be so?
Quite plainly labeled *ESCARGOTS.*

Then, as you evenly divided   65
Delicacies unknown before,
Even the youngest was provided
With a small portion of his own—
A kindness he's still grateful for,
Who sees a line distinctly drawn   70
From diverse canapés and *torten°*
Through Eliot° to later Auden.°

III

Those afternoons of cakes and laughter
Faded to evenings that ended
With your invariant departure   75
For downtown and for company
More worldly-wise than that provided

---

46 **Oscar Wilde** Irish poet and dramatist (1854–1900), Wilde was charged with "homosexual offenses" under Britain's Criminal Law Amendment, found guilty, and sentenced to two years in prison.   46 **Walter Pater** (1839–1894), British essayist and critic, also homosexual   47 *putti* (Italian), in art, winged cherubs   61 **Smithfield ham** a prized, salt-cured smoked ham from Smithfield, Virginia   71 *torten* (German), plural of *torte*, a rich, layered cake   72 **Eliot** T.S. Eliot (1888–1965), American poet who became a British citizen   72 **Auden** W. H. Auden (1907–1973), British poet

By your provincial family;
Although I kept my nose in books,
I caught the grown-ups' knowing looks.   80

No matter what their glances meant,
Their explanations gave you cover;
The Interfaith Impediment
To me, at least, seemed plausible:
Your fiancée (*not* your lover)   85
Was a Jewish or a Catholic girl
Whose parents would not let her wed
A Protestant—our Uncle Fred.

Your long engagement having failed,
You bore with equanimity   90
Whatever grief its loss entailed.
That was a fiction through and through,
I realize: it had to be;
Back then I thought that it was true,
And even now want in some sense   95
For it to be not *just* pretense—

I break off and an upraised brow
Furrows my own: "*What's that you said?*"
I'm really not sure that *I* know,
But *you* must—you're the analyst.   100
"*His nephew wanted Uncle Fred
Straight with an unacknowledged twist,
To be spared the humiliation
Of queerdom by association.*"

A liberal for my whole life,   105
I'm more than willing to believe
The very worst about myself:
Was I so timid that I'd wanted
A likely fiction to deceive
The childhood friends who would have taunted?   110
Of course—but that scenario
Assumes I would have had to know,

Which wasn't very likely, was it?
He died. The years went by. I guessed
What had been hidden in his closet,   115

The knowledge I had come so near,
The truth that could not be expressed.
It was his death that I thought queer.
I use the word in its old sense.
I think he died of the pretense.   120

    IV

His death, recounted, soon assumed
Sufficient plausibility;
We mourned and our lives resumed.
And yet it left a residue
Behind—a need for secrecy,   125
The knot a child tries to undo
By tugging at—this doesn't work:
The knot just tightens with each jerk.

Familiar silence, a white noise
Made up of what cannot be said,   130
Affirming all that it denies;
In its refusal, volumes speak,
Are eloquent, could they be read:
To this young scholar, they were Greek,
Unfathomable on their shelves.   135
My life went on. It tried on selves,

Adjusting them until they fit
My aptitudes or sense of style,
And on those days I thought of it,
His death became one reason why   140
I ought to jog that extra mile
Or give up (on the umpteenth try)
The weed that killed him, as I thought.
Silence would seem to have won out,

Until, when almost all who knew   145
The secret were themselves deceased,
It was at last my mother who
One afternoon abruptly said,
"It wasn't cardiac arrest—
Somebody killed your Uncle Fred,   150
Beat him to death so brutally
That when your father claimed him, he

Could only recognize him by
The bloodstained clothing that he wore—
The coroner agreed to lie."   155
To lie? Because he had been killed?
But who killed Freddie? Where? What for?
Some questions answered, others stilled
By her final revelation:
"The men's room at Grand Central Station."   160

     V

The first scene had to be revised:
No longer dying instantly
But torturously brutalized,
You fade out slowly, underneath
Accumulating agony   165
Which only ends with your last breath.
I am unable to repair
That treachery or your despair;

The brother who collapsed and died,
The other who continued, grieving;   170
Justice, which you have been denied,
And silence, by which you were blamed;
The years that passed with me believing
In lies of which I am ashamed;
The savagery that still deprives: 175
Your absence from my children's lives,

Your troubled presence in my own,
Encumbering me with the ghost
Of someone inchoately known.
I light one of your candlesticks   180
(The other one has gotten lost)
And watch intently as the wax
Pools steadily beneath the flame
Then overflows its shallow dam

To run in rivulets upon   185
The figure of Angelic Youth
Whose bronze features seem to frown
In anger—or is he just bored?
"*He was no beauty, in all truth,*

But still the best I could afford;   190
The friendless nightmare of my death
Can never be set right, and yet

Within your life, I still persist,
An influence that you call good
And find few reasons to resist,   195
And many to be grateful for;
Alive, I would feel gratitude
Myself, with nothing to deplore,
Nothing to alter or amend,
As I felt even at the end;   200

But even as a welcome guest
Within the swiftly moving lives
Of those who knew and loved me best
I am now changed past recognition,
A figure that somehow survives   205
The boundaries of its condition,
A fiction that your words renew;
Now let me go, and you go too."

                                                          —2002

B. H. Fairchild (b. 1942)

B. H. Fairchild was born in Houston, Texas, and grew up in small towns in Texas, Oklahoma, and Kansas. He studied at the University of Kansas and the University of Tulsa. His poetry collections include The Art of the Lathe *(1998), which depicts factory life in a Midwestern town, and for which he received the 1999 Kingsley Tufts Poetry Award. Fairchild also has written* Such Holy Song *(1980), a study of William Blake. He currently lives in California.*

Beauty

> Therefore,
> Their sons grow suicidally beautiful . . .
> —*James Wright*, "Autumn Begins in
> Martin's Ferry, Ohio"

I.

We are at the Bargello° in Florence, and she says,
what are you thinking? and I say, *beauty*, thinking
of how very far we are now from the machine shop
and the dry fields of Kansas, the treeless horizons
of slate skies and the muted passions of roughnecks   5
and scrabble farmers drunk and romantic enough
to weep more or less silently at the darkened end
of the bar out of, what else, loneliness, meaning
the ache of thwarted desire, of, in a word, *beauty*,
or rather its absence, and it occurs to me again   10
that no male member of my family has ever used
this word in my hearing or anyone else's except
in reference, perhaps, to a new pickup or dead deer.
This insight, this backward vision, first came to me
as a young man as some weirdness of the air waves   15
slipped through the static of our new Motorola
with a discussion of *beauty* between Robert Penn Warren°

---

1 Bargello an Italian national art museum   **17 Robert Penn Warren** (1905–1989), American poet and novelist

and Paul Weiss° at Yale College. We were in Kansas
eating barbecue-flavored potato chips and waiting
for *Father Knows Best*° to float up through the snow   20
of rural TV in 1963. I felt transported, stunned.
Here were two grown men discussing "beauty"
seriously and with dignity as if they and the topic
were as normal as normal topics of discussion
between men such as soybean prices or why   25
the commodities market was a sucker's game
or Oklahoma football or Gimpy Neiderland
almost dying from his hemorrhoid operation.
They were discussing beauty and tossing around
allusions to Plato and Aristotle° and someone   30
named Pater,° and they might be homosexuals.
That would be a natural conclusion, of course,
since here were two grown men talking about "beauty"
instead of scratching their crotches and cursing
the goddamned government trying to run everybody's   35
business. Not a beautiful thing, that. The government.
Not beautiful, though a man would not use that word.
One time my Uncle Ross from California called my mom's
Sunday dinner centerpiece "lovely," and my father
left the room, clearly troubled by the word "lovely"   40
coupled probably with the very idea of California
and the fact that my Uncle Ross liked to tap-dance.
The light from the venetian blinds, the autumn,
silver Kansas light laving the table that Sunday,
is what I recall now because it was beautiful,   45
though I of course would not have said so then, *beautiful*,
as so many moments forgotten but later remembered
come back to us in slants and pools and uprisings of light,
beautiful in itself, but more beautiful mingled
with memory, the light leaning across my mother's   50
carefully set table, across the empty chair
beside my Uncle Ross, the light filtering down
from the green plastic slats in the roof of the machine shop

---

18 **Paul Weiss** (1901–2002), American philosopher known for his work in metaphysics   20 ***Father
Knows Best*** situation comedy that ran from 1954 to 1962   30 **Plato and Aristotle** Ancient Greek
philosophers   31 **Pater** Walter Pater (1839–1894), British essayist and critic

where I worked with my father so many afternoons,
standing or crouched in pools of light and sweat with men   55
who knew the true meaning of labor and money and other
hard, true things and did not, did not ever, use the word, *beauty*.

II.

Late November, shadows gather in the shop's north end,
and I'm watching Bobby Sudduth do piece work on the Hobbs.°
He fouls another cut, *motherfucker, fucking bitch machine,*   60
and starts over, sloppy, slow, about two joints away
from being fired, but he just doesn't give a shit.
He sets the bit again, white wrists flashing in the lamplight
and showing botched, blurred tattoos, both from a night
in Tijuana, and continues his sexual autobiography,   65
that's right, fucked my own sister, and I'll tell you, bud,
it wasn't bad. Later, in the Philippines, the clap:
as far as I'm concerned, any man who hasn't had V.D.
just isn't a man. I walk away, knowing I have just heard
the dumbest remark ever uttered by man or animal.   70
The air around me hums in a dark metallic bass,
light spilling like grails of milk as someone opens
the mammoth shop door. A shrill, sullen truculence
blows in like dust devils, the hot wind nagging
my blousy overalls, and in the sideyard the winch truck   75
backfires and stalls. The sky yellows. Barn sparrows cry
in the rafters. That afternoon in Dallas Kennedy is shot.

Two weeks later sitting around on rotary tables
and traveling blocks whose bearings litter the shop floor
like huge eggs, we close our lunch boxes and lean back   80
with cigarettes and watch smoke and dust motes rise and drift
into sunlight. All of us have seen the newscasts,
photographs from *Life*, have sat there in our cavernous rooms,
assassinations and crowds flickering over our faces,
some of us have even dreamed it, sleeping through   85
the TV's drone and flutter, seen her arm reaching
across the lank body, black suits rushing in like moths,
and the long snake of the motorcade come to rest,

59 Hobbs a metal working lathe made by the Hobbs Manufacturing Company

then the announcer's voice as we wake astonished in the dark.
We think of it now, staring at the tin ceiling like a giant screen,   90
what a strange goddamned country, as Bobby Sudduth
arches a wadded Fritos bag at the time clock and says,
Oswald, from that far, you got to admit, that shot was a beauty.

III.

The following summer. A black Corvette gleams like a slice
of onyx in the sideyard, driven there by two young men   95
who look like Marlon Brando° and mention Hollywood
when Bobby asks where they're from. The foreman, my father,
has hired them because we're backed up with work, both shop
and yard strewn with rig parts, flat-bed haulers rumbling
in each day lugging damaged drawworks, and we are desperate.   100
The noise is awful, a gang of roughnecks from a rig
on down-time shouting orders, our floor hands knee-deep
in the drawwork's gears heating the frozen sleeves and bushings
with cutting torches until they can be hammered loose.
The iron shell bangs back like a drum-head. Looking   105
for some peace, I walk onto the pipe rack for a quick smoke,
and this is the way it begins for me, this memory,
this strangest of all memories of the shop and the men
who worked there, because the silence has come upon me
like the shadow of cranes flying overhead as they would   110
each autumn, like the quiet and imperceptible turning
of a season, the shop has grown suddenly still here
in the middle of the workday, and I turn to look
through the tall doors where the machinists stand now
with their backs to me, the lathes whining down together,   115
and in the shop's center I see them standing in a square
of light, the two men from California, as the welders
lift their black masks, looking up, and I see their faces first,
the expressions of children at a zoo, perhaps,
or after a first snow, as the two men stand naked,   120
their clothes in little piles on the floor as if they
are about to go swimming, and I recall how fragile
and pale their bodies seemed against the iron and steel

96 Marlon Brando (1924–2004), stage and screen actor best known for roles in which he exuded a brooding masculinity

of the drill presses and milling machines and lathes.
I did not know the word, *exhibitionist*, then, and so   125
for a moment it seemed only a problem of memory,
that they had *forgotten* somehow where they were,
that this was not the locker room after the game,
that they were not taking a shower, that this was not
the appropriate place, and they would then remember,   130
and suddenly embarrassed, begin shyly to dress again.
But they did not, and in memory they stand frozen
and poised as two models in a drawing class,
of whom the finished sketch might be said, though not by me
nor any man I knew, to be beautiful, they stand there   135
forever, with the time clock ticking behind them,
time running on but not moving, like the white tunnel
of silence between the snap of the ball and the thunderclap
of shoulder pads that never seems to come and then
there it is, and I hear a quick intake of breath   140
on my right behind the Hobbs and it is Bobby Sudduth
with what I think now was not just anger but a kind
of terror on his face, an animal wildness
in the eyes and the jaw tight, making ropes in his neck
while in a long blur with his left hand raised and gripping   145
an iron file he is moving toward the men who wait
attentive and motionless as deer trembling in a clearing,
and instantly there is my father between Bobby
and the men as if he were waking them after a long sleep,
reaching out to touch the shoulder of the blonde one   150
as he says in a voice almost terrible in its gentleness,
its discretion, *you boys will have to leave now.*
He takes one look at Bobby who is shrinking back
into the shadows of the Hobbs, then walks quickly back
to his office at the front of the shop, and soon   155
the black Corvette with the orange California plates
is squealing onto Highway 54 heading west into the sun.

  IV.

So there they are, as I will always remember them,
the men who were once fullbacks or tackles or guards
in their three-point stances knuckling into the mud,   160
hungry for highschool glory and the pride of their fathers,

eager *to gallop terribly against each other's bodies,*°
each man in his body looking out now at the nakedness
of a body like his, men who each autumn had followed
their fathers into the pheasant-rich fields of Kansas   165
and as boys had climbed down from the Allis-Chalmers°
after plowing their first straight furrow, licking the dirt
from their lips, the hand of the father resting lightly
upon their shoulder, men who in the oven-warm winter
kitchens of Baptist households saw after a bath the body   170
of the father and felt diminished by it, who that same
winter in the abandoned schoolyard felt the odd intimacy
of their fist against the larger boy's cheekbone
but kept hitting, ferociously, and walked away
feeling for the first time the strength, the *abundance,*   175
of their own bodies. And I imagine the men
that evening after the strangest day of their lives,
after they have left the shop without speaking
and made the long drive home alone in their pickups,
I see them in their little white frame houses on the edge   180
of town adrift in the long silence of the evening turning
finally to their wives, touching without speaking the hair
which she has learned to let fall about her shoulders
at this hour of night, lifting the white nightgown
from her body as she in turn unbuttons his work shirt   185
heavy with the sweat and grease of the day's labor until
they stand naked before each other and begin to touch
in a slow choreography of familiar gestures their bodies,
she touching his chest, his hand brushing her breasts,
and he does not say the word "beautiful" because   190
he cannot and never has, and she does not say it
because it would embarrass him or any other man
she has ever known, though it is precisely the word
I am thinking now as I stand before Donatello's David°
with my wife touching my sleeve, *what are you thinking?*   195
and I think of the letter from my father years ago
describing the death of Bobby Sudduth, a single shot
from a twelve-gauge which he held against his chest,

---

162 *to gallop terribly against each other's bodies* a line from James Wright's poem "Autumn Begins
in Martin's Ferry, Ohio" (see page 145)   166 **Allis-Chalmers** a brand of tractors   194 **Donatello's
David** nude statue by the Italian artist Donatello (1386–1466), depicting the young Biblical King
David brandishing Goliath's sword above the head of the dead giant

the death of the heart, I suppose, *a kind of terrible beauty*,
as someone said of the death of Hart Crane,° though that is   200
surely a perverse use of the word, and I was stunned then,
thinking of the damage men will visit upon their bodies,
what are you thinking? she asks again, and so I begin
to tell her about a strange afternoon in Kansas,
about something I have never spoken of, and we walk   205
to a window where the shifting light spreads a sheen
along the casement, and looking out, we see the city
blazing like miles of uncut wheat, the farthest buildings
taken in their turn, and the great dome, the way
the metal roof of the machine shop, I tell her,   210
would break into flame late on an autumn day, with such beauty.

—1998

Gla∂yơ Car∂iff (b. 1942)

*Gladys Cardiff is a member of the Cherokee nation. She grew up in
Seattle, Washington, and studied at the University of Washington and
Western Michigan University. She teaches creative writing and literature at
Oakland University.*

Combing

Bending, I bow my head
And lay my hand upon
Her hair, combing, and think
How women do this for
Each other. My daughter's hair   5
Curls against the comb,
Wet and fragrant—orange
Parings. Her face, downcast,
Is quiet for one so young.

---

200 Hart Crane (1899–1932), American poet who committed suicide by jumping from the deck of a steamship

I take her place. Beneath 10
My mother's hands I feel
The braids drawn up tight
As a piano wire and singing,
Vinegar rinsed. Sitting
Before the oven I hear 15
The orange coils tick
The early hour before school.

She combed her grandmother
Mathilda's hair using
A comb made out of bone. 20
Mathilda rocked her oak wood
Chair, her face downcast,
Intent on tearing rags
In strips to braid a cotton
Rug from bits of orange 25
And brown. A simple act,

Preparing hair. Something
Women do for each other,
Plaiting the generations.

—1976

Beautiful Zombies

Kanane'ski Amayehi, Fishing Spider, speaks:

There are things more terrible than death.
To see the turtle tribe swim by,
huge eyes half-dead yet brimmed with tears,
following, always following 5
some hazy possibility

is to see the manner of my own
predation magnified. Dim-buzz,
punching fang and venom volt,
and all the senses washed away. But theirs 10
is a communal self-inflicted bite.

As they were once, they were the watery
world's artisans. They studied
the designs of water, the surface tension
of still pools, wind-dapple and deep   15
whorl of moon-called water.

And as they learned, the patterns grew
upon their bodies so that they and water
seemed one. Their numbers increased, their forays
lengthened. If one was hurt, it thought   20
into itself the intricacies

of water, and sewed itself back up.
Everyone knows only a turtle
can loosen a turtle's bite. They thought:
"We are living calendars. Time   25
and we are one. Time heals our wounds."

They no longer studied water. Their bodies
thickened, became deeply
engraved. They slowed down, forgot the trick
of mending themselves. They live a half-   30
life of perpetual noon. They cast no shadow.

—1999

Sharon Olds (b. 1942)

*Sharon Olds displays a candor in dealing with the intimacies of family ro-
mance, covering three generations, that has made her one of the chief contemporary heirs to the confessional tradition. Her first collection,* Satan
Says *(1980), was awarded the inaugural San Francisco Poetry Center
Award and established Olds's distinctive voice, and her characteristic use
of lushly sensuous, often explicit, imagery. Her second volume,* The Dead
and the Living, *won the 1983 Lamont Poetry Prize and the National Book
Critics Circle Award. Born in San Francisco, she studied at Stanford University and Columbia. Olds currently resides in New York City, and
teaches at New York University and in the NYU workshop program at
Goldwater Hospital on New York's Roosevelt Island. A powerful and dramatic reader, she is much in demand on the lecture circuit.*

The One Girl
at the Boys' Party

When I take my girl to the swimming party
I set her down among the boys. They tower and
bristle, she stands there smooth and sleek,
her math scores unfolding in the air around her.
They will strip to their suits, her body hard and   5
indivisible as a prime number,
they'll plunge in the deep end, she'll subtract
her height from ten feet, divide it into
hundreds of gallons of water, the numbers
bouncing in her mind like molecules of chlorine   10
in the bright blue pool. When they climb out,
her ponytail will hang its pencil lead
down her back, her narrow silk suit
with hamburgers and french fries printed on it
will glisten in the brilliant air, and they will   15
see her sweet face, solemn and
sealed, a factor of one, and she will
see their eyes, two each,
their legs, two each, and the curves of their sexes,
one each, and in her head she'll be doing her   20

wild multiplying, as the drops
sparkle and fall to the power of a thousand from her body.

—*1984*

The Girl

They chased her and her friend through the woods
and caught them in a small clearing, broken
random bracken, a couple of old mattresses,
the dry ochre of foam rubber,
as if the place had been prepared.   5
The thin one with black hair
started raping her best friend,
and the blond one stood above her,
thrust his thumbs back inside her jaws, she was 12,
stuck his penis in her mouth and throat   10
faster and faster and faster.
Then the black-haired one stood up—
they lay like pulled-up roots at his feet,
two naked 12-year-old girls, he said
Now you're going to know what it's like   15
to be shot 5 times and slaughtered like a pig,
and they switched mattresses,
the blond was raping and stabbing her friend,
the black-haired one sticking inside her
in one place and then another,   20
the point of his gun pressed deep into her waist,
she felt a little click in her spine and a
sting like 7-Up in her head and then he
pulled the tree-branch across her throat
and everything went dark,   25
the gym went dark, and her mother's kitchen,
even the globes of light on the rounded
lips of her mother's nesting bowls went dark.

When she woke up she was lying on the cold
iron-smelling earth, she was under the mattress,   30
pulled up over her like a
blanket at night,

she saw the body of her best friend
and she began to run,
she came to the edge of the woods and she stepped   35
out from the trees, like a wound debriding,
she walked across the field to the tracks
and said to the railway brakeman *Please, sir. Please, sir.*

At the trial she had to say everything—
her big sister taught her the words—   40
she had to sit in the room with them and
point to them. Now she goes to parties
but does not smoke, she is a cheerleader,
she throws her body up in the air
and kicks her legs and comes home and does the dishes   45
and her homework, she has to work hard in math,
the night over the roof of her bed
filled with white planets. Every night she
prays for the soul of her best friend and
then thanks God for life. She knows   50
what all of us want never to know
and she does a cartwheel, the splits, she shakes the
shredded pom-poms in her fists.

                                                                —1987

I Go Back to May 1937

I see them standing at the formal gates of their colleges,
I see my father strolling out
under the ochre sandstone arch, the
red tiles glinting like bent
plates of blood behind his head, I   5
see my mother with a few light books at her hip
standing at the pillar made of tiny bricks with the
wrought-iron gate still open behind her, its
sword-tips black in the May air,
they are about to graduate, they are about to get married,   10
they are kids, they are dumb, all they know is they are
innocent, they would never hurt anybody.
I want to go up to them and say Stop,

don't do it—she's the wrong woman,
he's the wrong man, you are going to do things   15
you cannot imagine you would ever do,
you are going to do bad things to children,
you are going to suffer in ways you never heard of,
you are going to want to die. I want to go
up to them there in the late May sunlight and say it,   20
her hungry pretty blank face turning to me,
her pitiful beautiful untouched body,
his arrogant handsome blind face turning to me,
his pitiful beautiful untouched body,
but I don't do it. I want to live. I   25
take them up like the male and female
paper dolls and bang them together
at the hips like chips of flint as if to
strike sparks from them, I say
Do what you are going to do, and I will tell about it.   30

—*1987*

Topography

After we flew across the country we
got in bed, laid our bodies
delicately together, like maps laid
face to face, East to West, my
San Francisco against your New York, your   5
Fire Island against my Sonoma, my
New Orleans deep in your Texas, your Idaho
bright on my Great Lakes, my Kansas
burning against your Kansas your Kansas
burning against my Kansas, your Eastern   10
Standard Time pressing into my
Pacific Time, my Mountain Time
beating against your Central Time, your
sun rising swiftly from the right my
sun rising swiftly from the left your   15
moon rising slowly from the left my
moon rising slowly from the right until
all four bodies of the sky

burn above us, sealing us together,
all our cities twin cities,   20
all our states united, one
nation, indivisible, with liberty and justice for all.

                                                        —*1987*

Marilyn Hacker (b. 1942)

Marilyn Hacker is best known for literary formalism and her lesbian ac-
tivism. Her many poetic honors include the Poets' Prize for her Selected
Poems, 1965–1990 *(1994) and the National Book Award for* Presentation
Piece *(1974). Born in New York City, Hacker grew up in the Bronx and*
began college at New York University at the age of fifteen. While still an
undergraduate, she married the science fiction writer Samuel Delaney.
Over the next decade, Hacker and Delaney separated, and both became
known as outspoken gay writers. Hacker has edited a number of literary
journals including The Kenyon Review, Thirteen Moon *(a feminist liter-*
ary magazine now located at SUNY Albany), The Little Magazine, *and*
Quark, *a science fiction journal. Hacker divides her time between New*
York and Paris, and teaches at the City College of New York.

Wagers

I bet you don't wear shoulder pads in bed.
I bet when we get over, we'll be *bad!*
I bet you blush all over when you come.

Although the butch coach gave them out, and said,
they're regulation issue for the team,   5
I bet you don't wear shoulder pads in bed;

and if I whispered something just unseemly enough, I could make your ears turn red.
I bet you blush all over when you come

to where I say, I slept on what we did,   10
and didn't, then undressed you in a dream.
I bet you don't wear shoulder pads in bed.

I bet my blue pajamas split a seam
while I thought of my hand on you instead.
I bet you blush all over when you come.   15

Maybe I'll spend Bastille Day feeling bad,
deferring fireworks till the troops get home
—I bet you don't wear shoulder pads in bed.

Don't give me any; just promise me some.
I'm having nicer nightmares than I had.   20
I bet you blush all over when you come,

but I can bide my time until it's bid-
dable (though, damn, you make me squirm;
I bet you don't wear shoulder pads in bed),

wait till the strawberries are ripe for cream,   25
and get to give, for having kept my head.
I bet you blush all over when you come.
I bet you don't wear shoulder pads in bed.

—1986

Ghazal° on Half a Line by Adrienne Rich

In a familiar town, she waits for certain letters,
working out the confusion and the hurt in letters.

Whatever you didn't get—the job, the girl—
rejections are inevitably curt in letters.

This is a country with a post office   5
where one can still make oneself heard in letters.

(Her one-street-over neighbor's Mme de Sévigné°
who almost always had the last word in letters.)

Was the disaster pendant from a tongue
one she might have been able to avert in letters?   10

Still, acrimony, envy, lust, disdain
are land mines the unconscious can insert in letters.

Ghazal Ancient Persian verse form made up of couplets. The opening rhyme recurs in the second line of each succeeding couplet   **7 Mme de Sévigné** (1626–1696), French noblewoman known for her letters

Sometimes more rage clings to a page than she would claim—
it's necessary to remain alert in letters

(an estranged friend donated to a library   15
three decades of her dishing out the dirt in letters)

and words which resonate and turn within
the mind can lie there flattened and inert in letters.

The tightest-laced precisely-spoken celibate
may inadvertently shrug off her shirt in letters.   20

Ex-lovers who won't lie down naked again
still permit themselves to flirt in letters.

What does Anonymous compose, unsigned
at night, after she draws the curtain? Letters.

—2003

Omelette

> You can't break eggs without making an omelette
> *—That's what they tell the eggs.*
> *—Randall Jarrell, "A War"*

First, chop an onion and sauté it separately
in melted butter, unsalted, preferably.
    Add mushrooms (add girolles° in autumn)
    Stir until golden and gently wilted.

Then, break the eggs as neatly as possible,   5
crack! on the copper lip of the mixing bowl;
    beat, frothing yolks and whites together,
    thread with a filet of cream. You've melted

more butter in a scrupulous seven-inch
iron skillet: pour the mixture in swiftly, keep   10
    flame high as edges puff and whiten.
    Lower the flame to a reminiscence.

When I was twenty, living near Avenue
D,° there were Sunday brunches at four o'clock.

3 **girolles** wild mushrooms 14 **Avenue D** in New York City

Eggs were the necessary protein   15
hangovers (bourbon and pot) demanded.

Style: that's what faggots (that's what they called themselves)
used to make dreary illness and poverty
    glitter. Not scrambled eggs, not fried eggs:
    Jamesian° omelettes, skill and gesture.   20

Soon after, "illness" wouldn't mean hangovers.
How many of those glamorous headachy
    chefs sliding perfect crescents onto
    disparate platters are middle-aged now?

Up, flame, and push the edges in carefully: 25
egg, liquid, flows out toward the perimeter.
    Now, when the center bubbles thickly
    spoon in the mushroom and onion mixture—

though the Platonic ideal omelette
has only hot, loose egg at its heart, with fresh   30
    herbs, like the one that Lambert Strether°
    lunched on, and fell for that lost French lady.

Those were the lunchtime omelettes Claire and I
(three decades after the alphabet avenue
    brunch) savored at the women's bookshop/   35
    salon de thé,° our manila folders

waiting for coffee— Emily Dickinson's°
rare tenses and amphibious metaphors.
    Browned, molten gold ran on the platter:
    a homely lyric, with salad garland.   40

Outside, it rained in June, or was spring for a
brief February thaw. Now the bookshop's one
    more Left Bank restaurant, with books for
    "atmosphere": omelettes aren't served there. . . .

With (you've been using it all along) a wood   45
spatula, flip one half of the omelette

---

20 **Jamesian** reminiscent of novelist Henry James   31 **Lambert Strether** A character in Henry James's (see line 20) novel *The Ambassadors*, Lambert Strether is an American who travels to France to spy on a family scion who is having an affair with a Frenchwoman   36 **salon de thé** tea room   37 **Emily Dickinson** American poet (1830–1886)

over the girolle-garnished other.
Eat it with somebody you'll remember.

—*2003*

Sydney Lea (b. 1942)

Sydney Lea writes masterful lyric and narrative poems set in impoverished rural New England. The founder and long-time editor of the New England Review *and a member of the graduate faculty of Vermont College, Lea received the 1998 Poets' Prize for* To the Bone: New and Selected Poems. *A longtime resident of Vermont, he has written essays on responsible hunting and dog-training, collected in* Hunting the Whole Way Home *(1994).*

Young Man Leaving Home

Over the dropped eggs and hash, his elders
poured unaccustomed benedictions.

The morning broke fair, but they
insisted on sensing rain.

That last spring, after so many,   5
the tree with the rope swing blossomed,

random plum blooms dropping groundward
where the playhouse leaned.

Later, the tracks with their switchbacks among
the shanties outside the station   10

had a somewhat surprising Protestant look
of a hopeless proposition.

Adieu: to the father who fobbed and fondled
his watch, at the end of his chain,

whose simple grief no halting final   15
declaration seemed to soften;

to the mother feigning unpatience
with the lateness of the train.

They. Tree. House. Yard.
All had called for his valediction,   20

but now was already the hour prior
to greeting whatever it is that this is,

hour of assembly, of public instead
of certain longed-for private kisses,

hour of livered grandmothers, aunts,   25
whose cheeks the plain tears stained . . .

It passed in the fashion of dreams, at once
chaotic and sluggish.

En route: in silence, he hailed The Future,
that unimaginable lode of riches,   30

this hero, composed of a dozen young rebels
out of thin novels, groaning with luggage.

—1980

Hunter's Sabbath: Hippocratic

the gauzy lichen here   took years
to mask this granite   patient earth
I know I will not save   nor cure
invading   yet today my path
as often will be hare's   and deer's   5
and cat's   described by seat and track
thin trail out   thin trail back
that I may leave   no greater scar
than they incise   on scarp and peak
in easy passing   unpursued   10
nor greater wound   than weather makes
in any less than   fevered mood
today I will not prey   nor storm
my way may do   no earthly good
but let it do at least   no harm   15

—1996

Louise Glück (b. 1943)

Louise Glück is known for spare and dramatic lyric poems frequently informed by mythology, history, and fairy tales. Of the pared-down quality of her verse, she has written, "I am attracted to ellipsis, to the unsaid, to suggestion, to eloquent, deliberate silence." Glück also is noteworthy for the ways in which she varies her poetic attack from book to book, so that each collection stands as a distinct project with its own ambitions and strategies. Recipient of the National Book Critics Circle Award for The Triumph of Achilles *(1985), the Pulitzer Prize and the Poetry Society of America's William Carlos Williams Prize for* The Wild Iris *(1992), and the PEN/Martha Albrand Award for her collection of essays,* Proofs and Theories *(1994), she grew up in Long Island and was educated at Sarah Lawrence College and Columbia University. Glück served as Poet Laureate from 2003 to 2004. She teaches at Williams College and lives in Cambridge, Massachusetts.*

Mock Orange

It is not the moon, I tell you.
It is these flowers
lighting the yard.

I hate them.
I hate them as I hate sex,   5
the man's mouth
sealing my mouth, the man's
paralyzing body—

and the cry that always escapes,
the low, humiliating   10
premise of union—

In my mind tonight
I hear the question and pursuing answer
fused in one sound
that mounts and mounts and then   15
is split into the old selves,
the tired antagonisms. Do you see?
We were made fools of.

And the scent of mock orange
drifts through the window.   20

How can I rest?
How can I be content
when there is still
that odor in the world?

—*1985*

The Reproach

You have betrayed me, Eros.
You have sent me
my true love.

On a high hill you made
his clear gaze;   5
my heart was not
so hard as your arrow.

What is a poet
without dreams?
I lie awake; I feel   10
actual flesh upon me,
meaning to silence me—
Outside, in the blackness
over the olive trees,
a few stars.   15

I think this is a bitter insult:
that I prefer to walk
the coiled paths of the garden,
to walk beside the river
glittering with drops   20
of mercury. I like to lie
in the wet grass beside the river,
running away, Eros,
not openly, with other men,
but discreetly, coldly—   25

All my life
I have worshiped the wrong gods.
When I watch the trees
on the other side,
the arrow in my heart   30
is like one of them,
swaying and quivering.

—1985

Daisies

Go ahead: say what you're thinking. The garden
is not the real world. Machines
are the real world. Say frankly what any fool
could read in your face: it makes sense
to avoid us, to resist   5
nostalgia. It is
not modern enough, the sound the wind makes
stirring a meadow of daisies: the mind
cannot shine following it. And the mind
wants to shine, plainly, as   10
machines shine, and not
grow deep, as, for example, roots. It is very touching,
all the same, to see you cautiously
approaching the meadow's border in early morning,
when no one could possibly   15
be watching you. The longer you stand at the edge,
the more nervous you seem. No one wants to hear
impressions of the natural world: you will be
laughed at again; scorn will be piled on you.
As for what you're actually   20
hearing this morning: think twice
before you tell anyone what was said in this field
and by whom.

—1992

Ellen Bryant Voigt (b. 1943)

Ellen Bryant Voigt is a native of Virginia, and grew up on a farm. She studied piano seriously from an early age, and trained as a concert pianist before earning a degree from the University of Iowa's Writers' Workshop. In addition to her six books of poetry, Voigt has published The Flexible Lyric *(1999), a collection of essays on poetic craft, in which she has written that "poetry's first allegiance is to music." In 2000, the Vermont Symphony Orchestra premiered "Voices of 1918," a commissioned work based on Voigt's book* Kyrie *(1995). Voigt, who lives in Vermont, has taught poetry at a number of colleges in New England and the South.*

Daughter

There is one grief worse than any other.

When your small feverish throat clogged, and quit,
I knelt beside the chair on the green rug
and shook you and shook you,
but the only sound was mine shouting you back,   5
the delicate curls at your temples,
the blue wool blanket,
your face blue,
your jaw clamped against remedy—

how could I put a knife to that white neck?   10
With you in my lap,
my hands fluttering like flags,
I bend instead over your dead weight
to administer a kiss so urgent, so ruthless,
pumping breath into your stilled body,   15
counting out the rhythm for how long until
the second birth, the second cry
oh Jesus that sudden noisy musical inhalation
that leaves me stunned
by your survival.   20

—*1983*

Lesson

Whenever my mother, who taught
small children forty years,
asked a question, she
already knew the answer.
"Would you like to" meant   5
you would. "Shall we" was
another, and "Don't you think."
As in "Don't you think
it's time you cut your hair."

So when, in the bare room,   10
in the strict bed, she said,
"You want to see?" her hands
were busy at her neckline,
untying the robe, not looking
down at it, stitches   15
bristling where the breast
had been, but straight at me.

I did what I always did:
not weep—she never wept—
and made my face a kindly   20
whitewashed wall, so she
could write, again, whatever
she wanted there.

                                                        —2002

The Others

Our two children grown, now
is when I think
of the others:
                    two more times
the macrocephalic sperm battered   5
its blunt cell forward, rash
leap to the viscous egg—
                    marriage

from our marriage, earth and fire—
and what then,   10
        in the open
synapse from God's finger
to Adam's hand?
        The soul
sent back: 15
      our lucky
or unlucky lost, of whom
we never speak.

—*2002*

Michael Palmer (b. 1943)

Michael Palmer writes poems that defy conventions of logic and syntax in an effort to defamiliarize language and unsettle the reader. Born in New York City, Palmer has written numerous books, including Codes Appearing: Poems 1979–1988 *(2001),* The Promises of Glass *(2000), and* The Lion Bridge: Selected Poems 1972–1995 *(1998). Palmer has received a Guggenheim Foundation fellowship and two grants from the Literature Program of the National Endowment for the Arts. He lives in San Francisco.*

Voice and Address

You are the owner of one complete thought

Its sons and daughters
march toward the capital

There are growing apprehensions to the south

It is ringed about   5
by enclaves of those who have escaped

You would like to live somewhere else

away from the exaggerated music
in a new, exaggerated shirt

a place where colored stones have no value   10

This hill is temporary
but convenient for lunch

Does she mean that the afternoon should pass

in such a manner
not exactly rapidly   15

and with a studied inattention

He has lost his new car
of which you were, once,

a willing prisoner

a blister in your palm   20
identical with the sky's bowl

reflected in the empty sentence

whose glare we have completely shed
ignoring its freshness

The message has been sent   25

across the lesser fractures in the glass
where the listeners are expendable

The heart is thus flexible

now straight now slightly bent
and yesterday was the day for watching it   30

from the shadow of its curious house

Your photo has appeared
an island of calm

in a sea of priapic doubt

You are the keeper of one secret thought   35
the rose and its thorn no longer stand for

You would like to live somewhere

but this is not permitted
You may not even think of it

lest the thinking appear as words   40

and the words as things
arriving in competing waves

from the ruins of that place

—1984

A word is coming up on the screen

A word is coming up on the screen, give me a moment. In the mean-time let me tell you a little something about myself. I was born in Passaic° in a small box flying over Dresden° one night, lovely fig-urines. Things mushroomed after that. My cat has twelve toes, like poets in Boston. Upon the microwave she sits, hairless. The children 5 they say, you are no father but a frame, waiting for a painting. Like, who dreamed you up? Like, gag me with a spoon. Snow falls—win-ter. Things are aglow. One hobby is Southeast Asia, nature another. As a child I slept beneath the bed, fists balled. A face appeared at the window, then another, the same face. We skated and dropped, 10 covering our heads as instructed. Then the music began again, its certainty intact. The true dancers floated past. They are alive to this day, as disappearing ink. After the storm we measured the shore. I grew to four feet then three. I drove a nail through the page and awoke smiling. That was my first smile. In a haze we awaited the 15 next. You said, "Interior colors." You said, "Antinucleons." You said, "Do not steal my words for your work." Snow falls—winter. She hands out photographs of the Union dead. Things are aglow. I traded a name for what followed it. This was useless. The palace of our house has its columns, its palms. A skull in a handcart. I re- 20 moved a tongue and an arm, but this was useless. On Tuesday Freud° told me, "I believe in beards and women with long hair. Do not fall in love." Is there discourse in the tropics? Does the central motif stand out clearly enough? In this name no letters repeat, so it cannot be fixed. Because it's evening I remember memory now. 25 Your English I do not speak. A word is coming up on the screen.

—1988

3 **Passaic** in New Jersey   3 **Dresden** in Germany   22 **Freud** Sigmund Freud (1856–1939), Austrian psychiatrist, founder of psychoanalysis

Untitled

O you in that little bark
What is the relation of the painting to its title

The painting bears no relation to its title
The tiny boat bears

nameless people across   5
water that is infinitely dark

darker even than snow on paving stones
darker than faces in shadow on a boat

The boat is called Blunder, or Nothing, or Parallel Lines
The poem was called I Forget, then Empire, then Game of Cards   10

a game played yesterday in milky light
light which played across the players' faces

and the arcane faces of the cards
There is no relation between the painting and its title

The painting came first then its title   15
The players are playing cards in a little boat

They are asleep and it is dark
Their dream is called The Orderly Electrons

One traveler dreams she does not belong
Another dreams with his eyes wide open   20

like a solemn philosopher
dead from an act of thought

Two more lie with limbs intertwined
The painting has no title

though it has been signed Keeper of the Book   25
the signature obviously forged

for D.S.

—1995

James Tate (b. 1943)

James Tate writes a unique brand of comically surrealistic poetry that has remained constant throughout his career. He was born in Kansas City, Missouri. His first book, The Lost Pilot, *won the Yale Younger Poets Award in 1966, when its author was still a student in the Iowa Writers' Workshop. Tate's* Selected Poems *received the Pulitzer Prize in 1992, and his collection* Worshipful Company of Fletchers *(1994) received the National Book Award. Tate also has published a novel,* Lucky Darryl *(1977), and a short story collection,* Hottentot Ossuary *(1974). He has taught poetry at the University of California, Berkeley; Columbia University; Emerson College; and the University of Massachusetts, Amherst.*

The Lost Pilot

for my father, 1922–1944

Your face did not rot
like the others—the co-pilot,
for example, I saw him

yesterday. His face is corn-
mush: his wife and daughter,   5
the poor ignorant people, stare

as if he will compose soon.
He was more wronged than Job.°
But your face did not rot

like the others—it grew dark,   10
and hard like ebony:
the features progressed in their

distinction. If I could cajole
you to come back for an evening,
down from your compulsive   15

orbiting, I would touch you,
read your face as Dallas,
your hoodlum gunner, now,

---

8 Job Biblical patriarch afflicted by God as a test of his faith

with the blistered eyes, reads
his braille editions. I would   20
touch your face as a disinterested

scholar touches an original page.
However frightening, I would
discover you, and I would not

turn you in; I would not make   25
you face your wife, or Dallas,
or the co-pilot, Jim. You

could return to your crazy
orbiting, and I would not try
to fully understand what   30

it means to you. All I know
is this: when I see you,
as I have seen you at least

once every year of my life,
spin across the wilds of the sky   35
like a tiny, African god,

I feel dead. I feel as if I were
the residue of a stranger's life,
that I should pursue you.

My head cocked toward the sky,   40
I cannot get off the ground,
and, you, passing over again,

fast, perfect, and unwilling
to tell me that you are doing
well, or that it was mistake   45

that placed you in that world,
and me in this; or that misfortune
placed these worlds in us.

—1967

The Blue Booby

The blue booby lives
on the bare rocks
of Galápagos°
and fears nothing.
It is a simple life: 5
they live on fish,
and there are few predators.
Also, the males do not
make fools of themselves
chasing after the young   10
ladies. Rather,
they gather the blue
objects of the world
and construct from them

a nest—an occasional   15
Gaulois° package,
a string of beads,
a piece of cloth from
a sailor's suit. This
replaces the need for   20
dazzling plumage;
in fact, in the past
fifty million years
the male has grown
considerably duller,   25
nor can he sing well.
The female, though,

asks little of him—
the blue satisfies her
completely, has   30
a magical effect
on her. When she returns
from her day of
gossip and shopping,
she sees he has found her   35
a new shred of blue foil:

3 **Galápagos** Pacific archepelago   16 **Gaulois** or Gauloises, French cigarettes sold in a bright blue
package

for this she rewards him
with her dark body,
the stars turn slowly
in the blue foil beside them   40
like the eyes of a mild savior.

—1970

Teaching the Ape to Write Poems

They didn't have much trouble
teaching the ape to write poems:
first they strapped him into the chair,
then tied the pencil around his hand
(the paper had already been nailed down).   5
Then Dr. Bluespire leaned over his shoulder
and whispered into his ear:
"You look like a god sitting there.
Why don't you try writing something?"

—1972

Robert Morgan (b. 1944)

*Robert Morgan is a native of the mountains of North Carolina, and has
retained a large measure of regional ties in his poetry. One of his collections,* Sigodlin (1990), *takes its title from an Appalachian word for things
that are built slightly out of square.* Gap Creek: The Story of a Marriage
(1999), *a novel of turn-of-the-century mountain life, was a bestseller in
2000, and was featured in Oprah Winfrey's book club. In 1971, Morgan
began teaching at Cornell University. He lives in Freeville, New York.*

Mountain Bride

They say Revis found a flatrock
on the ridge just
perfect for a natural hearth,
and built his cabin with a stick

and clay chimney right over it. 5
On their wedding night he lit
the fireplace to dry away the mountain
chill of late spring, and flung on

applewood to dye
the room with molten color while 10
he and Martha that was a Parrish
warmed the sheets between the tick

stuffed with leaves and its feather
cover. Under that wide hearth
a nest of rattlers, 15
they'll knot a hundred together,

had wintered and were coming awake.
The warming rock
flushed them out early.
It was she 20

who wakened to their singing near
the embers and roused him to go look.
Before he reached the fire
more than a dozen struck

and he died yelling her to stay 25
on the big four-poster.
Her uncle coming up the hollow
with a gift bearham two days later

found her shivering there
marooned above a pool 30
of hungry snakes,
and the body beginning to swell.

—1979

Sigodlin

When old carpenters would talk of buildings
out of plumb or out of square, they always
said they were sigodlin, as though anti-

sigodlin meant upright and square, at proper
angles as a structure should be, true to   5
spirit level, plumb line, erect and sure
from the very center of the earth, firm
and joined solid, orthogonal and right,
no sloping or queasy joints, no slouching
rafters or sills. Those men made as they were: 10
the heavy joists and studs yoked perfectly,
and showing the dimensions themselves, each
mated pair of timbers to embody
and enact the crossing of space in its
real extensions, the vertical to be   15
the virtual pith of gravity, horizontal
aligned with the surface of the planet at
its local tangent. And what they fitted
and nailed or mortised into place, downright
and upstanding, straight up and down and flat   20
as water, established the coordinates
forever of their place in creation's
fabric, in a word learned perhaps from
masons who heard it in masonic rites
drawn from ancient rosicrucians° who   25
had the term from the Greek mysteries'
love of geometry's power to say,
while everything in the real may lean just
the slightest bit sigodlin or oblique,
the power whose center is everywhere.   30

—1990

25 **rosicrucianos** a mystical society that claims ancient Egyptian orgins

Shirley Geok-lin Lim (b. 1944)

Shirley Geok-lin Lim writes poetry, fiction, and criticism. Born in Malacca, Malaya, she grew up in poverty and was abandoned by her mother. Her love of the English language over her native tongue earned her the disapproval of the teachers at the Catholic convent school she attended. Lim, who won a scholarship to the University of Malaysia, went on to earn a Ph.D. in English and American literature from Brandeis University. Among the White Moon Faces: An Asian-American Memoir of Homelands *(1996) won her attention both in the United States and Asia. Like her poetry, her prose explores questions of identity and national origin.*

Pantoun° for Chinese Women

"At present, the phenomena of butchering, drowning and leaving to die female infants have been very serious."

(*The People's Daily, Peking, March 3rd, 1983*)

They say a child with two mouths is no good.
In the slippery wet, a hollow space,
Smooth, gumming, echoing wide for food.
No wonder my man is not here at his place.

In the slippery wet, a hollow space,   5
A slit narrowly sheathed within its hood.
No wonder my man is not here at his place:
He is digging for the dragon jar of soot.

That slit narrowly sheathed within its hood!
His mother, squatting, coughs by the fire's blaze   10
While he digs for the dragon jar of soot.
We had saved ashes for a hundred days.

His mother, squatting, coughs by the fire's blaze.
The child kicks against me mewing like a flute.
We had saved ashes for a hundred days.   15
Knowing, if the time came, that we would.

Pantoun Malayan term for the pantoum, a verse form in which the second and fourth lines of each stanza recur as the first and third lines of the stanza that follows

The child kicks against me crying like a flute
Through its two weak mouths. His mother prays
Knowing when the time comes that we would,
For broken clay is never set in glaze.   20

Through her two weak mouths his mother prays.
She will not pluck the rooster nor serve its blood,
For broken clay is never set in glaze:
Women are made of river sand and wood.

She will not pluck the rooster nor serve its blood.   25
My husband frowns, pretending in his haste
Women are made of river sand and wood.
Milk soaks the bedding. I cannot bear the waste.

My husband frowns, pretending in his haste.
Oh clean the girl, dress her in ashy soot!   30
Milk soaks our bedding, I cannot bear the waste.
They say a child with two mouths is no good.

—*1989*

Riding into California

If you come to a land with no ancestors
to bless you, you have to be your own
ancestor. The veterans in the mobile home
park don't want to be there. It isn't easy.
Oil rigs litter the land like giant frozen birds.   5
Ghosts welcome us to a new life, and
an immigrant without home ghosts
cannot believe the land is real. So you're
grateful for familiarity, and Bruce Lee°
becomes your hero. Coming into Fullerton,   10
everyone waiting at the station is white.
The good thing about being Chinese on Amtrak
is no one sits next to you. The bad thing is
you sit alone all the way to Irvine.

—*1998*

9 Bruce Lee (1940–1973), martial artist and film star from Hong Kong

Starlight Haven

Susie Wong was at the Starlight Haven,
the Good Times Bar and Sailors Home.
It was always dark at noon:
you had to blink three times before
you could see Susie standing by   5
the washed chutney jar half-filled
with ten and twenty-cent coins.
When the bar was empty her eyes were sad
and she'd mop the formica tables,
dry a row of tall Anchor Pilsner°   10
glasses. The wet cloth slap-slapped
like Susie's japanese slippers
over the dirty floor.
Then the swing-doors
bang and the darkness is full of white   15
uniforms, full of cold Tigers°
sweating in warm air-conditioning.
I think of the flutter in Susie's pulse.
Buy a drink, Tommy boy! G.I. Joe!
Yankee Doodle! Howdy Doody! Romeo!   20
and suddenly Johnny Mathis°
like black magic is crooning "Chances Are."
Her girlish voice is soft and happy,
soft like a tubby belly after
six babies and ten years of beat-up   25
marriage, happy as only Singapore
Susie Wongs can be, when Johnny
and Ray are rocking the bottles
and their tops pop off and the chutney
jar is singing chink, chink.   30

The red-faced brawny men are laughing
at her voice. Quack, quack, they laugh
so hard they spill Tigers over
the plastic counter. Quack, quack, fuck, fuck.
Susie looks at the bar-man who makes   35

10 **Anchor Pilsner** brand of beer   21 **Johnny Mathis** (b. 1935), American vocalist
16 **tigers beer** brewed in singapore

his coolie eyes dumb black stones
and wipes up the yellow puddles
without a grunt.
Thirty years later
I hear mother singing "In the sweet   40
bye and bye." She is a Jesus woman
grown up from bar-girl. Sailors and Tommies
have disappeared from her Memory Lane.
I still keep the bracelet mother gave me,
gold saved from beer spilled on the clean   45
tables, her clean lap. I savor the taste
of that golden promise, never to love men
in white who laugh, quack, quack.

—*1998*

Dick Davis   (b. 1945)

*Dick Davis is the foremost translator worldwide of Persian into English,
and the author of many books of restrained, formally elegant poems. Born
in Portsmouth, England, he studied at King's College, Cambridge. In
1970, while teaching in Greece, he took a trip to Iran, fell ill, and was
nursed back to health by the Iranian woman who eventually became his
wife. For eight years, Davis remained in Iran, studying Persian and teaching at the University of Tehran. After the revolution in 1979, he returned
with his family to England and earned a Ph.D. in medieval Persian literature from the University of Manchester. He has published translations
from Italian (prose) and Persian (prose and verse) and edited numerous
academic works. Davis currently teaches Persian at Ohio State University.*

Duchy and Shinks

For Catherine Tufariello and Jeremy Telman

Duchy and Shinks, my father's maiden aunts,
Lived at the seaside and kept house together:
They bicycled in every kind of weather
And looked across the waves to far-off France.
Routine had made their days a stately dance,   5

A spinsters' *pas de deux*, with every feather
Where it ought to be: no one asked them whether
They liked a life with nothing left to chance.

They showed me photographs of long ago—
Two English roses in a chorus line: 10
I said, "They're lovely" as I sipped my tea.
They were, too—at the *Folies*,° second row,
Or downstage, glittering in a grand design,
With every feather where it ought to be.

—2002

Farewell to the Mentors

Old bachelors to whom I've turned
    For comfort in my life,
I find you less than useful now
    I've children and a wife;

And though you're great on *Weltschmerz*,° loss,   5
    Lust, irony, old age,
I draw a blank when looking for
    Advice on teenage rage;

On sibling rivalry and rows
    I can't begin to rate you,   10
You're silent when it comes to screams
    Of "Dad, I really hate you."

So get you gone, Fitz.,° Edgar,° Wystan,°
    And dear old Housman° too;
It's clear that at this juncture I   15
    Need other guides than you.

—2002

12 **Folies** the *Folies-Bergere*, a famous Parisian revue featuring scantily-clad chorus girls
5 **Weltschmerz** (German), sadness over the world's evils   13 **Fitz.** Edward Fitzgerald (1809–1883),
British poet and translator of Omar Khayyam's *Rubaiyat*   13 **Edgar** Edgar Bowers (1924–2000),
American poet   13 **Wystan** Wystan Hugh (W. H.) Auden (1907–1973), British poet   14 **Housman**
A. E. Housman (1859–1936), British poet

A Monorhyme
for the Shower

Lifting her arms to soap her hair
Her pretty breasts respond—and there
The movement of that buoyant pair
Is like a spell to make me swear
Twenty-odd years have turned to air;   5
Now she's the girl I didn't dare
Approach, ask out, much less declare
My love to, mired in young despair.

Childbearing, rows, domestic care—
All the prosaic wear and tear   10
That constitute the life we share—
Slip from her beautiful and bare
Bright body as, made half aware
Of my quick surreptitious stare,
She wrings the water from her hair   15
And turning smiles to see me there.

—*2002*

Kay Ryan (b. 1945)

Kay Ryan writes spare and highly original poems dense with rhyme and wordplay. Of her writing process and the brevity of her poems, she says: ". . . the way I write is to melt all the materials in my brain at once, like those cyclotrons in which they get atomic matter really hot and get it to do weird things. I have so many things that I like to do at once, that I can't do very long poems. It's hard to sustain." A lifelong Californian, Ryan grew up in the San Joaquin Valley and the Mojave Desert. After studying at UCLA and the University of California, Irvine, she took a job teaching basic writing skills at the College of Marin, where she teaches today. Ryan has been awarded two Pushcart Prizes, and her collection Flamingo Watching *was a finalist for the 1995 Lenore Marshall Poetry Prize, awarded by the American Academy of Poets; in 2004 she was awarded the Ruth Lilly Award.*

Turtle

Who would be a turtle who could help it?
A barely mobile hard roll, a four-oared helmet,
she can ill afford the chances she must take
in rowing toward the grasses that she eats.
Her track is graceless, like dragging   5
a packing-case places, and almost any slope
defeats her modest hopes. Even being practical,
she's often stuck up to the axle on her way
to something edible. With everything optimal,
she skirts the ditch which would convert   10
her shell into a serving dish. She lives
below luck-level, never imagining some lottery
will change her load of pottery to wings.
Her only levity is patience,
the sport of truly chastened things.   15

—*1994*

Bestiary

A bestiary catalogs
bests. The mediocres
both higher and lower
are suppressed in favor
of the singularly savage   5
or clever, the spectacularly
pincered, the archest
of the arch deceivers
who press their advantage
without quarter even after   10
they've won as of course they would.
Best is not to be confused with *good*—
a different creature altogether,
and treated of in the goodiary—
a text alas lost now for centuries.   15

—*1996*

Drops in the Bucket

At first
each drop
makes its
own pock
against the tin.   5
In time
there is a
thin lacquer
which is
layered and   10
relayered
till there's
a quantity
of water
with its   15
own skin

and sense
of purpose,
shocked at
each new violation   20
of its surface.

—2000

Mockingbird

Nothing whole
is so bold,
we sense. Nothing
not cracked is
so exact and   5
of a piece. He's
the distempered
emperor of parts,
the king of patch,
the master of   10
pastiche, who so
hashes other birds'
laments, so minces
their capriccios, that
the dazzle of dispatch   15
displaces the originals.
As though brio
really does beat feeling,
the way two aces
beat three hearts   20
when it's cards
you're dealing.

—2000

Leon Stokesbury (b. 1945)

Leon Stokesbury was born in Oklahoma City, and grew up in Silsbee, Texas. He has taught creative writing and literature at several southern universities, and currently teaches in the graduate creative writing program at Georgia State University in Atlanta. His poetry collections include Autumn Rhythm: New and Selected Poems, *which won the 1996 Poets' Prize. He also has edited anthologies of contemporary Southern poetry and the poetry of World War II. Known for his skill as a performer, Stokesbury has given readings at over one hundred colleges and universities.*

To His Book

Wafer; thin and hard and bitter pill I
   Take from time to time; pillow I have lain
      Too long on; holding the brief dreams, the styled
Dreams, the nightmares, shadows, red flames high
   High up on mountains; wilted zinnias, rain   5
      On dust, and great weight, the dead dog, and wild
Onions; mastodonic woman who knows how,—
   I'm tired of you, tired of your insane
      Acid eating in the brain. Sharp stones, piled
Particularly, I let you go. Sink, or float, or fly now,   10
      Bad child.

—*1976*

Day Begins at Governor's Square Mall

Here, newness is all. Or almost all. And like
a platterful of pope's noses° at a White House dinner,
I exist apart. But these trees now—
how do you suppose they grow this high in here?
They look a little like the trees I sat beneath in 1959   5
waiting with my cheesecloth net for butterflies.

2 pope's nose rural expression for the tail-end of a chicken

It was August and it was hot. Late summer,
yes, but already the leaves in trees were
flecked with ochers and the umbers of the dead.
I sweated there for hours, so driven,   10
so immersed in the forest's shimmering life,
that I could will my anxious self not move
for half a day—just on the imagined chance
of making some slight part of it my own.
Then they came. One perfect pair of just-hatched   15
black-and-white striped butterflies. The white
lemon-tipped with light, in shade
then out, meandering. Zebra swallowtails,
floating, drunk in the sun, so rare to find
their narrow, fragile, two-inch tails intact.   20
At that moment I could only drop my net and stare.
The last of August. 1959. But these trees, now,
climb up through air and concrete never hot or cold.
And I suspect the last lepidoptera that found
themselves in here were sprayed then swept away.   25
Everyone is waiting though, as before a storm—
anticipating something. Do these leaves never fall?

Now, and with a mild surprise, faint
music falls. But no shop breaks open yet.
The people, like myself, range aimlessly;   30
the air seems thick and still. Then, lights blink on;
the escalators jerk and hum. And in the center, at
the exact center of the mall, a jet of water spurts
twenty feet straight up, then drops and spatters
in a shallow pool where signs announce that none   35
may ever go. O bright communion! O new cathedral!
where the appetitious, the impure, the old, the young,
the bored, the lost, the dumb, with wide dilated eyes°
advance with offerings to be absolved and be made clean.
Now, the lime-lit chainlink fronts from over one hundred   40
pleasant and convenient stalls and stores are rolled away.
Now, odors of frying won tons come wafting up from
Lucy Ho's Bamboo Garden. And this music, always
everywhere, yet also somehow strangely played as if

38 dilated eyes "I remember I wrote this poem shortly after rereading Wordsworth's 'Tintern Abbey' and then seeing George A. Romero's 1978 horror film *Dawn of the Dead* for the first time" [Author's note]

not to be heard, pours its soft harangue down now.   45
The people wander forward now. And the world begins.

—*1986*

The Day Kennedy Died

Suppose on the day Kennedy died you had
a vision. But this was no inner movie
with a plot or anything like it. Not
even very visual when you get down
to admitting what actually occurred.   5
About two-thirds of the way through 4th period
Senior Civics, fifteen minutes before
the longed-for lunchtime, suppose you stood up
for no good reason—no reason at all really—
and announced, as you never had before,   10
to the class in general and to yourself
as well, "Something. Something is happening.
I see. Something coming. I can see. I . . ."

And that was all. You stood there: blank.
The class roared. Even Phyllis Hoffpaur, girl   15
most worshipped by you from afar that year,
turned a vaguely pastel shade of red
and smiled, and Richard Head, your best friend,
Dick Head to the chosen few, pulled you down
to your desk whispering, "Jesus, Man! Jesus   20
Christ!" Then you went numb. You did not know
for sure what had occurred. But less than one hour
later, when Stella (despised) Vandenburg, teacher
of twelfth grade English, came sashaying
into the auditorium, informing, left and right,   25
as many digesting members of the student body
as she could of what she had just heard,
several students began to glance at you,
remembering what you'd said. A few pointed,
whispering to their confederates, and on that   30

disturbing day they slinked away in the halls.
Even Dick Head did not know what to say.

In 5th period Advanced Math, Principal
Crawford played the radio over the intercom
and the school dropped deeper into history.   35
For the rest of that day, everyone slinked away—
except for the one moment Phyllis Hoffpaur
stared hard, the look on her face asking,
assuming you would know, "Will it be ok?"

And you did not know. No one knew.   40
Everyone staggered back to their houses
that evening aimless and lost, not knowing,
certainly sensing something had been
changed forever. *Silsbee High forever!*
That is our claim! Never, no never!   45
Will we lose our fame! you often sang.
But this was to be the class of 1964,
afraid of the future at last, who would select,
as the class song, Terry Stafford's *Suspicion.*
And this was November—even in Texas   50
the month of failings, month of sorrows
—from which we saw no turning.
It would be a slow two-months slide until
the manic beginnings of the British Invasion,°
three months before Clay's° ascension to the throne,   55
but all you saw walking home that afternoon
were the gangs of gray leaves clotting the curbs
and culverts, the odors of winter forever
in the air: cold, damp, bleak, dead, dull:
dragging you toward the solstice like a tide.   60

—*2004*

54 **British Invasion** British rock bands, such as The Beatles, became popular in the U.S. in 1964
55 **Clay's** Cassius Clay (Muhammed Ali) became heavyweight champion on February 25, 1964

Marilyn Nelson (b. 1946)

Marilyn Nelson is the author of The Homeplace *(1990), a sequence of poems on family history.* The Homeplace *is remarkable for its sensitive exploration of the mixed white and black bloodlines in the poet's family history. Nelson was born in Cleveland, Ohio, to Melvin M. Nelson, one of the famed Tuskegee airmen, and Johnnie Mitchell Nelson, a teacher. Brought up on military bases, she began writing in elementary school. She holds degrees from the University of California, Davis; the University of Pennsylvania; and the University of Minnesota. Her collection of new and selected poems,* The Fields of Praise, *received the 1998 Poets' Prize. Nelson teaches at the University of Connecticut, and in 2001 she was named poet laureate of the state of Connecticut.* Carver: A Life in Poems, *a poetic biography of George Washington Carver, appeared in 2001.*

The Ballad of Aunt Geneva

Geneva was the wild one.
Geneva was a tart.
Geneva met a blue-eyed boy
and gave away her heart.

Geneva ran a roadhouse.   5
Geneva wasn't sent
to college like the others:
Pomp's° pride her punishment.

She cooked out on the river,
watching the shore slide by,   10
her lips pursed into hardness,
her deep-set brown eyes dry.

They say she killed a woman
over a good black man
by braining the jealous heifer   15
with an iron frying pan.

They say, when she was eighty,
she got up late at night

8 Pomp's in *The Homeplace,* Geneva is one of Pomp Atwood's seven children

and sneaked her old, white lover in
to make love, and to fight.   20

First, they heard the tell-tale
singing of the springs,
then Geneva's voice rang out:
I need to buy some things,

So next time, bring more money.   25
And bring more moxie, too.
I ain't got no time to waste
on limp white mens like you.

Oh yeah? Well, Mister White Man,
it sure might be stone-white,   30
but my thing's white as it is.
And you know damn well I'm right.

Now listen: take your heart pills
and pay the doctor mind.
If you up and die on me,   35
I'll whip your white behind.

They tiptoed through the parlor
on heavy, time-slowed feet.
She watched him, from her front door,
walk down the dawnlit street.   40

Geneva was the wild one.
Geneva was a tart.
Geneva met a blue-eyed boy
and gave away her heart.

                                                        —1990

Lonely Eagles

For Daniel "Chappie" James, General USAF
and for the 332nd Fighter Group

Being black in America
was the Original Catch,
so no one was surprised
by 22:°

4 22 a reference to Joseph Heller's World War II novel *Catch-22*

The segregated airstrips,   5
separate camps.
They did the jobs
they'd been trained to do.

Black ground-crews kept them in the air;
black flight-surgeons kept them alive;   10
the whole Group removed their headgear
when another pilot died.

They were known by their names:
"Ace" and "Lucky,"
"Sky-hawk Johnny," "Mr. Death."   15
And by their positions and planes.
Red Leader to Yellow Wing-man,
do you copy?

If you could find a fresh egg
you bought it and hid it   20
in your dopp-kit or your boot
until you could eat it alone.
On the night before a mission
you gave a buddy
your hiding-places   25
as solemnly
as a man dictating
his will.
There's a chocolate bar
in my Bible;   30
my whiskey bottle
is inside my bed-roll.

In beat-up Flying Tigers
that had seen action in Burma,
they shot down three German jets.   35
They were the only outfit
in the American Air Corps
to sink a destroyer
with fighter planes.
Fighter planes with names   40
like "By Request."
Sometimes the radios
didn't even work.

They called themselves
"Hell from Heaven." 45
This Spookwaffe.°
My father's old friends.

It was always
maximum effort:
A whole squadron 50
of brother-men
raced across the tarmac
and mounted their planes.

    My tent-mate was a guy named Starks.
    The funny thing about me and Starks 55
    was that my air mattress leaked,
    and Starks' didn't.
    Every time we went up,
    I gave my mattress to Starks
    and put his on my cot. 60

    One day we were strafing a train.
    Strafing's bad news:
    you have to fly so low and slow
    you're a pretty clear target.
    My other wing-man and I 65
    exhausted our ammunition and got out.
    I recognized Starks
    by his red tail
    and his rudder's trim-tabs.
    He couldn't pull up his nose. 70
    He dived into the train
    and bought the farm.

    I found his chocolate,
    three eggs, and a full fifth
    of his hoarded-up whiskey. 75
    I used his mattress
    for the rest of my tour.

    It still bothers me, sometimes:
    I was sleeping
    on his breath. 80

—*1990*

46 Spookwaffe a play on Luftwaffe (German Air Force)

Minor Miracle

Which reminds me of another knock-on-wood
memory. I was cycling with a male friend,
through a small midwestern town. We came to a 4-way
stop and stopped, chatting. As we started again,
a rusty old pick-up truck, ignoring the stop sign,   5
hurricaned past scant inches from our front wheels.
My partner called, "Hey, that was a 4-way stop!"
The truck driver, stringy blond hair a long fringe
under his brand-name beer cap, looked back and yelled,
        "You fucking niggers!"   10
And sped off.
My friend and I looked at each other and shook our heads.
We remounted our bikes and headed out of town.
We were pedaling through a clear blue afternoon
between two fields of almost-ripened wheat   15
bordered by cornflowers and Queen Anne's lace
when we heard an unmuffled motor, a honk-honking.
We stopped, closed ranks, made fists.
It was the same truck. It pulled over.
A tall, very much in shape young white guy slid out: 20
greasy jeans, homemade finger tattoos, probably
a Marine Corps boot-camp footlockerful
of martial arts techniques.

"What did you say back there!" he shouted.
My friend said, "I said it was a 4-way stop.   25
You went through it."
"And what did I say?" the white guy asked.
"You said: 'You fucking niggers.'"
The afternoon froze.

"Well," said the white guy,   30
shoving his hands into his pockets
and pushing dirt around with the pointed toe of his boot,
"I just want to say I'm sorry."
He climbed back into his truck
and drove away.   35

—*1997*

Thomas Lux (b. 1946)

*Thomas Lux is the only child of a milkman and a Sears, Roebuck switch-
board operator, neither of whom graduated from high school. Born in
Northampton, Massachusetts, and raised on a dairy farm, Lux spent
many childhood afternoons in his town's public library. His first book,*
Memory's Handgrenade *(1972), was published soon after he graduated
from Emerson College in Boston. Lux, who also has studied at the Iowa
Writers' Workshop, taught for many years at Sarah Lawrence College and
in the Warren Wilson low-residence M.F.A. program. In 2001, he became
the first holder of the McEver Chair at Georgia Institute of Technology's
Ivan Allen College. The rueful humor of Lux's poems is often evident in
their titles—for example, "Walt Whitman's Brain Dropped on Laboratory
Floor," "Commercial Leech Farming Today," and "Pecked to Death by
Swans."*

Kwashiorkor; Marasmus

An unknown river whose banks drip feathers,
orchid petals, wherein live fish
mysterious; a medieval scholar, humanist
scamp. No, a rare, rich dish, thick

with crème fraîche;° the local junior high   5
known for annual bake sales.
A beautiful African princess, two
thousand cows her dowry; a town

in New Jersey. A defunct balm
or salve; a tree whose boat-shaped leaves   10
are prized for love potions. A long-forgotten,
one-sided battle won easily by imperialists;

a ship lost rounding the Horn,°
not a single spar or beam washed ashore.
A name but no face   15
from a dream; a rich uncle

---

5 **crème fraîche** (French), a thick cream used in soups and sauces   13 **the Horn** Cape Horn, at the
southern tip of South America

kids are named after in hopes of . . .
An Arab pastry; a lower prophet,
saint of bad luck and the empty beggar's bowl.
Two more words, by heart, to learn.   20

—*1990*

Refrigerator, 1957

More like a vault—you pull the handle out
and on the shelves: not a lot,
and what there is (a boiled potato
in a bag, a chicken carcass
under foil) looking dispirited,   5
drained, mugged. This is not
a place to go in hope or hunger.
But, just to the right of the middle
of the middle door shelf, on fire, a lit-from-within red,
heart red, sexual red, wet neon red,   10
shining red in their liquid, exotic,
aloof, slumming
in such company: a jar
of maraschino cherries. Three-quarters
full, fiery globes, like strippers   15
at a church social. Maraschino cherries, maraschino,
the only foreign word I knew. Not once
did I see these cherries employed: not
in a drink, nor on top
of a glob of ice cream,   20
or just pop one in your mouth. Not once.
The same jar there through an entire
childhood of dull dinners—bald meat,
pocked peas and, see above,
boiled potatoes. Maybe   25
they came over from the old country,
family heirlooms, or were status symbols
bought with a piece of the first paycheck
from a sweatshop,
which beat the pig farm in Bohemia,   30
handed down from my grandparents

to my parents
to be someday mine,
then my child's?
They were beautiful   35
and, if I never ate one,
it was because I knew it might be missed
or because I knew it would not be replaced
and because you do not eat
that which rips your heart with joy.   40

—*1997*

Yusef Komunyakaa (b. 1947)

Yusef Komunyakaa has written memorably on a wide range of subjects, including jazz and his service during the Vietnam War. A native of Boga-lusa, Louisiana, he was the eldest of five children. After graduating from high school, he enlisted in the Army to begin a tour of duty in Vietnam. He served as a correspondent for and editor of The Southern Cross, *a mili-tary newspaper, and received the Bronze Star for his work as a journalist. Komunyakaa studied at the University of Colorado, Colorado State Uni-versity, and the University of California, Irvine. He has taught in the New Orleans public school system and at the University of New Orleans; Indi-ana University, Bloomington; and Princeton University.* Neon Vernacular: New and Selected Poems *(1993) won the Pulitzer Prize in 1994, and* Pleasure Dome: New and Collected Poems *appeared in 2001.*

Facing It

My black face fades,
hiding inside the black granite.
I said I wouldn't,
dammit: No tears.
I'm stone. I'm flesh.   5
My clouded reflection eyes me
like a bird of prey, the profile of night
slanted against morning. I turn
this way—the stone lets me go.
I turn this way—I'm inside   10
the Vietnam Veterans Memorial

again, depending on the light
to make a difference.
I go down the 58,022 names,
half-expecting to find   15
my own in letters like smoke.
I touch the name Andrew Johnson;
I see the booby trap's white flash.
Names shimmer on a woman's blouse
but when she walks away   20
the names stay on the wall.
Brushstrokes flash, a red bird's
wings cutting across my stare.
The sky. A plane in the sky.
A white vet's image floats   25
closer to me, then his pale eyes
look through mine. I'm a window.
He's lost his right arm
inside the stone. In the black mirror
a woman's trying to erase names: 30
No, she's brushing a boy's hair.

—1988

My Father's Love Letters

On Fridays he'd open a can of Jax°
After coming home from the mill,
& ask me to write a letter to my mother
Who sent postcards of desert flowers
Taller than men. He would beg,   5
Promising to never beat her
Again. Somehow I was happy
She had gone, & sometimes wanted
To slip in a reminder, how Mary Lou
Williams' "Polka Dots & Moonbeams"°   10
Never made the swelling go down.

---

1 **Jax** brand of beer brewed in New Orleans   10 **Polka Dots & Moonbeams** song recorded by jazz
pianist and composer Mary Lou Williams (1910–1981)

His carpenter's apron always bulged
With old nails, a claw hammer
Looped at his side & extension cords
Coiled around his feet.   15
Words rolled from under the pressure
Of my ballpoint: Love,
Baby, Honey, Please.
We sat in the quiet brutality
Of voltage meters & pipe threaders,   20
Lost between sentences . . .
The gleam of a five-pound wedge
On the concrete floor
Pulled a sunset
Through the doorway of his toolshed.   25
I wondered if she laughed
& held them over a gas burner.
My father could only sign
His name, but he'd look at blueprints
& say how many bricks   30
Formed each wall. This man,
Who stole roses & hyacinth
For his yard, would stand there
With eyes closed & fists balled,
Laboring over a simple word, almost   35
Redeemed by what he tried to say.

—1992

Ode to the Maggot

Brother of the blowfly
& godhead, you work magic
Over battlefields,
In slabs of bad pork

& flophouses. Yes, you   5
Go to the root of all things.
You are sound & mathematical.
Jesus Christ, you're merciless

With the truth. Ontological & lustrous,
You cast spells on beggars & kings   10
Behind the stone door of Caesar's tomb
Or split trench in a field of ragweed.

No decree or creed can outlaw you
As you take every living thing apart. Little
Master of earth, no one gets to heaven   15
Without going through you first.

—*2000*

Molly Peacock (b. 1947)

*Molly Peacock uses poetic form to give shape to raw and difficult subject
matter, including her father's alcoholism and her experiences as an abused
child. Born in Buffalo, New York, she studied at the State University of
New York at Binghamton and at Johns Hopkins University. In addition to
many books of poetry, she has published prose including* Paradise, Piece
by Piece *(1998), a literary memoir about her decision not to have children,
and* How to Read a Poem . . . and Start a Poetry Circle *(1999). She also
edited the anthology,* The Private I: Privacy in a Public World *(2001). A
former president of the Poetry Society of America, she helped pioneer the
"Poetry in Motion" series which displays poems in New York City buses
and subway cars. Poet-in-residence at the Poet's Corner, Cathedral of St.
John the Divine in Manhattan, Peacock lives in London, Ontario, and in
New York City.*

Buffalo

Many times I wait there for my father,
in parking lots of bars or in the bars
themselves, drinking a cherry Coke, Father
joking with a bartender who ignores
him, except to take the orders. I think   5
of the horrible discipline of bartenders,
and how they must feel to serve, how some shrink
from any conversation to endure
the serving, serving, serving of disease.

I think I would be one of these, eternally   10
hunched around myself, turning to appease
monosyllabically in the dimness. To flee
enforced darkness in the afternoon
wasn't possible, where was I to go?
Home was too far to walk to, my balloon,   15
wrinkling in the front seat in the cold, too
awful to go out and play with. Many
times I wait there for Daddy, stupefied
with helpless rage. *Looks old for her age*, any
one of the bartenders said. Outside, the wide   20
endlessly horizontal vista raged
with sun and snow: it was Buffalo, gleaming
below Great Lakes. Behind bar blinds we were caged,
some motes of sunlight cathedrally beaming.

—1989

Why I Am Not a Buddhist

I love desire, the state of want and thought
of how to get; building a kingdom in a soul
requires desire. I love the things I've sought—
you in your beltless bathrobe, tongues of cash that loll
from my billfold—and love what I want: clothes,   5
houses, redemption. Can a new mauve suit
equal God? Oh no, desire is ranked. To lose
a loved pen is not like losing faith. Acute
desire for nut gateau° is driven out by death,
but the cake on its plate has meaning,   10
even when love is endangered and nothing matters.
For my mother, health; for my sister, bereft,
wholeness. But why is desire suffering?
Because want leaves a world in tatters?
How else but in tatters should a world be?   15
A columned porch set high above a lake.
Here, take my money. A loved face in agony,
the spirit gone. Here, use my rags of love.

—1995

9 **nut gateau** a cake

A Favor of Love

"Thank you for making this sacrifice,"
I say to my husband as I run to Kim's market.
Never mind what the sacrifice is.
Sacrifices between husbands and wives are private,
and fill a person with simple, healing water.   5
Kim's buzzes with Sunday night customers
as into the plastic basket go
watercress, asparagus, garlic, pecans
when a girl throws herself through the plastic door flaps
tears streaming down her face while her boyfriend   10
catapults past the troughs of oranges screaming,
Water! Water!
And Mr. Kim peers down his quizzical nose
and Mrs. Kim stands in mountain pose

openly hating the girl for dying of an overdose   15
among the lemons, mangoes, papayas, and limes
of the country of her family's origins
plunging among the plums and dying there
the color of a plum beneath her dark hair
for the girl is turning purple.   20
From the back of the store by the water the boyfriend
shouts that she's swallowed a lollipop head.
Now she is almost the color of an eggplant,
and young Mr. Kim by the register is asking her,
"Should I call 911?" in a pleasant, insistent whisper,   25
"Should I call 911?"
Big sound should boom from her, but only a bubble
squeaks at her lips. "Call 911!" I speak for her
raising my woollen arm, aiming for her
shoulder blades where I whack, whack her again,   30
and no lollipop pops out. But sound bellows out!
Like idiots everywhere, her boyfriend shouts
Calm down, Calm down, forcing water into her throat,
which must help dissolve the candy my backslap dislodged.
"Where's that Choking Victims poster you're supposed to hang?" 35
the boyfriend demands of young Mr. Kim.
"I'll cancel 911," he says.
"Where is that lady?" the sobbing girl is asking.

Right here, I say, *I am right here behind you.*
    I am putting endive in my basket.   40
    As she grabs me in a bear hug,
      her face has a human color

and it is a hard face, strong and horsey.
    "Oh Mommy!" she shouts.
As my sister was dying she called me Mommy.   45
    I stand in a mountain pose,
and she smiles up from a pile of plastic baskets.
    "My name is Marisol!" she spouts.
    My name is Molly!
(I'm afraid she might hear those *l*'s as *m*'s.)   50
    "Thank you for saving my life!"
Now don't eat any more lollipops, I say mommily,
    closing the cosmic circle begun at breakfast
when my husband made the promise I won't reveal.
    Grown human beings making sacrifices   55
    return to the universe a favor of love.

                                —*2002*

Jim Hall (b. 1947)

Jim Hall is one of the most brilliantly inventive comic poets in recent years. He also has written a successful series of crime novels set in south Florida, beginning with Under Cover of Daylight *in 1987. Born in Hopkinsville, Kentucky, Hall studied at Florida Presbyterian College (now Eckerd College), Johns Hopkins, and the University of Utah. He teaches at Florida International University, and lives in Key Largo.*

Maybe Dats Your Pwoblem Too

All my pwoblems,
who knows, maybe evwybody's pwoblems
is due to da fact, due to da awful twuth
dat I am SPIDERMAN.

I know, I know. All da dumb jokes: 5
No flies on you, ha ha,
and da ones about what do I do wit all
doze extwa legs in bed. Well, dat's funny yeah.
But you twy being
SPIDERMAN for a month or two. Go ahead.   10

You get doze cwazy calls fwom da
Gubbener askin you to twap some booglar who's
only twying to wip off color T.V. sets.
Now, what do I cawre about T.V. sets?
But I pull on da suit, da stinkin suit,   15
wit da sucker cups on da fingers,
and get my wopes and wittle bundle of
equipment and den I go flying like cwazy
acwoss da town fwom woof top to woof top.

Till der he is. Some poor dumb color T.V. slob   20
and I fall on him and we westle a widdle
until I get him all woped. So big deal.

You tink when you SPIDERMAN
der's sometin big going to happen to you.
Well, I tell you what. It don't happen dat way.   25
Nuttin happens. Gubbener calls, I go.
Bwing him to powice, Gubbener calls again,
like dat over and over.

I tink I twy sometin diffunt. I tink I twy
sometin excitin like wacing cawrs. Sometin to make   30
my heart beat at a difwent wate.
But den you just can't quit being sometin like
SPIDERMAN.
You SPIDERMAN for life. Fowever. I can't even
buin my suit. It won't buin. It's fwame wesistent.   35
So maybe dat's youwr pwoblem too, who knows.
Maybe dat's da whole pwoblem wif evwytin.
Nobody can buin der suits, dey all fwame wesistent.
Who knows?

—1980

Sperm Count

On the bright slide a thousand
of them squiggle. Some set off
for the edge of this flat world,
some spin in a frenzy as if they know
this isn't where they were meant to be.   5
And there are the dead ones,
the two-headed or tailless ones.
The jig is up for them.
No marathon swim. No happy cry:
I'm here! Look what I've brought!   10

What are we anyway
if it can all be sent in one
microscopic slithering? I have,
as I peer at a thousand versions
of myself, every conceivable predictable   15
response. I am clearly more than
anything one of them can deliver.
I side with the two-headed ones.
They, at least, had some new idea.

When later I am home and cleaning out   20
old trunks, old letters, scraps of
writing, things I can't bear to read
or part with, things that have swum
as far as they can and have come to
nothing, I think again of the ones   25
that finally make it.
They would be the very ones
I would never have as friends:
dogged, mean enough to bump their twins aside.
The will to wriggle up the last hostile twist   30
of tube. The blind brutal ignorance to believe
the message that they carry
should be passed on at all.

—1986

White Trash

Now it's styrofoam pellets
that blow across the yard.
They settle in the new grass
like the eggs of Japanese toys.
It's a kind of modern snowing.   5

The boy next door opened a box,
took out the precious present
and shook these white spun plastic
droplets into the wind.
It's how his family thinks.   10

Hundreds of them. Shaped like
unlucky fetuses or the brains
of TV stars.
Now they burrow in the lawn,
defy the rake, wriggle like the toes
of the shallow buried.   15

They'll be there when we're gone.
Bright tumors, rooted in the dark.
Crowding the dirt. Nothing makes them
grow. But nothing kills them either.

—1986

Amy Uyematsu (b. 1947)

Amy Uyematsu is the granddaughter of Japanese immigrants. Raised in Los Angeles's Little Tokyo neighborhood, she majored in mathematics at UCLA, where she helped pioneer an Asian-American studies program. She has published two poetry collections: Nights of Fire, Nights of Rain *(1998) and* 30 Miles from J-Town *(1992), for which she received the Nicholas Roerich Poetry Prize. Uyematsu's 1969 essay "The Emergence of Yellow Power in America" drew connections between the burgeoning Asian-American struggle for political power and the more established Black Power movement.*

Lessons from Central America

Always start with the male children.

Give them candy, Coca Cola, and guns.

Tell them secrets.
Teach them to doubt everything,
especially fathers and priests.   5
Show them what happens to men
who won't listen to reason
and necessity.

Take them to the grave of warm skulls.
Make them watch all the ways   10
for torturing a sister.

Do not trust them
too long with their mothers,
but do give them bread
and shoes for their feet.   15

—*1998*

Ai (b. 1947)

Ai writes realistic dramatic monologues that often reveal the agonies of characters trapped in unfulfilling or even dangerous lives. With her gallery of social misfits, she is the contemporary heir to the tradition begun by Robert Browning. Of mixed Japanese, African, Choctaw, and Irish extraction, Ai was born Florence Anthony in the American Southwest. She received the 1978 Lamont Poetry Selection of the Academy of American Poets for her second book, Killing Floor, *and an American Book Award from the Before Columbus Foundation for her third collection,* Sin *(1986). In 1999,* Vice *received the National Book Award for Poetry. Ai lives in Tucson, Arizona.*

Child Beater

Outside, the rain, pinafore of gray water, dresses the town
and I stroke the leather belt,
as she sits in the rocking chair,
holding a crushed paper cup to her lips.
I yell at her, but she keeps rocking;   5
back, her eyes open, forward, they close.
Her body, somehow fat, though I feed her only once a day,
reminds me of my own just after she was born.
It's been seven years, but I still can't forget how I felt.
How heavy it feels to look at her.   10

I lay the belt on a chair
and get her dinner bowl.
I hit the spoon against it, set it down
and watch her crawl to it,
pausing after each forward thrust of her legs   15
and when she takes her first bite,
I grab the belt and beat her across the back
until her tears, beads of salt-filled glass, falling,
shatter on the floor.

I move off. I let her eat,   20
while I get my dog's chain leash from the closet.
I whirl it around my head.

O daughter, so far, you've only had a taste of icing,
are you ready now for some cake?

—*1973*

She Didn't Even Wave

For Marilyn Monroe

I buried Mama in her wedding dress
and put gloves on her hands,
but I couldn't do much about her face,
blue-black and swollen,
so I covered it with a silk scarf.   5
I hike my dress up to my thighs
and rub them,
watching you tip the mortuary fan back and forth.
Hey. Come on over. Cover me all up
like I was never here. Just never.   10
Come on. I don't know why I talk like that.
It was a real nice funeral. Mama's.
I touch the rhinestone heart pinned to my blouse.
Honey, let's look at it again.
See. It's bright like the lightning that struck her. 15

I walk outside
and face the empty house.
You put your arms around me. Don't.
Let me wave goodbye.
Mama never got a chance to do it.   20
She was walking toward the barn
when it struck her. I didn't move;
I just stood at the screen door.
Her whole body was light.
I'd never seen anything so beautiful.   25

I remember how she cried in the kitchen
a few minutes before.
She said, *God. Married.*
I don't believe it, Jean, I won't.

He takes and takes and you just give.   30
At the door, she held out her arms
and I ran to her.
She squeezed me so tight:
I was all short of breath.
And she said, *don't do it.*   35
In ten years, your heart will be eaten out
and you'll forgive him, or some other man, even that
and it will kill you.
Then she walked outside.
And I kept saying, I've got to, Mama,   40
hug me again. Please don't go.

—*1979*

Timothy Steele   (b. 1948)

Timothy Steele has written a successful scholarly study of the rise of free
verse, Missing Measures *(1990), and is perhaps the most skillful craftsman*
of the contemporary New Formalist poets. Born in Burlington, Vermont,
Steele earned his B.A. at Stanford and his Ph.D. from Brandeis University,
where he studied under the formalist poet J. V. Cunningham. Steele's hon-
ors include a Guggenheim fellowship, a Peter I. B. Lavan Younger Poets
Award from the Academy of American Poets, and the Los Angeles PEN
Center's Literary Award for poetry. He has lived for a number of years in
Los Angeles, where he teaches at California State University, Los Angeles.

Life Portrait

thinking of Dora Spenlow and David Copperfield°

Her pensive figure charms, as does the lisp
And coaxing baby talk she sometimes plies.
Yet his devotion wanes. What beckons him?
       The customary will-o'-the-wisp—
A dreamed-up soul mate, beautiful and wise?   5

Dora Spenlow and David Copperfield characters in Charles Dickens's novel *David Copperfield*

No matter: what it comes to, in the end,
Is that when in mock-plaintive moments she
Says, "Don't forget, bad boy, your little friend,"
He fails to catch the import of the plea.

She dies; in time he marries his ideal,   10
And forges to success. Yet the detail
Of his fulfillment never quite convinces.
    And it's her presence he will feel
Hiking up switchbacks of a mountain trail.
The daffodil, bowed at the canyon's rim,   15
Will drop a bead of water like a note
From its toy trumpet blossom, his eyes will swim,
And he'll feel a thick hot tightness in his throat.

He's one, now, with the greedy overreachers.
She sat, hands on his shoulder, chin on them,   20
Then ran a thoughtful finger down his profile,
    As if to remind him of his features.
Height shows the small lake as a sparkling gem,
And shows as threads the streams that spill and bend
And join and part along the valley's floor.   25
He once forgot, bad boy, his little friend,
Although he won't forget her any more.

                                     —1986

Sapphics° Against Anger

Angered, may I be near a glass of water;
May my first impulse be to think of Silence,
Its deities (who are they? do, in fact, they
        Exist? etc.).

May I recall what Aristotle says of   5
The subject: to give vent to rage is not to

Sapphics stanza form named after Sappho (c. 650 B.C.)

Release it but to be increasingly prone
       To its incursions.

May I imagine being in the Inferno,
Hearing it asked: "Virgilio mio,° who's   10
That sulking with Achilles there?" and hearing
       Virgil say: "Dante,

That fellow, at the slightest provocation,
Slammed phone receivers down, and waved his arms like
A madman. What Attila did to Europe,   15
       What Genghis Khan did

To Asia, that poor dope did to his marriage."
May I, that is, put learning to good purpose,
Mindful that melancholy is a sin, though
       Stylish at present.   20

Better than rage is the post-dinner quiet,
The sink's warm turbulence, the streaming platters,
The suds rehearsing down the drain in spirals
       In the last rinsing.

For what is, after all, the good life save that   25
Conducted thoughtfully, and what is passion
If not the holiest of powers, sustaining
       Only if mastered.

                              —*1986*

Social Reform

A prince of rational behavior,
Satan informs us that our Savior
Remarks we'll always have the poor,
Which moral saves expenditure.
We'll always have the poor? Okay.   5
Yet, looked at whole, the text will say

---

10 Virgilio mio Dante is addressing Virgil, his guide through hell

Something more lenitive, and truer.
We'll have the poor: let's make them fewer.

—1986

Albert Goldbarth (b. 1948)

Albert Goldbarth writes wildly digressive poems that explore the detritus of contemporary life. Born in Chicago, he studied at the University of Illinois at Chicago Circle, the Iowa Writers' Workshop, and the University of Utah. Goldbarth began his long teaching career at Elgin Community College in Illinois; he also has taught at Cornell University, Syracuse University, University of Texas at Austin, and at Wichita State University. His collection Heaven and Earth: A Cosmology *(1991) received the National Book Critics Circle Award. Goldbarth also received the OSU Press/The* Journal *Award for the poetry collection* Popular Culture *(1989). His other books include the collections* Arts and Sciences *(1986),* Across the Layers *(1993), and* The Gods *(1993), and two collections of essays,* A Sympathy of Souls *(1990) and* Great Topics of the World *(1994).*

Dog, Fish, Shoes (or Beans)

"I was a shmooshled little girl," my Aunt Elena says.
"I'm seventeen, I have a shape from a matzoh ball,
boomp boomp boomp I walk. So no wonder, Glicka
with big soft eyes like stewed prunes
has a boyfriend, he would jump through hoops of fire   5
for her if his wizzle was dipped in kerosene first,
and Pearl has a boyfriend, Misha does, Rebekka
whose body goes in and out like an accordion, hooy
she could walk down the street and the trolleys
fall out of their tracks. But poor Elena, me,   10
boohoo boohoo with the tears all shpritzing, don't
laugh from my story, it's very sad. So what
does Elena do on Saturday night, with everybody else

in front of the radio holding hands to ukelele songs?
Elena, the poor shmo, baby-sits for people   15
in her building. On the third floor are the Morrises,
with a dog a cocker spaniel—like a bowling ball
of dirty fur and always yapping, I
hated it—and a goldfish. And so for *them*
I don't even *baby*-sit, they would hire somebody   20
I swear to wipe the dog's tush if they could.
So I stay up there, I feed the fish and the dog.
I clean the box, I listen like an idiot
to the ukelele serenades like everyone else, and I cry.
Good; so this is my Saturday date. One night,   25
does it *rain?*—like Noah's Flood of a rain.
From nowhere, a Noah's Flood all of a sudden.
I run to close the bedroom window—*whoops,*
and down the three floors goes the goldfish bowl
with Miss Goldilox, which the name is a joke,   30
like lox the fish, but a goldfish. It lands
in a puddle. I think to myself, 'In a puddle?
Could beeeee . . . this little fishy's heart still beats.' So I
run downstairs—" "—*But,*" my Uncle Mo
takes over, "she leaves the door to the apartment open.   35
This is Important: remember. Meanwhile,
a certain very handsome young man—" "—oh, handsome
like a *blintz* that got run over—" "—is delivering
a wagon of shoes from the Jewish Poor Relief Fund—"
"—shoes? it was canned goods—" "—listen   40
in *your* story maybe it's canned goods, *mine* it's shoes—"
"—okay, Mr. Memory, but I'm telling you I see
these little cans with the pears and the whaddayacallem beans
on the labels—" "—shoes, it was shoes, it was shoes,
up past your winkus in shoes, do you hear me—"   45
"—don't laugh—" "—so anyway—" "—feh!—" "—where
was I—" "—don't interrupt—" "—and I said
'Pardon me Miss but is this poor shivering
cocker spaniel yours?'—" "—and here we are to tell you
this story Fifty Years Later!" Then we always said: 50
Did you go upstairs and kiss? And they always
never answered: "The fish, by the way, we never found."
"So you see?" she'd add. "Nothing is hopeless."

                                                                              —*1999*

Rarefied

> This sweater is made from only the finest, softest
> underhairs of the Mongolian camel.
>
> —*From a mail-order catalogue*

"Fancy-schmancy," my father would have said,
whose snazziest sweater was still a déclassé
synthetic from the sweatshops of Taiwan. My friend
Deloris, however, who really owns such clothes,
would say "exquisite" or "sublime"—her opened closet's   5
row of shoulders teases late-day bedroomlight
along *such* textures, there are days when the laboring brain
and throbbing crotch appear to us to be not much more
than her wardrobe's tasteful accessories. ". . . woven
from genital-down of prepubescent yeti, and then   10
hand-sewn in our undersea domes." "Untouched
by anyone other than albino elves, this wool is. . . ."

———

Rarefied—to Helthi Hart, the diet guru, it's
a cup of clear organic cauliflower broth. And for
the Emperor Excessia, it's a mad dessert of swans' tongues   15
—there were, what? ten thousand?—dipped in a slip
of stiffening honey and set out to await the banqueteers
like a field of fresh shoots they could graze.
Some Roman party hosts had great roped bowls of snow
brought from the mountaintops to entertain their guests   20
with dishes of rose-petal sherbet and chilled roe.
They might even allow the household slaves to slide
leftover snow along the burning welts the ropes ate
into their shoulders all down the mountainside.

———

Afterward it was an unrecognizable tatter.   25
But an image of my father's worn-thin Bargain City
"all-weather" jacket is still whole in its polyester glory.
This is what happened: the alley dog (he later called the thing
a "cur") had cornered Livia, and she screamed once,

with a seven-year-old's unselfconscious terror.   30
And then my father was there, with his jacket wound around his arm,
and a rock. When it was over, he tore the sleeves off, tied the poor dog
quiet and, after comforting Livia, they both kneeled down
to comfort the dog. He was like that. And the jacket
that served as weapon and restraint?—was like him,   35
every day of his life. It did what was needed.

————————

I misread "migraine." Which of the two
would we call the most rarefied? "Margarine"?
Or maybe comparison isn't the point. A ghost
is a person rarefied through the fine, fine colander   40
death; that doesn't make, for most of us, extinction
an ideal. It was hard to think of Frank and Deloris
divorcing, since it was hard to imagine the two of them
engaging in *anything* so mundane as sex or rage or envy
with the rest of the hoi polloi.° They seemed unearthly   45
in close to a literal way, like radio waves. And yet divorce
they did. They found *something* real they could unjoin,
hertz from hertz until there just was air.

————————

A dream: We own the softest of the soft
Mongolian camel underhair sweaters. One day   50
(we *think* we're doing the "right thing") we release it
into the wild, to romp with its brother and sister
desert sweaters, out where it "belongs."
You know, however, what happens by now: it's unfit
to fend for itself amid that hardened herd.   55
They beat it. It's hungry. It crawls back
into the city, mewing, curling up at night against a door
my father opens and, seeing something in need, he brings it inside,
wraps it in flannel. That's how he was.
He'd give you the cheap shirt off his back.   60

                                                              —*2001*

————————

45 **hoi polloi** the masses (Greek)

Wendy Rose (b. 1948)

*Wendy Rose has written of the American Indian movement of the 1960s
and 1970s, and of coming to terms with her own mixed cultural lineage.
Born in Oakland, California, Rose is of Hopi, Miwok, English, Scottish,
Irish, and German extraction. She began writing poetry after dropping out
of high school and becoming involved in San Francisco's bohemian artistic
circles. Later, Rose studied at Cabrillo and Contra Costa junior colleges,
and completed a Ph.D. in anthropology at the University of California,
Berkeley. She has served as coordinator of the American Indian Studies
Program at Fresno City College. Also a visual artist, Rose has published
ten collections of poems.*

Robert

> I am death, the destroyer of worlds . . . the
> physicists have known sin and this is a knowl-
> edge they cannot lose.
> —*J. Robert Oppenheimer,° 1945*

the lines of your arteries
begin to glow   making maps
finger follows afraid &
firm   pale like the alamagordo sky
the white lizards in the sand   5

are you humming or is it
a wayward insect or the tremble
of your deepest bones. los alamos
trinity   alamagordo°   (frail robert)
jornada del muerto°   you crouch   10
in the bunker   hands to your eyes
your light gray business suit   porkpie hat
loosened tie   speaking to
transparent friends or to no one

J. Robert Oppenheimer (1904–1967), director of the Manhattan Project which developed the first
atomic bomb   **9 alamagordo** in New Mexico, site of the first atomic blast   **10 jornada del muerto** a
barren stretch of desert; Spanish for "route of the dead"

in particular   15
it's amazing
how the tools, the technology
trap one
   & you are amazed at the welts
   so wide on your wrists, those chains   20
   enormous from your belt.
   not even your wife was awake
   morning pivot of your life
   the radio groaned   you twisted
   the knob feeling for   25
   an end to feeling   but the voice
   said anyway how your kids went screaming
   from the crotch of the plane
   mouth-first onto play yard & roof top
   & garden & temple, onto hair & flesh   30
   onto steel & clay   leaving you
   leaving you   leaving you
   your own fingerprints   in the ashes
   your vomit   your tears

—1985

Alfalfa Dance

Warm afternoons
smell of alfalfa
green in the air
       I pretend
       I am graceful   5
       and thin,
        tie my hair
with sage ribbons
squash blossoms
sandy roots for toeshoes   10
Hopi ballerina
       whose hands flutter
       into fiddles and flutes,
       who steps from room to room
       curtains closed   15

walking through
knee-high thistle
in San Francisco
prance and bow
      elk doe   20
      waiting at the redbud
      for applause
      or for the stones to move
beetles skittering
from beneath   25
or fragrant
with the earth
      steam
      in the sun
      lift   30
      one obsidian hoof
nose directly
into the wind
dance away
from humanity   35
      —1994

Grandmother Rattler

who coils in my bones,
what were you thinking
that summer night
when you found the warm road
on the edge of the canyon   5
and stopped just there
exactly at the center
where the pickups and cars
and evening walkers would see
your spiral upon spiral,   10
hear the singing voice
of your tail,
see your black head
rising?

When I stopped my car   15
and walked up to you,
arms spread and hands open,
why didn't you move?
Why didn't you slide down the stones
among the white oaks   20
and single tall stems
of soaproot?

When those white people stopped,
leaned out of their truck,
whistled and hooted,   25
did you not recognize Owl among them
calling to me over and over,
"Kill it! Kill it!"   I would not, of course,
but still you would not move
even to save your life   30
but sang all the louder,
your body quaking
with rage.

Then the woman came out
of her house just there,   35
saw you, ran back,
picked up the heaviest shovel
she could find, pushed her way past
where I tried to shield you,
and said she would kill you   40
if I would not,
said she had horses down the hill
that might get bit, or she might die
if you were allowed
to live out the night.   45

O Grandmother.
What did I become?
The German mother who closed her ears
to the sound of neighbors
as they choked and burned?   50
Uniformed boy in a silver room,
his finger hovering over one small button
to kill thousands he will never see,

elders and infants he will only know
by the magic devil word "enemy"?   55
I know only this.
I took the shovel
wanting to spare you a death
at their hands, brought it down edgewise
on your soft red neck, cleanly sliced   60
the head from the body,
felt a shadow pass
over my womb.

Ever since
there is a dream   65
where opals outline
the shape of diamonds
on my back.
My mouth opens
and your high   70
whistling hum
bleeds out;
my tongue
licks the air.

—2002

Heather McHugh (b. 1948)

*Heather McHugh has published several books of poetry and translations,
including* Hinge & Sign: Poems 1968–1993 *(1994). Born to Canadian
parents in San Diego, California, she grew up in Virginia, and studied at
Harvard University and the University of Denver. McHugh teaches at
Warren Wilson College and the University of Washington in Seattle.*

Better or Worse

I.

Daily, the kindergarteners
passed my porch. I loved
their likeness and variety,
their selves in line like little

monosyllables, but huggable—   5
I wasn't meant

to grab them, ever,
up into actual besmooches or down
into grubbiest tumbles, my lot was not
to have them, in the flesh.   10
Was it better or worse to let
their lovability go by untouched, and just
watch over their river of ever-
inbraiding relations? I wouldn't
mother them or teach. We couldn't be   15
each other's others; maybe,
at removes, each other's each.

    II.

Each toddler had a hand-hold on
a loop of rope, designed to haul
the whole school onward   20
in the sidewalk stream—
like pickerel through freshets,
at the pull of something else's will, the children
spun and bobbled, three years old and four
(or were they little drunken Buddhas,   25
buoyant, plump?). They looked
now to the right, now to the sky, and now
toward nothing (nothing was too small)—
they followed a thread of destination,
chain of command, order of actual rope that led   30

to what? Who knew?

For here and now in one child's eye there was a yellow truck,
and in another's was a burning star; but from my own
    perspective,
overhead, adult, where trucks and suns had lost their luster,
they were one whole baby-rush toward   35
a target, toward the law
of targets, fledge
in the wake of an arrowhead;

a bull's-eye bloomed, a red
eight-sided sign. What   40

did I wish them?
Nothing I foresaw.

—*1994*

A Physics

When you get down to it, Earth
has our own great ranges
of feeling—Rocky, Smoky, Blue—
and a heart that can melt stones.

The still pools fill with sky,   5
as if aloof, and we have eyes
for all of this—and more, for Earth's
reminding moon. We too are ruled

by such attractions—spun and swaddled,
rocked and lent a light. We run   10
our clocks on wheels, our trains
on time. But all the while we want

to love each other endlessly—not only for
a hundred years, not only six feet up and down.
We want the suns and moons of silver   15
in ourselves, not only counted coins in a cup. The whole

idea of love was not to fall. And neither was
the whole idea of God. We put him well
above ourselves, because we meant,
in time, to measure up.   20

—*1994*

The Size of Spokane

The baby isn't cute. In fact he's
a homely little pale and headlong
stumbler. Still, he's one
of us—the human beings
stuck on flight 295 (Chicago to Spokane);   5
and when he passes my seat twice

at full tilt this then that direction,
I look down from Lethal Weapon 3 to see
just why. He's

running back and forth   10
across a sunblazed circle on
the carpet—something brilliant, fallen
from a porthole. So! it's light
amazing him, it's only light, despite
some three and one   15
half hundred
people, propped in rows
for him to wonder at; it's light
he can't get over, light he can't
investigate enough, however many   20
zones he runs across it,
flickering himself.

The umpteenth time
I see him coming, I've had
just about enough; but then   25
he notices me noticing and stops—
one fat hand on my armrest—to
inspect the oddities of me.

           *

Some people cannot hear.
Some people cannot walk.   30
But everyone was
sunstruck once, and set adrift.
Have we forgotten how
astonishing this is? so practiced all our senses
we cannot imagine them? foreseen instead of seeing   35
all the all there is? Each spectral port,
each human eye

is shot through with a hole, and everything we know
goes in there, where it feeds a blaze. In a flash

the baby's old; Mel Gibson's hundredth comeback seems   40
less clever; all his chases and embraces
narrow down, while we

fly on (in our
plain radiance of vehicle)

toward what cannot stay small forever.   45

—1994

Lynn Emanuel (b. 1949)

*Lynn Emanuel combines influences as diverse as film noir and the novels
of Italo Calvino and Gertrude Stein. Born in Mt. Kisco, New York, to an
artist father and a businesswoman mother, she has lived in North Africa,
Europe, and the Near East. She holds degrees from Bennington College,
the City College of New York, and the University of Iowa. Emanuel has
received the National Poetry Series Award, and has been featured in the
Pushcart Prize Anthology and Best American Poetry. She has taught at the
Bread Loaf Writers' Conference, the Bennington Writers Workshops, and
the University of Pittsburgh, where she directs the Writing Program.*

Frying Trout while Drunk

Mother is drinking to forget a man
Who could fill the woods with invitations:
Come with me he whispered and she went
In his Nash Rambler, its dash
Where her knees turned green   5
In the radium dials of the '50s.
When I drink it is always 1953,
Bacon wilting in the pan on Cook Street
And mother, wrist deep in red water,
Laying a trail from the sink   10
To a glass of gin and back.
She is a beautiful, unlucky woman
In love with a man of lechery so solid
You could build a table on it
And when you did the blues would come to visit.   15
I remember all of us awkwardly at dinner,
The dark slung across the porch,
And then mother's dress falling to the floor,

Buttons ticking like seeds spit on a plate.
When I drink I am too much like her—   20
The knife in one hand and in the other
The trout with a belly white as my wrist.
I have loved you all my life
She told him and it was true
In the same way that all her life   25
She drank, dedicated to the act itself,
She stood at this stove
And with the care of the very drunk
Handed him the plate.

                                                              —1984

The Sleeping

I have imagined all this:
In 1940 my parents were in love
And living in the loft on West 10th
Above Mark Rothko° who painted cabbage roses
On their bedroom walls the night they got married.   5

I can guess why he did it.
My mother's hair was the color of yellow apples
And she wore a velvet hat with her pajamas.

I was not born yet. I was remote as starlight.
It is hard for me to imagine that   10
My parents made love in a roomful of roses
And I wasn't there.

But now I am. My mother is blushing.
This is the wonderful thing about art.
It can bring back the dead. It can wake the sleeping   15
As it might have late that night
When my father and mother made love above Rothko
Who lay in the dark thinking *Roses, Roses, Roses.*

                                                              —1984

4 **Mark Rothko** (1903–1970), American abstract expressionist painter

Outside Room Six

Down on my knees again, on the linoleum outside room six,
I polish it with the remnant of Grandpa's union suit,
and once again dead Grandma Fry looks down on me
from Paradise and tells me from the balcony of wrath
I am girlhood's one bad line of credit.   5

Every older girl I know is learning how to in a car,
while here I am, eye at the keyhole, watching Raoul,
who heats my dreams with his red hair, lights up my life
with his polished brogues, groans *Jesus, Jesus*.
I am little and stare into the dark until the whole small   10

town of lust emerges. I stare with envy, I stare and stare.
Now they are having cocktails. The drinks are dim lagoons
beneath their paper parasols. The air is stung with orange,
with lemon, a dash of Clorox, a dash of bitters;
black square, white square goes the linoleum.   15

—1992

David St. John (b. 1949)

David St. John writes narrative poems that engage the senses with an intensity usually reserved for the lyric. His many honors include fellowships from the National Endowment for the Arts, the John Simon Guggenheim Memorial Foundation, and the American Academy in Rome, and a grant from the Ingram Merrill Foundation. His work has been published in numerous literary magazines including the New Yorker, *the* Paris Review, Poetry, The American Poetry Review, Antaeus, Harper's, *and the* New Republic, *and has been widely anthologized. He has taught creative writing at Oberlin and Johns Hopkins and currently teaches at the University of Southern California. He lives in Venice, California.*

I Know

> The definition of beauty is easy; it is what leads
> to desperation.
>
> —*Valéry*

I know the moon is troubling;

Its pale eloquence is always such a meddling,
Intrusive lie. I know the pearl sheen of the sheets
Remains the screen I'll draw back against the night;

I know all of those silences invented for me approximate   5
Those real silences I cannot lose to daylight . . .
I know the orchid smell of your skin

The way I know the blackened path to the marina,
When gathering clouds obscure the summer moon—
Just as I know the chambered heart where I begin.   10

I know too the lacquered jewel box, its obsidian patina;
The sexual trumpeting of the diving, sweeping loons . . .
I know the slow combinations of the night, & the glow

Of fireflies, deepening the shadows of all I do not know.

—*1994*

My Tea with Madame Descartes

She'd said let's have tea
Because she believed I was English; she meant,
　　　　Of course, not tea but her usual sequence
Of afternoon aperitifs, in slender glasses the length
　　　　Of a finger, and only slightly wider.　　　　　　5
　　　　　　We met near the Odéon° because, she said,
For her, all the cafés in Montparnasse° were haunted still;
　　　　Just like, she added, the old days with S——.
I'd spent the morning looking through the file drawers
　　　　Of the *Herald Tribune*, leafing through early reviews　　10
　　　　　　Of Madame's stage days, then dozens of articles
About her books of photographs, her memoirs, the late novel
　　　　That embarrassed several continents. Here and there,
I'd run across a few glossy photos of Madame herself
　　　　　　Thrown into the file, always with yet　　　　15
Another notable lovestruck admirer at her slender, bare elbow.
　　　　When I walked in, still a little blinded by
The September sunlight, I didn't notice her at first, tucked
　　　　Along the far wall, a leisurely veil
Of cigarette smoke steadily latticing the air before her;　　20
　　　　Then I caught her unmistakable reflection
In one of the square mirrored pillars, those regal cheekbones,
　　　　The nearly opaque, sea-blue eyes
That'd commandeered both men and newspapers for forty years,
　　　　　　Simply lifting to meet mine . . .　　　　25
As I introduced myself, my apologies for my late arrival
　　　　Waved away like so much smoke,
　　　　I noticed that the silver of her hair was laced
With an astonishing gold, like those threads woven so deftly
　　　　Throughout a tapestry to trap the light;　　　30
In that dim café, the gold fired as delicately as filaments
　　　　Of beaten leaf in a Byzantine mosaic. Beneath her

---

6 **Odéon** hotel in Paris　7 **Montparnasse** neighborhood in Paris known for cafés that attracted artists and intellectuals

Quite carefully constructed mask,
The islands of rouge mapping soft slopes of powder,
Beneath the precise calm she'd expertly painted for herself   35
Before the mirror, I could see
Why scandal had tattooed even the air she'd
Walked through. I'd never seen a beauty like hers, riveting
As the Unicorn's
Soft eye. There's so much we name as beautiful   40
Simply to dismiss it, cage it, desire then dispense with it—
Yet her beauty was singular,
Volcanic, viscous . . . as inevitable as lava moving slowly
Toward you. Even those few lines in her face
Seemed as delicate as those left by a leaf's edge, drawn by   45
A child through the sand. Her beauty
Was so close to a vengeance—one exacted by the world
Upon those of us so ordinary, so weak, we can barely
Admit its existence. So I just sat there, a notebook
At hand; I took out my micro pocket recorder, placing it   50
Between us. She lit up a filtered Gitane;°
Then she began: "I suppose I think the War years
Were the worst, always seeing some of one's
Old friends in swank restaurants lifting glasses
To the Germans at adjoining tables, while the others   55
Had all disappeared into the Underground.° At times, it was
So hard to know who still
Might be alive. After the war, I took several lovers;
Then, the fatigue set in. I married a sweet but stupid man,
A lawyer for Lanvin and Charvet;° I slowly   60
Went mad, truly mad, living that way—
But getting out was almost accidental.
One fall, my friend Lee Miller° happened to pass through Paris;
In the old days, I'd modeled nude for her crowd—
'Dusting off the lazy angels'   65
We called the parties we threw then. That visit, Lee
Gave me an old Rolliflex° she'd outgrown,
And I thought, one day, flipping through those

---

51 **Gitane** French brand of cigarette   56 **Underground** French resistance during World War II
60 **Lanvin and Charvet** boutiques   63 **Lee Miller** (1907–1977), American photographer of the
1920s, 30s, and 40s   67 **Rolliflex** brand of camera

Old pieces of hers from *Vogue* and *Life*, I'd like
  To do that! About this time, my dull husband decided   70
We'd visit his brother, a sniffy diplomat off rotting
    In Saigon. So, I packed my Rolliflex, knowing
  That was that; when my husband went back to Paris,
I kissed him goodbye and took the train to Tibet—Lhasa—
    Then on to Bangkok, Argentina, Chile . . .   75
Just everywhere. The whole while, I was learning
    What the lens of my eye meant in the world.
I began to keep some journals too; slowly, I acquired
  What's politely called *a kind of reputation.* Then,
I could get in anywhere—the refugee camps, prisons, anywhere!   80
    Nobody would say *no* to me, the woman
  With the famous eye, 'that daunting feminine aperture'
One pig of an editor called it. You know, the only photos
    People remember are the most
  Grotesque: the young African shepherd girl, hanging   85
By a loop of barbed wire; that charred carapace of a soldier's
  Corpse, stretched out over the white coals
    Of St. Lawrence's faithful grill° . . .
Those heads of Buddhist monks nodding on a row of bamboo
  spikes.
    Do you need more? I'm tired. Thank God that, in Saigon,   90
I threw caution right out along the winds;
      For such an illogical woman
I suppose that's the last 'logical' thing I've ever done.
  And now," she said, "put your notebook down; I've
    Decided to take your picture."   95
Out of her purse, she pulled a spy-sized Minox,° the kind
  With a drawbridge lens. As the tiny camera unfolded,
    The eye of its castle widening slowly
Before her consoling wink, I simply sat back, trying somehow
  To smile, to look worldly, desirable, nonchalant—   100
My hands so self-consciously gripping the small café table
    Which Madame had so easily turned.

              —1994

---

88 St. Lawrence's faithful grill St. Lawrence, a third century saint and martyr, was roasted to death on a grill because he refused to renounce his religion **96 Minox** brand of camera

Sarah Cortez (b. 1950)

Sarah Cortez grew up in Houston, Texas, and holds degrees in psychology and religion, classical studies, and accounting. She is a deputy constable in Harris County, Texas. She also serves as Visiting Scholar at the University of Houston's Center for Mexican-American Studies. Her poetic debut, How to Undress A Cop *(2000), features bold and sensuous poems about policing the streets of Houston.*

Tu Negrito °

She's got to bail me out,
he says into the phone outside the holding cell.
She's going there tomorrow anyway for Mikey.
Tell her she's got to do this for me.

He says into the phone outside the holding cell,   5
Make sure she listens. Make her feel guilty, man.
Tell her she's got to do this for me.
She can have all my money, man.

Make sure she listens. Make her feel guilty, man.
Tell her she didn't bail me out the other times.   10
She can have all my money, man.
She always bails out Mikey.

Tell her she didn't bail me out the other times.
I don't got no one else to call, cousin.
She always bails out Mikey.   15
Make sure you write all this down, cousin.

I don't got no one else to call, cousin.
I really need her now.
Make sure you write this all down, cousin.
Page her. Put in code 333. That's me.   20

I really need her now.
Write down "Mommie." Change it from "Mom."

Tu Negrito your little dark one (Spanish)

Page her. Put in code 333. That's me.
Write down "*Tu Negrito*." Tell her I love her.

Write down "Mommie." Change it from "Mom."   25
I'm her littlest. Remind her.
Write down "*Tu Negrito*." Tell her I love her.
She's got to bail me out.

                                                    —*2000*

Undressing a Cop

Do it first in your mind.
Many times. Linger over
details. Eye each piece
of shiny metal, thick black
leather, muscled bicep. Take   5

control when you start. Your
sure fingers will unhook
the square silver buckle
in front and listen to breath
change. You will unsnap keepers. Lower   10

gun belt to the floor while
unzipping Regulation trousers.
Before reaching inside, undo the
shirt's top button, unzip the front
flap hiding the chest. Kiss   15

underneath the badge's place. The silver
you've stared at—an engraved star
with blocked numbers that means your lover
may die for the State. Wonder what
it's like to be called by a number. Peel   20

back the shirt and drop it
on the floor. Pull up a V-necked white
T-shirt and suck the nipples, a surprise
of pink vulnerable flesh, alive, soft,
tender, bringing light into your mouth. Feel   25

the curve of rounded flesh
against your cheek. Lower your hands.
Tease the wet hardness aching inside
dark navy-blue trousers. Pick
a spot. Decide what you want.   30
Ride until you come. Don't try

to touch a heart or reach inside
guts. Instead, observe and maintain
the silence, your own backbone
rigid even while loving   35
and being loved.

—2000

Rodney Jones (b. 1950)

Rodney Jones has written eight books of poetry, including Kingdom of the
Instant *(2002) and* Elegy for the Southern Drawl *(1999). Born on a farm
in Hartselle, Alabama, Jones grew up in Falkville, a town in northern Al-
abama, and studied at the University of Alabama at Tuscaloosa and the
University of North Carolina, Greensboro. He teaches at Southern Illinois
University Carbondale.*

On the Bearing
of Waitresses

Always I thought they suffered, the way they huffed
through the Benzedrine light of waffle houses,
hustling trays of omelettes, gossiping by the grill,
or pruning passes like the too prodigal buds of roses,
and I imagined each come home to a trailer court,   5
the yard of bricked-in violets, the younger sister
pregnant and petulant at her manicure, the mother
with her white Bible, the father sullen in his corner.
Wasn't that the code they telegraphed in smirks?
And wasn't this disgrace, to be public and obliged,   10
observed like germs or despots about to be debunked?

Unlikely brides, apostles in the gospel of stereotypes,
their future was out there beyond the parked trucks,
between the beer joints and the sexless church,
the images we'd learned from hayseed troubadours—   15
perfume, grease, and the rending of polarizing loves.
But here in the men's place, they preserved a faint
decorum of women and, when they had shuffled past us,
settled in that realm where the brain approximates
names and rounds off the figures under uniforms.   20
Not to be honored or despised, but to walk as spies would,
with almost alien poise in the imperium of our disregard,
to go on steadily, even on the night of the miscarriage,
to glide, quick smile, at the periphery of appetite.
And always I had seen them listening, as time brought   25
and sent them, hovering and pivoting as the late
orders turned strange, *blue garden, brown wave.* Spit
in the salad, wet socks wrung into soup, and this happened.
One Sunday morning in a truckstop in Bristol, Virginia,
a rouged and pancaked half-Filipino waitress   30
with hair dyed the color of puffed wheat and mulberries
singled me out of the crowd of would-be bikers
and drunken husbands guzzling coffee to sober up
in time to cart their disgusted wives and children
down the long street to the First Methodist Church.   35
Because I had a face she trusted, she had me wait
that last tatter of unlawful night that hung there
and hung there like some cast-off underthing
caught on the spikes of a cemetery's wrought-iron fence.
And what I had waited for was no charm of flesh,   40
not the hard seasoning of luck, or work, or desire,
but all morning, in the sericea° by the filthy city lake,
I suffered her frightened lie, how she was wanted
in Washington by the CIA, in Vegas by the FBI—
while time shook us like locks that would not break.   45
And I did not speak, though she kept pausing to look
back across one shoulder, as though she were needed
in the trees, but waxing her slow paragraphs into
chapters, filling the air with her glamour and her shame.

—1989

42 **sericea** a common weed

Winter Retreat: Homage to Martin Luther King, Jr.

There is a hotel in Baltimore where we came together,
we black and white educated and educators,
for a week of conferences, for important counsel
sanctioned by the DOE° and the Carter administration,
to make certain difficult inquiries, to collate notes   5
on the instruction of the disabled, the deprived,
the poor, who do not score well on entrance tests,
who, failing school, must go with mop and pail
skittering across the slick floors of cafeterias,
or climb dewy girders to balance high above cities,   10
or, jobless, line up in the bone cold. We felt
substantive burdens lighter if we stated it right.
Very delicately, we spoke in turn. We walked
together beside the still waters of behaviorism.
Armed with graphs and charts, with new strategies   15
to devise objectives and determine accountability,
we empathetic black and white shone in seminar rooms.
We enunciated every word clearly and without accent.
We moved very carefully in the valley of the shadow
of the darkest agreement error. We did not digress.   20
We ascended the trunk of that loftiest cypress
of Latin grammar the priests could never
successfully graft onto the rough green chestnut
of the English language. We extended ourselves
with that sinuous motion of the tongue that is half   25
pain and almost eloquence. We black and white
politely reprioritized the parameters of our agenda
to impact equitably on the Seminole and the Eskimo.
We praised diversity and involvement, the sacrifices
of fathers and mothers. We praised the next white   30
Gwendolyn Brooks° and the next black Robert Burns.°
We deep made friends. In that hotel we glistened

---

4 DOE Department of Education   **31 Gwendolyn Brooks** (1917–2000), African-American poet
31 Robert Burns (1759–1796), Scottish poet

over the *pommes au gratin*° and the *poitrine de veau.*°
The morsels of lamb flamed near where we talked.
The waiters bowed and disappeared among the ferns.   35
And there is a bar there, there is a large pool.
Beyond the tables of the drinkers and raconteurs,
beyond the hot tub brimming with Lebanese tourists
and the women in expensive bathing suits doing laps,
if you dive down four feet, swim out far enough,   40
and emerge on the other side, it is sixteen degrees.
It is sudden and very beautiful and colder
than thought, though the air frightens you at first,
not because it is cold, but because it is visible,
almost palpable, in the fog that rises from difference.   45
While I stood there in the cheek-numbing snow,
all Baltimore was turning blue. And what I remember
of that week of talks is nothing the record shows,
but the revelation outside, which was the city
many came to out of the fields, then the thought   50
that we had wanted to make the world kinder,
but, in speaking proudly, we had failed a vision.

—*1989*

33 *pommes au gratin* potatoes baked with cheese   33 *poitrine de veau* brisket of veal

Julia Alvarez (b. 1950)

Julia Alvarez published her first collection, Homecoming, *in 1984. It contained both free verse and "33," a sequence of thirty-three sonnets on the occasion of the poet's thirty-third birthday. Her poetry collection* The Other Side/El Otro Lado *(1995) has won acclaim, but she is perhaps best known for her novels, which include* How the Garcia Girls Lost Their Accents *(1991),* In the Time of the Butterflies *(1994), and* ¡Yo! *(1997). Alvarez was born in New York City. Her family moved to the Dominican Republic soon after her birth, and returned to the United States ten years later, the result of her father's involvement with an unsuccessful attempt to overthrow the Trujillo dictatorship. Alvarez has been a poet-in-the-schools in Kentucky, Delaware, and North Carolina. She currently teaches at Middlebury College in Vermont.*

from "33"

HE: Age doesn't matter when you're both in love!
SHE: You say that now, wait till you've had enough.
HE: I love for keeps. I'll never let you down.
SHE: You lie, my dear, you'll lay me in the ground.
HE: Statistics say I'll probably die first.   5
SHE: Statistics say most couples get divorced.
HE: Better to love and lose than not at all.
SHE: Better to read the writing on the wall!
HE: You go by loss, you might as well not live.
SHE: Or live, single, and psychoanalyzed.   10
HE: It breaks my heart to hear you talk that way.
SHE: (Boy in her arms, wiping his tears away,
prescribes the cure for existential ache)
Come in, my sweet, and have some birthday cake.

—1984

How I Learned to Sweep

My mother never taught me sweeping. . . .
One afternoon she found me watching
t.v. She eyed the dusty floor

boldly, and put a broom before
me, and said she'd like to be able 5
to eat her dinner off that table,
and nodded at my feet, then left.
I knew right off what she expected
and went at it. I stepped and swept;
the t.v. blared the news; I kept 10
my mind on what I had to do,
until in minutes, I was through.
Her floor was as immaculate
as a just-washed dinner plate.
I waited for her to return 15
and turned to watch the President,
live from the White House, talk of war:
in the Far East our soldiers were
landing in their helicopters
into jungles their propellers 20
swept like weeds seen underwater
while perplexing shots were fired
from those beautiful green gardens
into which these dragonflies
filled with little men descended. 25
I got up and swept again
as they fell out of the sky.
I swept all the harder when
I watched a dozen of them die . . .
as if their dust fell through the screen 30
upon the floor I had just cleaned.
She came back and turned the dial;
the screen went dark. *That's beautiful,*
she said, and ran her clean hand through
my hair, and on, over the window- 35
sill, coffee table, rocker, desk,
and held it up—I held my breath—
That's beautiful, she said, impressed,
she hadn't found a speck of death.

—*1984*

Bilingual Sestina

Some things I have to say aren't getting said
in this snowy, blond, blue-eyed, gum-chewing English:
dawn's early light sifting through *persianas*° closed
the night before by dark-skinned girls whose words
evoke *cama, aposento, sueños*° in *nombres*°   5
from that first world I can't translate from Spanish.

Gladys, Rosario, Altagracia—the sounds of Spanish
wash over me like warm island waters as I say
your soothing names: a child again learning the *nombres*
of things you point to in the world before English   10
turned *sol, sierra, cielo, luna* to vocabulary words—
sun, earth, sky, moon. Language closed

like the touch-sensitive *morivivi*° whose leaves closed
when we kids poked them, astonished. Even Spanish
failed us back then when we saw how frail a word is   15
when faced with the thing it names. How saying
its name won't always summon up in Spanish or English
the full blown genie from the bottled *nombre.*

Gladys, I summon you back by saying your *nombre.*
Open up again the house of slatted windows closed   20
since childhood, where *palabras*° left behind for English
stand dusty and awkward in neglected Spanish.
Rosario, muse of *el patio,*° sing in me and through me say
that world again, begin first with those first words

you put in my mouth as you pointed to the world—   25
not Adam, not God, but a country girl numbering
the stars, the blades of grass, warming the sun by saying,
¡Qué calor!° as you opened up the morning closed
inside the night until you sang in Spanish,
Estas son las mañanitas,° and listening in bed, no English   30

yet in my head to confuse me with translations, no English
doubling the world with synonyms, no dizzying array of words
—the world was simple and intact in Spanish—

---

3 persianas blinds   **5 sueños** beds, apartment, dreams   **5 nombres** names   **13 morivivi** Caribbean plant   **21 palabras** words   **23 el patio** the courtyard   **28 ¡Qué calor!** How hot it is!   **30 Estas son las mañanitas** These are the little tomorrows

luna, sol, casa, luz, flor,° as if the *nombres*
were the outer skin of things, as if words were so close   35
one left a mist of breath on things by saying

their names, an intimacy I now yearn for in English—
words so close to what I mean that I almost hear my Spanish
heart beating, beating inside what I say *en inglés.*°

—*1995*

Carolyn Forché (b. 1950)

*Carolyn Forché is best known for her poetry of witness, exemplified by her
second collection,* The Country Between Us *(1982), which describes her experiences in war-torn El Salvador. A Detroit native, Forché studied at Michigan State University and Bowling Green State University. Her first collection,* Gathering the Tribes *(1976), won the Yale Younger Poets Award. In
1977, she traveled to Spain to translate the work of Salvadoran-exiled poet
Claribel Alegría, and upon her return, received a John Simon Guggenheim
Memorial Foundation Fellowship, which enabled her to travel to El Salvador, where she worked as a human rights advocate.* The Country Between
Us *received the Lamont Selection of the Academy of American Poets.
Forché, who also edited the anthology* Against Forgetting: Twentieth-Cen-
tury Poetry of Witness *(1993), received the Edita and Ira Morris Hiroshima
Foundation for Peace and Culture Award, in recognition of her work on be-
half of human rights and the preservation of memory and culture.*

The Colonel

What you have heard is true. I was in his house.° His wife carried a
tray of coffee and sugar. His daughter filed her nails, his son went
out for the night. There were daily papers, pet dogs, a pistol on the
cushion beside him. The moon swung bare on its black cord over
the house. On the television was a cop show. It was in English.   5
Broken bottles were emedded in the walls around the house to
scoop the kneecaps from a man's legs or cut his hands to lace. On
the windows there were gratings like those in liquor stores. We had
dinner, rack of lamb, good wine, a gold bell was on the table for

34 luna, sol, casa, luz, flor moon, son, house, light, flowers   **39 en inglés** in English
1 his house in El Salvador

calling the maid. The maid brought green mangoes, salt, a type of   10
bread. I was asked how I enjoyed the country. There was a brief
commercial in Spanish. His wife took everything away. There was
some talk then of how difficult it had become to govern. The parrot
said hello on the terrace. The colonel told it to shut up, and pushed
himself from the table. My friend said to me with his eyes: say   15
nothing. The colonel returned with a sack used to bring groceries
home. He spilled many human ears on the table. They were like
dried peach halves. There is no other way to say this. He took one
of them in his hands, shook it in our faces, dropped it into a water
glass. It came alive there. I am tired of fooling around he said. As   20
for the rights of anyone, tell your people they can go fuck themselves. He swept the ears to the floor with his arm and held the last
of his wine in the air. Something for your poetry, no? he said. Some
of the ears on the floor caught this scrap of his voice. Some of the
ears on the floor were pressed to the ground.   25

—1982

Expatriate

American life, you said, is not possible.
Winter in Syracuse, Trotsky° pinned
to your kitchen wall, windows facing
a street, boxes of imported cigarettes.
The film *In the Realm of the Senses*,   5
and piles of shit burning and the risk
of having your throat slit. Twenty-year-old poet.
To be in love with some woman who cannot speak
English, to have her soften your back with oil
and beat on your mattress with grief and pleasure   10
as you take her from behind, moving beneath you
like the beginning of the world.
The black smell of death as blood and glass
is hosed from the street and the beggar holds
his diminishing hand to your face.   15
It would be good if you could wind up
in prison and so write your prison poems.
Good if you could marry the veiled face

2 **Trotsky** Leon Trotsky (1879–1940), Russian revolutionary and Soviet politician

and jewelled belly of a girl who could
cook Turkish meat, baste your body   20
with a wet and worshipful tongue.
Istanbul, you said, or *Serbia*, mauve
light and mystery and passing for other
than American, a *Kalashnikov*° over
your shoulder, spraying your politics   25
into the flesh of an enemy become real.
You have been in Turkey a year now.
What have you found? Your letters
describe the boring ritual of tea,
the pittance you are paid to teach   30
English, the bribery required for so much
as a postage stamp. Twenty-year-old poet,
Hikmet° did not choose to be Hikmet.

—1982

For the Stranger

Although you mention Venice
keeping it on your tongue like a fruit pit
and I say yes, perhaps Bucharest, neither of us
really knows. There is only this train
slipping through pastures of snow,   5
a sleigh reaching down
to touch its buried runners.
We meet on the shaking platform,
the wind's broken teeth sinking into us.
You unwrap your dark bread   10
and share with me the coffee
sloshing into your gloves.
Telegraph posts chop the winter fields
into white blocks, in each window
the crude painting of a small farm.   15
We listen to mothers scolding
children in English as if

---

24 *Kalasnikov* AK-47, Russian-made assault rifle   33 **Hikmet** Nâzim Hikmet (1902–1963), Turkish
poet and social critic. Condemned by his nation for his anti-fascist activities, he spent sixteen years in
prison and subsequently lived in exile in the Soviet Union and other socialist countries

we do not understand a word of it—
sit still, sit still.

There are few clues as to where   20
we are: the baled wheat scattered
everywhere like missing coffins.
The distant yellow kitchen lights
wiped with oil.
Everywhere the black dipping wires   25
stretching messages from one side
of a country to the other.
The men who stand on every border
waving to us.

Wiping ovals of breath from the windows   30
in order to see ourselves, you touch
the glass tenderly wherever it holds my face.
Days later, you are showing me
photographs of a woman and children
smiling from the windows of your wallet.   35

Each time the train slows, a man
with our faces in the gold buttons
of his coat passes through the cars
muttering the name of a city. Each time
we lose people. Each time I find you   40
again between the cars, holding out
a scrap of bread for me, something
hot to drink, until there are
no more cities and you pull me
toward you, sliding your hands   45
into my coat, telling me
your name over and over, hurrying
your mouth into mine.
We have, each of us, nothing.
We will give it to each other.   50

                                                              —*1982*

Jorie Graham (b. 1950)

Jorie Graham has received a MacArthur Foundation fellowship and a Pulitzer Prize for her book of selected poems, The Dream of the Unified Field *(1995). Her previous collections include* Erosion *(1983) and* The End of Beauty *(1987), and she has edited the poetry anthologies* Earth Took of Earth: 100 Great Poems of the English Language *(1996) and* The Best American Poetry 1990. *Born in New York City, she grew up in Italy and studied at the Sorbonne, Columbia University, and the University of Iowa. She has taught at the Iowa Writers' Workshop and currently serves as the Boylston Professor of Rhetoric and Oratory at Harvard University. While Graham's early poems are fairly conventional examples of lyrical free verse, her later works are experimental.*

At Luca Signorelli's Resurrection of the Body°

See how they hurry
    to enter
their bodies,
    these spirits.
Is it better, flesh,   5
    that they

should hurry so?
    From above
the green-winged angels
    blare down   10
trumpets and light. But
    they don't care,

they hurry to congregate,
    they hurry
into speech, until   15

Luca Signorelli (c. 1445–1523), Renaissance painter. His fresco *Resurrection of the Body* is in a cathedral in Orvieto, Italy

it's a marketplace,
it is humanity. But still
    we wonder

in the chancel
    of the dark cathedral,   20
is it better, back?
    The artist
has tried to make it so: each tendon
    they press

to re-enter   25
    is perfect. But is it
perfection
    they're after,
pulling themselves up
    through the soil   30

into the weightedness, the color,
    into the eye
of the painter? Outside
    it is 1500,
all round the cathedral   35
    streets hurry to open

through the wild
    silver grasses . . . .
The men and women
    on the cathedral wall   40
do not know how,
    having come this far,

to stop their
    hurrying. They amble off
in groups, in   45
    couples. Soon
some are clothed, there is
    distance, there is

perspective. Standing below them
    in the church   50
in Orvieto, how can we
    tell them

to be stern and brazen
    and slow,

that there is no   55
    entrance,
only entering. They keep on
    arriving,
wanting names,
    wanting   60

happiness. In his studio
    Luca Signorelli
in the name of God
    and Science
and the believable   65
    broke into the body

studying arrival.
    But the wall
of the flesh
    opens endlessly,   70
its vanishing point so deep
    and receding

we have yet to find it,
    to have it
stop us. So he cut   75
    deeper,
graduating slowly
    from the symbolic

to the beautiful. How far
    is true?   80
When his one son
    died violently,°
he had the body brought to him
    and laid it

on the drawing-table,   85
    and stood
at a certain distance

82 according to an anecdote recorded by Italian painter and biographer Giorgio Vasari, (1511–1574), after Signorelli's son was killed the painter had his body brought to him so that he could study it and preserve it in his drawings

awaiting the best
  possible light, the best depth
    of day,   90

then with beauty and care
    and technique
and judgment, cut into
    shadow, cut
into bone and sinew and every   95
    pocket

in which the cold light
    pooled.
It took him days,
    that deep   100
caress, cutting,
    unfastening,

until his mind
    could climb into
the open flesh and   105
    mend itself.

                                                          —1983

I Watched a Snake

hard at work in the dry grass
    behind the house
catching flies. It kept on
    disappearing.
And though I know this has   5
    something to do

with lust, today it seemed
    to have to do
with work. It took it almost half
    an hour to thread   10
roughly ten feet of lawn,
    so slow

between the blades you couldn't see
    it move. I'd watch

its path of body in the grass go 15
    suddenly invisible
only to reappear a little
    further on

black knothead up, eyes on
    a butterfly. 20
This must be perfect progress where
    movement appears
to be a vanishing, a mending
    of the visible

by the invisible—just as we 25
    stitch the earth,
it seems to me, each time
    we die, going
back under, coming back up. . . .
    It is the simplest 30

stitch, this going where we must,
    leaving a not
unpretty pattern by default. But going
    out of hunger

for small things—flies, words—going 35
    because one's body

goes. And in this disconcerting creature
    a tiny hunger,
one that won't even press
    the dandelions down, 40
retrieves the necessary blue-
    black dragonfly

that has just landed on a pod . . .
    all this to say
I'm not afraid of them 45
    today, or anymore
I think. We are not, were not, ever
    wrong. Desire

is the honest work of the body,
    its engine, its wind. 50
It too must have its sails—wings
    in this tiny mouth, valves

in the human heart, meanings like sailboats
    setting out

over the mind. Passion is work   55
    that retrieves us,
lost stitches. It makes a pattern of us,
    it fastens us
to sturdier stuff
    no doubt.   60

—1983

Two Paintings by Gustav Klimt°

Although what glitters
    on the trees
row after perfect row,
    is merely
the injustice   5
    of the world,

the chips on the bark of each
    beech tree
catching the light, the sum
    of these delays   10
is the beautiful, the human
    beautiful,

body of flaws.
    The dead
would give anything   15
    I'm sure,
to step again onto
    the leafrot,

into the avenue of mottled shadows,
    the speckled   20

Gustav Klimt (1862–1918), Austrian painter

broken skins. The dead
    in their sheer
open parenthesis, what they
    wouldn't give

for something to lean on   25
    that won't
give way. I think I
    would weep
for the moral nature
    of this world,   30

for right and wrong like pools
    of shadow
and light you can step in
    and out of
crossing this yellow beech forest,   35
    this *buchen-wald*,

one autumn afternoon, late
    in the twentieth
century, in hollow light,
    in gaseous light. . . .   40
To receive the light
    and return it

and stand in rows, anonymous,
    is a sweet secret
even the air wishes   45
    it could unlock.
See how it pokes at them
    in little hooks,

the blue air, the yellow trees.
    Why be afraid?   50
They say when Klimt
    died suddenly
a painting, still
    incomplete,

was found in his studio,   55
    a woman's body
open at its point of

entry,
rendered in graphic,
    pornographic,   60

detail—something like
    a scream
between her legs. Slowly,
    feathery,
he had begun to paint   65
    a delicate

garment (his trademark)
    over this mouth
of her body. The mouth
    of her face   70
is genteel, bored, feigning a need
    for sleep. The fabric

defines the surface,
    the story,
so we are drawn to it,   75
    its blues
and yellows glittering
    like a stand

of beech trees late
    one afternoon   80
in Germany, in fall.
    It is called
Buchenwald,° it is
    1890. In

the finished painting   85
    the argument
has something to do
    with pleasure.

        —*1983*

83 **Buchenwald** Nazi concentration camp

Mekeel McBride (b. 1950)

Mekeel McBride teaches English at the University of New Hampshire and works part-time as a floor-guard and birthday-party specialist at Happy Wheels Roller Rink. She lives in Kittery, Maine. Her playful poems occasionally flirt with the surreal, but also are concerned with finding the extraordinary in everyday life.

Aubade

She wakes long before he does. A fierce shock
of love forces her to look away. Light
the color of gray silk settles among
the dark fronds of a Phoenix palm. Asleep
he laughs, as if in whatever world's   5
now his own, someone dances drunkenly
with an Alaskan bear, or, on a dare
kisses the mayor's bald head, leaving
a perfect red lip print that will amuse
the sparrows for hours. She watches him sleep   10
for almost an hour and although he
does not laugh again, nor wake, he talks
a kind of dream-prattle that has in it
parrots and a dove-grey slate still dusty
with the chalk of childhood. She cannot see   15
his face buried in the pillow but thinks
how in that pillow he must leave some
residue of dream: a name, a scar, parts
of a song in which two people now are
dancing. His red hair flares against   20
the plain white pillowcase: a benign fire,
rich as any color Rembrandt° ever
loved, the first deep whisper of the rising sun.

—1983

---

22 **Rembrandt** Rembrandt Harmenszoon van Rijn (1606–1669), Dutch painter and draftsman

If that Boaty Pink Cadillac from 1959 with the Huge Fins

the one that takes up almost two lanes as it swims by,
if it were mine, I'd let you ride in it. I'd pick you up right now,
at your front door. I'd just sit there for awhile, hoping
you'd look out the window for a weather test, whatever, and see me
in that huge pink that exists-nowhere-in-nature-czarina of a car.   5

And you'd fly out the door as if a holiday were happening right
in your driveway, as if that millionaire from the old tv show
had finally found your house after all these years, as if God
had said, OK, for the next day despair's going to have to hold
somebody else's soul hostage.   10

You'd swing open the Cadillac door, pearly as the nail polish
of Miss Lana Turner,° who is now deceased but whose glamour
will never leave us. And wherever you wanted to go, well,
I'd take you there because there's enough gas
in this beauty to get us to Texas or San Francisco   15

or a good viewing of the shuttle going starward which is what
this bygone baby is, a dream machine with real wheels,
white walls spiffier than anybody's poetry moon,
prettier than Mazda or Toyota, even Infiniti.
A chrome castle soaked in salmony sunrise, a huge pink   20

thumbs-down to the rat-box subcompact of modern life.
This 1959 Cadillac floating steamy and unstoppable down the road
like a comet the color of Jayne Mansfield's° lipstick,
melting around corners leaving behind violet flags of old exhaust.
Did I see that? a pedestrian says to himself, What *was* that . . .   25

---

12 Lana Turner (1921–1995), American movie star   **23 Jayne Mansfield** (1933–1967), also an
American movie actress

Well, I'll tell you, that was love's submarine taking its time,
sashaying through the black lack of imagination
all around us. That was me wanting to get you wherever
you want to go and you going right along with it,
in the pink-as-flamingoes chrome cool boat-us-home Cadillac.   30

—2001

Kettle

An old woman gets tired of her sad face
so she fills her soup bowl with fresh water
then stares into that small lake until she sees
her reflection floating there but softened.
She smiles and when she does that,   5
her sadness gets tricked into the bowl,
surprised to be lightened a little at last.
Then she takes that bowl into high grass
and leaves it there for the rough tongues
of homeless cats to scratch across;   10
for starlight to mend itself in.
Now, who knows whether she is old
or young, this woman who tricks away despair.
She's laughing as she peels the wrinkled skins
from red potatoes, dropping them moon   15
by moon into evening's kettle: new root soup.

—2001

Emily Grosholz (b. 1950)

Emily Grosholz teaches philosophy and African-American studies at Pennsylvania State University. Born and raised in the Philadelphia suburbs, she has traveled in Italy and Greece and lived in Germany, France, and England. Grosholz has published philosophical works as well as four books of poetry. Her poems are often informed by her interest in mathematics and philosophy.

Letter from Germany

Though it is only February, turned
less than a week ago,
and though the latitude is upward here
of Newfoundland's north shore,
Mother, spring is out. It's almost hot,   5
simmering above and underground,
and in my veins! where your blood also runs.
The hazels dangle down
green flowery catkins, and the alders too,
those bushy, water-loving trees,   10
have a like ornament, in purple-red.
Spring is so forward here.
Snowbells swing in garden beds;
the pussy willows that you liked to bring
inside, to force their silver fur,   15
are open in the air;
witch hazel in the formal park,
still leafless, wears a ribbon-petaled bloom
of yellow and pale orange.
Once or twice I've walked through clouds   20
of insects by the river to the east
of town; the ducks are back on the canal
now that the ice is gone, loud and in love.
I wish that I could bring you here
to see this fast, unseasonable spring;   25
I wish that I could write a letter home.
But since a year you are not anywhere,
not even underground,

so that the words I might have written down
I say aloud into the atmosphere   30
of pollen and fresh clouds.
I say the litany of my desires,
and wonder, knowing better, if you hear
through some light-rooted organ of the air.

—*1984*

November

for Dick Davis

My friend, it seems as if we know at last
we won't be here much longer.
Crossing the mountain of a hundred years
we've gained the shadow side. Against our faces
Boreas° falls, the breath of nothingness.   5

The Chinese sages recommend reflection:
characters like willows
bend to the river where cold water flows
unceasingly, changing its fluid mind
with every passing cloud or boat or leaf.   10

What's left behind? Only a few brief verses.
Come to visit soon, and drink a glass
of wine and watch the woods behind my house
decant the autumn moon
overblown and gold on the horizon.   15

—*2003*

5 **Boreas** the north wind

Dana Gioia (b. 1950)

Dana Gioia is the first poet to serve as chair of the National Endowment for the Arts. Born and raised in Los Angeles, he made a successful career in business before devoting himself full-time to writing. The editor of several textbooks and anthologies, Gioia also is an influential critic; his essay "Can Poetry Matter?" stimulated much discussion when it appeared in The Atlantic. *His third collection of poems,* Interrogations at Noon *(2001), won the American Book Award.*

The Next Poem

How much better it seems now
than when it is finally done—
the unforgettable first line,
the cunning way the stanzas run.

The rhymes soft-spoken and suggestive   5
are barely audible at first,
an appetite not yet acknowledged
like the inkling of a thirst.

While gradually the form appears
as each line is coaxed aloud—   10
the architecture of a room
seen from the middle of a crowd.

The music that of common speech
but slanted so that each detail
sounds unexpected as a sharp   15
inserted in a simple scale.

No jumble box of imagery
dumped glumly in the reader's lap
or elegantly packaged junk
the unsuspecting must unwrap.   20

But words that could direct a friend
precisely to an unknown place,
those few unshakeable details
that no confusion can erase.

And the real subject left unspoken   25
but unmistakable to those
who don't expect a jungle parrot
in the black and white of prose.

How much better it seems now
than when it is finally written.   30
How hungrily one waits to feel
the bright lure seized, the old hook bitten.

—*1991*

Planting a Sequoia

All afternoon my brothers and I have worked in the orchard,
Digging this hole, laying you into it, carefully packing the soil.
Rain blackened the horizon, but cold winds kept it over the Pacific,
And the sky above us stayed the dull gray
Of an old year coming to an end.   5

In Sicily a father plants a tree to celebrate his first son's birth—
An olive or a fig tree—a sign that the earth has one more life to bear.
I would have done the same, proudly laying new stock into my father's
    orchard,
A green sapling rising among the twisted apple boughs,
A promise of new fruit in other autumns.   10

But today we kneel in the cold planting you, our native giant,
Defying the practical custom of our fathers,
Wrapping in your roots a lock of hair, a piece of an infant's birth cord,
All that remains above earth of a first-born son,
A few stray atoms brought back to the elements.   15

We will give you what we can—our labor and our soil,
Water drawn from the earth when the skies fail,
Nights scented with the ocean fog, days softened by the circuit of bees.
We plant you in the corner of the grove, bathed in western light,
A slender shoot against the sunset.   20

And when our family is no more, all of his unborn brothers dead,
Every niece and nephew scattered, the house torn down,
His mother's beauty ashes in the air,

I want you to stand among strangers, all young and ephemeral to you,
Silently keeping the secret of your birth.   25

                                                                —*1991*

Elegy with Surrealist°
Proverbs as Refrain

"Poetry must lead somewhere," declared Breton.°
He carried a rose inside his coat each day
to give a beautiful stranger— "Better to die of love
than love without regret." And those who loved him
soon learned regret. "The simplest surreal act   5
is running through the street with a revolver
firing at random." Old and famous, he seemed *démodé*.
There is always a skeleton on the buffet.

Wounded Apollinaire° wore a small steel plate
inserted in his skull. "I so loved art," he smiled,   10
"I joined the artillery." His friends were asked to wait
while his widow laid a crucifix across his chest.
Picasso° hated death. The funeral left him so distressed
he painted a self-portrait. "It's always other people,"
remarked Duchamp,° "who do the dying."   15
I came. I sat down. I went away.

Dali° dreamed of Hitler as a white-skinned girl—
impossibly pale, luminous and lifeless as the moon.
Wealthy Roussel° taught his poodle to smoke a pipe.
"When I write, I am surrounded by radiance.   20
My glory is like a great bomb waiting to explode."
When his valet refused to slash his wrists,
the bankrupt writer took an overdose of pills.

Surrealist a movement in the arts that flourished in Paris after World War I; the writers and painters in the poem were associated with it   **1 Breton** Andre Breton (1896–1966), French poet and critic, and one of the founders of the Surrealist movement in art, which sought to reject the morals of bourgeois society. Breton worked to incorporate the unconscious mind into writing and art   **9 Apollinaire** Guillaume Apollinaire (1880–1918), French poet   **13 Picasso** Pablo Picasso (1881–1973), Spanish painter and sculptor   **15 Duchamp** Marcel Duchamp (1887–1968), French/American conceptual artist   **17 Dali** Salvador Dali (1904–1989), Spanish painter   **19 Roussel** Raymound Roussel (1877–1933), French writer

There is always a skeleton on the buffet.

Breton considered suicide the truest art,   25
though life seemed hardly worth the trouble to discard.
The German colonels strolled the Île de la Cité—°
some to the Louvre, some to the Place Pigalle.
"The loneliness of poets has been erased," cried Éluard,°
in praise of Stalin.° "Burn all the books," said dying Hugo Ball.°   30
There is always a skeleton on the buffet.
I came. I sat down. I went away.

                               —2001

Timothy Murphy (b. 1951)

Timothy Murphy, a former student of Robert Penn Warren at Yale, returned to his native North Dakota to make a career as a venture capitalist and partner in a farm that produces 850,000 hogs a year. Unpublished until his mid-forties, Murphy brought four collections to print during the 1990s. His poetry collections include The Deed of Gift *(1998),* Set the Ploughshare Deep *(2000), and* Very Far North *(2002). His verse translation of* Beowulf, *done in collaboration with Alan Sullivan, appears in* The Longman Anthology of British Literature. *Written in a distinctive poetic voice, alert with intelligence and dense with rhyme and wordplay, Murphy's poems often tell of the harshness of life in the high plains.*

The Track of a Storm

Bastille Day, 1995

We grieve for the twelve trees we lost last night,
pillars of our community, old friends
and confidants dismembered in our sight,
stripped of their crowns by the unruly winds.
There were no baskets to receive their heads,   5
no women knitting by the guillotines,

27 **Ile de la Cité** a site in Paris, as are the Louvre and Place Pigalle   29 **Eluard** Paul Eluard (1895–1952), French poet   30 **Stalin** Joseph Stalin (1879–1953), Soviet Communist leader who sought to destroy his perceived political opposition by executing or imprisoning millions of ordinary citizens   30 **Hugo Ball** (1886–1927), German poet

only two sleepers rousted from their beds
by fusillades of hailstones on the screens.
Her nest shattered, her battered hatchlings drowned,
a stunned and silent junko watches me   10
chainsawing limbs from corpses of the downed,
clearing the understory of debris
while supple saplings which survived the blast
lay claim to light and liberty at last.

                                        —1998

Case Notes

for Dr. Richard Kolotkin

MARCH 7, 2002

Raped at an early age
by older altar boy.
"Damned by the Church to Hell,
never to sire a son,
perhaps man's greatest joy,"   5
said father in a rage.
Patient was twenty-one.
Handled it pretty well.

MARCH 14, 2002

Curiously, have learned
patient was Eagle Scout.   10
Outraged that Scouts have spurned
each camper who is "out."
Questioned if taunts endured
are buried? "No, immured."

MARCH 21, 2002

Immersed in verse and drink   15
when he was just sixteen,
turned to drugs at Yale.
Patient began to sink,

to fear he was a "queen,"
a "queer" condemned to fail   20
or detox in a jail.

APRIL 1, 2002

Into a straight town
he brought a sober lover.
"Worked smarter, drank harder
to stock an empty larder,"   25
wrote poetry, the cover
for grief he cannot drown.

APRIL 9, 2002

Uneasy with late father,
feared for by his mother,
lover, and younger brother.   30
Various neuroses,
but no severe psychosis.
Precarious prognosis.

—2004

Andrew Hudgins (b. 1951)

Andrew Hudgins has demonstrated his poetic skills in a wide variety of po-
ems, including a book-length sequence of dramatic monologues, After the
Lost War *(1988), written in the voice of Sidney Lanier, the greatest South-*
ern poet of the late nineteenth century. Born in Texas to a military family,
Hudgins moved often during his childhood. His family moved back to the
South permanently when he was in junior high, eventually winding up in
Montgomery, Alabama, where Hudgins attended high school. At Hunting-
don College, he discovered the poetry of T. S. Eliot and began reading po-
etry independently. After working briefly as a junior high school teacher, he
studied at the University of Alabama, Syracuse University, and the Iowa
Writers' Workshop. Hudgins has taught at the University of Cincinnati,
and currently teaches at Ohio State University. His work blends the humor-
ous with the deeply serious, and the profane with the sacred.

Air View of an Industrial Scene

There is a train at the ramp, unloading people
who stumble from the cars and toward the gate.
The building's shadows tilt across the ground
and from each shadow juts a longer one
and from that shadow crawls a shadow of smoke   5
black as just-plowed earth. Inside the gate
is a small garden and someone on his knees.
Perhaps he's fingering the yellow blooms
to see which ones have set and will soon wither,
clinging to a green tomato as it swells.   10
The people hold back, but are forced to the open gate,
and when they enter they will see the garden
and some, gardeners themselves, will yearn
to fall to their knees there, untangling vines,
plucking at weeds, cooling their hands in damp earth. 15
They're going to die soon, a matter of minutes.
Even from our height, we see in the photograph
the shadow of the plane stamped dark and large

on Birkenau,° one black wing shading the garden.
We can't tell which are guards, which prisoners.   20
We're watchers. But if we had bombs we'd drop them.

—1985

Where the River Jordan° Ends

She put two flowered hair clasps in my hair.
They held. I was amazed. Though Daddy thought
I should be wearing ribbons on my head
he couldn't make them stay. One Christmas Day
he saved the ribbons left from opening gifts   5
and looped them through my curls. We went to church,
where Aunt Bess snickered, picked them from my hair
and off my neck. She told Daddy, *Jerome,*
she's festooned like a nigger Christmas tree.
But Mrs. Shores knew everything! She smiled   10
and smoothed my hair around the flowered clasps.
Her husband had invited Daddy down
to preach a week's revival at his church,
and she, since I was almost thirteen, let me
drink coffee when the men were off at work.   15

Their son took me and Sis into the church.
We ran around the aisles till we got tired,
then shucked our shoes and socks, sat on the rail,
and dangled feet into the River Jordan—
a painting on the wall that seemed to flow   20
into the baptistery. We splashed around,
got wet, then stripped down to our birthday suits,
and leapt into the font. We went berserk.
We were cannonballing off the rail
when Daddy threw the double doors apart.   25
We jumped into the font and held our breaths.
When I came up, Daddy was standing there,

19 Birkenau German concentration camp in World War II
River Jordan in which Jesus was baptized

waiting. I flinched. Instead he touched my cheek:
Put on your clothes, Elizabeth Marie.
And then I saw the tears. I cried all day.   30
That night as I sat staring at the wall
behind my father, where the Jordan ends,
I heard God's voice and went to be immersed,
trembling and happy in a paper robe,
and Daddy hugged my body to his chest.   35
I left a wet, dark shadow on his suit.
I wanted to be saved again. Again.

—1985

Heat Lightning in a Time of Drought

My neighbor, drunk, stood on his lawn and yelled,
Want some! Want some! He bellowed it as cops
cuffed him, shoved him in their back seat—*Want some!*—
and drove away. Now I lie here awake,
not by choice, listening to the crickets' high   5
electric trill, urgent with lust. Heat lightning flashes.
The crickets will not, will not stop. I wish
that I could shut the window, pull the curtain, sleep.
But it's too hot. *Want some!* He screamed it till
I was afraid I'd made him up to scream   10
what I knew better than to say out loud
although it's August-hot and every move
bathes me in sweat and we are careless,
careless, careless, every one of us,
and when my neighbor screams out in his yard   15
like one dog howling for another dog,
I call the cops, then lie in my own sweat,
remembering the woman
who, at a party on a night this hot,
walked up to me, propped her chin on my chest,   20
and sighed. She was a little drunk, the love-light
unshielded in her eyes. We fell in love.
One day at supper the light fixture dropped,

exploded on the table. Glass flew around us,
a low, slow-motion blossoming of razors.   25
She was unhurt till I reached out my hand
—left hand—to brush glass from her face.
Two drops of blood ran down her cheek.
On TV, I'd seen a teacher dip a rose
in liquid nitrogen. When he withdrew it,   30
it smoked, frozen solid. He snapped one petal, frail
as isinglass, and then, against the table,
he shattered it. The whole rose blew apart.
Like us. And then one day the doorbell rang.
A salesman said, *Watch this!* He stripped my bed   35
and vacuumed it. The nozzle sucked up two
full, measured cups of light gray flakes. He said,
That's human skin. I stood, refusing the purchase,
stood staring at her flesh and mine commingled
inside the measuring cup, stood there and thought,   40
*She's been gone two years, she's married, and all this time
her flesh has been in bed with me.* Don't laugh.
Don't laugh. That's what the Little Moron says
when he arrives home early from a trip
and finds his wife in bed with someone else.   45
The man runs off. The Little Moron puts
a pistol to his own head, cocks the hammer.
His wife, in bed, sheets pulled up to her breasts,
starts laughing. *Don't you laugh!* he screams. *Don't laugh—
you're next.* It is the wisest joke I know because   50
the heart's a violent muscle, opening
and closing. Who knows what we might do:
by night, the craziness of dreams; by day,
the craziness of logic. Listen!
My brother told me of a man wheeled, screaming,   55
into the ward, a large Coke bottle rammed
up his ass. I was awed: there is no telling
what we'll do in our fierce drive to come together.
The heart keeps opening and closing like a mine
where fire still burns, a century underground,   60
following the veins of black coal, rearing up
to take a barn, a house, a pasture. Although
I wish that it would rain tonight, I fret
about the heat lightning that flicks and glitters

on the horizon as if it promised rain. 65
It can't. But I walk outside, stand on parched grass,
and watch it hungrily—all light, all dazzle—
remembering how we'd drive out past the town's light,
sit on the hood, and watch great thunderheads
huge as a state—say, Delaware—sail past. Branched 70
lightning jagged, burst the dark from zenith to horizon.
We stared at almost nothing: some live oaks,
the waist-high corn. Slow raindrops smacked the corn,
plopped in the dirt around us, drummed the roof,
and finally reached out, tapped us on the shoulders. 75
We drove home in the downpour, laughed, made love
—still wet with rain—and slept. But why stop there?
Each happy memory leads me to a sad one:
the friend who helped me through my grief by drinking
all of my liquor. And when, at last, we reached 80
the wretched mescal, he carefully sliced off
the worm's black face, ate its white body, staggered
onto this very lawn, and racked and heaved
until I helped him up. *You're okay, John.*
You've puked it out. "No, man—you're wrong. That worm 85
ain't ever coming out." Heat lightning flashes.
No rain falls and no thunder cracks the heat.
No first concussion dwindles to a long
low rolling growl. I go in the house, lie down,
pray, masturbate, drift to the edge of sleep. 90
I wish my soul were larger than it is.

—1991

Joy Harjo (b. 1951)

Joy Harjo is one of the leading voices in contemporary Native-American poetry. Born in Tulsa, Oklahoma, she has a rich multicultural heritage: Her father was Creek and her mother Cherokee, French, and Irish. At sixteen, Harjo moved to the Southwest to study at the Institute of American Indian Arts, where she switched her major from art to poetry. She also holds degrees from the University of New Mexico and the Iowa Writers' Workshop, and has taught at the Institute of American Indian Arts, Arizona State University, the University of Colorado, and the University of New Mexico. She has written teleplays, public service announcements, and scripts for educational television, and has edited several literary journals including the High Plains Literary Review. *A powerful performer, Harjo has been profiled on Bill Moyers's television series,* The Power of the Word. *Her band, The Real Revolution, combines music with poetry.*

She Had Some Horses

She had some horses.

She had horses who were bodies of sand.
She had horses who were maps drawn of blood.
She had horses who were skins of ocean water.
She had horses who were the blue air of sky.   5
She had horses who were fur and teeth.
She had horses who were clay and would break.
She had horses who were splintered red cliff.

She had some horses.

She had horses with eyes of trains.   10
She had horses with full, brown thighs.
She had horses who laughed too much.
She had horses who threw rocks at glass houses.
She had horses who licked razor blades.

She had some horses.   15

She had horses who danced in their mothers' arms.
She had horses who thought they were the sun and their
     bodies shone and burned like stars.
She had horses who waltzed nightly on the moon.

She had horses who were much too shy, and kept quiet
    in stalls of their own making.

She had some horses.   20

She had horses who liked Creek° Stomp Dance songs.
She had horses who cried in their beer.
She had horses who spit at male queens who made them afraid of
    themselves.
She had horses who said they weren't afraid.
She had horses who lied.   25
She had horses told the truth, who were stripped
    bare of their tongues.

She had some horses.

She had horses who called themselves, "horse."
She had horses who called themselves, "spirit," and kept
    their voices secret and to themselves.
She had horses who had no names.   30
She had horses who had books of names.

She had some horses.

She had horses who whispered in the dark, who were afraid to speak.
She had horses who screamed out of fear of the silence, who
    carried knives to protect themselves from ghosts.
She had horses who waited for destruction.   35
She had horses who waited for resurrection.

She had some horses.

She had horses who got down on their knees for any savior.
She had horses who thought their high price had saved them.
She had horses who tried to save her, who climbed in her
    bed at night and prayed as they raped her.   40

She had some horses.

She had some horses she loved.
She had some horses she hated.

These were the same horses.

—*1983*

21 **Creek** Native American tribe

Song for the Deer and Myself to Return On

This morning when I looked out the roof window
before dawn and a few stars were still caught
in the fragile weft of ebony night
I was overwhelmed. I sang the song Louis taught me:
a song to call the deer in Creek,° when hunting,   5
and I am certainly hunting something as magic as deer
in this city far from the hammock of my mother's belly.
It works, of course, and deer came into this room
and wondered at finding themselves
in a house near downtown Denver.   10
Now the deer and I are trying to figure out a song
to get them back, to get all of us back,
because if it works I'm going with them.
And it's too early to call Louis
and nearly too late to go home.   15

—*1990*

5 Creek Native American tribal language

Judith Ortiz Cofer (b. 1952)

Judith Ortiz Cofer writes poetry, fiction, and essays that explore her Puerto Rican heritage, seeking to reconcile her original culture with her adopted one. Born in Hormigueros, a rural village in Puerto Rico, Ortiz Cofer moved to Paterson, New Jersey, as a young child. Because her father was in the U.S. Navy, Ortiz Cofer and her mother and siblings returned periodically to the island while his fleet was on maneuvers. She studied at Augusta College and Florida Atlantic University, and currently teaches at the University of Georgia and lives on a farm in rural Louisville, Georgia.

The Latin Deli: An Ars Poetica°

Presiding over a formica counter,
plastic Mother and Child magnetized
to the top of an ancient register,
the heady mix of smells from the open bins
of dried codfish, the green plantains   5
hanging in stalks like votive offerings,
she is the Patroness of Exiles,
a woman of no-age who was never pretty,
who spends her days selling canned memories
while listening to the Puerto Ricans complain   10
that it would be cheaper to fly to San Juan
than to buy a pound of Bustelo coffee here,
and to Cubans perfecting their speech
of a "glorious return" to Havana—where no one
has been allowed to die and nothing to change until then;   15
to Mexicans who pass through, talking lyrically
of *dólares*° to be made in El Norte°—
                                        all wanting the comfort
of spoken Spanish, to gaze upon the family portrait
of her plain wide face, her ample bosom   20
resting on her plump arms, her look of maternal interest
as they speak to her and each other

Ars Poetica the art of poetry (Latin) **17 dólares** dollars **17 El Norte** the North

of their dreams and their disillusions—
how she smiles understanding,
when they walk down the narrow aisles of her store   25
reading the labels of packages aloud, as if
they were the names of lost lovers: *Suspiros,*°
Merengues,° the stale candy of everyone's childhood.

                                       She spends her days
slicing *jamón y queso*° and wrapping it in wax paper   30
tied with string: plain ham and cheese
that would cost less at the A&P, but it would not satisfy
the hunger of the fragile old man lost in the folds
of his winter coat, who brings her lists of items
that he reads to her like poetry, or the others,   35
whose needs she must divine, conjuring up products
from places that now exist only in their hearts—
closed ports she must trade with.

                                                   —1993

The Lesson of the Teeth

I heard my mother say it once
in the kitchen—that to dream of teeth
means death is coming, rattling
its bag of bones as a warning to all
to say a "Credo" every night before sleeping.   5

One day, as a child, seeking the mystery
of my Aunt Clotilde's beauty,
I slipped into her bedroom without knocking.
She was sitting at her vanity,
combing her long black hair everyone said   10
I'd inherited. A set of false teeth
floated in a jar beside her. In horror,
I looked up into the face of a sunken-cheeked hag
in the mirror—then ran all the way home.

She must have seen me but never let on.   15
Her face filled with flesh appeared often

27 Suspiros meringue cookies; "suspiros" is Spanish for "sighs" **28 Merengues** traditional Puerto Rican candy made from whipped egg whites and castor sugar **30 jamón y queso** ham and cheese

at our place. But her smile
sent a little current of icy fear up my spine—
that message they say you receive
when someone steps on your grave.   20

—*1993*

Naomi Shihab Nye (b. 1952)

*Naomi Shihab Nye, a dedicated world traveler and humanitarian, has read
her poetry in Bangladesh and the Middle East, promoting international
understanding through the arts. The daughter of a Palestinian father and
an American mother, she has written many poems informed by her Palestinian ancestry, and has translated contemporary Arabic poetry. Raised in
St. Louis, Jerusalem, and San Antonio, Nye received her B.A. from Trinity
University in San Antonio, Texas, where she still lives. Her poetry collections include* Fuel *(1998),* Red Suitcase *(1994), and* Hugging the Jukebox
(1982). A regular columnist for Organica, *Nye has been featured on two
PBS poetry specials:* The Language of Life: A Festival of Poets *and* The
United States of Poetry. *She writes songs and children's books, and edits
prose anthologies. She also has worked for more than twenty-eight years
as a visiting writer in schools at all levels.*

The Traveling Onion

It is believed that the onion originally came from
India. In Egypt it was an object of worship—
why I haven't been able to find out. From Egypt
the onion entered Greece and on to Italy, thence
into all of Europe.

—*Better Living Cookbook*

When I think how far the onion has traveled
just to enter my stew today, I could kneel and praise
all small forgotten miracles,
crackly paper peeling on the drainboard,
pearly layers in smooth agreement,   5
the way knife enters onion, straight
and onion falls apart on the chopping block,
a history revealed.

And I would never scold the onion
for causing tears.   10
It is right that tears fall
for something small and forgotten.
How at meal, we sit to eat,
commenting on texture of meat or herbal aroma
but never on the translucence of onion,   15
now limp, now divided,
or its traditionally honorable career:
For the sake of others,
disappear.

—1986

Yellow Glove

What can a yellow glove mean in a world of motorcars and
governments?

I was small, like everyone. Life was a string of precautions: Don't
kiss the squirrel before you bury him, don't suck candy, pop balloons,
drop watermelons, watch TV. When the new gloves appeared one   5
Christmas, tucked in soft tissue, I heard it trailing me: Don't lose
the yellow gloves.

I was small, there was too much to remember. One day, waving at a
stream—the ice had cracked, winter chipping down, soon we would
sail boats and roll into ditches—I let a glove go. Into the stream,   10
sucked under the street. Since when did streets have mouths?
I walked home on a desperate road. Gloves cost money. We didn't
have much. I would tell no one. I would wear the yellow glove that
was left and keep the other hand in a pocket. I knew my mother's
eyes had tears they had not cried yet and I didn't want to be the one 15
to make them flow. It was the prayer I spoke secretly, folding socks,
lining up donkeys in windowsills. I would be good, a promise made to
the roaches who scouted my closet at night. If you don't get in my
bed, I will be good. And they listened. I had a lot to fulfill.

The months rolled down like towels out of a machine. I sang   20
and drew and fattened the cat. Don't scream, don't lie, don't cheat, don't
fight—you could hear it anywhere. A pebble could show you how to
be smooth, tell the truth. A field could show how to sleep without
walls. A stream could remember how to drift and change—the next
June I was stirring the stream like a soup, telling my brother dinner   25
would be ready if he'd only hurry up with the bread, when I saw it.
The yellow glove draped on a twig. A muddy survivor. A quiet flag.

Where had it been in the three gone months? I could wash it, fold it
in my winter drawer with its sister, no one in that world would ever
know. There were miracles on Harvey Street. Children walked   30
home in yellow light. Trees were reborn and gloves traveled far, but
returned. A thousand miles later, what can a yellow glove mean in a
world of bankbooks and stereos?

Part of the difference between floating and going down.

—1986

Mark Jarman (b. 1952)

Mark Jarman was born in Mount Sterling, Kentucky, and has lived in Scotland, California, and Tennessee, where he currently teaches at Vanderbilt University. Jarman studied at the University of California, Santa Cruz and the Iowa Writers' Workshop. With Robert McDowell, he edited The Reaper, *a magazine specializing in narrative poetry. At the relatively young age of twenty-two, Jarman published a poetry chapbook entitled* Tonight Is the Night of the Prom. *He has since published eight full-length collections, including* Questions for Ecclesiastes, *which won the Lenore Marshall Poetry Prize for 1998, and* Unholy Sonnets (2000). *Both volumes consider the role of God and religion in contemporary life. With David Mason, Jarman coedited* Rebel Angels: 25 Poets of the New Formalism. *His essays have been collected by Story Line Press and in the University of Michigan Press's Poets on Poetry series.*

After Disappointment

To lie in your child's bed when she is gone
Is calming as anything I know. To fall
Asleep, her books arranged above your head,
Is to admit that you have never been
So tired, so enchanted by the spell   5
Of your grown body. To feel small instead
Of blocking out the light, to feel alone,
Not knowing what you should or shouldn't feel,
Is to find out, no matter what you've said
About the cramped escapes and obstacles   10
You plan and face and have to call the world,
That there remain these places, occupied
By children, yours if lucky, like the girl
Who finds you here and lies down by your side.

—1997

Ground Swell

Is nothing real but when I was fifteen,
Going on sixteen, like a corny song?
I see myself so clearly then, and painfully—
Knees bleeding through my usher's uniform
Behind the candy counter in the theater   5
After a morning's surfing; paddling frantically
To top the brisk outsiders coming to wreck me,
Trundle me clumsily along the beach floor's
Gravel and sand; my knees aching with salt.
Is that all that I have to write about?   10
You write about the life that's vividest.
And if that is your own, that is your subject.
And if the years before and after sixteen
Are colorless as salt and taste like sand—
Return to those remembered chilly mornings,   15
The light spreading like a great skin on the water,
And the blue water scalloped with wind-ridges,
And—what was it exactly?—that slow waiting
When, to invigorate yourself, you peed
Inside your bathing suit and felt the warmth   20
Crawl all around your hips and thighs,
And the first set rolled in and the water level
Rose in expectancy, and the sun struck
The water surface like a brassy palm,
Flat and gonglike, and the wave face formed.   25
Yes. But that was a summer so removed
In time, so specially peculiar to my life,
Why would I want to write about it again?
There was a day or two when, paddling out,
An older boy who had just graduated   30
And grown a great blonde moustache, like a walrus,
Skimmed past me like a smooth machine on the water,
And said my name. I was so much younger,
To be identified by one like him—
The easy deference of a kind of god   35
Who also went to church where I did—made me
Reconsider my worth. I had been noticed.
He soon was a small figure crossing waves,

The shawling crest surrounding him with spray,
Whiter than gull feathers. He had said my name   40
Without scorn, just with a bit of surprise
To notice me among those trying the big waves
Of the morning break. His name is carved now
On the black wall in Washington, the frozen wave
That grievers cross to find a name or names.   45
I knew him as I say I knew him, then,
Which wasn't very well. My father preached
His funeral. He came home in a bag
That may have mixed in pieces of his squad.
Yes, I can write about a lot of things   50
Besides the summer that I turned sixteen.
But that's my ground swell. I must start
Where things began to happen and I knew it.

                                        —*1997*

Rita Dove (b. 1952)

Rita Dove won the Pulitzer Prize in 1987 for Thomas and Beulah, *a sequence of lyric poems about her grandparents' lives in Ohio. One of the most important voices of contemporary African-American poetry, she served as Poet Laureate of the United States from 1993 to 1995. Born in Akron, Ohio, Dove holds degrees from Miami University of Ohio and the Iowa Writers' Workshop. In addition to her seven poetry collections, she has published a book of short stories,* Fifth Sunday *(1985), a novel,* Through the Ivory Gate *(1992), a collection of essays,* The Poet's World *(1995), and a play,* The Darker Face of the Earth, *which premiered in 1996 at the Oregon Shakespeare Festival and was subsequently produced at the Kennedy Center in Washington, D.C., and at the Royal National Theatre in London.* Seven for Luck, *her song cycle for soprano and orchestra, with music by John Williams, was premiered by the Boston Symphony Orchestra at Tanglewood in 1998. For the White House's 1999/2000 New Year's celebration, Dove gave a live reading at the Lincoln Memorial, accompanied by John Williams's music, an event included in Steven Spielberg's documentary* The Unfinished Journey. *Dove is Commonwealth Professor of English at the University of Virginia in Charlottesville.*

Adolescence—III

With Dad gone, Mom and I worked
The dusky rows of tomatoes.
As they glowed orange in sunlight
And rotted in shadow, I too
Grew orange and softer, swelling out   5
Starched cotton slips.

The texture of twilight made me think of
Lengths of Dotted Swiss.° In my room
I wrapped scarred knees in dresses
That once went to big-band dances;   10
I baptized my earlobes with rosewater.
Along the window-sill, the lipstick stubs
Glittered in their steel shells.

Looking out at the rows of clay
And chicken manure, I dreamed how it would happen: 15

8 Dotted Swiss type of sheer fabric

He would meet me by the blue spruce,
A carnation over his heart, saying,
"I have come for you, Madam;
I have loved you in my dreams."
At his touch, the scabs would fall away.   20
Over his shoulder, I see my father coming toward us:
He carries his tears in a bowl,
And blood hangs in the pine-soaked air.

—*1980*

After Reading *Mickey In The Night Kitchen*° For The Third Time Before Bed

I'm in the milk and the milk's in me! . . . I'm Mickey!

My daughter spreads her legs
to find her vagina:
hairless, this mistaken
bit of nomenclature
is what a stranger cannot touch   5
without her yelling. She demands
to see mine and momentarily
we're a lopsided star
among the spilled toys,
my prodigious scallops   10
exposed to her neat cameo.

And yet the same glazed
tunnel, layered sequences.
She is three; that makes this
innocent. *We're pink!*   15
she shrieks, and bounds off.

Mickey In The Night Kitchen picture book by Maurice Sendak

Every month she wants
to know where it hurts
and what the wrinkled string means
between my legs. *This is good blood*   20
I say, but that's wrong, too.
How to tell her that it's what makes us—
black mother, cream child.
That we're in the pink
and the pink's in us.   25

            —1989

American Smooth

We were dancing—it must have
been a foxtrot or a waltz,
something romantic but
requiring restraint,
rise and fall, precise   5
execution as we moved
into the next song without
stopping, two chests heaving
above a seven-league
stride—such perfect agony   10
one learns to smile through,
ecstatic mimicry
being the sine qua non°
of American Smooth.
And because I was distracted   15
by the effort of
keeping my frame
(the leftward lean, head turned
just enough to gaze out
past your ear and always   20
smiling, smiling),
I didn't notice
how still you'd become until
we had done it

13 **sine qua non** an essential part (Latin)

(for two measures? 25
four?)— achieved flight,
that swift and serene
magnificence,
before the earth
remembered who we were 30
and brought us down.

—*2004*

Alberto Ríos (b. 1952)

Alberto Ríos was born in Nogales, Arizona, the son of a Mexican-American father and an English-born mother. He received a B.A. and an M.F.A. in creative writing from the University of Arizona, and won the Walt Whitman Award of the Academy of American Poets for his first book, Whispering to Fool the Wind *(1982). He also has written a collection of short stories,* The Iguana Killer: Twelve Stories of the Heart, *which won the Western States Book Award in 1984.* Capirotada *(1999), his memoir about growing up on the Mexican-American border, received the Latino Literary Hall of Fame Book Award for the best biography of the year. His poetry has been set to classical and popular music, including a cantata by James DeMars called "Toto's Say." Ríos was featured in the documentary* Birthwrite: Growing Up Hispanic. *He lives in Chandler, Arizona, and is Regents Professor of English at Arizona State University.*

Madre Sofía°

My mother took me because she couldn't
wait the second ten years to know.
This was the lady rumored to have been
responsible for the box-wrapped baby
among the presents at that wedding, 5
but we went in, anyway, through the curtains.
Loose jar-top, half turned
and not caught properly in the threads
her head sat mimicking its original intention
like the smile of a child hitting himself. 10

Madre Sofía Mother Sofía; "Sofia" is the Greek word for wisdom

Central in that head grew unfamiliar poppies
from a face mahogany, eyes half yellow
half gray at the same time, goat and fog,
slit eyes of the devil, his tweed suit, red
lips, and she smelled of smoke, cigarettes,   15
but a diamond smoke, somehow; I inhaled
sparkles, but I could feel them, throat, stomach.
She did not speak, and as a child
I could only answer, so that together
we were silent, cold and wet, dry and hard;   20
from behind my mother pushed me forward.
The lady put her hand on the face
of a thin animal wrap, tossing that head
behind her to be pressured incredibly
as she sat back in the huge chair and leaned.   25
And then I saw the breasts as large as her
head, folded together, coming out of her dress
as if it didn't fit, not like my mother's.
I could see them, how she kept them
penned up, leisurely, in maroon feed bags,   30
horse nuzzles of her wide body,
but exquisitely penned up
circled by pearl reins and red scarves.
She lifted her arm, but only with the tips
of her fingers motioned me to sit opposite.   35
She looked at me but spoke to my mother
words dark, smoky like the small room,
words coming like red ants stepping occasionally
from a hole on a summer day in the valley,
red ants from her mouth, her nose, her ears,   40
tears from the corners of her cinched eyes.
And suddenly she put her hand full on my head
pinching tight again with those finger tips
like a television healer, young Oral Roberts°
half standing, quickly, half leaning   45
those breasts swinging toward me
so that I reach with both my hands to my lap
protecting instinctively whatever it is
that needs protection when a baseball is thrown

---

44 **Oral Roberts** (born 1918), Pentecostal minister and televangelist

and you're not looking but someone yells,   50
the hand, then those breasts coming toward me
like the quarter-arms of the amputee Joaquin
who came back from the war to sit
in the park, reaching always for children
until one day he had to be held back.   55
I sat there, no breath, and could see only
hair around her left nipple, like a man.
Her clothes were old.
Accented, in a language whose spine had been
snapped, she whispered the words of a city   60
witch, and made me happy, alive like a man:
The future will make you tall.

—1982

The Purpose of Altar Boys

Tonio told me at catechism
the big part of the eye
admits good, and the little
black part is for seeing
evil—his mother told him   5
who was a widow and so
an authority on such things.
That's why at night
the black part gets bigger.
That's why kids can't go out   10
at night, and at night
girls take off their clothes
and walk around their
bedrooms or jump on their
beds or wear only sandals   15
and stand in their windows.
I was the altar boy
who knew about these things,
whose mission on some Sundays
was to remind people of   20
the night before as they
knelt for Holy Communion.

To keep Christ from falling
I held the metal plate under chins,
while on the thick   25
red carpet of the altar
I dragged my feet
and waited for the precise
moment: plate to chin
I delivered without expression   30
the Holy Electric Shock,
the kind that produces
a really large swallowing
and makes people think.
I thought of it as justice.   35
But on other Sundays the fire
in my eyes was different,
my mission somehow changed.
I would hold the metal plate
a little too hard   40
against those certain same
nervous chins, and I
I would look
with authority down
the tops of white dresses.   45

—1982

Brad Leithauser (b. 1953)

Brad Leithauser wrote the ambitious novel-in-verse Darlington's Fall *(2002), as well as numerous poetry collections and novels. Born and raised in Detroit, Michigan, he attended Harvard College and Harvard Law School. He served for three years as a research fellow at the Kyoto Comparative Law Center in Japan, and also has lived in Italy, England, Iceland, and France. Leithauser currently teaches at Mount Holyoke College and lives in South Hadley, Massachusetts, with his wife, the poet Mary Jo Salter.*

A Quilled Quilt, A Needle Bed

Under the longleaf pines
The curved, foot-long needles have
Woven a thatchwork quilt—threads,
Not patches, windfall millions
Looped and overlapped to make   5
The softest of needle beds.

The day's turned hot, the air
Coiling around the always
Cool scent of pine. As if lit
From below, a radiance   10
Milder yet more clement than
The sun's, the forest-carpet

Glows. It's a kind of pelt:
Thick as a bear's, tawny like
A bobcat's, more wonderful   15
Than both—a maize labyrinth
Spiraling down through tiny
Chinks to a caked, vegetal

Ferment where the needles
Crumble and blacken. And still   20
The mazing continues . . . whorls

Within whorls, the downscaling
Yet-perfect intricacies
Of lichens, seeds and crystals.

—1982

The Odd Last Thing
She Did

A car is idling on the cliff.
Its top is down. Its headlights throw
A faint, bright ghost-shadow glow
On the pale air. On the shore, so far
Below that the waves' push-and-drag   5
Is dwindled to a hush—a kind
Of oceanic idle—the sea
Among the boulders plays a blind-
Fold game of hide and seek,
Or capture the flag. The flag   10
Swells and sways. The car
Is empty. A Friday, the first week
Of June. Nineteen fifty-three.

A car's idling on the cliff,
But surely it won't be long before   15
Somebody stops to investigate
And things begin to happen fast:
Men, troops of men will come,
Arrive with blazing lights, a blast
Of sirens, followed by still more   20
Men. Though not a soul's in sight,
The peace of the end of the late
Afternoon—the sun down, but enough light
Even so to bathe the heavens from
Horizon to shore in a deep   25
And delicate blue—will not keep.

Confronted with such an overload
Of questions (most beginning, *Why would she* . . .

So gifted, bright, and only twenty-three),
Attention will come to fix upon   30
This odd last thing she did: leaving
The car running, the headlights on.
She stopped—it will transpire—to fill
The tank a mere two miles down the road.
(Just sixteen, the kid at the station will   35
Quote her as saying, "What a pity
You have to work *today*! It's not right . . .
What weather! Goodness, what a night
It'll be!" He'll add: "She sure was pretty.")

Was there a change of plan?   40
Why the stop for gas? Possibly
She'd not yet made up her mind? Or
Had made it up but not yet settled
On a place? Or could it be she knew
Where she was headed, what she would do—   45
And wanted to make sure the car ran
For hours afterward? Might the car not be,
Then, a sort of beacon, a lighthouse-
In-reverse, meant to direct one not
Away from but toward the shore   50
And its broken boulders, there to spot
The bobbing white flag of a blouse?

Her brief note, which will appear
In the local *Leader*, contains a phrase
("She chanted snatches of old lands")   55
That will muddle the town for three days,
Until a Professor E. H. Wade
Pins it to Ophelia°—and reprimands
The police, who, this but goes to show,
Have not the barest knowledge of Shakespeare,   60
Else would never have misread "lauds"
As "lands." A Detective Gregg Messing
Will answer, tersely, "Afraid
It's not our bailiwick. Missing
Persons, yes; missing poems, no."   65

---

58 Ophelia suicidal maiden in Shakespeare's *Hamlet*

(What's truly tragic's never allowed
To stand alone for long, of course.
At each moment there's a crowd
Of clowns pressing in: the booming ass
At every wake who, angling a loud   70
Necktie in the chip dip,
Airs his problems with intestinal gas,
Or the blow-dried bonehead out to sell
Siding to the grieving mother . . . Well,
Wade sent the *Leader* another *brief word:*   75
"Decades of service to the Bard now force
Me to amend the girl's little slip.
'Chaunted' not 'chanted' is the preferred . . .")

Yet none of her unshakable entourage
—Pedants, pundits, cops without a clue,   80
And a yearning young grease monkey—are
Alerted yet. Still the empty car
Idles, idles on the cliff, and night
Isn't falling so much as day
Is floating out to sea . . . Soon, whether   85
She's found or not, her lights will draw
Moths and tiny dark-winged things that might
Be dirt-clumps, ashes. Come what may,
The night will be lovely, as she foresaw,
The first stars easing through the blue,   90
Engine and ocean breathing together.

—1998

Harryette Mullen (b. 1953)

Harryette Mullen writes poems that revel in the music of language, veering playfully between logic and nonsense. Nevertheless, she claims, "I intend the poem to be meaningful: to allow, or suggest, to open up, or insinuate possible meanings, even in those places where the poem drifts between intentional utterance and improvisational wordplay." Born in Florence, Alabama, Mullen grew up in Fort Worth, Texas, and holds degrees from the University of Texas, Austin, and the University of California, Santa Cruz. She has taught in the Texas Commission on the Arts' Artists in the Schools, and at Cornell University, and currently teaches African-American literature and creative writing at the University of California, Los Angeles. Her books include Muse & Drudge *(1995),* S*PeRM**K*T *(1992),* Trimmings *(1991), and* Tree Tall Woman *(1981).*

Any Lit

You are a ukulele beyond my microphone
You are a Yukon beyond my Micronesia
You are a union beyond my meiosis
You are a unicycle beyond my migration
You are a universe beyond my mitochondria   5
You are a Eucharist beyond my Miles Davis°
You are a euphony beyond my myocardiogram
You are a unicorn beyond my Minotaur
You are a eureka beyond my maitai
You are a Yuletide beyond my minesweeper   10
You are a euphemism beyond my myna bird
You are a unit beyond my mileage
You are a Yugoslavia beyond my mind's eye
You are a yoo-hoo beyond my minor key
You are a Euripides beyond my mime troupe   15
You are a Utah beyond my microcosm

You are a Uranus beyond my Miami
You are a youth beyond my mylar
You are a euphoria beyond my myalgia
You are a Ukrainian beyond my Maimonides°   20

6 Miles Davis (1926–1991), American jazz musican   **20 Maimonides** (1135–1204), Jewish
philosopher

You are a Euclid beyond my miter box
You are a Univac° beyond my minus sign
You are a Eurydice° beyond my maestro
You are a eugenics beyond my Mayan
You are a U-boat beyond my mind control   25
You are a euthanasia beyond my miasma
You are a urethra beyond my Mysore
You are a Euterpe° beyond my Mighty Sparrow
You are a ubiquity beyond my minority
You are a eunuch beyond my migraine   30
You are a Eurodollar beyond my miserliness
You are a urinal beyond my Midol
You are a uselessness beyond my myopia

—*2002*

Dim Lady

My honeybunch's peepers are nothing like neon. Today's special at
Red Lobster is redder than her kisser. If Liquid Paper is white, her
racks are institutional beige. If her mop were Slinkys, dishwater
Slinkys would grow on her noggin. I have seen table-cloths in
Shakey's Pizza Parlors, red and white, but no such picnic colors do   5
I see in her mug. And in some minty-fresh mouth-washes there is
more sweetness than in the garlic breeze my main squeeze wheezes.
I love to hear her rap, yet I'm aware that Muzak has a hipper beat.
I don't know any Marilyn Monroes. My ball and chain is plain
from head to toe. And yet, by gosh, my scrumptious Twinkie has as   10
much sex appeal for me as any lanky model or platinum movie idol
who's hyped beyond belief.

—*2002*

22 **Univac** an early computer   23 **Eurydice** the wife of the singer Orpheus in Greek mythology
28 **Euterpe** the Greek muse of music

Mark Doty (b. 1953)

Mark Doty is known for richly textured lyric poems that often draw from the cityscape of New York City and the seascape of Provincetown, Massachusetts. Doty has written six poetry collections, including My Alexandria *(1993), chosen by Philip Levine for the National Poetry Series. He also has published two memoirs:* Heaven's Coast *(1996), which describes his partner's death from an* AIDS*-related illness, and* Firebird *(1999), which explores his childhood from ages six to sixteen. Doty has taught creative writing at the Iowa Writers' Workshop, Vermont College, Brandeis University, Sarah Lawrence College, Columbia University, the University of Utah, and the University of Houston. He currently divides his time between Houston and Provincetown.*

Bill's Story

When my sister came back from Africa,
we didn't know at first how everything
had changed. After a while Annie
bought men's and boys' clothes in all sizes,
and filled her closets with little   5
or huge things she could never wear.

Then she took to buying out
theatrical shops, rental places on the skids,
sweeping in and saying, *I'll take everything.*
Dementia was the first sign of something   10
we didn't even have a name for,
in 1978. She was just becoming stranger

—all those clothes, the way she'd dress me up
when I came to visit. It was like we could go back
to playing together again, and get it right.   15
She was a performance artist, and she did
her best work then, taking the clothes to clubs,
talking, putting them all on, talking.

It was years before she was in the hospital,
and my mother needed something   20
to hold onto, some way to be helpful,
so she read a book called *Deathing*

(a cheap, ugly verb if ever I heard one)
and took its advice to heart;

she'd sit by the bed and say, *Annie,*   25
look for the light, look for the light.
It was plain that Anne did not wish
to be distracted by these instructions;
she came to, though she was nearly gone then,
and looked at our mother with what was almost certainly   30

annoyance. *It's a white light,*
Mom said, and this struck me
as incredibly presumptuous, as if the light
we'd all go into would be just the same.
Maybe she wanted to give herself up   35
to indigo, or red. If we can barely even speak

to each other, living so separately,
how can we all die the same?
I used to take the train to the hospital,
and sometimes the only empty seats   40
would be the ones that face backwards.
I'd sit there and watch where I'd been

waver and blur out, and finally
I liked it, seeing what you've left
get more beautiful, less specific.   45
Maybe her light was all that gabardine
and flannel, khaki and navy
and silks and stripes. If you take everything,

you've got to let everything go. Dying
must take more attention than I ever imagined.   50
Just when she'd compose herself
and seem fixed on the work before her,
Mother would fret, trying to help her
just one more time: *Look for the light,*

until I took her arm   55
and told her wherever I was in the world
I would come back, no matter how difficult
it was to reach her, if I heard her calling.
Shut up, mother, I said, and Annie died.

—*1993*

No

The children have brought their wood turtle
into the dining hall
because they want us to feel

the power they have
when they hold a house   5
in their own hands, want us to feel

alien lacquer and the little thrill
that he might, like God, show his face.
He's the color of ruined wallpaper,

of cognac, and he's closed,   10
pulled in as though he'll never come out;
nothing shows but the plummy leather

of the legs, his claws resembling clusters
of diminutive raspberries.
They know he makes night   15

anytime he wants, so perhaps
he feels at the center of everything,
as they do. His age,

greater than that of anyone
around the table, is a room   20
from which they are excluded,

though they don't mind,
since they can carry this perfect
building anywhere. They love

that he might poke out   25
his old, old face, but doesn't.
I think the children smell unopened,

like unlit candles, as they heft him
around the table, praise his secrecy,
holding to each adult face   30

his prayer,
the single word of the shell,
which is no.

—1993

Gjertrud Schnackenberg (b. 1953)

Gjertrud Schnackenberg was born in Tacoma, Washington, and educated at Mount Holyoke College. She has published five poetry collections, including Supernatural Love: Poems 1976–1992 *(2000). Her most recent book,* The Throne of Labdacus *(2000), which retells the myth of Oedipus in free verse, represents a departure from the lush, graceful, formalist poems of her early career.*

Nightfishing

The kitchen's old-fashioned planter's clock portrays
A smiling moon as it dips down below
Two hemispheres, stars numberless as days,
And peas, tomatoes, onions, as they grow
Under that happy sky; but though the sands   5
Of time put on this vegetable disguise,
The clock covers its face with long, thin hands.
Another smiling moon begins to rise.

We drift in the small rowboat an hour before
Morning begins, the lake weeds grown so long   10
They touch the surface, tangling in an oar.
You've brought coffee, cigars, and me along.
You sit still, like a monument in a hall,
Watching for trout. A bat slices the air
Near us, I shriek, you look at me, that's all,   15
One long sobering look, a smile everywhere
But on your mouth. The mighty hills shriek back.
You turn back to the hake, chuckle, and clamp
Your teeth on your cigar. We watch the black
Water together. Our tennis shoes are damp.   20
Something moves on your thoughtful face, recedes.
Here, for the first time ever, I see how,
Just as a fish lurks deep in water weeds,
A thought of death will lurk deep down, will show
One eye, then quietly disappear in you.   25
It's time to go. Above the hills I see
The faint moon slowly dipping out of view,

Sea of Tranquillity, Sea of Serenity,
Ocean of Storms° . . . You start to row, the boat
Skimming the lake where light begins to spread.   30
You stop the oars, midair. We twirl and float.

I'm in the kitchen. You are three days dead.
A smiling moon rises on fertile ground,
White stars and vegetables. The sky is blue.
Clock hands sweep by it all, they twirl around,   35
Pushing me, oarless, from the shore of you.

—1982

Signs

Threading the palm, a web of little lines
Spells out the lost money, the heart, the head,
The wagging tongues, the sudden deaths, in signs
We would smooth out, like imprints on a bed,

In signs that can't be helped, geese heading south,   5
In signs read anxiously, like breath that clouds
A mirror held to a barely open mouth,
Like telegrams, the gathering of crowds—

The plane's X in the sky, spelling disaster:
Before the whistle and hit, a tracer flare;   10
Before rubble, a hairline crack in plaster
And a housefly's panicked scribbling on the air.

—1985

Supernatural Love

My father at the dictionary-stand
Touches the page to fully understand
The lamplit answer, tilting in his hand

His slowly scanning magnifying lens,
A blurry, glistening circle he suspends   5
Above the word "Carnation." Then he bends

28 **Sea of Tranquillity . . . Ocean of Storms** lunar plains

So near his eyes are magnified and blurred,
One finger on the miniature word,
As if he touched a single key and heard

A distant, plucked, infinitesimal string,   10
"The obligation due to every thing
That's smaller than the universe." I bring

My sewing needle close enough that I
Can watch my father through the needle's eye,
As through a lens ground for a butterfly   15

Who peers down flower-hallways toward a room
Shadowed and fathomed as this study's gloom
Where, as a scholar bends above a tomb

To read what's buried there, he bends to pore
Over the Latin blossom. I am four,   20
I spill my pins and needles on the floor

Trying to stitch "Beloved" X by X.
My dangerous, bright needle's point connects
Myself illiterate to this perfect text

I cannot read. My father puzzles why   25
It is my habit to identify
Carnations as "Christ's flowers," knowing I

Can give no explanation but "Because."
Word-roots blossom in speechless messages
The way the thread behind my sampler does   30

Where following each X I awkward move
My needle through the word whose root is love.
He reads, "A pink variety of Clove,

Carnatio, the Latin, meaning flesh."
As if the bud's essential oils brush   35
Christ's fragrance through the room, the iron-fresh

Odor carnations have floats up to me,
A drifted, secret, bitter ecstasy,
The stems squeak in my scissors, *Child, it's me,*

He turns the page to "Clove" and reads aloud: 40
"The clove, a spice, dried from a flower-bud."
Then twice, as if he hasn't understood,

He reads, "From French, for *clou*, meaning a nail."
He gazes, motionless. "Meaning a nail."
The incarnation blossoms, flesh and nail,   45

I twist my threads like stems into a knot
And smooth "Beloved," but my needle caught
Within the threads, *Thy blood so dearly bought,*

The needle strikes my finger to the bone.
I lift my hand, it is myself I've sewn,   50
The flesh laid bare, the threads of blood my own,

I lift my hand in startled agony
And call upon his name, "Daddy daddy"—
My father's hand touches the injury

As lightly as he touched the page before,   55
Where incarnation bloomed from roots that bore
The flowers I called Christ's when I was four.

—*1985*

Michael Donaghy (b. 1954)

Michael Donaghy has earned the reputation of being a "poet's poet" for his witty, elegantly crafted verse. He was born in the Bronx, New York, but has lived in London since 1985. Donaghy studied at Fordham University and the University of Chicago, where he served as poetry editor of the Chicago Review. *His collection* Shibboleth *(1988) received the Whitbread Prize for Poetry and the Geoffrey Faber Memorial Prize. His other books include* Errata *(1993),* Dances Learned Last Night *(2000), and* Conjure *(2000). Donaghy teaches at City University and Birkbeck College and is a fellow of the Royal Society of Literature.*

Pentecost

The neighbours hammered on the walls all night,
Outraged by the noise we made in bed.
Still we kept it up until by first light
We'd said everything that could be said.

Undaunted, we began to mewl and roar   5
As if desire had stripped itself of words.

Remember when we made those sounds before?
When we built a tower° heavenwards
They were our reward for blasphemy.
And then again, two thousand years ago,   10
We huddled in a room in Galilee
Speaking languages we didn't know,
While amethyst uraeuses° of flame
Hissed above us. We recalled the tower
And the tongues. We knew this was the same,   15
But love had turned the curse into a power.

See? It's something that we've always known:
Though we command the language of desire,
The voice of ecstasy is not our own.
We long to lose ourselves amid the choir   20
Of the salmon twilight and the mackerel sky,
The very air we take into our lungs,
And the rhododendron's cry.

And when you lick the sweat along my thigh,
Dearest, we renew the gift of tongues.   25

—*1988*

Black Ice and Rain

Psalms 6.6

    Can I come in? I saw you slip away.
Hors d'oeuvres depress you, don't they? They do me.
And cocktails, jokes . . . such dutiful abandon.
Where the faithful observe immovable feasts
—boat races, birthdays, marriages, martyrdoms—   5
we're summoned to our lonely ceremonies any time:
B minor, the mouldiness of an old encyclopedia,
the tinny sun snapping off the playground swings,

---

8 tower the biblical tower of Babel. According to the book of Genesis, the peoples of earth spoke a single language until a group of men attempted to build a city with a tower reaching to heaven. God confused their language so they would no longer understand each other and scattered them over the face of the earth   **13 uraeuses** snake-like shapes

these are, though we can't know this, scheduled
to arrive that minute of the hour, hour of the day,   10
day of every year. Again, regular as brickwork,
comes the time the nurse jots on your chart
before she pulls the sheet across your face. Just so,
the past falls open anywhere—even sitting here with you.

Sorry. You remind me of a girl I knew.   15
I met her at a party much like this, but younger, louder,
the bass so fat, the night so sticky you could drown.
We shouted art at each other over soul
and cold beer in the crowded kitchen and I, at least,
was halfway to a kiss when she slipped   20
her arm around her friend.
I worked at liking him, and it took work,
and it never got any easier being harmless,
but we danced that night like a three-way game of chess
and sang to Curtis Mayfield° pumped so loud   25
that when I drove them home they could hardly
whisper to invite me up.

Their black walls smirked with Jesus on black velvet
—Jesus, Elvis, Mexican skeletons, big-eyed Virgins,
Rodin's° hands clasped in chocolate prayer—   30
an attitude of decor, not like this room of yours.
A bottle opened—tequila with a cringe of worm—
and she watched me.
Lighting a meltdown of Paschal candles,°
she watched me. He poured the drinks rasping   35
We're seriously into cultural detritus. At which, at last,
she smiled. Ice cubes cracked. The worm sank in my glass.
And all that long year we were joined at the hip.

I never heard them laugh. They had,
instead, this tic of scratching quotes in air—   40
like frightened mimes inside their box of style,
that first class carriage from whose bright window
I watched the suburbs of my life recede.

---

25 **Curtis Mayfield** (1942–1999), American soul musician   30 **Rodin** Auguste Rodin (1840–1917),
French sculptor   34 **Paschal candles** candles lit in the Roman Catholic observance of Easter

Exactly one year on she let me kiss her—once—
her mouth wine-chilled, my tongue a clumsy guest,   45
and after that the invitations dwindled.
By Christmas we were strangers. It was chance
I heard about the crash. He died at once.
Black ice and rain, they said. No news of her.

I can't remember why I didn't write.   50
Perhaps I thought she'd sold the flat and left.
Some nights midway to sleep I'm six years old.
Downstairs it's New Year's Eve. Drink and shrieks.
But my mother's lit the luminous plastic Jesus
to watch me through the night, which is why   55
I've got my pillow wrapped around my head.
I never hear the door. And when she speaks,
her thick-tongued anger rearing like a beast,
I feel my hot piss spreading through the sheets.
But when I wake, grown up, it's only sweat.   60
But if I dream, I bleed. A briar crown,
a fist prised open wide, a steadied nail,
a hammer swinging down—the past falls open
anywhere . . .
                    Ash Wednesday evening.   65
Driving by, I saw her lights were on.
I noticed both their names still on the buzzer
and when I rang I heard her voice. *Come in*—
        her nose was broken, her front teeth gone,
a rosary was twisted round her fists—   70
        —*Come in. I've been saying a novena.*
Inside, each crucifix and candle shone
transfigured in her chrysalis of grief.
She spoke about the crash, how she'd been driving,
how they had to cut her from the wreck . . .   75
and then she slipped and called me by his name.

Of those next hours I remember most
the silences between her sobs, the rain
against the skylight slowly weakening
to silence, silence brimming into sleep and dawn.   80
Then, having lain at last all night beside her,
having searched at last that black-walled room,

the last unopened chamber of my heart,
and found there neither pity nor desire
but an assortment of religious kitsch,   85
I inched my arm from under her and left.

  Since then, the calmest voice contains her cry
just within the range of human hearing
and where I've hoped to hear my name gasped out
from cradle, love bed, death bed, there instead   90
I catch her voice, her broken lisp, his name.
Since then, each night contains all others,
nested mirror-within-mirror, stretching back from then
to here and now, this party, this room, this bed,
where, in another life, we might have kissed.   95
Thank you, friend, for showing me your things—
you have exquisite taste—but let's rejoin your guests
who must by now be wondering where you've gone.

                                                  —2000

The River in Spate

          sweeps us both down its cold grey current.
Grey now as your father was when I met you,
I wake even now on that shore where once,
sweat slick and still, we breathed together—
in—soft rain gentling the level of the lake,   5
out—bright mist rising from the lake at dawn.
How long before we gave each other to sleep,
to air—drawing the mist up, exhaling the rain?
Though we fight now for breath and weaken
in the torrent's surge to the dark of its mouth,   10
you are still asleep in my arms by its source,
small waves lapping the gravel shore,
and I am still awake and watching you,
in wonder, without sadness, like a child.

                                                  —2000

Kim Addonizio (b. 1954)

Kim Addonizio is the author of four books of poetry, The Philosopher's Club *(1994),* Jimmy & Rita *(1997),* Tell Me *(2000), and* What Is This Thing Called Love *(2004), and a book of stories,* In the Box Called Pleasure *(1999). With Dorianne Laux, she coauthored* The Poet's Companion: A Guide to the Pleasures of Writing Poetry *(1997), a widely used book on craft. Her awards include two fellowships from the National Endowment for the Arts, a Pushcart Prize, and a Commonwealth Club Poetry Medal. Born in Washington, D.C., Addonizio earned a B.A. and an M.A. from San Francisco State University. A founding editor of the journal* Five Fingers Review, *Addonizio has worked as a waitress, tennis instructor, Kelly Girl, attendant for the disabled, and auto parts store bookkeeper. She currently teaches private workshops in the San Francisco Bay area. Addonizio's poems achieve a delicate balance between the confessional and the universal, and manage to be simultaneously lyrical and gritty.*

First Poem for You

I like to touch your tattoos in complete
darkness, when I can't see them. I'm sure of
where they are, know by heart the neat
lines of lightning pulsing just above
your nipple, can find, as if by instinct, the blue   5
swirls of water on your shoulder where a serpent
twists, facing a dragon. When I pull you
to me, taking you until we're spent
and quiet on the sheets, I love to kiss
the pictures in your skin. They'll last until   10
you're seared to ashes; whatever persists
or turns to pain between us, they will still
be there. Such permanence is terrifying.
So I touch them in the dark; but touch them, trying.

—*1994*

Fine

You're lucky. It's always them and not you. The family trapped in
the fire, the secretary slain in the parking lot holding her coffee and
Egg McMuffin, the ones rushed to emergency after the potluck.
You're lucky you didn't touch the tuna casserole, and went for the
baked chicken instead. Your friend with breast cancer that was   5
detected too late—metastasized to the lymph nodes, the lungs, a few
months to live—lucky there's no history in your family. Another
friend's fiancé, heart attack at forty-seven. You lie in bed at night,
your head on your lover's chest, and you're grateful. Your teenaged
daughter, unlike all her friends, hasn't become sullen or combative,   10
addicted to cigarettes or booze. She's not in the bathroom with her
finger down her throat to throw up dinner. You and your family are
fine. You're happy. It's like you're in your own little boat, just you,
sailing along, and the wind is up and nothing's leaking. All around
you you can see other boats filling up, flipping over, sliding under.   15
If you look into the water you can watch them for a while, going
down slowly, getting smaller and farther away. Soon, if nothing
happens to you, if your luck holds, really holds, you'll end up
completely alone.

—*2000*

Target

It feels so good to shoot a gun,
to stand with your legs apart
holding a nine millimeter in both hands
aiming at something that can't run.
Over and over I rip holes   5

in the paper target clamped to its hanger,
target I move closer with the flick of a switch
or so far away its center looks
like a small black planet in its white square
of space. It feels good to nestle a clip   10

of bullets against the heel of your hand,
to ratchet one into the chamber

and cock the hammer back and fire, the recoil
surging along your arms as the muzzle kicks up, as you keep
control. It's so good you no longer wonder   15

why some boys lift them from bottom drawers and boxes
at the backs of closets, and drive fast into lives
they won't finish, lean from their car windows and
let go a few rounds into whatever's out there.
You can hear what comes back as they speed away: 20

burst glass, or the high ring of struck steel,
or maybe moans. Now you want
to take the thing and hurl it into
the ocean, to wait until it drops down
through the dark and cold and lodges so deep   25

nothing could retrieve it. But you know it would
float back and wash up like a bottle
carrying a message from a dead man.
You stand there firing until the gun feels
light again, and innocent. And then you reload.   30

—2000

Mary Jo Salter (b. 1954)

Mary Jo Salter has traveled widely with her husband, poet and novelist Brad Leithauser, and has lived in Japan, Italy, and Iceland. A student of Elizabeth Bishop's at Harvard, Salter brings to her art a devotion to the poet's craft that mirrors that of her mentor. She has published five collections of poetry and The Moon Comes Home *(1989), a children's book. Educated at Harvard and at Cambridge University, she is an editor of* The Norton Anthology of Poetry *and an Emily Dickinson Lecturer in Humanities at Mount Holyoke College.*

Welcome to Hiroshima

is what you first see, stepping off the train:
a billboard brought to you in living English
by Toshiba Electric. While a channel
silent in the TV of the brain

projects those flickering re-runs of a cloud   5
that brims its risen columnful like beer
and, spilling over, hangs its foamy head,
you feel a thirst for history: what year

it started to be safe to breathe the air,
and when to drink the blood and scum afloat   10
on the Ohta River. But no, the water's clear,
they pour it for your morning cup of tea

in one of the countless sunny coffee shops
whose plastic dioramas advertise
mutations of cuisine behind the glass: 15
a pancake sandwich; a pizza someone tops

with a maraschino cherry. Passing by
the Peace Park's floral hypocenter (where
how bravely, or with what mistaken cheer,
humanity erased its own erasure),   20

you enter the memorial museum
and through more glass are served, as on a dish
of blistered grass, three mannequins. Like gloves
a mother clips to coatsleeves, strings of flesh

hang from their fingertips; or as if tied   25
to recall a duty for us, *Reverence*
the dead whose mourners too shall soon be dead,
but all commemoration's swallowed up

in questions of bad taste, how re-created
horror mocks the grim original,   30
and thinking at last *They should have left it all*
you stop. This is the wristwatch of a child.

Jammed on the moment's impact, resolute
to communicate some message, although mute,
it gestures with its hands at eight-fifteen   35
and eight-fifteen and eight-fifteen again

while tables of statistics on the wall
update the news by calling on a roll
of tape, death gummed on death, and in the case
adjacent, an exhibit under glass   40

is glass itself: a shard the bomb slammed in
a woman's arm at eight-fifteen, but some
three decades on—as if to make it plain
hope's only as renewable as pain,

and as if all the unsung   45
debasements of the past may one day come
rising to the surface once again—
worked its filthy way out like a tongue.

                                                    —1985

Dead Letters

I

Dear Mrs. Salter: Congratulations! You
(no need to read on—yet I always do)
may have won the sweepstakes, if you'll send . . .
Is this how it must end?
Or will it ever end? The bills, all paid,   5
come monthly anyway, to cheer the dead.
BALANCE: decimal point and double o's
like pennies no one placed upon your eyes.
I never saw you dead—you simply vanished,
your body gone to Science, as you wished: 10
I was the one to send you there, by phone,
on that stunned morning answering the blunt
young nurse who called, wanting to "clear the room."
"Take her," I said, "I won't be coming in"—
couldn't bear to see your cherished face with more   15
death in it than was there five days before.
But now, where are you really? From the mail
today, it seems, you might almost be well:
*Dear Patient: It's been three years since your eyes
were checked . . .* A host of worthy causes vies   20
for your attention: endangered wildlife funds,
orphans with empty bowls in outstretched hands,
political prisoners, Congressmen. The *LAST
ISSUE*s of magazines are never last.
And now you've shored up on some realtors' list,   25

since word went out you've "moved" to my address:
Dear New Apartment Owner: If you rent . . .
Mother, in daydreams sometimes I am sent
to follow you, my own forwarding text
Dear Mrs. Salter's Daughter: You are next.   30

—*1989*

David Mason   (b. 1954)

David Mason is best known for the title poem of The Country I Remember
*(1996), a long narrative about the life of a Civil War veteran and his
daughter. The poem has been performed in a theatrical version. Mason
edited, with Mark Jarman,* Rebel Angels *(1996), an anthology of recent poetry written in traditional forms, and also coedited, with John Frederick
Nims, the fourth edition of the popular poetry textbook,* Western Wind
*(1999). Born in Bellingham, Washington, Mason left The Colorado College
after his freshman year to unload crab and shrimp boats in Dutch Harbor,
Alaska. After that, he hitchhiked through the British Isles before returning
to school and beginning a novel set in Alaska. In 1979, his older brother
Douglas was killed in a climbing accident on Washington state's Mount
Shuksan; this incident has been a central one in Mason's life and poetry.
Mason has lived in Rochester, New York; Moorhead, Minnesota; and a
fishing village in Greece. He currently teaches at The Colorado College.*

Song of the Powers

Mine, said the stone,
mine is the hour.
I crush the scissors,
such is my power.
Stronger than wishes,   5
my power, alone.

Mine, said the paper,
mine are the words
that smother the stone
with imagined birds,   10
reams of them, flown
from the mind of the shaper.

Mine, said the scissors,
mine all the knives
gashing through paper's   15
ethereal lives;
nothing's so proper
as tattering wishes.

As stone crushes scissors,
as paper snuffs stone   20
and scissors cut paper,
all end alone.
So heap up your paper
and scissor your wishes
and uproot the stone   25
from the top of the hill.
They all end alone
as you will, you will.

—1996

The Collector's Tale

When it was over I sat down last night,
shaken, and quite afraid I'd lost my mind.
The objects I have loved surrounded me
like friends in such composed society
they almost rid the atmosphere of fright.   5
I collected them, perhaps, as one inclined
to suffer other people stoically.

That's why, when I found Foley at my door—
not my shop, but here at my private home,
the smell of bourbon for his calling card—   10
I sighed and let him in without a word.
I'd only met the man two months before
and found his taste as tacky as they come,
his Indian ethic perfectly absurd.

The auction house in St. Paul where we met   15
was full that day of cherry furniture.
I still can't tell you why he'd chosen me

to lecture all about his Cherokee
obsessions, but I listened—that I regret.
My patience with a stranger's geniture   20
compelled him to describe his family tree.

He told me of his youth in Oklahoma,
his white father who steered clear of the Rez,°
a grandma native healer who knew herbs
for every illness. Nothing like the 'burbs,   25
I guess. He learned to tell a real toma-
hawk from a handsaw, or lift his half-mad gaze
and "entertain" you with some acid barbs.

So he collected Indian artifacts,
the sort that sell for thousands in New York.   30
Beadwork, war shirts, arrowheads, shards of clay
beloved by dealers down in Santa Fe.
He lived to corner strangers, read them tracts
of his invention on the careful work
he would preserve and pridefully display.   35

Foley roamed the Great Plains in his van,
his thin hair tied back in a ponytail,
and people learned that he was smart enough
to deal. He made a living off this stuff,
became a more authenticated man.   40
But when he drank he would begin to rail
against the white world's trivializing fluff.

Last night when he came in, reeking of smoke
and liquor, gesticulating madly
as if we'd both returned from the same bar,   45
I heard him out a while, the drunken bore,
endured his leaning up against my oak
credenza there, until at last I gladly
offered him a drink and a kitchen chair.

I still see him, round as a medicine ball   50
with a three-day beard, wearing his ripped jeans
and ratty, unlaced Nikes without socks.

23 Rez reservation

I see him searching through two empty packs
and casting them aside despite my scowl,
opening a third, lighting up—he careens   55
into my kitchen, leaving boozy tracks.

I offered brandy. He didn't mind the brand
or that I served it in a water glass.
He drank with simple greed, making no show
of thanks, and I could see he wouldn't go.   60
He told me nothing happened as he planned,
how he left Rasher's tiny shop a mess.
I killed him, Foley said. *You got to know.*

*

You know the place. Grand Avenue. The Great
White Way they built over my people's bones   65
after the western forts made stealing safe.
Safe for that fucking moneyed generation
F. Scott Fitzgerald° tried to write about—
and here was Rasher, selling off such crap
no self-respecting dealer'd waste his time.   70

I heard he had good beadwork, Chippewa,
but when I went in all I saw was junk.
I'm thinking, Christ, the neighbors here must love him,
the one dusty-shuttered place on the block
and inside, counters filled with silver plate   75
so tarnished Mother wouldn't touch it, irons
with fraying cords and heaps of magazines.

He had the jawbone of a buffalo
from South Dakota, an old Enfield rifle,
a horn chair (or a cut-rate replica),   80
German Bible, a blue-eyed Jesus framed
in bottlecaps—I mean he had everything
but paint-by-number sunsets, so much junk
I bet he hadn't made a sale in years.

You got to know this guy—skinny bald head   85
and both his hands twisted from arthritis.

---

68 **F. Scott Fitzgerald** (1896–1940), American novelist

I wouldn't give his place a second look
except I heard so much about this beadwork.
He leads me to a case in the back room.
I take a look. The stuff is fucking new,   90
pure Disneyland, not even off the Rez.

Foley's glass was empty; I poured him more
to buy time while I thought of some excuse
to get him out of here. If homicide
indeed were his odd tale's conclusion, I'd   95
rather let him pass out on my floor,
then dash upstairs and telephone the police.
I wouldn't mind if "fucking" Foley fried.

It's crap, he said. *I tell this slimy coot*
he doesn't know an Indian from a dog.   100
I can't believe I drove five hundred miles
to handle sentimental tourist crap.
He rolled himself upright in my kitchen chair
and looked at me with such complete disdain
that I imagined Mr. Rasher's stare.   105

I knew the man. We dealers somehow sense
who we trust and who the characters are.
I looked at my inebriated guest
and saw the fool-as-warrior on a quest
for the authentic, final recompense   110
that would rub out, in endless, private war,
all but his own image of the best.

Pretty quick I see I hurt his feelings.
He gets all proud on me and walks around
pointing at this and that,   115
a World's Fair pin, a Maris° autograph,
and then he takes me to a dark wood cupboard
and spins the combination on the lock
and shows me what's inside. The old man

shows me his motherfucking pride and joy.   120
I look inside his cupboard and it's there

---

116 Maris Roger Maris (1934–1985), outfielder for the New York Yankees

all right—a black man's head with eyes sewn shut—
I mean this fucker's real, all dried and stuffed,
a metal ashtray planted in the skull.
I look and it's like the old man's nodding.   125
Yeah, yeah, you prick, now tell me this is nothing.

He's looking at me looking at this head,
telling me he found it in a house
just up the street. Some dead white guy's estate
here in the liberal north allowed this coot   130
whatever his twisted little hands could take,
and then he hoards it away for special guests.
I didn't say a thing. I just walked out.

Now Foley filled his glass, drinking it down.
His irises caught fire as he lit up.   135
I sat across from him and wiped my palms
but inside I was setting off alarms
as if I should alert this sleeping town
that murder lived inside it. I could stop
the story now, I thought, but nothing calms   140

a killer when he knows he must confess,
and Foley'd chosen me to hear the worst.
Weird, he said, looking straight at me beyond
his burning cigarette. I got so mad.
Like all I thought of was a hundred shelves   145
collecting dust in Rasher's shop, and how
a dead man's head lay at the center of it.

I had to get a drink. Some yuppie bar
that charged a fortune for its cheapest bourbon.
I'm in there while the sun sets on the street   150
and people drop in after leaving work.
I look at all these happy people there
laughing, anyway; maybe they aren't happy—
the well-dressed women tossing back their hair,

the men who loosen their designer ties   155
and sip their single malts—living on bones
of other people, right?
And two blocks down the street, in Rasher's shop,
a head where someone flicked his ashes once,

because of course a darky can't be human, 160
and someone's family kept that darky's head.

These genteel people with their decent souls
must have been embarrassed finding it,
and Rasher got it for a fucking song
and even he could never sell the thing. 165
No, he showed it to me just to get me,
just to prove I hadn't seen it all.
Well, he was right, I hadn't seen it all.

I didn't know the worst that people do
could be collected like a beaded bag, 170
bad medicine or good, we keep the stuff
and let it molder in our precious cases.
Some fucker cared just how he dried that head
and stitched the skin and cut the hole in the top—
big medicine for a man who liked cigars. 175

It's just another piece of history,
human, like a slave yoke or a scalping knife,
and maybe I was drunk on yuppie booze,
but I knew some things had to be destroyed.
Hell, I could hardly walk, but I walked back, 180
knocked on Rasher's door until he opened,
pushed him aside like a bag of raked-up leaves.

Maybe I was shouting, I don't know.
I heard him shouting at my back, and then
he came around between me and the case, 185
a little twisted guy with yellow teeth
telling me he'd call the fucking cops.
I found the jawbone of that buffalo.
I mean I must have picked it up somewhere,

maybe to break the lock, but I swung hard 190
and hit that old fucker upside the head
and he went down so easy I was shocked.
He lay there moaning in a spreading pool
I stepped around. I broke that old jawbone
prizing the lock, but it snapped free, and I 195
snatched out the gruesome head.

I got it to my van all right, and then
went back to check on Rasher. He was dead.
For a while I tried to set his shop on fire
to see the heaps of garbage in it burn,   200
but you'd need gasoline to get it going
and besides, I couldn't burn away the thought
of that weird thing I took from there tonight.

It's out there, Foley said. *I'm parked outside*
a few blocks down—I couldn't find your house.   205
I knew you'd listen to me if I came.
I knew you'd never try to turn me in.
You want to see it? No? I didn't either,
and now I'll never lose that goddamned head,
even if I bury it and drive away.   210

                              *

By now the bluster'd left his shrinking frame
and I thought he would vomit in my glass,
but Foley had saved strength enough to stand,
while I let go of everything I'd planned—
the telephone, police and bitter fame   215
that might wash over my quiet life and pass
away at some inaudible command.

I thought of all the dead things in my shop.
No object I put up was poorly made.
Nothing of mine was inhumane, although   220
I felt death in a kind of undertow
pulling my life away. *Make it stop*,
I thought, as if poor Foley had betrayed
our best ideals. Of course I let him go.

The truth is, now he's left I feel relieved.   225
I locked the door behind him, but his smell
has lingered in my hallway all these hours.
I've mopped the floor, washed up, moved pots of flowers
to places that he touched. If I believed,
I would say Foley had emerged from hell.   230
I ask for help, but the silent house demurs.

—2004

Ginger Andrews (b. 1956)

Ginger Andrews won Story Line Press's 1999 Nicholas Roerich Poetry Prize for her book, An Honest Answer, *which explores the difficulties of life in a lumber town of the Pacific Northwest. Born in North Bend, Oregon, she cleans houses for a living, and is a janitor and Sunday school teacher at North Bend Church of Christ.*

Primping in the Rearview Mirror

after a solid ten-minute bout of tears,
hoping that the Safeway man who stocks the shelves
and talked to you once for thirty minutes about specialty jams,
won't ask if you're all right, or tell you you look like shit
and then have to apologize as he remembers that you don't   5
like cuss words and you don't date ex-prison guards
because you're married. The truth is you're afraid
this blue-eyed charismatic sexist hunk of a reject just might
trigger another round of tears, that you'll lean into him
right in front of the eggs and milk, crying like a baby,   10
your face buried in his chest just below the two opened
buttons of his tight white knit shirt, his big cold hands
pressed to the small of your back, pulling you closer
to whisper that everything will be all right.

—*2002*

Forrest Hamer (b. 1956)

Forrest Hamer is the author of Call and Response *(1995). Born in North Carolina, he studied at Yale and the University of California, Berkeley. A psychologist, he lectures in psychology and social welfare at UC Berkeley.*

Erection

I wanted them bad: the mail-order x-ray glasses
that looked straight through clothes to bodies

of those in my class, of the old-lady teacher
who wore miniskirts and an opened blouse, of grownups

whose eyes stopped meeting mine. I wanted to see   5
a privacy clothes know: the geography of the possible.

I waited.

And when the glasses hadn't come, and each day's
disappointment stung like slaps,

I worried that other people could see hard-ons hidden   10
by long-tailed shirts worn outside the pants,

by a walk-become-a-race, or by the distraction
of stubborness and anger. And arrogance.

Wondered if they could see how timid the penis
otherwise seemed, how fat still my chest was,   15

making improbable breasts. Wondered if they could
see the tenseness of no-more-but-not-yet,

of sleep-erupting dreams having nothing to do with the body
and everything, desire becoming specific.

And when the glasses still hadn't come   20
and there was cause to doubt their existence,

I began to imagine what I might see,
bodies nothing like those I have seen.

—1995

Li-Young Lee (b. 1957)

Li-Young Lee was born in Jakarta, Indonesia, to Chinese parents. His father, the subject of many of Lee's poems, had been a personal physician to Mao Zedong before moving the family to Indonesia, where he helped found Gamaliel University. In 1959, the family fled Indonesia to escape a dictatorial regime that had imprisoned Lee's father for a year and a half. The family lived in Hong Kong, Macau, and Japan before settling in the United States, where Lee's father served as a Presbyterian minister. Lee studied at the University of Pittsburgh, the University of Arizona, and the State University of New York at Brockport. The City in Which I Love You, *the second of his three published collections, was the 1990 Lamont Poetry Selection. He also has written a prose memoir,* The Winged Seed: A Remembrance *(1995), which received an American Book Award. He lives in Chicago.*

Persimmons

In sixth grade Mrs. Walker
slapped the back of my head
and made me stand in the corner
for not knowing the difference
between *persimmon* and *precision*.   5
How to choose

persimmons. This is precision.
Ripe ones are soft and brown-spotted.
Sniff the bottoms. The sweet one
will be fragrant. How to eat: 10
put the knife away, lay down newspaper.
Peel the skin tenderly, not to tear the meat.
Chew the skin, suck it,
and swallow. Now, eat
the meat of the fruit,   15
so sweet,
all of it, to the heart.

Donna undresses, her stomach is white.
In the yard, dewy and shivering
with crickets, we lie naked,   20
face-up, face-down.

I teach her Chinese.
Crickets: *chiu chiu*. Dew: I've forgotten.
Naked: I've forgotten.
Ni, wo: you and me.   25
I part her legs,
remember to tell her
she is beautiful as the moon.

Other words
that got me into trouble were   30
fight and *fright*, *wren* and *yarn*.
Fight was what I did when I was frightened,
fright was what I felt when I was fighting.
Wrens are small, plain birds,
yarn is what one knits with.   35
Wrens are soft as yarn.
My mother made birds out of yarn.
I loved to watch her tie the stuff;
a bird, a rabbit, a wee man.

Mrs. Walker brought a persimmon to class   40
and cut it up
so everyone could taste
a *Chinese apple*. Knowing
it wasn't ripe or sweet, I didn't eat
but watched the other faces.   45

My mother said every persimmon has a sun
inside, something golden, glowing,
warm as my face.

Once, in the cellar, I found two wrapped in newspaper,
forgotten and not yet ripe.   50
I took them and set both on my bedroom windowsill,
where each morning a cardinal
sang, *The sun, the sun.*

Finally understanding
he was going blind,   55
my father sat up all one night
waiting for a song, a ghost.
I gave him the persimmons,
swelled, heavy as sadness,
and sweet as love.   60

This year, in the muddy lighting
of my parents' cellar, I rummage, looking
for something I lost.
My father sits on the tired, wooden stairs,
black cane between his knees,   65
hand over hand, gripping the handle.

He's so happy that I've come home.
I ask how his eyes are, a stupid question.
All gone, he answers.

Under some blankets, I find a box.   70
Inside the box I find three scrolls.
I sit beside him and untie
three paintings by my father:
Hibiscus leaf and a white flower.
Two cats preening.   75
Two persimmons, so full they want to drop from the cloth.

He raises both hands to touch the cloth,
asks, *Which is this?*

This is persimmons, Father.

Oh, the feel of the wolftail on the silk,   80
the strength, the tense
precision in the wrist.
I painted them hundreds of times
eyes closed. These I painted blind.
Some things never leave a person: 85
scent of the hair of one you love,
the texture of persimmons,
in your palm, the ripe weight.

—1986

H. L. Hix (b. 1960)

H. L. Hix writes poems in experimental form, bridging the seemingly irreconcilable New Formalist and Language Poetry movements. He has published three poetry collections: Perfect Hell *(1996),* Rational Numbers *(2000), and* Surely As Birds Fly *(2002). He has also translated the poems of Eugenijus Alisanka and published several books of literary criticism, including* Spirits Hovering Over the Ashes: Legacies of Postmodern Theory *(1995) and* As Easy as Lying *(2002). Hix is vice president of academic affairs at the Cleveland Institute of Art.*

from "Orders of Magnitude"

#46

I make it my principle to watch you
undress. When you bend for a sock, I count
your vertebrae. I know your underwear
from ten feet, I have pet names for each pair:
Lucky, Climber, Omigod. I make it   5
my principle to be first in bed, last
to close my eyes. I count your breaths. Some nights
I reach a thousand before I can stop.
If I could die watching you, I would make
it my principle to shorten my life.   10

#48

Songs surround us, but we hardly hear them.
Laughing girls speak in rapid Japanese.
The neighbor's sprinkler fortes for the part
of its arc that frets the climbing rose. Crows
bicker. One woman practices her scales,   15
a cappella. Another sobs. Windchimes
domino the direction of each gust.
A broom rasps across warped, weathered porch boards.
I did it, Mama, a child says. Songs fall
on us as feathers fall on a river.   20

#83

How do you like paradise so far? Stay.
Its charm burns off like morning rain. Crabs clean
these rocks by hand. You will regret feelings
so exquisite. Earth screamed our birth with fire:
the end will come when the sea loses count.   25
One god named the old island, another
will name the new. Teach me to lay my eggs
in sand, I'll teach you to breathe in the sea.
Watch for the silhouetted shearwater
at sunset zipping the horizon closed.   30

—*2000*

Denise Duhamel (b. 1961)

*Denise Duhamel is known for her irreverent humor and the incisiveness
with which she writes about popular culture and women's issues. Duhamel
was born in Woonsocket, Rhode Island, and educated at Emerson College
and Sarah Lawrence College. Her most recent title is* Queen for a Day: Selected and New Poems *(2001). Her other books include* Exquisite Politics
(with Maureen Seaton, 1997), Kinky *(1997),* Girl Soldier *(1996), and*
How the Sky Fell *(1996). She is married to the poet Nick Carbó, and
teaches at Florida International University in Miami.*

Ego

I just didn't get it—
even with the teacher holding an orange (the earth) in one hand
and a lemon (the moon) in the other,
her favorite student (the sun) standing behind her with a flashlight.
I just couldn't grasp it—   5
this whole citrus universe, these bumpy planets revolving so slowly
no one could even see themselves moving.
I used to think if I could only concentrate hard enough
I could be the one person to feel what no one else could,
sense a small tug from the ground, a sky shift, the earth changing
    gears.   10
Even though I was only one minispeck on a speck,

even though I was merely a pinprick in one goosebump on the orange,
I was sure then I was the most specially perceptive, perceptively
    sensitive.
I was sure then my mother was the only mother to snap—
"The world doesn't revolve around you!"   15
The earth was fragile and mostly water
just the way the orange was mostly water if you peeled it
just the way I was mostly water if you peeled me.
Looking back on that third-grade science demonstration,
I can understand why some people gave up on fame or religion or
    cures—   20
especially people who have an understanding
of the excruciating crawl of the world,
who have a well-developed sense of spatial reasoning
and the tininess that it is to be one of us.
But not me—even now I wouldn't mind being god, the force   25
who spins the planets the way I spin a globe, a basketball, a yo-yo.
I wouldn't mind being that teacher who chooses the fruit,
or that favorite kid who gives the moon its glow.

                       —2001

Catherine Tufariello (b. 1963)

Catherine Tufariello is the author of Keeping My Name *(2004) and the fine-press chapbook* Annunciations *(2001). She grew up in Tonawanda, New York, and studied English literature at SUNY–Buffalo and Cornell University. She lives in Ualparaiso, Indiana.*

Useful Advice

You're 37? Don't you think that maybe
It's time you settled down and had a baby?

No wine? Does this mean happy news? I knew it!

Hey, are you sure you two know how to do it?

All Dennis has to do is look at me   5
And I'm knocked up.

Some things aren't meant to be.
It's sad, but try to see this as God's will.

I've heard that sometimes when you take the Pill . . .

Does he wear boxers? Briefs are bad for sperm.

A former partner at my husband's firm   10
Who tried for years got pregnant when she stopped
Working so hard.

               Why don't you two adopt?
You'll have one of your own then, like my niece.

At work I heard about this herb from Greece—

My sister swears by dong quai.° Want to try it?   15

Forget the high-tech stuff. Just change your diet.

Yoga is good for that. My cousin Carol—

It's true! Too much caffeine can make you sterile.

They have these ceremonies in Peru—

You mind my asking, is it him or you?   20

Have you tried acupuncture? Meditation?

It's in your head. Relax! Take a vacation
And have some fun. You think too much. Stop trying.

Did I say something wrong? Why are you crying?

                      —2004

---

15 dong quai aromatic herb grown in China, Korea, and Japan, reputed to be an all-purpose woman's tonic

Greg Williamson (b. 1964)

Greg Williamson is the author of two books of poetry, The Silent Partner
(1994) and Errors in the Script *(2001). Born in Nashville, Tennessee,
Williamson studied at Vanderbilt University and the Writing Seminars at
Johns Hopkins University, where he now teaches.*

Kites at the Washington Monument

> What's up, today, with our lovers?
> —W. D. Snodgrass

At fingertip control
    These state-of-the-art stunt kites
Chandelle, wingover, and roll
    To dive from conspicuous heights,

Whatever the pilots will,   5
    While the wowed audience follows
As the kites come in for the kill
    And slice up the air like swallows.

But, look, across the park
    Someone has put together—   10
What is it? It looks like a lark
    Tossed up into the weather.

It's homemade out of paper
    That tumbles and bobs like a moth
On another meaningless caper.   15
    Why, it's a bit of froth

Spun on a blue lake,
    A name or a wrinkled note
Dropped into the wake
    Of an ocean-going boat.   20

But still it pulls itself higher
    As he would pull it back.
The line goes tight as wire,
    Or sags, falling, and goes slack,

And while the audience claps   25
    At the aerobatic buzz,
It flutters, quiets, then it snaps.
    But that's about all it does.

Flying its tail of rags
    Above these broken lands,   30
It's one of those white flags
    For things that are out of our hands,

The hoisted colors of
    Attenuated hope,
The handkerchief of a love   35
    That's come to the end of its rope.

When the line breaks, the string
    Floats to the ground in the wind.
He stands there watching the thing
    Still holding up his end   40

As the kite heads into the sky
    Like a sail leaving a slip.
The rags wave goodbye.
    They're scarves at the back of a ship.

—2001

Rafael Campo (b. 1964)

Rafael Campo teaches medicine at Harvard Medical School and practices at the Beth Israel Hospital of Boston, with an emphasis on serving Latinos and the gay, lesbian, and bisexual communities, and on HIV/AIDS medicine. He studied at Amherst College and Harvard Medical School and completed his medical residency at the University of California, San Francisco, at the peak of the AIDS epidemic. His poetry collections include The Other Man Was Me *(1994),* Diva *(1999), and* Landscape With Human Figure *(2002). His essays on poetry and medicine have been collected in* The Poetry of Healing: A Doctor's Education in Empathy, Identity, and Desire *(1997).*

Oysters

Your concentration while you're shucking them
Is fierce: they fight against your prying blade,
As if intent to guard some plumbless gem
Of truth. I squeeze some fruit for lemonade;
The yellow rinds become a fragrant pile.   5
More scraping from the deck, a stifled curse—
You bring me one, the frilly muscle pale,
Defeated, silent in its briny juice
Like sweat expended in the effort to
Remain inviolate. I slurp it down,   10
One dose of aphrodisiac, and you
Return to your grim work, all Provincetown
Draped out below you, edge of the known world.
I see what is left: bone-white, hollow-shelled.

—2002

Christian Wiman (b. 1966)

Christian Wiman became the eleventh editor of Poetry *magazine, the nation's oldest poetry journal, in 2003. An essayist as well as a poet, Wiman has taught at Northwestern University, Stanford University, the Prague School of Economics, and Lynchburg College in Virginia.*

Afterwards

> . . . it is no great distance
> From slimness to cool water.
> —*Ovid*

There is nothing left for anyone to hold.
The days are long and mild, and parts
of herself are drifting imperceptibly
into them. She almost remembers rain,
each drop colder than she is, clearer.   5
Her face becomes the face of everyone
who looks into her, her longings their own.
When she feels the warm bodies of children
swimming inside of her, or lovers
under the shadows on her skin,   10
she wants to carry them all down
into her deepest reaches. They leave
silvered with tears. On clear nights she wears
the moon like a soft jewel and dreams
of a world as still and silent as she is.   15
The least touch leaves her whole body trembling.

—*1998*

Sherman Alexie (b. 1966)

Sherman Alexie cowrote the screenplay for Smoke Signals, *the independent film based on a short story from his collection* The Lone Ranger and Tonto Fistfight in Heaven *(1993). A Spokane/Coeur d'Alene Indian, Alexie grew up on Spokane Indian Reservation. Born hydrocephalic, he underwent brain surgery and survived, despite doctors' predictions. He studied at Gonzaga University and Washington State University. Shortly after graduating from WSU, Alexie published his first two poetry collections,* The Business of Fancydancing *(1991) and* I Would Steal Horses *(1993). He also has published two novels,* Reservation Blues *(1995) and* Indian Killer *(1996). A popular stand-up performer, Alexie has made television appearances on* Politically Incorrect, 60 Minutes II, *and* NOW *with Bill Moyers. In 1998, he took part in the* PBS Lehrer News Hour *"Dialogue on Race with President Clinton."*

The Exaggeration of Despair

I open the door

(this Indian girl writes that her brother tried to hang himself
with a belt just two weeks after her other brother did hang himself

and this Indian man tells us that back in boarding school,
five priests took him into a back room and raped him repeatedly   5

and this homeless Indian woman begs for quarters, and when I ask
her about her tribe, she says she's horny and bends over in front of me

and this homeless Indian man is the uncle of an Indian man
who writes for a large metropolitan newspaper, and so now I know
   them both

and this Indian child cries when he sits to eat at our table   10
because he had never known his own family to sit at the same table

and this Indian woman was born to an Indian woman
who sold her for a six-pack and a carton of cigarettes

and this Indian poet shivers beneath the freeway
and begs for enough quarters to buy pencil and paper   15

and this fancydancer passes out at the powwow
and wakes up naked, with no memory of the evening, all of his
   regalia gone

and this is my sister, who waits years for an eagle, receives it
and stores it with our cousins, who then tell her it has disappeared

and this is my father, whose own father died on Okinawa,° shot   20
by a Japanese soldier who must have looked so much like him

and this is my father, whose mother died of tuberculosis
not long after he was born, and so my father must hear coughing
   ghosts

and this is my grandmother who saw, before the white men came,
three ravens with white necks, and knew our God was going to
   change)   25

and invite the wind inside.

                                                                —*1996*

---

20 **Okinawa** Japanese island, site of the last World War II battle between the United States and Japan

Diane Thiel (b. 1967)

Diane Thiel has received several national awards, including the Robert Frost Award and the Robinson Jeffers Award. Her first collection, Echolocations (2000), *was the winner of the thirteenth annual Nicholas Roerich Poetry Prize. She also has published the poet's guide* Writing Your Rhythm: Using Nature, Culture, Form and Myth (2001). *Born in Coral Gables, Florida, Thiel grew up in Miami Beach and has traveled extensively throughout Europe and South America, most recently as a Fulbright scholar in Odessa. She has taught creative writing for over ten years—at Brown University, Florida International University, the University of Miami, and, currently, at the University of New Mexico. She has also taught for many years in a National Science Foundation interdisciplinary program—Ecology for Urban Students—and for the Miami Book Fair's poet-in-the-schools program.*

The Minefield

He was running with his friend from town to town.
They were somewhere between Prague and Dresden.
He was fourteen. His friend was faster
and knew a shortcut through the fields they could take.
He said there was lettuce growing in one of them,   5
and they hadn't eaten all day. His friend ran a few lengths ahead,
like a wild rabbit across the grass,
turned his head, looked back once,
and his body was scattered across the field.

My father told us this, one night,   10
and then continued eating dinner.

He brought them with him—the minefields.
He carried them underneath his good intentions.
He gave them to us—in the volume of his anger,
in the bruises we covered up with sleeves.   15
In the way he threw anything against the wall—
a radio, that wasn't even ours,
a melon, once, opened like a head.
In the way we still expect, years later and continents away,
that anything might explode at any time,   20

and we would have to run on alone
with a vision like that
only seconds behind.

—2000

A. E. Stallings (b. 1968)

A. E. Stallings is the author of Archaic Smile, *chosen for the 1999 Richard Wilbur Award by Dana Gioia. Written exclusively in received forms, the book is noteworthy for the vigor and humor with which Stallings rewrites classical myths. Raised in Decatur, Georgia, Stallings studied at the University of Georgia and Oxford University. She composed the Latin lyrics for the opening music of the Paramount film* Sum of All Fears, *and currently is at work on a verse translation of Lucretius'* De Rerum Natura. *Stallings also serves as an editor for the* Atlanta Review. *She lives in Athens, Greece, with her husband, John Psaropoulos, editor of the* Athens News.

Hades Welcomes His Bride°

Come now, child, adjust your eyes, for sight
Is here a lesser sense. Here you must learn
Directions through your fingertips and feet
And map them in your mind. I think some shapes
Will gradually appear. The pale things twisting   5
Overhead are mostly roots, although some worms
Arrive here clinging to their dead. Turn here.
Ah. And in this hall will sit our thrones,
And here you shall be queen, my dear, the queen
Of all men ever to be born. No smile?   10
Well, some solemnity befits a queen.
These thrones I have commissioned to be made
Are unlike any you imagined; they glow

Hades . . . In ancient Greek mythology, Hades, lord of the underworld, fell in love with and abducted Persephone, daughter of the Olympian gods Zeus and Demeter, the goddess of fertility. Because she ate six pomegranate seeds while underground, Persephone was fated to spend half of each year in the underworld; her yearly return to her mother represents the return of spring

Of deep-black diamonds and lead, subtler
And in better taste than gold, as will suit   15
Your timid beauty and pale throat. Come now,
Down these winding stairs, the air more still
And dry and easier to breathe. Here is a room
For your diversions. Here I've set a loom
And silk unraveled from the finest shrouds   20
And dyed the richest, rarest shades of black.
Such pictures you shall weave! Such tapestries!
For you I chose those three thin shadows there,
And they shall be your friends and loyal maids,
And do not fear from them such gossiping   25
As servants usually are wont. They have
Not mouth nor eyes and cannot thus speak ill
Of you. Come, come. This is the greatest room;
I had it specially made after great thought
So you would feel at home. I had the ceiling   30
Painted to recall some evening sky—
But without the garish stars and lurid moon.
What? That stark shape crouching in the corner?
Sweet, that is to be our bed. Our bed.
Ah! Your hand is trembling! I fear   35
There is, as yet, too much pulse in it.

—1999

Suji Kwock Kim (b. 1968)

Suji Kwock Kim received the 2002 Walt Whitman Award for Notes from
the Divided Country, *an exploration of the Japanese occupation of Korea,
and of the Korean War and its aftermath. The daughter of immigrants,
Kim grew up in Poughkeepsie, New York. She studied at Yale; the Iowa
Writers' Workshop; Seoul National University, where she was a Fulbright
scholar; and Stanford University, where she was a Stegner fellow. Kim is
coauthor of* Private Property, *a multimedia play produced at the Edin-
burgh Festival Fringe and featured on BBC-TV. She lives in San Francisco
and New York.*

Occupation

The soldiers
are hard at work
building a house.
They hammer
bodies into the earth   5
like nails,
they paint the walls
with blood.
Inside the doors
stay shut, locked   10
as eyes of stone.
Inside the stairs
feel slippery,
all flights go down.
There is no floor: 15
only a roof,
where ash is falling—
dark snow,
human snow,
thickly, mutely   20
falling.
Come, they say.
This house will
last forever.
You must occupy it.   25

And you, and you—
And you, and you—
Come, they say.
There is room
for everyone.   30

—*2003*

Wilmer Mills (b. 1969)

Wilmer Mills operated a sawmill in Sewanee, Tennessee until recently becoming a student in seminary. His childhood was spent in rural Brazil, where his parents served as agricultural missionaries for the Presbyterian Church. He studied at the University of the South. His first book, Light for the Orphans *(2002), contains many longer narrative poems and dramatic monologues spoken by a variety of voices.*

Ghost Story

He wakes the women of the neighborhood
By pressing down on them at night, each one
The kind of person everyone believes.
Men say, "She wouldn't make things up like that."
But no one really argues their accounts   5
Of phantom hands that push down on their breasts
As if to drown them in their mattresses.
The fact that only women see the man
Is proof enough for me. I've always found
A way to see the truth in women's stories,   10
Believing everything.
                        Tonight my roof
Has brightened of a sudden under rain,
Strange rain that falls straight down
As if to push the color of my tin
So deeply through my pillow I will dream   15
Of mallard heads, dark green of Charleston shutters.
And somewhere on my road or others near,

The broken ghost of someone lonelier
Than I could ever be will stand beside
A woman's bed and bear down with his hands   20
Until she wakes.
                That part is always true,
The moment she recounts how horrified
She lay beneath his strength, afraid to breathe.
So in my bed below the shape of rain
I say a prayer for them that each will wake   25
In time to live and tell the terror's tale
Each morning, like a dream that sisters share,
Though miles apart, and everyone believes.

                                     —*2002*

Morri Creech (b. 1970)

Morri Creech has an impressive poetic range. His first collection, Paper
Cathedrals *(2001), contains both dramatic monologues and personal
lyrics. Creech studied at Winthrop University in South Carolina and at
McNeese State University in Louisiana, where he currently teaches.*

Broken Glass

In 1970 my father returned
to the sweetness of desolation,
wandering past rows of mobile homes,
past the hulls of cars
splayed in the wheatgrass   5
that whiskered their silent engines,
past the skeletons of stripped machines,
dismantled harrows,
to the pine grove where shattered glass
gleamed beneath a bed of straw needles.   10
I had never been there before,
never seen the blazing fragments,
small as I was,

with a handful of rocks in my pocket
for the moment when my father   15
lined the bottles like years
against a rotten stump
and reared back to hurl the first stone.
I had never seen him raise his hand
against the world.   20
But the emptied bottles
of bourbon and scuppernong wine
flashed beneath the trees,
and he burned to splinter them all
to a heap of slivers.   25
He pitched the curve,
the fastball, the slider, the knuckle.
He left nothing intact, that man whose life
was an arrangement of tools
hung in a garage   30
for repairing bush hogs and cultivators;
his mind whirled
beyond the gears of perfect machinery,
and he reveled in the dust
and gravity of human error,   35
shouting as he threw each stone
with all the rage he could muster.
Feet planted firm,
he ground the pitcher's mound dirt into his palms,
rubbed them together,   40
then wound up the sidewind
and fractured the barrier
between him and the weeds
springing up around the dead-rooted pine,
chanting the names of his heroes,   45
those faded figures
from the box of trading cards in his closet,
chanting them in the language
of failure, oblivious to me
standing next to him, silent and afraid—   50
until at last he grew tired,
hefted me onto his shoulders,
and headed back

toward the O-rings and gaskets
that required his attention,   55
back toward his ordered life,
leaving the wreckage behind him,
scattered and shining.

—2001

Beth Ann Fennelly (b. 1971)

Beth Ann Fennelly wrote Open House, *which received the 2001 Kenyon
Review Prize. Raised in a suburb north of Chicago, she studied at the University of Notre Dame and the University of Arksansas. She has taught at
Knox College in Galesburg, Illinois, and the University of Mississippi, and
is married to the fiction writer Tom Franklin.*

Asked for a Happy Memory of Her Father, She Recalls Wrigley Field°

His drinking was different in sunshine,
as if it couldn't be bad. Sudden, manic,
he swung into a laugh, bought me
two ice creams, said *One for each hand.*

Half the hot inning I licked Good Humor   5
running down wrists. My bird-mother
earlier, packing my pockets with sun block,
has hopped her warning: *Be careful.*

So, pinned between his knees, I held
his Old Style° in both hands   10
while he streaked the lotion on my cheeks
and slurred *My little Indian princess.*

Wrigley Field Chicago baseball field   **10 Old Style** brand of beer

Home run: the hairy necks of men in front
jumped up, thighs torn from gummy green bleachers
to join the violent scramble. Father   15
held me close and said *Be careful,*

be careful. But why should I be full of care
with his thick arm circling my shoulders,
with a high smiling sun, liké a home run,
in the upper right-hand corner of the sky?   20

—2001

Appendix A:
Literary Movements

A Field Guide to
Contemporary American Poetry

Writing in the *Dictionary of Literary Biography Yearbook* in 1986, critic Ronald Baughman published "A Field Guide to Recent Schools of American Poetry." Baughman noted that the Modernist orthodoxy that prevailed during the first half of the 20th century met with serious challenges at the beginning of the second half: "After World War II, most American poets rebelled against the requirements for poetry established by Eliot and the New Criticism and instead placed emphasis on the writer's personality, the writer's self. This reversal is perhaps the single most important occurrence in the poetry of the postwar decades." Baughman's taxonomy divided American poets among several "schools" which shared little save that their members were contemporary with one another, and he identified eight key groups of contemporary American poets. These were (using his capitalizations) the Academics, the Concretists, the Confessionalists, the Black Mountain School, the Deep Imagists, the New York School, the Beat Generation, and practitioners of the New Black Aesthetic. While readers may wish to consult the full text of Baughman's essay for his comments on the most prominent individual members, a few general statements should perhaps be made about these groups, which seemed so clearly defined only a couple of decades ago but now, in the first decade of a new century, may require further qualifications and revisions.

First, most of the individual writers mentioned by Baughman are now in their 70s and 80s, having published collected editions that represent the summing up of their careers. They have won the important prizes, and a few have served as Poet Laureate, a position established in 1986 and filled since that time by poets born as early as 1905 (Robert Penn Warren) and as recently as 1952 (Rita Dove). The current laureate, Ted Koosner (b. 1939), like his immediate predecessors—Louise Glück (b. 1943), Billy Collins (b. 1941), Robert Pinsky (b. 1940), and Robert Hass (b. 1941)—represents a generation who were raised in the 1950s and who completed their educations and began their publishing careers in the 1960s and 1970s. While one still looks with expectations to the publication of books by senior poets like Richard Wilbur, Anthony Hecht, Adrienne Rich, or Carolyn Kizer, it is unlikely that they will depart significantly from their established manners in any new work. Throughout the 1980s and 1990s one sensed that the torch was being passed to the next generation.

Second, and perhaps more important, many members of the younger generation of poets would perhaps be reluctant to identify themselves as members of the schools identified by Baughman. For example, it is unlikely that any contemporary poet under fifty would refer to himself or herself as a "confessionalist," though the term "post-confessional," like "post-modern," is now common in critical discourse. Most of these poets, who were learning their craft when Baughman's schools were at their height, absorbed diverse influences in their early careers and have arrived at poetic styles which may not be readily distinguishable from one another. Indeed, the stylistic qualities of many contemporary American poets seem very different from those of the high modernists and even those of the generation that came to prominence after World War II. A relaxed, conversational idiom; a restrained rhetoric which employs local tropes sparingly (the simile predominates); and fairly uniform free verse lines, more often than not arranged in uniform stanzas, characterize the work of many contemporary poets. The poetic barricades of this younger generation have more often been raised along lines of gender, sexual, or ethnic identity than according to the dictates of modernist aesthetic manifestoes like Ezra Pound's famous Imagist program. To cite only one case, forty years ago it was fairly safe to say that Beat poets held in common certain countercultural attitudes toward middle-class American society and also put identifiable aesthetic principles to work in their poetry: demotic free verse or the incorporation of jazz rhythms, for example. Today one would be reluctant to make any such generalizations beyond noting, say, that women poets tend to write on gender-related issues more than male poets do; that African-American poets and those of other ethnic groups often examine social injustices in American society; that Native-American poets frequently share some of the same ritualistic approaches to the natural world; or that many gay poets have adopted the rhetoric of the long tradition of protest poetry. Put in the simplest possible terms, much American poetry of the early 1950s focused on *cultural* issues; much poetry written since has focused on *social* ones.

Still, certain younger poets show some affinities to the schools of the older generation, and it may be useful to discuss briefly these poetic lines of descent. The Academic poets of the 1950s, who produced a rhymed, metrical poetry of wit and linguistic precision, with a wide cultural (mostly European) reference, are often cited as the forebears of today's New Formalists, and the activities and occasional polemics of this latter group have attracted quite a bit of critical attention and no small amount of controversy. Perhaps because they have chosen to travel somewhat outside the mainstream of many of their contemporaries, they have often been discussed by critics in political terms, even though there seems little that connects them beyond a dedication—with considerable latitude—to writing in meter; they actually represent many diverse lifestyles and different political points of view. According to some critics, they break with the older academic formalists in their preference for popular, demotic forms of culture and, in general, their idioms and cultural frames of reference will likely strike readers as somewhat more familiar than those of their elders.

Concretism garnered some public exposure in the popular media a few decades ago, but it has remained, for the most part, a literary curiosity. An aesthetic that uses words as visual icons formed into interesting shapes on the page is unlikely to elicit much serious critical response, and, indeed, many of the productions of concrete poets are perhaps more suitable for gallery display than for the pages of books. If the Concretists have any heirs in the present scene, they are the poets of the Language group (originally named after a journal in which the work of many of them early appeared). According to critic Marjorie Perloff, the *avant garde* poets of 1950s proclaimed that "Form is never more than an extension of content." For the Language poet, this aphorism becomes, in critic Jonathan Holden's words, "Theory is never more than the extension of practice." Indeed, there often have been strong alliances between these poets and the post-modern literary theorists who have come to prominence in American graduate programs in recent times. Still, the ambitions of Language poetry reach beyond the constraints of academia; its proponents argue that poetry can subvert the prevailing social order by subverting the conventions of language.

The Confessional poets of the 1960s remain one of the chief influences on the poets of this generation, though the effects of confessional novelty, in an age of a popular culture when few if any subjects are taboo, have made it increasingly difficult for poets to shock readers with explicit personal revelations. When Robert Lowell, scion of Boston gentility and winner of American poetry's most coveted awards, revealed, in *Life Studies* (1959), that "my mind's not right," publishing poems detailing family dysfunction, marital woes, alcoholism, mental illness, and psychotherapy, the reading public, perhaps feeling that such candor was long overdue, was fascinated. Sylvia Plath's suicide in 1963 caused her posthumous collection *Ariel* (1965) to be valued all the more highly by women who heard, in its bitterest moments, a cry that could have issued from their own lips, and Anne Sexton, revealing the hidden anxieties of suburban America, inspired a generation of women who came of age on the cusp of the feminist era. Some thirty years ago, in *The Confessional Poets*, critic Robert Phillips described the typical confessional poem, stressing its therapeutic, personal, and alienated qualities. Most younger American poets have at one time or another written poems in this vein. Indeed, the autobiographical narrative/lyric has become a staple of our poetry, and, today, contemporary poets of the mainstream feel free to reveal their most intimate moments. It would be safe to say that virtually every poet writing today has learned from and at times imitated the candor of the first generation of Confessionalist poets.

Two of Baughman's groups, the Black Mountain School and the Deep Imagists, have retained relatively little direct influence in the contemporary scene, though many of their members are still writing. The former, named after a group of poets who studied at Black Mountain College with Charles Olsen in the 1950s and taking their impetus, to some degree, from the "American Grain" poetics of William Carlos Williams, promoted an experimental "projective verse" and explored various theories of open form and composition by "fields" or "breath-units." While Language Poets frequently cite as influential the visually-oriented poems of Creeley and Olson, it is difficult to think of many poets writing today who are passionate about the metrical matters raised by the Black Mountain poets, perhaps because poetry in open forms so completely pervades the contemporary canon of American poetry that the question is moot.

The Deep Imagists have also receded in their influence. Deep Image poetry had an important influence on many young poets in the early 1970s, when it seemed as though a new poetic idiom, heavily influenced by European and South American expressionsism and surrealism, had emerged. One critic dubbed it "Blymagism" after its chief supporter Robert Bly, but satirical comments did not keep it from entering the graduate poetry workshops and spawning hundreds of poems that seemed to have few ties to the British and American traditions. It should be noted that the startling dislocations of language and logic found in much Deep Image poetry followed hard on the psychedelic late 1960s and was fueled by the rage of the era of Vietnam War protests and Watergate; one of Bly's typical poems of the period describes President Lyndon Johnson's military advisors as "dressed as gamboling lambs." Such self-consciously bizarre tropes may seem dated today, though some contemporaries occasionally employ surrealistic or absurdist techniques as part of their larger poetic strategies.

The New York School, led by Frank O'Hara, Kenneth Koch, and John Ashbery, flowered in the late 1950s and early 1960s among writers who had close affinities with abstract expressionist painters like Jackson Pollock and Willem de Kooning. Like the Deep Imagists, the New York poets stressed subjectivity and the unconscious, but they infused their own surrealism with a comic spirit much more akin to the Dadaist experiments of Zurich than to Deep-Image high seriousness. Ashbery, whose reputation remains high among influential critics like Helen Vendler, Marjorie Perloff, and Harold Bloom, is surely one of the most discussed poets on the contemporary scene, but relatively few mainstream contemporary poets betray his direct influence. Most of the poets represented in *The New York Poets* (1970), an anthology edited by David Shapiro and Ron Padgett, have not advanced beyond the time and place that inspired their early prominence. O'Hara's influence, however, is clearly evident in the works of those younger writers identified as second generation New York School poets, a group that includes David Lehman, Denise Duhamel, and Dean Young.

Similarly, the poets of the Beat Generation also seem, from the perspective of a half century, products of a particular conjunction of circumstances (San Francisco in the early 1950s), and their period style of "hydrogen jukebox" rhetoric, to borrow a phrase of Allen Ginsberg's, seems now to reflect the discontents of the Eisenhower era. The Beats, like so many other figures that fifty years ago seemed on the outermost fringes of American poetry, have at long last become respectable. Today, it is difficult to imagine, given the graphic nature of the heavy metal and rap lyrics that one can hear anywhere, that Ginsberg's *Howl* was the focus of a censorship trial when it was first published. Perhaps more than that of the other groups, the Beats' agenda has been co-opted by franchised popular culture and has made its clearest marks on the participants of the "poetry slams" that became popular in the 1990s and on the performance-based lyrics of rappers and hip-hop artists.

The last of Baughman's schools, which he labels the New Black Aesthetic, must today be expanded to include members of other ethnic groups—Hispanics, Asian-Americans, and Native Americans being the most prominent—and it seems clear that no single aesthetic can adequately represent poets of such different origins. Multiculturalism has become one of the most important, and sometimes controversial, social and academic issues of our era, and its spirit has clearly affected the contents of anthologies and textbooks. As the population of the United States (and thus of the college classrooms) reflects an increasing diversity of ethnic backgrounds, it seems likely that future overviews of American poetry will surely include mention of more representatives of minority cultures, at least until that time, projected by demographers to arrive later in this century, when it is predicted that *every* American will be a member of a minority group.

Once the schools have been discussed and their descendants identified, what remains for the poets—and there are many of them—who demonstrate no clear ties to one particular group? If the definition of a truly *American* poetry dates from Ralph Waldo Emerson's "The Poet" (1844), then "the experience of each new age requires a new confession, and the world seems always waiting for its poet." That poet may arise, as most these days do, from a university creative writing program, or that poet, like Whitman and Dickinson, may somehow forge a new style largely on his or her own. It is, of course, impossible to say what the future holds—and the purpose of any anthology is to deal with a present that will rapidly become the past—but the situation today may be analogous to that of a century ago, when there was no consensus in either America or Great Britain about which poets, if any, were deserving of major status. The great voices of the Romantic and Victorian eras had grown silent, and the founders of modernism were still largely unpublished. In *The Fate of American Poetry* (1991), poet-critic Jonathan Holden argues that the "mainstream of American poetry . . . has continued to be, whether narrative or meditative, in a realist mode that is essentially egalitarian, university-based, and middle class, and to be written in a free verse that has, by and large, vastly improved since the sixties, evolved into a flexible medley of older prosodies so rich in echoes that it bears out Eliot's famous dictum that 'No verse is ever really free.'" Whether this modestly stated aesthetic has produced or will produce poems that will stand the test of time remains open to question. Still, if the past provides us any hints about the reliability of any field guide in mapping out the future, of the many poems that we have collected here more than a handful will survive for the delight and instruction of readers in distant places and times.

In the glossary below, we have provided additional information about the major schools that have influenced and continue to shape contemporary American poetry. Following each entry is a list, by no means exhaustive, of poets who have been linked to the respective group.

Glossary of Poetic Schools and Trends

Academic Formalism

In the 1950s, most American poetry was characterized by rhyme, regular meter, a sense of Anglo-American literary tradition, a dry wit, and a classical belief in the supremacy of the intellect. Such poems tended to compression, impersonality, careful craftsmanship, and occasionally ornate diction. Many of the poets associated with the academic formalism—Donald Justice, Richard Wilbur, Anthony Hecht, John Hollander, and X. J. Kennedy, for example—continued to use traditional poetic form even after the free-verse "revolution" of the 1960s, when the use of rhyme and meter became less prominent.

> *See Edgar Bowers, Anthony Hecht, Donald Justice, X. J. Kennedy, Carolyn Kizer, James Merrill, Howard Nemerov, Louis Simpson, Mona Van Duyn, Richard Wilbur, and Miller Williams.*

African-American Poetry

In the 1960s, the black-power movement sought to build on recent civil rights gains to increasingly empower black America. The related black arts movement used art to promote political change. Amiri Baraka, who coined the term "Black Arts" and who had been active as a beat poet under his earlier name, LeRoi Jones, opened a black-arts repertory school in Harlem to teach and produce plays that, in his words, "shattered the illusions of the American body politic, and awakened black people to the meaning of their lives." Black-arts poets—including the still-controversial Baraka, Nikki Giovanni, Larry Neal, and Sonia Sanchez—emphasized speech and performance, call and response, and the African-American vernacular. The wildly popular performance poetry movement owes a large debt to the black-arts movement in both style and substance. In recent decades, African-American poets have worked in a wide variety of styles and have written on an equally wide variety of themes, but many younger poets are visibly influenced by the protest poetry of their predecessors.

> *See Ai, Gerald Barrax, Lucille Clifton, Toi Derricotte, Rita Dove, Forrest Hamer, Michael Harper, Yusef Komunyakaa, Harryette Mullen, and Marilyn Nelson.*

Beat Poetry

Borrowed from the slang of jazz musicians and street hustlers, "beat" originally meant down and out, but writer Jack Kerouac also claimed a spiritual dimension for the word, using it to describe a beatific state. Reacting against post-World War II middle-class materialism and conformity, as well as the predominant aesthetic of academic formalism, Kerouac and his fellow Beats (a group which included Allen Ginsberg, Gregory Corso, Gary Snyder, and Diane DiPrima) sought transcendence by embracing jazz (then considered "low" culture) and such counter-cultural phenomena as illegal drugs and Zen Buddhism. Generally meant to be performed and heard, Beat poems often sought to shock their audience out of complacency. Ginsberg's *Howl*, for example, made liberal use of bold, explicit homosexual imagery. The United States government reacted to *Howl* by seizing 520 copies and putting the book's publisher, Lawrence Ferlinghetti, on trial for obscenity. He was acquitted, and *Howl* has gone on to become a staple of college reading lists. The Beat influence lives on in the Spoken Word poetry movement.

> *See Charles Bukowski, Gregory Corso, Allen Ginsberg, and Gary Snyder.*

The Black-Arts Movement

See African-American Poetry.

Black Mountain

Black Mountain College, in rural North Carolina, was the unlikely center of a mid-century artistic upheaval. Black Mountain's faculty included such esteemed figures as architect Walter Gropius, painters Willem de Kooning and Robert Motherwell, and composer John Cage, as well as a number of experimental poets including Charles Olson, Robert Duncan, and Robert Creeley. Olson's theory of "Projective Verse," which promoted open forms and composition by "fields," and claimed that "the poem itself must, at all points, be a high energy-construct and, at all points, an energy-discharge," provided a rationale for the composition of open forms, and was widely admired among free-verse poets. "Some Notes on Organic Form," an essay by poet Denise Levertov, also associated with Black Mountain, provided an alternate way of describing how free verse might be composed in claiming that "there is a form in all things (and in our experience) which the poet can discover and reveal." While Olson and Creeley's importance to mainstream poetry has waned somewhat over the last few decades, experimentalists—including the Language poets—still frequently cite them as crucial influences.

See Hayden Carruth, Robert Creeley, and Denise Levertov.

Confessionalism

As its name indicates, confessional poetry features the use of private—even shocking—autobiographical material. Early confessional poets (including W. D. Snodgrass, Robert Lowell, Sylvia Plath and Anne Sexton) wrote openly about mental illness, infidelity, dysfunctional families, and alcoholism, ushering in an age of personal revelation. While some critics have dismissed confessionalism as mere gut-spilling, the reader's feeling of being addressed directly and honestly is, of course, an illusion. Sharon Olds—one of the many contemporary poets writing in the tradition of Lowell and Sexton—favors the term "apparently personal," which underscores her contention that even poems based on autobiography employ artifice.

See Kim Addonizio, Sharon Olds, Sylvia Plath, Anne Sexton and W. D. Snodgrass,

Cowboy Poetry

A type of performance poetry, cowboy poems are informed by the oral tradition of the American west. These poets—often experienced cowboys or, at least, rural Westerners—recite traditional poems from memory, aiming to entertain and to pass on lore about their rapidly-disappearing way of life. The poems generally use rhyme and extremely regular meter to emphasize their aural qualities. Although several recent anthologies have been dedicated to cowboy poetry, the most important showcase for this work is the annual National Cowboy Poetry Gathering in Elko, Nevada, which lasts nine days and regularly draws an audience of thousands.

Deep Image

Deep-image poetry applies the theories of psychoanalyst Carl Jung to poetry. Like his contemporary, Sigmund Freud, Jung believed that the unconscious reveals itself in symbols, and he was particularly interested in a collective unconscious, a set of symbols and images shared by members of a culture. Influenced by Jung and by South American and European surrealist poets, deep imagists like Robert Bly called for a more passionate, less rational poetry that favored imaginative leaps over logic, and emotion over reason. Generally concerned with landscape and natural imagery, deep-image poems tend to depict a sinking into things—water, darkness, or death—and a consequent fuller understanding of life and the self.

See Robert Bly, Louise Glück, Charles Simic, and James Wright

Ecological Poetry

A term used to describe poetry that focuses on ecological issues and the environment. While early American poets like William Cullen Bryant and Ralph Waldo Emerson often focused on the natural world for their subject matter and inspiration, in recent decades increased awareness of a threatened global environment has prompted many contemporary poets to address, even more directly, ecological themes.

See W. S. Merwin, Mary Oliver, Pattiann Rogers, Gary Snyder, and Richard Wilbur.

Expansive Poetry

Encompassing both the new formalism and the new narrative, the term expansive poetry has been used to describe contemporary poets who draw on the traditional tools of poetry (rhyme, received forms, regular meter, and storytelling) in an effort to expand poetry's scope beyond that of the first-person, semi-confessional lyric poem common over the last three decades.

See New Formalism and New Narrative.

Feminist Poetics

With the emergence of the women's movement, a number of women writers began working to define themselves in relationship to a literary tradition that had long marginalized the female voice. Enacting the 1960s maxim that "the personal is the political," women writers frequently turned to their own lives as a starting point for scrutinizing the power relationship between the sexes. In her 1986 treatise *Stealing the Language*, Alicia Suskin Ostriker sought to define feminist poetics, arguing that certain thematic preoccupations—including revisionist mythmaking and the poetics of the body—were common to women. Closely identified with feminist poetics are activist poets like Adrienne Rich, Audre Lorde, June Jordan, and Marge Piercy, whose politically charged poems seek to transform the culture at large.

See Kim Addonizio, Lucille Clifton, Carolyn Forche, Marilyn Hacker, Carolyn Kizer, Denise Levertov, Sharon Olds, Molly Peacock, Sylvia Plath, Adrienne Rich, and Anne Sexton.

Hip Hop or Rap

The origins of hip-hop or rap poetry extend back to African oral tradition, and, more recently to the black-arts movement. In early 1970s, urban poets known as m.c.'s began "rapping," or reciting rhymes to the backbeat of d.j.-manipulated turntables or drum machines. Though rap poems generally have four strong stresses per line, the lines can be as long or as short as the poet chooses. Early rap often addressed political themes and life on the inner-city streets, but themes of rap and hip-hop music have largely shifted to sex, violence, and conspicuous consumption since the early 1990s when hip hop was absorbed by the mainstream of American culture.

Identity poetics

This term describes poetry that explores the poet's experience as a member of a disempowered group. While the black arts movement provides the first example of an explicitly identity-based literary movement, the term identity poetics embraces feminist poetry, queer poetics, Asian-, Hispanic-, and Native American writing, and other work arising out of a poet's racial, ethnic, or gender identity.

See Julia Alvarez, Rafael Campo, Lucille Clifton, Judith Ortiz Cofer, Mark Doty, Rita Dove, Marilyn Hacker, Joy Harjo, Suji Kwock Kim, Yusef Komunyakaa, Shirley Geok-lin Lim, James Merrill, Haryette Mullen, Adrienne Rich, and Alberto Ríos. Also see African-American Poetry and Feminist Poetics.

Iowa Writers' Workshop School

The first—and still the most prestigious—creative writing degree program in the United States, the Iowa Writers' Workshop has trained many of the nation's most honored poets and has been a model for most other graduate creative writing programs. As a result, the Iowa Writers' Workshop has become associated with the type of poems most often produced by the process known as "workshopping," in which student poems are subjected to group critiques. From the 1970s through the 1980s, the "workshop poem"—the neo-confessional, free-verse lyric, sometimes bearing traces of the deep imagists—was the very type of the contemporary poem, and was featured in American literary magazines to the exclusion of almost any other kind. While the face of American poetry has in recent years grown more varied, the Iowa-influenced poem still dominates the poetry scene.

> *See Jorie Graham, Michael S. Harper, Donald Justice, Philip Levine, Thomas Lux, Gerald Stern, Thomas Lux, Ellen Bryant Voigt, W. D. Snodgrass, and Jorie Graham.*

Language Poetry

Named for the experimental poetry journal $L=A=N=G=U=A=G=E$, Language poetry sets out to thwart expectations, and in doing so to help readers "develop a new order of thinking," according to Charles Bernstein, one of the magazine's editors. Drawing on postmodern literary theories, linguistics, and semiotics, poets like Lyn Hejinian, Leslie Scalapino, Ron Silliman, and Michael Palmer stress the role of the reader who brings new perceptions to the text, creating it anew as he or she reads. Interested in fragments, nonsense, and breaking language down to its smallest components (phonemes and even letters), these poets often cite Ezra Pound, Gertrude Stein, Charles Olson, and Louis Zukofsky as their influences. Language poets also see a political element to their aesthetics, claiming that their nonlinear constructs undermine the English language, and in doing so, thwart the prevailing social and political order. Although practitioners of this movement consider themselves experimental and cutting-edge, Language poetry emerged in the early 1970s and is firmly rooted in academe, with many of its practitioners holding positions at established graduate writing programs like SUNY Buffalo and the University of Pennsylvania.

> *See Michael Palmer, Susan Howe, Harryette Mullen, and H. L. Hix.*

Multicultural Poetics

Beginning with the Harlem Renaissance of the 1920s, anthologies of African-American poetry containing the work of Gwendolyn B. Bennett, Arna Bontemps, Countee Cullen, Jessie Faucet, Langston Hughes, Claude McKay, Alice Dunbar Nelson, and others began to appear, and in the 1940s two African-American woman poets, Margaret Walker and Gwendolyn Brooks, came to prominence. Further developments in African-American poetry are summarized above, but in the late 1960s other identifiable groups began to gain prominence in the American canon—Native Americans, Hispanic-Americans, Asian-Americans, and others—in many cases appearing in anthologies which focused on the poetry of a single ethnic segment with the aim of exploring the complex diversity of American society.

> *See Ai, Sherman Alexie, Julia Alvarez, Gerald Barrax, Rafael Campo, Gladys Cardiff, Lucille Clifton, Judith Ortiz Cofer, Sarah Cortez, Rhina Espaillat, Suji Kwock Kim, Shirley Geok-lin Lim, Joy Harjo, Michael S. Harper, Yusef Komunyakaa, Li-Young Lee, Harryette Mullen, Marilyn Nelson, Naomi Shihab Nye, Alberto Ríos, Wendy Rose, and Amy Uyematsu.*

New Formalism

In the late 1970s and early 1980s, a handful of poets born since 1940 began independently experimenting with rhyme, regular meter, and traditional poetic forms like the sonnet and villanelle. In a controversial essay titled "Can Poetry Matter," one of these poets, Dana Gioia, accused contemporary poets of writing mostly for each other, and in doing so, of having become "a subculture of specialists." The new formalists consciously desire to widen poetry's readership by harkening back to the long tradition of English-language verse.

> See *Julia Alvarez, Dana Gioia, Emily Grosholz, Marilyn Hacker, Brad Leithauser, David Mason, Timothy Murphy, Molly Peacock, Mary Jo Salter, and Timothy Steele.*

New Narrative

The new-narrative movement began in 1981, when poets Mark Jarman and Robert McDowell founded *The Reaper*, a journal promoting the return of storytelling in poetry. *The Reaper* asserted that poems should offer the entertainment value—including characters and a gripping plot—of well-crafted fiction. The new-narrative movement, like the new formalism, attempted to bring poetry to a wider readership.

> See *B. H. Fairchild, Andrew Hudgins, Mark Jarman, David Mason, and Marilyn Nelson.*

New York School

The Manhattan art scene of the 1950s and early 1960s was home to a handful of poets—chief among them John Ashbery, Frank O'Hara, Kenneth Koch, and James Schuyler—who socialized and often collaborated with abstract impressionist painters like Larry Rivers, Fairfield Porter and Jane Freilicher. Like the deep imagists, the New York poets looked to the French surrealists, and were interested in the unconscious. Unlike the deep Imagists, however, Ashbery and company valued irony and wit, and often composed their poems in a spirit of playful collaboration. O'Hara's casually conversational voice lives on in the work of second-generation New York school-poets like Denise Duhamel and David Lehman (who wrote *The Last Avant-Garde*, an extended study of the New York school), while Ashbery's poems frequently are claimed as an influence by Language poets.

> See *John Ashbery, Denise Duhamel, Edward Field, and Frank O'Hara.*

Regionalism

In the early 20th century, poets like Edwin Arlington Robinson and Robert Frost, following the writers of local-color realism of the 19th century, were seen as chroniclers of New England life, while other poets like Carl Sandburg and Edgar Lee Masters were seen as spokespersons for the Midwest. Perhaps because of the increased urbanization of American life, identification with a geographical region, with the possible exceptions of the South and the West, does not occupy the prominence it once did, but many poets continue to explore the life and landscapes of parts of the United States outside major urban areas.

> See *Betty Adcock, A. R. Ammons, Ginger Andrews, Hayden Carruth, Fred Chappell, James Dickey, B. H. Fairchild, John Haines, Andrew Hudgins, Richard Hugo, Rodney Jones, Yusef Komunyakaa, Maxine Kumin, Sydney Lea, Robert Morgan, Gary Snyder, Miller Williams, and James Wright.*

Spoken Word/Performance Poetry

A product of the early 1990s coffee house scene (most notably at Manhattan's Nuyorican Poets Café and Venice, California's Beyond Baroque), spoken word emerged from "poetry slams" in which poets perform their work, competing for audience approval. Spoken-word poets write for the stage and not the page, often infusing their performances with humor and politically charged anger. The enormous mainstream popularity of spoken word is visible everywhere in mainstream culture. Coffeehouse poetry readings are increasingly popular, and spoken-word pieces have been featured in commercials for The Gap, at the rock festival Lollapalooza, on MTV, and even on Broadway, where *Def Poetry Jam* enjoyed a successful run.

Stand-Up Poetry

Like other performance poets, stand-up poets aim to entertain, using accessible language and humor. Unlike some performance poetry, however, the work of stand-up poets like Billy Collins, Ron Koertge, and Allison Joseph also functions on the page, where a single reading is often enough to yield meaning and pleasure.

> *See Billy Collins and Edward Field.*

Stanford School

For many years, the poet and controversial critic Yvor Winters (1900-1968) taught literature and creative writing at Stanford University, at the time one of the few universities in the country that offered such a curriculum. Winters, who began his writing career as a free-verse Imagist poet, turned in later life to a rigid neo-classicism that seemed at odds with most of the main currents of modernism, arguing against the intuitive qualities of romanticism and practicing a poetics that favored a strict formalism, the clear statement of ideas and moral opinions, and the preeminence of reason. Poets like J. V. Cunningham and critics like Donald Stanford are often cited as prime "Wintersians," but the list of poets whom he taught and influenced (and the poets whom these poets taught and influenced in turn) is long, even though many of them later moved away from his influence.

> *See Edgar Bowers, Dick Davis, Dana Gioia, Thom Gunn, Donald Hall, Robert Hass, Donald Justice, Philip Levine, Robert Pinsky, and Timothy Steele.*

Surrealism

Mainly a product of South America and Europe, surrealist poetry tried to liberate the imagination and explore the unconscious. Toward this end, surrealist poets experiment with automatic writing, dream imagery, free association, and bizarre, often jarring, juxtapositions.

> *See Robert Bly, Russell Edson, Donald Justice, Charles Simic, and James Tate. Also see Deep Image.*

Appendix B: Major Prizes

Bollingen Prize in Poetry

Administered by Yale University and the Bollingen Foundation, this award recognizes artistic achievement.

1949 Ezra Pound
1950 Wallace Stevens
1951 John Crowe Ransom
1952 Marianne Moore
1953 Archibald MacLeish and William Carlos Williams
1954 W. H. Auden
1955 Léonie Adams and Louise Bogan
1956 Conrad Aiken
1957 Allen Tate
1958 e. e. cummings
1959 Theodore Roethke
1960 Delmore Schwartz
1961 Yvor Winters
1962 John Hall Wheelock and Richard Eberhart
1963 Robert Frost
1965 Horace Gregory
1967 Robert Penn Warren
1969 John Berryman and Karl Shapiro
1971 Richard Wilbur and Mona Van Duyn

1973 James Merrill
1975 Archie Randolph Ammons
1977 David Ignatow
1979 W. S. Merwin
1981 Howard Nemerov and May Swenson
1983 Anthony Hecht and John Hollander
1985 John Ashbery and Fred Chappell
1987 Stanley Kunitz
1989 Edgar Bowers
1991 Laura Riding Jackson and Donald Justice
1993 Mark Strand
1995 Kenneth Koch
1997 Gary Snyder
1999 Robert Creeley
2001 Louise Glück
2003 Adrienne Rich

National Book Award for Poetry 1950–2003

(Awards began in 1950)
1950 *Paterson: Book III and Selected Poems*—William Carlos Williams
1951 *The Auroras of Autumn*—Wallace Stevens
1952 *Collected Poems*—Marianne Moore
1953 *Collected Poems, 1917–1952*—Archibald MacLeish
1954 *Collected Poems*—Conrad Aiken
1955 *The Collected Poems of Wallace Stevens*—Wallace Stevens
1956 *The Shield of Achilles*—W. H. Auden
1957 *Things of the World*—Richard Wilbur
1958 *Promises: Poems, 1954–1956*—Robert Penn Warren
1959 *Words for the Wind*—Theodore Roethke
1960 *Life Studies*—Robert Lowell
1961 *The Woman at the Washington Zoo*—Randall Jarrell
1962 *Poems*—Alan Dugan
1963 *Traveling Through the Dark*—William Stafford
1964 *Selected Poems*—John Crowe Ransom
1965 *The Far Field*—Theodore Roethke
1966 *Buckdancer's Choice: Poems*—James Dickey
1967 *Nights and Days*—James Merrill

1968 *The Light Around the Body*—Robert Bly
1969 *His Toy, His Dream, His Rest*—John Berryman
1970 *The Complete Poems*—Elizabeth Bishop
1971 *To See, To Take*—Mona Van Duyn
1972 *Selected Poems Frank O'Hara: The Collected Poems of Frank O'Hara*—Howard Moss
1973 *Collected Poems, 1951–1971*—A. R. Ammons
1974 *The Fall of America: Poems of these States, 1965–1971*—Allen Ginsberg
Diving into the Wreck: Poems 1971–1972—Adrienne Rich
1975 *Presentation Piece*—Marilyn Hacker
1976 *Self-portrait in a Convex Mirror*—John Ashbery
1977 *Collected Poems, 1930–1976*—Richard Eberhart
1978 *The Collected Poems of Howard Nemerov*—Howard Nemerov
1979 *Mirabell: Book of Numbers*—James Merrill
1980 *Ashes*—Philip Levine
1981 *The Need to Hold Still*—Lisel Mueller
1982 *Life Supports: New and Collected Poems*—William Bronk
1983 *Selected Poems*—Galway Kinnell
Country Music: Selected Early Poems—Charles Wright
1984-1990 No award
1991 *What Work Is*—Philip Levine
1992 *New & Selected Poems*—Mary Oliver
1993 *Garbage*—A. R. Ammons
1994 *A Worshipful Company of Fletchers*—James Tate
1995 *Passing Through: The Later Poems*—Stanley Kunitz
1996 *Scrambled Eggs & Whiskey*—Hayden Carruth
1997 *Effort at Speech: New & Selected Poems*—William Meredith
1998 *This Time: New and Selected Poems*—Gerald Stern
1999 *Vice: New & Selected Poems*—Ai
2000 *Blessing the Boats: New and Selected Poems 1988-2000*—Lucille Clifton

2001 *Poems Seven: New and Complete Poetry*—Alan Dugan
2002 *In the Next Galaxy*—Ruth Stone
2003 *The Singing*—C.K. Williams

The National Book Critics Circle Award for Poetry

1981 *A Coast of Trees*—A. R. Ammons
1982 *Antarctic Traveler*—Katha Pollitt
1983 *Changing Light at Sandover*—James Merrill
1984 *The Dead and the Living*—Sharon Olds
1985 *The Triumph of Achilles*—Louise Gluck
1986 *Wild Gratitude*—Edward Hirsch
1987 *Flesh and Blood*—C. K. Williams
1988 *That One Day*—Donald Hall
1989 *Transparent Gestures*—Rodney Jones
1990 *Bitter Angel*—Amy Gerstler
1991 *Heaven and Earth: A Cosmology*—Albert Goldbarth
1992 *Collected Shorter Poems 1946-1991*—Hayden Carruth
1993 *My Alexandria*—Mark Doty
1994 *Rider*—Mark Rudman
1995 *Time and Money*—William Matthews
1996 *Sun Under Wood*—Robert Hass
1997 *Black Zodiac*—Charles Wright
1998 *The Bird Catcher*—Marie Ponsot
1999 *Ordinary Words*—Ruth Stone
2000 *Carolina Ghost Woods*—Judy Jordan
2001 *Saving Lives*—Albert Goldbarth
2002 *Early Occult Memory Systems of the Lower Midwest*—B. H. Fairchild

Pulitzer Prize for Poetry 1945–2003

1945 *V-Letter and Other Poems*—Karl Shapiro
1946 No award
1947 *Lord Weary's Castle*—Robert Lowell
1948 *The Age of Anxiety*—W. H. Auden
1949 *Terror and Decorum*—Peter Viereck
1950 *Annie Allen*—Gwendolyn Brooks
1951 *Complete Poems*—Carl Sandburg
1952 *Collected Poems*—Marianne Moore
1953 *Collected Poems 1917-1952*—Archibald MacLeish
1954 *The Waking*—Theodore Roethke
1955 *Collected Poems*—Wallace Stevens
1956 *Poems - North & South*—Elizabeth Bishop
1957 *Things of This World*—Richard Wilbur
1958 *Promises: Poems 1954-1956*—Robert Penn Warren
1959 *Selected Poems 1928-1958*—Stanley Kunitz
1960 *Heart's Needle*—W. D. Snodgrass
1961 *Times Three: Selected Verse From Three Decades*—Phyllis McGinley
1962 *Poems*—Alan Dugan
1963 *Pictures from Breughel*—the late William Carlos Williams
1964 *At The End Of The Open Road*—Louis Simpson
1965 *77 Dream Songs*—John Berryman
1966 *Selected Poems*—Richard Eberhart
1967 *Live or Die*—Anne Sexton
1968 *The Hard Hours*—Anthony Hecht
1969 *Of Being Numerous*—George Oppen
1970 *Untitled Subjects*—Richard Howard
1971 *The Carrier of Ladders*—William S. Merwin
1972 *Collected Poems*—James Wright
1973 *Up Country*—Maxine Kumin
1974 *The Dolphin*—Robert Lowell
1975 *Turtle Island*—Gary Snyder
1976 *Self-Portrait in a Convex Mirror*—John Ashbery
1977 *Divine Comedies*—James Merrill
1978 *Collected Poems*—Howard Nemerov
1979 *Now and Then*—Robert Penn Warren
1980 *Selected Poems*—Donald Justice
1981 *The Morning of the Poem*—James Schuyler
1982 *The Collected Poems*—the late Sylvia Plath (a posthumous publication)
1983 *Selected Poems*—Galway Kinnell
1984 *American Primitive*—Mary Oliver

1985 *Yin*—Carolyn Kizer
1986 *The Flying Change*—Henry Taylor
1987 *Thomas and Beulah*—Rita Dove
1988 *Partial Accounts: New and Selected Poems*—William Meredith
1989 *New and Collected Poems*—Richard Wilbur
1990 *The World Doesn't End*—Charles Simic
1991 *Near Changes*—Mona Van Duyn
1992 *Selected Poems*—James Tate
1993 *The Wild Iris*—Louise Glück
1994 *Neon Vernacular: New and Selected Poems*—Yusef Komunyakaa

1995 *The Simple Truth*—Philip Levine
1996 *The Dream of the Unified Field*—Jorie Graham
1997 *Alive Together: New and Selected Poems*—Lisel Mueller
1998 *Black Zodiac*—Charles Wright
1999 *Blizzard of One*—Mark Strand
2000 *Repair*—C.K. Williams
2001 *Different Hours*—Stephen Dunn
2002 *Practical Gods*—Carl Dennis
2003 *Moy Sand and Gravel*—Paul Muldoon

Acknowledgments

Betty Adcock, "Digression on the Nuclear Age" reprinted by permission of Louisiana State University Press from *Beholdings: Poems of Betty Adcock* by Betty Adcock. Copyright © 1988 by Betty Adcock. "To a Young Feminist Who Wants to Be Free" and "Voyages" reprinted by permission of Louisiana State University Press from *The Difficult Wheel: Poems* by Betty Adcock. Copyright © 1995 by Betty Adcock.

Kim Addonizio, "First Poem for You" from *The Philosopher's Club*. Copyright © 1994 by Kim Addonizio. Reprinted with the permission of BOA Editions, Ltd. "Fine" and "Target" from *Tell Me*. Copyright © 2000 by Kim Addonizio. Reprinted with the permission of BOA Editions, Ltd.

Ai, "Child Beater" and "She Didn't Even Wave" from *Vice*. Copyright © 1999 by Ai. Used by permission of W. W. Norton & Company, Inc.

Sherman Alexie, "The Exaggeration of Despair" reprinted from *The Summer of Black Widows* © 1996 by Sherman Alexie, by permission of Hanging Loose Press.

Julia Alvarez, "33" and "How I Learned to Sweep" from *Homecoming*. Copyright © 1984, 1996 by Julia Alvarez. Published by Plume, an imprint of Dutton Signet, a division of Penguin Books USA, Inc.; originally published by Grove Press. Reprinted by permission of Susan Bergholz Literary Services, New York. All rights reserved. "Bilingual Sestina" from *The Other Side/El Otro Lado*. Copyright © 1995 by Julia Alvarez. Published by Plume/Penguin, a division of Penguin Group (USA). Reprinted by permission of Susan Bergholz Literary Services, New York. All rights reserved.

A. R. Ammons, "Corsons Inlet" copyright © 1963 by A. R. Ammons. "First Carolina Said-Song" and "The Foot-Washing" from *Collected Poems 1951-1971* by A. R. Ammons. Copyright © 1972 by A. R. Ammons. Used by permission of W. W. Norton & Company, Inc.

Ginger Andrews, "Primping in the Rearview Mirror" from *Hurricane Sisters* by Ginger Andrews. Reprinted with permission of the author and Story Line Press (www.storylinepress.com).

John Ashbery, "Farm Implements and Rutabagas in a Landscape" from *The Double Dream of Spring* by John Ashbery. Copyright © 1970, 1969, 1968, 1967, 1966 by John Ashbery. Reprinted by permission of Georges Borchardt, Inc. "The Other Tradition" from *Houseboat Days*, by John Ashbery. Copyright © 1975, 1976, 1977 by John Ashbery. Reprinted by permission of Georges Borchardt, Inc. "Paradoxes and Oxymorons" from *Shadow Train*, by John Ashbery. Copyright © 1980, 1981 by John Ashbery. Reprinted by permission of Georges Borchardt, Inc. "The Gods of Fairness," "This Room" and "Toy Symphony" from *Your Name Here* by John Ashbery. Copyright © 2000 by John Ashbery. Reprinted by permission of Farrar, Straus and Giroux, LLC.

Gerald Barrax, "Strangers Like Us: Pittsburgh, Raleigh, 1945-1985" and "Pittsburgh, 1948: The Music Teacher" reprinted by permission of Louisiana State University Press from *From a Person Sitting in Darkness: New and Selected Poems* by Gerald Barrax. Copyright © 1998 by Gerald Barrax.

Robert Bly, "After Drinking All Night with a Friend, We Go Out in a Boat at Dawn to See Who Can Write the Best Poem" from *Silence in the Snowy Fields*, © 1962 by Robert Bly. Reprinted by permission of Wesleyan University Press. "For My Son, Noah, Ten Years Old" from *The Man in the Black Coat Turns* by Robert Bly, copyright © 1981 by Robert Bly. Used by permission of Doubleday, a division of Random House, Inc. "The Scandal" from *Morning Poems* by Robert Bly. Copyright © 1997 by Robert Bly. Reprinted by permission of HarperCollins Publishers Inc.

Edgar Bowers, "The Astronomers of Mont Blanc," "Mary" and "A Fragment: the Cause" from *Collected Poems* by Edgar Bowers, copyright © 1997 by Edgar Bowers. Used by permission of Alfred A. Knopf, a division of Random House, Inc.

Charles Bukowski, "my father" from *Septuagenarian Stew: Stories & Poems* by Charles Bukowski. Copyright © 1990 by Charles Bukowski. Reprinted by permission of HarperCollins Publishers Inc. "the great escape" from *Sifting through the Madness for the Word, the Line, the Way: New Poems* by Charles Bukowski and edited by John Martin. Copyright © 2003 by Linda Lee Bukowski. Reprinted by permission of HarperCollins Publishers Inc.

Rafael Campo, "Oysters" from *Landscape with Human Figure* by Rafael Campo. Copyright, 2002, Rafael Campo. All rights reserved. Used by permission of Duke University Press.

Gladys Cardiff, "Combing" from *To Frighten a Storm* by Gladys Cardiff. Copper Canyon

Press, 1976. Reprinted by permission of the author. "Beautiful Zombies" from *A Bare Unpainted Table* by Gladys Cardiff. New Issues Press, 1999. Reprinted by permission of the author.

Hayden Carruth, "Woodsmoke at 70" from *Collected Shorter Poems 1946-1991*. Copyright © 1992 by Hayden Carruth. Reprinted with the permission of Copper Canyon Press, P. O. Box 271, Port Townsend, WA 98368-0271. "Pittsburgh" from *Scrambled Eggs & Whiskey: Poems 1991-1995*. Copyright © 1995 by Hayden Carruth. Reprinted with the permission of Copper Canyon Press, P. O. Box 271, Port Townsend, WA 98368-0271.

Jared Carter, "Drawing the Antique," "Interview" and "The Purpose of Poetry" from *After the Rain* by Jared Carter. Copyright © 1993 by Jared Carter. Reprinted by permission of the Cleveland State University Poetry Center.

Fred Chappell, "My Grandmother Washes Her Feet" reprinted by permission of Louisiana State University Press. From *Midquest: A Poem* by Fred Chappell. Copyright © 1981 by Fred Chappell. "Narcissus and Echo" reprinted by permission of Louisiana State University Press from *Source: Poems* by Fred Chappell. Copyright © 1985 by Fred Chappell. "Ave Atque Vale" reprinted by permission of Louisiana State University Press from *C: Poems* by Fred Chappell. Copyright © 1993 by Fred Chappell.

Amy Clampitt, "The Kingfisher," "What the Light Was Like" and "Nothing Stays Put" from *The Collected Poems of Amy Clampitt* by Amy Clampitt, copyright © 1997 by the Estate of Amy Clampitt. Used by permission of Alfred A. Knopf, a division of Random House, Inc.

Lucille Clifton, "homage to my hips" first published in *Two-Headed Woman*, copyright © 1980 by The University of Massachusetts Press, published by The University of Massachusetts Press. Now appears in *Good Woman: Poems and a Memoir 1969-1980*, copyright © 1987 by Lucille Clifton, published by BOA Editions, Ltd. Reprinted by permission of Curtis Brown, Ltd. "wishes for sons" from *Quilting: Poems 1987-1990*. Copyright © 1991 by Lucille Clifton. Reprinted with the permission of BOA Editions, Ltd. "lee" from *The Terrible Stories*. Copyright © 1996 by Lucille Clifton. Reprinted with the permission of BOA Editions, Ltd.

Judith Ortiz Cofer, "The Latin Deli: An Ars Poetica" by Judith Ortiz Cofer is reprinted with permission from the publisher of *The Americas Review* (Houston: Arte Público Press – University of Houston, 1991). "The Lesson of the Teeth" from *The Latin Deli: Prose and Poetry* by Judith Ortiz Cofer. ©

1993 by Judith Ortiz Cofer. Reprinted by permission of The University of Georgia Press.

Billy Collins, "Schoolsville" from *The Apple That Astonished Paris* by Billy Collins. Copyright © 1988 by Billy Collins. Reprinted by permission of the University of Arkansas Press. "Nostalgia" is from *Questions About Angels*, by Billy Collins, © 1991. Reprinted by permission of the University of Pittsburgh Press. "Litany," copyright © 2002 by Billy Collins, from *Nine Horses* by Billy Collins. Used by permission of Random House, Inc.

Gregory Corso, "Marriage" from *The Happy Birthday of Death*, copyright © 1960 by New Directions Publishing Corp. Reprinted by permission of New Directions Publishing Corp.

Sarah Cortez, "Tu Negrito" and "Undressing a Cop" by Sarah Cortez are reprinted with permission from the publisher of *How to Undress a Cop* (Houston: Arte Público Press – University of Houston, 2000). Copyright © 2000 by Sarah Cortez.

Morri Creech, "Broken Glass" from *Paper Cathedrals* by Morri Creech. Kent State University Press, copyright © 2001 by Morri Creech. Reprinted by permission of the author.

Robert Creeley, "Naughty Boy," "I Know a Man," "Oh No" and "The Language" from *The Collected Poems of Robert Creeley: 1945-1975*. Copyright © 1983 The Regents of the University of California. Reprinted by permission of the University of California Press.

Dick Davis, "Duchy and Shinks," "Farewell to the Mentors" and "A Monorhyme for the Shower" from *Belonging: Poems by Dick Davis*. Reprinted with the permission of Swallow Press/Ohio University Press, Athens, Ohio.

Toi Derricotte, "The Feeding" from *The Empress of the Death House* by Toi Derricotte. Lotus Press, copyright © 1978 by Toi Derricotte. Reprinted by permission of the author. "On the Turning Up of Unidentified Black Female Corpses" is from *Captivity*, by Toi Derricotte, © 1989. Reprinted by permission of the University of Pittsburgh Press. "Black Boys Play the Classics" is from *Tender*, by Toi Derricotte, © 1997. Reprinted by permission of the University of Pittsburgh Press.

James Dickey, "The Heaven of Animals" from *Drowning with Others*, © 1962 by James Dickey. Reprinted by permission of Wesleyan University Press. "Adultery" and "The Sheep Child" from *Falling, May Day Sermon, and Other Poems*, © 1981 by James Dickey. Reprinted by permission of Wesleyan University Press.

Tom Disch, "The Rapist's Villanelle" and "Zewhyexary" from *ABCDEFG HIJKLM NOPQRST UVWXYZ* by Tom Disch.

Hutchinson, 1981. Reprinted by permission of the author. "Ballade of the New God" from *The Dark Horse* (1996). Reprinted by permission of the author.

Michael Donaghy, "Pentecost" from *Dances Learned Last Night: Poems 1975-1995* by Michael Donaghy. Macmillan, London, UK, 2000. Reprinted by permission of the publisher. "Black Ice and Rain" and "The River in Spate" from *Conjure* by Michael Donaghy. Macmillan, London, UK, 2000. Reprinted by permission of the publisher.

Mark Doty, "Bill's Story" and "No" from *My Alexandria: Poems.* Copyright 1993 by Mark Doty. Used with permission of the poet and the University of Illinois Press.

Rita Dove, "Adolescence-III" from *The Yellow House on the Corner*, Carnegie-Mellon University Press, © 1980 by Rita Dove. Reprinted by permission of the author. "After Reading Mickey in the Night Kitchen for the Third Time Before Bed," from *Grace Notes* by Rita Dove. Copyright © 1989 by Rita Dove. Used by permission of the author and W. W. Norton & Company, Inc. "American Smooth" from *The New Yorker*, Condé Nast Publications, © 2003 by Rita Dove. Reprinted by permission of the author.

Alan Dugan, "On a Seven-Day Diary," "Love Song: I and Thou," "Tribute to Kafka for Someone Taken" and "Surviving the Hurricane" from *Poems Seven: New and Complete Poetry* by Alan Dugan. Copyright © 2001 by Alan Dugan. Reprinted by permission of Seven Stories Press.

Denise Duhamel, "Ego" is from *Queen for a Day*, by Denise Duhamel, © 2001. Reprinted by permission of the University of Pittsburgh Press.

Stephen Dunn, "The Sacred Life" from *Between Angels* by Stephen Dunn. Copyright © 1989 by Stephen Dunn. Used by permission of W. W. Norton & Company, Inc. "A Secret Life" from *Landscape at the End of the Century* by Stephen Dunn. Copyright © 1991 by Stephen Dunn. Used by permission of W. W. Norton & Company, Inc. "The Sexual Revolution" from *Different Hours* by Stephen Dunn. Copyright © 2000 by Stephen Dunn. Used by permission of W. W. Norton & Company, Inc.

Russell Edson, "An Old Man in Love" and "When the Ceiling Cries" from *The Very Thing That Happens*, copyright © 1964 by New Directions Publishing Corp. Reprinted by permission of New Directions Publishing Corp. "Ape" from *The Tunnel: Selected Poems*, FIELD Poetry Series v. 3, Copyright 1994 by Russell Edson. Reprinted by permission of Oberlin College Press.

Lynn Emanuel, "Frying Trout while Drunk," "The Sleeping" and "Outside Room Six" from *The Dig and Hotel Fiesta*. Copyright 1984, 1992, 1995 by Lynn Emanuel. Used

with permission of the poet and the University of Illinois Press.

Rhina P. Espaillat, "Visiting Day" from *Lapsing to Grace* by Rhina P. Espaillat. Bennett & Kitchel, copyright © 1992 by Rhina P. Espaillat. Reprinted by permission of the author. "Bra" and "Reservation" from *Where Horizons Go* by Rhina P. Espaillat. Copyright © 1998 by Truman State University Press. Reprinted by permission of the author and the publisher.

B. H. Fairchild, "Beauty" from *The Art of the Lathe.* Copyright © 1998 by B. H. Fairchild. Reprinted with the permission of Alice James Books.

Beth Ann Fennelly, "Asked for a Happy Memory of Her Father, She Recalls Wrigley Field" from *Open House: Poems* by Beth Ann Fennelly. Zoo Press, 2002. Reprinted by permission of Zoo Press and the author.

Edward Field, "The Bride of Frankenstein" and "The Dog Sitters" from *Counting Myself Lucky: Selected Poems 1963-1992* by Edward Field. Black Sparrow Press, copyright © 1992 by Edward Field. Reprinted by permission of the author.

Carolyn Forché, "The Colonel" and "Expatriate," copyright © 1981 by Carolyn Forché. "For the Stranger" copyright © 1978 by Carolyn Forché, from *The Country Between Us* by Carolyn Forché. "The Colonel" originally appeared in *Women's International Resource Exchange*. "For the Stranger" originally appeared in The New Yorker. Reprinted by permission of HarperCollins Publishers Inc.

Allen Ginsberg, "America" copyright © 1956, 1959 by Allen Ginsberg. "Howl, Part I" copyright © 1955 by Allen Ginsberg. "A Supermarket in California" copyright © 1955 by Allen Ginsberg, from *Collected Poems 1947-1980* by Allen Ginsberg. Reprinted by permission of HarperCollins Publishers Inc.

Dana Gioia, "Planting a Sequoia" and "The Next Poem" copyright 1991 by Dana Gioia. Reprinted from *The Gods of Winter* with the permission of Graywolf Press, Saint Paul, Minnesota. "Elegy with Surrealist Proverbs as Refrain" copyright 2001 by Dana Gioia. Reprinted from *Interrogations at Noon* with the permission of Graywolf Press, Saint Paul, Minnesota.

Louise Glück, "Mock Orange" and "The Reproach" from *The Triumph of Achilles* as taken from *The First Four Books of Poems* by Louise Glück. Copyright 1968, 1971, 1972, 1973, 1974, 1975, 1976, 1977, 1978, 1979, 1980, 1985, 1995 by Louise Glück. Reprinted by permission of HarperCollins Publishers Inc. "Daisies" from *The Wild Iris* by Louise Glück. Copyright © 1993 by Louise Glück. Reprinted by permission of HarperCollins Publishers Inc.

Albert Goldbarth, "Dog, Fish, Shoes (or Beans)" from *Troubled Lovers in History: A Sequence of Poems* by Albert Goldbarth. Copyright © 1999 by Ohio State University Press. Reprinted by permission of the publisher. "Rarefied" from *Saving Lives: Poems* by Albert Goldbarth. Copyright © 2001 by Ohio State University Press. Reprinted by permission of the publisher.

Jorie Graham, "At Luca Signorelli's Resurrection of the Body," "I Watched a Snake" and "Two Paintings by Gustav Klimt" from *Erosion* by Jorie Graham. © 1983 Princeton University Press. Reprinted by permission of Princeton University Press.

Emily Grosholz, "Letter from Germany" reprinted by permission from *The Hudson Review, Vol. XXXII, No. 3* (Autumn 1979). Copyright 1979 by Emily R. Grosholz. Republished in The River Painter (University of Illinois Press, 1984). "November" reprinted by permission from *The Hudson Review, Vol. LVI, No. 1* (Spring 2003). Copyright 2003 by Emily R. Grosholz.

Thom Gunn, "In the Tank," "From the Wave" and "Terminal" from *Collected Poems* by Thom Gunn. Copyright © 1994 by Thom Gunn. Reprinted by permission of Farrar, Straus and Giroux, LLC., and Faber and Faber Ltd.

Marilyn Hacker, "Wagers" from *Love, Death, and the Changing of the Seasons* by Marilyn Hacker. Copyright © 1986 by Marilyn Hacker. Reprinted by permission of Frances Collin, Literary Agent. "Ghazal on Half a Line by Adrienne Rich" and "Omelette" from *Desesperanto* by Marilyn Hacker. Copyright © 2003 by Marilyn Hacker. Used by permission of W. W. Norton & Company, Inc.

John Haines, "Life in an Ashtray" and "Rain Country" copyright 1993 by John Haines. Reprinted from *The Owl in the Mask of the Dreamer* with the permission of Graywolf Press, Saint Paul, Minnesota.

Jim Hall, "Maybe Dats Your Pwoblem Too" reprinted from *The Mating Reflex*: by permission of Carnegie Mellon University Press © 1980 by Jim Hall. "Sperm Count" and "White Trash" reprinted from *False Statements*: by permission of Carnegie Mellon University Press © 1986 by Jim Hall.

Forrest Hamer, "Erection" from *Call & Response*. Copyright © 1995 by Forrest Hamer. Reprinted with the permission of Alice James Books.

Joy Harjo, "She Had Some Horses" from the book *She Had Some Horses* by Joy Harjo. Copyright © 1983, 1997 Thunder's Mouth Press. Appears by permission of the publisher, Thunder's Mouth Press, A division of Avalon Publishing Group. "Song for the Deer and Myself to Return On" from *In Mad Love and War*, © 1990 by Joy Harjo. Reprinted by permission of Wesleyan University Press.

Michael S. Harper, "Black Study" from *Dear John, Dear Coltrane: Poems*. Copyright 1970 by Michael S. Harper. Used with permission of the poet and the University of Illinois Press. "Dear John, Dear Coltrane" and "We Assume: On the Death of Our Son, Reuben Masai Harper" from *Songlines in Michaeltree: New and Collected Poems*. Copyright 2000 by Michael S. Harper. Used with permission of the poet and the University of Illinois Press.

Robert Hass, "Meditation at Lagunitas" from *Praise* by Robert Hass. Copyright © 1979 by Robert Hass. Reprinted by permission of HarperCollins Publishers Inc. "A Story About the Body" from *Human Wishes* by Robert Hass. Copyright © 1989 by Robert Hass. Reprinted by permission of Harper-Collins Publishers Inc. "Forty Something" from *Sun Under Wood* by Robert Hass. Copyright © 1996 by Robert Hass. Reprinted by permission of HarperCollins Publishers Inc.

Anthony Hecht, "The Dover Bitch: A Criticism of Life," "A Hill," "More Light! More Light!" and "Third Avenue in Sunlight" from *Collected Earlier Poems* by Anthony Hecht, copyright © 1990 by Anthony E. Hecht. Used by permission of Alfred A. Knopf, a division of Random House, Inc. "The Book of Yolek" from *The Transparent Man* by Anthony Hecht, copyright © 1990 by Anthony E. Hecht. Used by permission of Alfred A. Knopf, a division of Random House, Inc.

H. L. Hix, "Orders of Magnitude" from *Rational Numbers* by H. L. Hix. Truman State University Press, 2000. Reprinted by permission of the author and the publisher.

Daniel Hoffman, "Rats," "Bob" and "Violence" reprinted by permission of Louisiana State University Press from *Beyond Silence: Selected Shorter Poems, 1948-2003* by Daniel Hoffman. Copyright © 2003 by Daniel Hoffman.

Susan Howe, "Closed Fist Withholding an Open Palm" from *Frame Structures*, copyright © 1974, 1975, 1978, 1979, 1996 by Susan Howe. Reprinted by permission of New Directions Publishing Corp.

Andrew Hudgins, "Air View of an Industrial Scene" and "Where the River Jordan Ends" from *Saints and Strangers* by Andrew Hudgins. Copyright © 1985 by Andrew Hudgins. Reprinted by permission of Houghton Mifflin Company. All rights reserved. "Heat Lightning in a Time of Drought" from *The Never-Ending: New Poems* by Andrew Hudgins. Copyright © 1991 by Andrew Hudgins. Reprinted by permission of Houghton Mifflin Company. All rights reserved.

Richard Hugo, "Bay of Recovery" and "Degrees of Gray in Philipsburg" Copyright © 1973 by

Richard Hugo. "My Buddy" from *Making Certain It Goes On: The Collected Poems of Richard Hugo* by Richard Hugo. Copyright © 1984 by The Estate of Richard Hugo. Used by permission of W. W. Norton & Company, Inc.

Mark Jarman, "After Disappointment" and "Ground Swell" from *Questions for Ecclesiastes* by Mark Jarman. Reprinted with permission of the author and Story Line Press (www.storylinepress.com).

Rodney Jones, "On the Bearing of Waitresses" and "Winter Retreat: Homage to Martin Luther King, Jr." from *Transparent Gestures* by Rodney Jones. Copyright © 1989 by Rodney Jones. Reprinted by permission of Houghton Mifflin Company. All rights reserved.

Donald Justice, "Counting the Mad," "But That Is Another Story," "Men at Forty" and "American Scenes (1904-1905)" from *New and Selected Poems* by Donald Justice, copyright © 1995 by Donald Justice. Used by permission of Alfred A. Knopf, a division of Random House, Inc.

X. J. Kennedy, "First Confession," "In a Prominent Bar in Secaucus One Day," "Little Elegy" and "Cross Ties" from *Cross Ties: Selected Poems* by X. J. Kennedy. University of Georgia Press, copyright © 1985 by X. J. Kennedy. Reprinted by permission of the author. "September Twelfth, 2001" from *The Lords of Misrule: Poems 1992-2001*, p. 88. © 2002 X. J. Kennedy. Reprinted with permission of The Johns Hopkins University Press.

Suji Kwock Kim, "Occupation" reprinted by permission of Louisiana State University Press from *Notes from the Divided Country: Poems* by Suji Kwock Kim. Copyright © 2003 by Suji Kwock Kim.

Galway Kinnell, "After Making Love We Hear Footsteps," "Goodbye" and "Saint Francis and the Sow" from *Mortal Acts, Mortal Words* by Galway Kinnell. Copyright © 1980 by Galway Kinnell. Reprinted by permission of Houghton Mifflin Company. All rights reserved.

Carolyn Kizer, "The Ungrateful Garden," "Bitch" and "Pro Femina: Part Three" from *Cool, Calm and Collected: Poems 1960-2000*. Copyright © 2001 by Carolyn Kizer. Reprinted with the permission of Copper Canyon Press, P. O. Box 271, Port Townsend, WA 98368-0271.

Yusef Komunyakaa, "Facing It" from *Dien Cai Dau*, © 1988 by Yusef Komunyakaa. Reprinted by permission of Wesleyan University Press. "My Father's Love Letters" from *Magic City*, © 1992 by Yusef Komunyakaa. Reprinted by permission of Wesleyan University Press. "Ode to the Maggot" from *Talking Dirty to the Gods* by Yusef Komunyakaa. Copyright © 2000 by Yusef Komunyakaa. Reprinted by permission of Farrar, Straus and Giroux, LLC.

Ted Kooser, "Abandoned Farmhouse," "The Salesman" and "Selecting a Reader" are from *Sure Signs: New and Selected Poems*, by Ted Kooser, © 1980. Reprinted by permission of the University of Pittsburgh Press.

Maxine Kumin, "Morning Swim." Copyright © 1965 by Maxine Kumin, "Woodchucks" copyright © 1972 by Maxine Kumin, from *Selected Poems 1960-1990* by Maxine Kumin. Used by permission of W. W. Norton & Company, Inc. "Noted in The New York Times" from *Nurture: Poems* by Maxine Kumin. Copyright © 1989 by Maxine W. Kumin. Reprinted by permission of The Anderson Literary Agency Inc. "Oblivion" from *The Long Marriage* by Maxine Kumin. Copyright © 2000 by Maxine Kumin. Used by permission of W. W. Norton & Company, Inc.

Sydney Lea, "Young Man Leaving Home" and "Hunter's Sabbath: Hippocratic." From *To the Bone: New and Selected Poems*. Copyright 1996 by Sydney Lea. Used with permission of the poet and the University of Illinois Press.

Li-Young Lee, "Persimmons" from *Rose*. Copyright © 1986 by Li-Young Lee. Reprinted with the permission of BOA Editions, Ltd.

Brad Leithauser, "A Quilled Quilt, A Needle Bed" from *Hundreds of Fireflies* by Brad Leithauser, copyright © 1981 by Brad Leithauser. Used by permission of Alfred A. Knopf, a division of Random House, Inc. "The Odd Last Thing She Did" from *The Odd Last Thing She Did* by Brad Leithauser, copyright © 1998 by Brad Leithauser. Used by permission of Alfred A. Knopf, a division of Random House, Inc.

Denise Levertov, "The Secret" copyright © 1964 by Denise Levertov. "What Were They Like?" and "Song for Ishtar" copyright © 1966 by Denise Levertov, from *Poems 1960-1967* by Denise Levertov. Reprinted by permission of New Directions Publishing Corp.

Philip Levine, "Animals Are Passing from Our Lives" from *Not This Pig*, © 1968 by Philip Levine. Reprinted by permission of Wesleyan University Press. "They Feed They Lion" from *They Feed They Lion and The Names of the Lost* by Philip Levine. "They Feed They Lion," copyright © 1968, 1969, 1970, 1971, 1972 by Philip Levine. "The Names of the Lost," copyright © 1976 by Philip Levine. Used by permission of Alfred A. Knopf, a division of Random House, Inc. "You Can Have It" from *New Selected Poems* by Philip Levine, copyright © 1991 by Philip Levine. Used by permission of Alfred A. Knopf, a division of Random House, Inc. "What Work Is" from *What Work Is* by Philip Levine, copyright © 1992 by Philip Levine. Used by

Naomi Shihab Nye, "The Traveling Onion" and "Yellow Glove" from *Yellow Glove* by Naomi Shihab Nye. Breitenbush Books, 1986. Reprinted by permission of the author.

Frank O'Hara, "Why I Am Not a Painter" from *Collected Poems* by Frank O'Hara, copyright © 1971 by Maureen Granville-Smith, Administratrix of the Estate of Frank O'Hara. Used by permission of Alfred A. Knopf, a division of Random House, Inc. "The Day Lady Died" and "Poem" from *Lunch Poems* by Frank O'Hara. City Lights Books, 1964. Reprinted by permission of the publisher.

Sharon Olds, "The One Girl at the Boys' Party" from *The Dead and the Living* by Sharon Olds, copyright © 1987 by Sharon Olds. Used by permission of Alfred A. Knopf, a division of Random House, Inc. "The Girl," "I Go Back to May 1937" and "Topography" from *The Gold Cell* by Sharon Olds, copyright © 1987 by Sharon Olds. Used by permission of Alfred A. Knopf, a division of Random House, Inc.

Mary Oliver, "The Black Snake" from *Twelve Moons* by Mary Oliver. Copyright © 1972, 1973, 1974, 1976, 1977, 1978, 1979 by Mary Oliver. By permission of Little, Brown and Company, (Inc.). "University Hospital, Boston" from *American Primitive* by Mary Oliver. Copyright © 1978, 1979, 1980, 1981, 1982, 1983 by Mary Oliver. By permission of Little, Brown and Company, (Inc.). "The Buddha's Last Instruction" from *House of Light* by Mary Oliver. Copyright © 1990 by Mary Oliver. Reprinted by permission of Beacon Press, Boston.

Michael Palmer, "Voice and Address" from *The Lion Bridge*, copyright © 1998 by Michael Palmer. Reprinted by permission of New Directions Publishing Corp. "A word is coming up on the screen…" from *Codes Appearing: Poems 1979-1988*, copyright © 1981, 1984, 1988 by Michael Palmer. Reprinted by permission of New Directions Publishing Corp. "Untitled" from *At Passages*, copyright © 1995 by New Directions Publishing Corp. Reprinted by permission of New Directions Publishing Corp.

Linda Pastan, "Ethics" copyright © 1981 by Linda Pastan. "Crocuses" and "1932-" from *Carnival Evening: New and Selected Poems 1968-1998* by Linda Pastan. Copyright © 1998 by Linda Pastan. Used by permission of W. W. Norton & Company, Inc.

Molly Peacock, "Buffalo" and "A Favor of Love" from *Cornucopia: New and Selected Poems* by Molly Peacock. Copyright © 2002 by Molly Peacock. Used by permission of W. W. Norton & Company, Inc. "Why I Am Not a Buddhist," from *Original Love* by Molly Peacock. Copyright © 1995 by Molly Peacock. Used by permission of W. W. Norton & Company, Inc.

Robert Phillips, "Running on Empty" from *Personal Accounts: New and Selected Poems 1966-1986* by Robert Phillips. Ontario Review Press, © 1986 by Robert Phillips. Reprinted by permission of the author. "The Stone Crab: A Love Poem" from *Breakdown Lane*, p. 32. © 1994 Robert Phillips. Reprinted with permission of The Johns Hopkins University Press. "Compartments" from *Spinach Days*, pp. 91-93. © 2000 Robert Phillips. Reprinted with permission of The Johns Hopkins University Press.

Robert Pinsky, "Shirt" and "The Want Bone" from *The Want Bone* by Robert Pinsky. Copyright © 1991 by Robert Pinsky. Reprinted by permission of HarperCollins Publishers Inc. "ABC" from *Jersey Rain* by Robert Pinsky. Copyright © 2000 by Robert Pinsky. Reprinted by permission of Farrar, Straus and Giroux, LLC.

Sylvia Plath, "The Colossus" from *The Colossus and Other Poems* by Sylvia Plath, copyright © 1962 by Sylvia Plath. Used by permission of Alfred A. Knopf, a division of Random House, Inc., and Faber and Faber Ltd. "Daddy" copyright © 1963 by Ted Hughes. "Edge," copyright © 1963 by Ted Hughes. "Lady Lazarus" copyright © 1963 by Ted Hughes. "The Moon and the Yew Tree" copyright © 1963 by Ted Hughes. "Morning Song" copyright © 1961 by Ted Hughes, from *Ariel* by Sylvia Plath. Reprinted by permission of HarperCollins Publishers Inc., and Faber and Faber Ltd.

Adrienne Rich, "Aunt Jennifer's Tigers" copyright © 2002, 1951 by Adrienne Rich. "Living in Sin" copyright © 2002, 1955 by Adrienne Rich. "Diving into the Wreck" copyright © 2002 by Adrienne Rich. Copyright © 1973 by W. W. Norton & Company, Inc. "Rape" copyright © 2002 by Adrienne Rich. Copyright © 1973 by W. W. Norton & Company, Inc., Part XIII "(Dedications)" from "An Atlas of the Difficult World" copyright © 2002, 1991 by Adrienne Rich, "Final Notations." Copyright © 2002, 1991 by Adrienne Rich, from *The Fact of a Doorframe: Selected Poems 1950-2001* by Adrienne Rich. Used by permission of the author and W. W. Norton & Company, Inc.

Alberto Ríos, "Madre Sofía" and "The Purpose of Altar Boys" from *Whispering to Fool the Wind*. Sheep Meadow Press, © 1982 by Alberto Ríos. Reprinted by permission of the author.

Pattiann Rogers, "Discovering Your Subject" and "Foreplay" in *Song of the World Becoming: New and Collected Poems, 1981-2001* (Minneapolis: Milkweed Editions, 2001). Copyright © 2001 by Pattiann Rogers. Reprinted with permission from Milkweed Editions.

Wendy Rose, "Robert" from *The Halfbreed Chronicles*. Copyright © 1985 by Wendy Rose. Reprinted with the permission of West End Press, Albuquerque, New Mexico. "Alfalfa Dance" from *Now Poof She Is Gone* by Wendy Rose. Firebrand Books, copyright © 1994 by Wendy Rose. Reprinted by permission of the author. "Grandmother Rattler" From *Itch Like Crazy*, by Wendy Rose, © 2002 Wendy Rose. Reprinted by permission of the University of Arizona Press.

Gibbons Ruark, "Polio," "The Visitor" and "Lecturing My Daughters" reprinted by permission of Louisiana State University Press from *Passing Through Customs: New and Selected Poems* by Gibbons Ruark. Copyright © 1999 by Gibbons Ruark.

Kay Ryan, "Turtle" from *Flamingo Watching* by Kay Ryan. Copper Beech Press, 1997. Reprinted by permission of the publisher. "Bestiary" from *Elephant Rocks* by Kay Ryan. Copyright © 1996 by Kay Ryan. Used by permission of Grove/Atlantic, Inc. "Drops in the Bucket" and "Mockingbird" from *Say Uncle* by Kay Ryan. Copyright © 2000 by Kay Ryan. Used by permission of Grove/Atlantic, Inc.

Mary Jo Salter, "Welcome to Hiroshima" From *Henry Purcell in Japan* by Mary Jo Salter, copyright © 1984 by Mary Jo Salter. Used by permission of Alfred A. Knopf, a division of Random House, Inc. "Dead Letters: Part I" from *Unfinished Painting* by Mary Jo Salter, copyright © 1989 by Mary Jo Salter. Used by permission of Alfred A. Knopf, a division of Random House, Inc.

Gjertrud Schnackenberg, "Nightfishing," "Signs" and "Supernatural Love" from *Supernatural Love: Poems 1976-1992* by Gjertrud Schnackenberg. Copyright © 2000 by Gjertrud Schnackenberg. Reprinted by permission of Farrar, Straus and Giroux, LLC.

Anne Sexton, "Unknown Girl in the Maternity Ward" from *To Bedlam and Part Way Back* by Anne Sexton. Copyright © 1960 by Anne Sexton, renewed 1988 by Linda G. Sexton. Reprinted by permission of Houghton Mifflin Company. All rights reserved. "All My Pretty Ones" from *All My Pretty Ones* by Anne Sexton. Copyright © 1962 by Anne Sexton, renewed 1990 by Linda G. Sexton. Reprinted by permission of Houghton Mifflin Company. All rights reserved. "In Celebration of My Uterus" from *Love Poems* by Anne Sexton. Copyright © 1967, 1968, 1969 by Anne Sexton. Reprinted by permission of Houghton Mifflin Company. All rights reserved. "Cinderella" from *Transformations* by Anne Sexton. Copyright © 1971 by Anne Sexton. Reprinted by permission of Houghton Mifflin Company. All rights reserved.

Charles Simic, "Fork" and "Stone" from *Charles Simic: Selected Early Poems* by Charles Simic. Copyright © 1999 by Charles Simic. Reprinted by permission of George Braziller, Inc. "I was stolen…" from *The World Doesn't End: Prose Poems*, copyright © 1987 by Charles Simic, reprinted by permission of Harcourt, Inc.

Louis Simpson, "To the Western World" from *A Dream of Governors*, © 1959 by Louis Simpson. Reprinted by permission of Wesleyan University Press. "American Poetry," "My Father in the Night Commanding No," "American Classic" and "Physical Universe" from *The Owner of the House: New Collected Poems 1940-2001*. Copyright © 2003 by Louis Simpson. Reprinted with the permission of BOA Editions, Ltd.

W. D. Snodgrass, "After Experience Taught Me…," "The Examination" and "Mementos, I" from *After Experience* by W. D. Snodgrass. Harper & Row, 1967. Reprinted by permission of the author.

Gary Snyder, "Hay for the Horses" and "Riprap" from *Riprap and Cold Mountain Poems* by Gary Snyder. Shoemaker & Hoard, 2003. Reprinted by permission of the publisher. "A Walk" from *The Back Country*, copyright © 1968 by Gary Snyder. Reprinted by permission of New Directions Publishing Corp. "The Bath" from *Turtle Island*, copyright © 1974 by Gary Snyder. Reprinted by permission of New Directions Publishing Corp.

David St. John, "I Know" and "My Tea with Madame Descartes" from *Study for the World's Body: Selected Poems* by David St. John. Copyright © 1994 by David St. John. Reprinted by permission of HarperCollins Publishers Inc.

A. E. Stallings, "Hades Welcomes His Bride" from *Archaic Smile: Poems* by A. E. Stallings. Copyright © 1999 by A. E. Stallings. Reprinted by permission of The University of Evansville Press.

Timothy Steele, "Life Portrait," "Sapphics Against Anger" and "Social Reform" from *Sapphics and Uncertainties: Poems 1970-1986* by Timothy Steele. Copyright © 1995 by Timothy Steele. Reprinted by permission of the University of Arkansas Press.

Gerald Stern, "Behaving Like a Jew," "The Dancing" and "The Sounds of Wagner," from *This Time: New and Selected Poems* by Gerald Stern. Copyright © 1998 by Gerald Stern. Used by permission of W. W. Norton & Company, Inc.

Leon Stokesbury, "To His Book" and "Day Begins at Governor's Square Mall" from *Autumn Rhythm: New and Selected Poems* by Leon Stokesbury. Copyright © 1996 by Leon Stokesbury. Reprinted by permission of the University of Arkansas Press. "The Day Kennedy Died" from *Crazyhorse, No. 65* (Spring-Summer 2004). Copyright © 2004 by

Leon Stokesbury. Reprinted by permission of the author.

Mark Strand, "Eating Poetry," "Keeping Things Whole" and "The Tunnel" from *Reasons for Moving; Darker; The Sargentville Notebook* by Mark Strand, copyright © 1973 by Mark Strand. Used by permission of Alfred A. Knopf, a division of Random House, Inc. "The Great Poet Returns" from *Blizzard of One* by Mark Strand, copyright © 1998 by Mark Strand. Used by permission of Alfred A. Knopf, a division of Random House, Inc.

James Tate, "The Lost Pilot" from *The Lost Pilot* by James Tate. Copyright © 1978 by James Tate. Reprinted by permission of HarperCollins Publishers Inc. "The Blue Booby" and "Teaching the Ape to Write Poems" from *Selected Poems* by James Tate. Wesleyan University Press, copyright © 1991 by James Tate. Reprinted by permission of the author.

Henry Taylor, "Artichoke" reprinted by permission of Louisiana State University Press from *The Flying Change* by Henry Taylor. Copyright © 1985 by Henry Taylor. "Understanding Fiction" reprinted by permission of Louisiana State University Press from *Understanding Fiction: Poems 1986-1996* by Henry Taylor. Copyright © 1996 by Henry Taylor.

Diane Thiel, "The Minefield" from *Echolocations* by Diane Thiel. Reprinted with permission of the author and Story Line Press (www.storylinepress.com).

Catherine Tufariello, "Useful Advice" from *Keeping My Name* by Catherine Tufariello. Texas Tech University Press, 2004. Reprinted by permission of the publisher and the author.

Amy Uyematsu, "Lessons from Central America" from *Nights of Fire, Nights of Rain* by Amy Uyematsu. Reprinted with permission of the author and Story Line Press (www.storyline-press.com).

Mona Van Duyn, "Letters from a Father" from *Selected Poems* by Mona Van Duyn, copyright © 2002 by Mona Van Duyn. Used by permission of Alfred A. Knopf, a division of Random House, Inc.

Ellen Bryant Voigt, "Daughter," from *The Forces of Plenty* by Ellen Bryant Voigt. Copyright © 1983 by Ellen Bryant Voigt. Used by permission of W. W. Norton & Company, Inc. "Lesson" and "The Others" from *Shadow of Heaven* by Ellen Bryant Voigt. Copyright © 2002 by Ellen Bryant Voigt. Used by permission of W. W. Norton & Company, Inc.

Richard Wilbur, "The Pardon" and "A Simile for Her Smile" from *Ceremony and Other Poems*, copyright 1950 and renewed 1978 by Richard Wilbur, reprinted by permission of Harcourt, Inc. "Year's End" from *Ceremony and Other Poems*, copyright 1949 and renewed 1977 by Richard Wilbur, reprinted by permission of Harcourt, Inc. "Love Calls Us to the Things of This World" and "Mind" from *Things of This World*, © 1956 and renewed 1984 by Richard Wilbur, reprinted by permission of Harcourt, Inc. "Advice to a Prophet" from *Advice to a Prophet and Other Poems*, copyright © 1959 and renewed 1987 by Richard Wilbur, reprinted by permission of Harcourt, Inc. "The Writer" from *The Mind-Reader*, copyright © 1971 by Richard Wilbur, reprinted by permission of Harcourt, Inc. "Hamlen Brook" from *New and Collected Poems*, copyright © 1987 by Richard Wilbur, reprinted by permission of Harcourt, Inc. "For C." from *Mayflies: New Poems and Translations*, copyright © 2000 by Richard Wilbur, reprinted by permission of Harcourt, Inc.

C. K. Williams, "Hood," "Hooks" and "Harm" from *Selected Poems* by C. K. Williams. Copyright © 1994 by C. K. Williams. Reprinted by permission of Farrar, Straus and Giroux, LLC.

Miller Williams, "Let Me Tell You" from *The Only World There Is* by Miller Williams, copyright © 1968, 1969, 1970, 1971 by Miller Williams. Used by permission of Dutton, a division of Penguin Group (USA) Inc. "The Book" reprinted by permission of Louisiana State University Press from *Living on the Surface: New and Selected Poems* by Miller Williams. Copyright © 1989 by Miller Williams. "The Curator" and "Folding His USA Today He Makes His Point in the Blue Star Cafe" reprinted from *Adjusting to the Light* by Miller Williams, by permission of the University of Missouri Press. Copyright © 1992 by Miller Williams.

Greg Williamson, "Kites at the Washington Monument" from *Errors in the Script: Poems* by Greg Williamson. Copyright © 2001 by Greg Williamson. Reprinted by permission of The Overlook Press.

Christian Wiman, "Afterwards" from *The Long Home* by Christian Wiman. Reprinted with permission of the author and Story Line Press (www.storylinepress.com).

James Wright, "Saint Judas" from Saint Judas, © 1959 by James Wright. Reprinted by permission of Wesleyan University Press. "Autumn Begins in Martins Ferry, Ohio," "A Blessing," "Lying in a Hammock at William Duffy's Farm in Pine Island, Minnesota" and "Two Poems About President Harding" from *The Branch Will Not Break*, © 1963 by James Wright. Reprinted by permission of Wesleyan University Press.

Index to Poets, Titles, and First Lines

Additional Titles of Interest

Note to Instructors: Any of these Penguin-Putnam, Inc., titles can be packaged with this book at a special discount. Contact your local Allyn & Bacon/Longman sales representative for details on how to create a Penguin-Putnam, Inc., Value Package.

Albee, *The Three Tall Women*

Allison, *Bastard Out of Carolina*

Alvarez, *How the García Girls Lost Their Accents*

Austen, *Persuasion*

Austen, *Pride & Prejudice*

Bellow, *The Adventures of Augie March*

Boyle, *Tortilla Curtain*

Cather, *My Antonia*

Cather, *O Pioneers!*

Cervantes, *Don Quixote*

Chopin, *The Awakening*

Conrad, *Nostromo*

DeLillo, *White Noise*

Desai, *Journey to Ithaca*

Douglass, *Narrative of the Life of Frederick Douglass*

Golding, *Lord of the Flies*

Hawthorne, *The Scarlet Letter*

Homer, *Iliad*

Homer, *Odyssey*

Huang, *Madame Butterfly*

Hulme, *Bone People*

Jen, *Typical American*

Karr, *The Liar's Club*

Kerouac, *On The Road*

Kesey, *One Flew Over the Cuckoo's Nest*

King, *Misery*

Larson, *Passing*

Lavin, *In a Cafe*

Marquez, *Love in the Time of Cholera*

McBride, *The Color of Water*

Miller, *Death of a Salesman*

Molière, *Tartuffe and Other Plays*

Morrison, *Beloved*

Morrison, *The Bluest Eye*

Morrison, *Sula*

Naylor, *Women of Brewster Place*

Orwell, *1984*

Postman, *Amusing Ourselves to Death*

Rayben, *My First White Friend*

Rose, *Lives on the Boundary*

Rose, *Possible Lives: The Promise of Public*

Rushdie, *Midnight's Children*

Shakespeare, *Four Great Comedies*

Shakespeare, *Four Great Tragedies*

Shakespeare, *Four Histories*

Shakespeare, *Hamlet*

Shakespeare, *King Lear*

Shakespeare, *Macbeth*

Shakespeare, *Othello*

Shakespeare, *Twelfth Night*

Shelley, *Frankenstein*

Silko, *Ceremony*

Solzhenitsyn, *One Day in the Life of Ivan Denisovich*

Sophocles, *The Three Theban Plays*

Spence, *The Death of Woman Wang*

Steinbeck, *Grapes of Wrath*

Steinbeck, *The Pearl*

Stevenson, *Dr. Jekyll & Mr. Hyde*

Swift, *Gulliver's Travels*

Twain, *Adventures of Huckleberry Finn*

Wilde, *The Importance of Being Earnest*

Wilson, *Joe Turner's Come and Gone*

Wilson, *Fences*

Woolf, *Jacob's Room*